White Settler Reserve

White Settler Reserve

New Iceland and the Colonization of the Canadian West

RYAN EYFORD

UBC Press • Vancouver • Toronto

© UBC Press 2016

All rights reserved. No part of this publication may be reproduced, stored in a retrieval system, or transmitted, in any form or by any means, without prior written permission of the publisher, or, in Canada, in the case of photocopying or other reprographic copying, a licence from Access Copyright, www.accesscopyright.ca.

25 24 23 22 21 20 19 18 17   5 4 3 2

Printed in Canada on FSC-certified ancient-forest-free paper
(100% post-consumer recycled) that is processed chlorine- and acid-free.

Library and Archives Canada Cataloguing in Publication

Eyford, Ryan, author
    White settler reserve : New Iceland and the colonization of the Canadian West / Ryan Eyford.

Includes bibliographical references and index.
Issued in print and electronic formats.
ISBN 978-0-7748-3159-8 (pbk.). – ISBN 978-0-7748-3160-4 (pdf). –
ISBN 978-0-7748-3161-1 (epub). – ISBN 978-0-7748-3162-8 (mobi)

    1. Land settlement – Canada, Western – History – 19th century. 2. Land tenure – Canada, Western – History – 19th century. 3. Icelanders – Canada, Western – History – 19th century. 4. Colonists – Canada, Western – History – 19th century. 5. Immigrants – Canada, Western – History – 19th century. 6. Indians of North America – Land tenure – Canada, Western – History – 19th century. 7. Liberalism – Canada, Western – History – 19th century. 8. Canada, Western – Colonization – History – 19th century. 9. Canada, Western – Emigration and immigration – History – 19th century. I. Title.

FC3217.4.E93 2016	971.2'02	C2016-902764-3
		C2016-902765-1

Canadä

UBC Press gratefully acknowledges the financial support for our publishing program of the Government of Canada (through the Canada Book Fund), the Canada Council for the Arts, and the British Columbia Arts Council.

This book has been published with the help of a grant from the Canadian Federation for the Humanities and Social Sciences, through the Awards to Scholarly Publications Program, using funds provided by the Social Sciences and Humanities Research Council of Canada.

Printed and bound in Canada by Friesens
Set in Garamond by Artegraphica Design Co. Ltd.
Copy editor: Deborah Kerr
Cartographer: Eric Leinberger
Indexer: Lillian Ashworth

UBC Press
The University of British Columbia
2029 West Mall
Vancouver, BC V6T 1Z2

To Aleisha, Lilja, and Ben

Contents

List of Illustrations / viii

Acknowledgments / ix

Introduction / 3

1 Northern Dreamlands: Canadian Expansionism and Icelandic Migration / 22

2 Broken Townships: Colonization Reserves and the Dominion Lands System / 45

3 The First New Icelanders: Family Migration and the Formation of a Reserve Community / 73

4 Quarantined within a New Order: Smallpox and the Spatial Practices of Colonization / 96

5 "Principal Projector of the Colony": The Turbulent Career of John Taylor, Icelandic Agent / 120

6 Becoming British Subjects: Municipal Government and Citizenship / 142

7 "Freemen Serving No Overlord": Debt, Self-Reliance, and Liberty / 163

Conclusion / 186

Notes / 193

Bibliography / 231

Index / 248

Illustrations

Secretary John Lowe, Department of Agriculture, December 1889 / 4
Map of reserved land in Manitoba, 1870-86 / 6
Dr. James Spencer Lynch, c. 1870 / 39
Map of reserves and surveyed land in Manitoba, 1875 / 46
Dominion Lands Survey township grid / 53
John Taylor's "Plan Proposed for Icelandic Village," October 1875 / 66
Benedikt Arason's map of Víðirnesbyggð, January 1879 / 70
Map of the *sýsla* (district) divisions in Iceland during the emigration period / 78
Símon Símonarson, Valdís Guðmundsdóttir, and their daughter, Jóhanna Guðrún, c. 1890 / 93
Reverend James Settee, Church of England missionary, n.d. / 97
Quarantine map of Manitoba and Keewatin, 1877 / 112
Joseph Monkman, n.d. / 118
John Taylor, Icelandic agent, n.d. / 121
Map of New Iceland showing the four *byggðir* (settlements), 1877 / 152
David Mills, minister of the interior, 1876-78 / 157
Jón Bjarnason, Sigtryggur Jónasson, Halldór Briem, and Páll Thorlaksson in Minneapolis, 1878 / 177
Icelandic Colony government loan acknowledgment / 180

Acknowledgments

My first acknowledgment is to Vogar, Manitoba. Vogar, meaning "coves" in Icelandic, is located on the eastern shore of Lake Manitoba in Treaty 2 territory. At the end of the nineteenth century, the Ojibwe and Metis residents of the region were confronted with an influx of immigrants from Iceland, including my great-great-grandparents Jörundur Sigurbjörnsson Eyford and Anna Jónasdóttir. The Icelanders claimed homesteads around the Dog Creek Indian Reserve. The farm where I spent the early part of my childhood sits between the reserve and the Metis village of Vogar. The spatial segregation of First Nations, Metis, and Euro-Canadians, established by the Dominion Lands Act and the Indian Act, was, and remains, an inescapable fact of life in the region. Although Vogar doesn't figure into this book directly, my origins in that place have unquestionably helped to shape my thinking about the history of colonization in Western Canada.

My second acknowledgment is to Jennifer S.H. Brown, who first helped me to think about that history from a scholarly perspective. In 1999, I was an undergraduate student in Professor Brown's "Natives and Newcomers" seminar at the University of Winnipeg. She suggested that I write my research paper on relations between Aboriginal people and Icelanders in the Manitoba Interlake. She also shared two unpublished papers on the subject by Anne Brydon and Winona Stevenson (now Wheeler) that guided me to some of the archival sources that remain central to this study. I want to thank Jennifer Brown for introducing me to the study of Indigenous history and for her generosity in sharing teaching materials when I returned to the University of Winnipeg as a faculty member in 2010.

She also did me the favour of putting me in contact with Ruth Christie, a Cree storyteller and descendant of both Joseph Monkman and John Ramsay who appear in the following chapters. My thanks go to Ruth for several enjoyable conversations about her ancestors and the many Indigenous-Icelandic connections around Lake Winnipeg.

This book has benefitted from the insightful critiques and sage advice of several outstanding historians. My list of debts to Adele Perry is too long to detail here. Suffice it to say that she gave generously of her time and expertise in helping me refine my ideas about the linkages between immigration and colonialism in Western Canada. Gerry Friesen pushed me to sharpen my arguments about the spatial dynamics of colonization over many lunches in St. John's College. In Iceland, Guðmundur Hálfdánarson provided helpful feedback on some early drafts and assisted me in applying for Icelandic research funding. Royden Loewen gave important encouragement, especially since we became department colleagues.

Many other friends and colleagues past and present in the history departments at the Universities of Manitoba and Winnipeg helped me in a variety of ways, including Donald A. Bailey, Roland Bohr, Jarvis Brownlie, Terry Cook, Sarah Elvins, Barry Ferguson, Jean Friesen, James Hanley, Esyllt Jones, Mary Jane McCallum, Leah Morton, Tom Nesmith, Nolan Reilly, Eliakim Sibanda, Greg Smith, and Ravi Vaitheespara. I also want to express my sincere thanks to Carol Adam, Lesley Cowan, Diana Defoort, Sandra Feguson, Angela Schippers, and Sylvie Winslow for their vital administrative work.

The research for this book, which was conducted not only in Winnipeg and Ottawa, but also in Barbados, Iceland, and the United Kingdom, could not have been undertaken without the generous support of several institutions and funding agencies, including the Social Sciences and Humanities Research Council of Canada, RANNÍS the Icelandic Centre for Research, the Canada Research Chair in Western Canadian Social History, the Department of History and Faculties of Arts and Graduate Studies at the University of Manitoba, St. John's College (University of Manitoba), and the University of Winnipeg Research Office. A special thanks goes to Kristina Guiguet for hosting me on two occasions when I was researching at Library and Archives Canada in Ottawa, and for being a dear friend.

Librarians and archivists at the Archives of Manitoba, Barbados Department of Archives, Landsbókasafn Íslands, Library and Archives Canada, the National Archives (UK), and the University of Manitoba

Acknowledgments xi

Archives and Special Collections provided vital assistance with research. I would particularly like to thank Chris Kotecki, Idelle Talbot, and Paula Warsaba at the Archives of Manitoba, and Sigrid Johnson, head of the Icelandic Collection at the University of Manitoba. Sigrid not only helped me access the collection but also provided me with office space. Thanks also to Bob Christopherson, Nelson Gerrard, the Hearn family, the late Donna Skardal, and Johanna Wilson for their generosity in sharing manuscript material and photographs from their private collections.

Conducting the research for this book required me to put considerable time and effort into learning Icelandic. Birna Bjarnadóttir, former chair in Icelandic at the University of Manitoba, enthusiastically supported me in that effort, including by speaking Icelandic with me during our many journeys together on the number 36 Winnipeg Transit bus. I benefitted from Helga Hilmisdóttir's superb skills as a language teacher through three undergraduate courses and a field course in Iceland. I also want to thank Guðrún Laufey Guðmundsdóttir, Úlfar Bragason, and the language instructors at the Árni Magnússon Institute for Icelandic Studies, where I completed the Summer Course in Modern Icelandic in 2007. Through no fault of any of those listed above, my knowledge of the language remains imperfect. Given this, I have relied on Ólafur Arnar Sveinsson and Nelson Gerrard for help with the translation of specific passages quoted here. Takk kærlega fyrir.

This book has been improved by feedback from colleagues and reviewers in a number of contexts. Earlier versions of the chapters were presented at conferences, including the Canadian Historical Association (Chapters 4, 5, 6), the Keewatin Graduate Student conference (Chapters 3 and 7), Western Canadian Studies (Chapter 2), and the núna/now Iceland/Canada Art Convergence (Chapter 1). I particularly want to thank Laurie Bertram, Sarah Carter, Ágústa Edwald, Robin Grazley, Paula Hastings, Laura Ishiguro, and Laura Madokoro, all of whom were among my co-presenters on panels at those meetings. Earlier versions of Chapters 4 and 5 were published in the *Journal of the Canadian Historical Association* (2006) and the edited collection *Within and Without the Nation: Canadian History as Transnational History* (2015). The former benefitted from the input of then JCHA editor Wendy Mitchinson and four anonymous reviewers, and the latter was improved by the comments and suggestions of the participants at the 2009 "Inside and Outside the Nation" Canadian history workshop and two anonymous reviewers. My sincere thanks also go to John Weaver for his insightful commentary on an early version of the full manuscript.

As a rookie author, I found UBC Press all that I could have hoped for in a publisher. Thank you to Darcy Cullen, first for encouraging me to submit a proposal, then for her patience through many delays on my part, and finally for her expert guidance in helping me move through the submission, review, and approval processes. The two anonymous reviewers gave the manuscript their careful attention and made several helpful suggestions for improvement. Thanks also to Lesley Erickson for seeing the book through to the finish line.

My final acknowledgments go to my family. My late *afi* (grandfather) Jörundur Árni Eyford tried to teach me not only Icelandic vocabulary but also the Saulteaux words he had learned from our Ojibwe neighbours. My mom Heather, dad Arnold, uncle Allan, brother Regan, sister Leanne, and many aunts, uncles, and cousins across Canada and in Iceland have all been interested in and supportive of my work through many years of study. Thank you to Aleisha Reimer, my partner and best friend, for her intelligence, strength, and tenacity, and for pushing me when I needed a push. All of the best things in my life, especially Lilja and Ben, I owe to her.

White Settler Reserve

Introduction

ON 18 SEPTEMBER 1877, the Canadian ministers of agriculture and the interior and their top deputies visited New Iceland, a reserve for Icelandic immigrants on the southwest shore of Lake Winnipeg. Two weeks later, the *Toronto Globe* published an account of this "ministerial inspection" that also included an overview of the troubled history of this "special experiment of immigrant colonization." Since the arrival of the first group of colonists in the fall of 1875, the Icelanders had endured hunger, crop failures, and disease, including an outbreak of smallpox that had put the colony under rigid quarantine for almost eight months. The anonymous *Globe* correspondent noted that though the Department of Agriculture's Immigration Branch had "spent and loaned ... large sums of public money ... to establish this settlement," its future was still in doubt. The article explained that the ministers had visited New Iceland to assess the situation for themselves and to determine whether government support for Icelandic immigration and colonization should continue.[1] This was a matter of politics as well as policy; opponents of Prime Minister Alexander Mackenzie's Liberal government had cited New Iceland as an example of a failed colonization policy. Critics accused government officials of making a grave error in the choice of colony site and characterized the Icelanders as an "effete and unprogressive race ... not equal to the struggle of life on this continent ... [They] must inevitabl[y] succumb to the fate of the 'least fit.'"[2]

The *Globe* article defended the government against the accusations of incompetence and portrayed the settlers in a favourable light. It described them as worthy colonists – an orderly, literate, and hardworking people

John Lowe (1824–1913), secretary of the Department of
Agriculture, a key figure in the establishment of New Iceland.
Library and Archives Canada, William Topley Collection, 1936–270.

intent on achieving social and material progress despite the difficulties they had faced. Casting aside all evidence to the contrary, it boldly declared that "the experiment of this colony may be pronounced a success."[3] This was hardly the assessment of a disinterested observer; in fact, the author of the article was none other than John Lowe, secretary of the Department of Agriculture, one of the officials who were principally responsible for organizing the colonization scheme.[4] However, Lowe's article was more than an attempt to whitewash the failures of this particular colony. It was also a defence of a whole mode of colonization in which the state took an active role in encouraging group immigration and settlement on reserved tracts of land. "Aided colonization in communities,"

Lowe asserted, "is nothing new on this continent. It has succeeded where it has been properly looked after."[5]

THIS BOOK EXAMINES THE role of land reserves for European immigrants in the colonization of the Canadian Northwest during the late nineteenth century. The practice of reserving land for European ethno-religious groups was an important part of Canada's immigration and land settlement policies in this period. Colonization reserves were part of a patchwork of reserved spaces in Manitoba and the North-West Territories. They were created simultaneously, and they shared borders with reserves for Indians, Metis people, and private corporations, such as the Hudson's Bay Company and the Canadian Pacific Railway.[6] Even areas that were open for homesteading by individuals were in effect reserved, in that they were designated for the exclusive use of incoming non-Aboriginal settlers. The 1876 Indian Act stipulated that "no Indian or non-treaty Indian ... shall be held capable of having acquired or acquiring a homestead ... right to ... any surveyed or unsurveyed lands."[7]

The reserve system developed out of a process of negotiation and contestation as Indigenous peoples pushed for the recognition of their claims to their traditional territories, and as European migrants, who could choose to relocate to any one of several settlement frontiers, negotiated the conditions under which they would settle in Canadian territory. The "Half-breed" reserves were created as a result of the 1870 Manitoba Act after the Red River Métis mounted an armed resistance to Canadian rule. Indian reserves were established as part of the southern numbered treaties between 1871 and 1877. From the Canadian state's perspective, the Manitoba Act and the treaties granted limited recognition to Indigenous property rights and minimized the threat of further armed conflict in the region, while at the same time legitimizing the appropriation and redistribution of territory for agricultural and commercial development.[8] The legal and administrative vehicle for that redistribution was the 1872 Dominion Lands Act, which established rules for homestead lands and, after 1874, colonization reserves. Administratively, the practice of reservation was carried out through the Department of the Interior. Whereas the department's Dominion Lands Branch created colonization reserves in concert with the Department of Agriculture's Immigration Branch, its Indian Affairs Branch negotiated treaties and allocated Indian reserves. After 1892, responsibility for immigration also came under the Department of the Interior's expansive mandate.

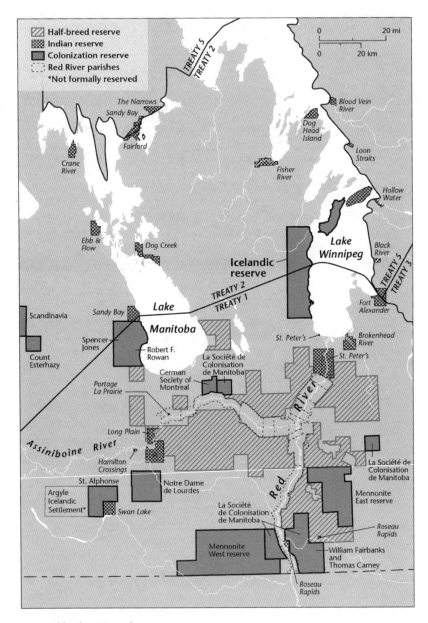

Reserved land in Manitoba, 1870–86

The southwest shore of Lake Winnipeg, in the Interlake region of what is now Manitoba, was established as a "reserve for Icelanders" by Order-in-Council in October 1875. This tract was one of the earliest colonization reserves in the Northwest.[9] It retained its reserve status until July 1897, when it was opened to "any class of settlers who may wish to locate in that vicinity."[10] The area had been identified as having potential as an agricultural settlement as early as 1858, when Canadian geologist Henry Youle Hind examined it during his Assiniboine and Saskatchewan expedition.[11] The Canadian government created the Icelandic reserve to encourage the increasing numbers of Icelandic immigrants arriving in Canadian ports to settle in the Northwest. During the mid-nineteenth century, a growing population and adverse environmental conditions put pressure on Iceland's traditional rural society. Thus, interest in emigration developed during the 1860s, and after 1870 a few individuals and small groups of young people began moving to Wisconsin. Only one of them, twenty-year-old Sigtryggur Jónasson, chose to settle in Canada. In 1873, the Scottish Canadian Allan Steamship Line helped transform Icelandic emigration into a mass movement of whole families. The dominion and Ontario governments worked with the Allan Line to redirect Icelandic migration to Canada by offering generous transportation subsidies. Early settlement experiments in Ontario were largely a failure, and in the spring of 1875 Baptist missionary John Taylor petitioned Ottawa to relieve the suffering of the Icelandic immigrants in the province. That summer the Departments of Agriculture and the Interior sent Taylor, Sigtryggur Jónasson, and four other Icelanders to examine lands in Manitoba or the North-West Territories with the goal of finding a suitable tract for an Icelandic colony. This group, called the Icelandic Deputation, selected an area along the west coast of Lake Winnipeg, extending fifty miles north from the 1870 provincial boundary. The first group of about 250 settlers arrived at Willow Point near the southern end of the reserve on 21 October 1875. They dubbed their colony Nýja Ísland (New Iceland) and soon founded the village of Gimli, named for the paradise where, according to ancient Norse myth, the gods and heroes would live after the end of the world. From its inception until the first decade of the twentieth century, New Iceland was important both as a destination for Icelandic migrants and as a mother colony that spawned other settlements in Canada and the United States. Between 1870 and 1914, approximately fifteen to twenty thousand Icelanders – roughly a quarter of Iceland's population – came to North America.[12] More than 80 percent of them settled initially in Canada.

The minister of the interior consented to the Icelanders' choice of reserve location despite pre-existing and competing claims from local Indigenous people to have one or more Indian reserves established in the same location.[13] The region was home to Cree, Ojibwe, and Metis people who combined hunting, fishing, and agriculture with involvement in the fur trade as trappers, suppliers of country produce, and wage-labourers.[14] By the early 1870s, permanent settlements had developed at several fur-trade posts and mission stations around Lake Winnipeg, including White Mud River in what became the Icelandic reserve.[15] The Ojibwe and Cree who negotiated Treaty 1 with the Canadian government in 1871 claimed the southwest shore of Lake Winnipeg as part of an extensive Indian reserve. However, Canadian negotiators, intent on keeping reserve size to a minimum, rejected their claim.[16] As a result, several people who lived in what became New Iceland received treaty annuities with the St. Peter's band, whose reserve was near the mouth of the Red River.[17] In 1874, a group of Cree from Norway House petitioned Lieutenant Governor Alexander Morris for a reserve in this location.[18] Government officials looked favourably upon this request until the Icelandic Deputation chose the site.[19] In the ensuing negotiations for Treaty 5, the Norway House Cree were redirected to Fisher River. A year later, the Canadian treaty negotiators rejected a request from the Indigenous residents of White Mud River, soon to be renamed Icelander's River by the colonists, that their settlement be designated as an Indian reserve.[20]

This book focuses on New Iceland to explore the ideas, practices, and processes that were integral to the building of a new colonial society in the Canadian Northwest between 1870 and 1900. It examines the internal dynamics of colonization by detailing the Icelandic colonists' relationship to the Indigenous people whom they displaced, to other settler groups, and to the Canadian government. In the process, it draws out the tensions between the designs and perceptions of government officials in Ottawa and Winnipeg, the administrative machinery of the state, and the lives and strategies of people at the local level as they attempted to navigate their shifting positions in the new order.

The central problem addressed in these pages is the uneasy fit between colonization reserves and the political, economic, and cultural logic of nineteenth-century liberalism, which, as Ian McKay argues, fundamentally shaped Canada in the century between 1840 and 1940.[21] According to McKay, Canada in this period was "simultaneously ... an *extensive* projection of liberal rule across a large territory and an *intensive* process of subjectification, whereby liberal assumptions are internalized and normalized within the dominion's subjects."[22] How do immigrant colonization reserves such as New Iceland, with their collective rights to land use and varying degrees of cultural autonomy, fit into this picture? Traditionally, it has been asserted that they do not fit at all: in the 1930s, political economist W.A. Mackintosh, echoing American historian Frederick Jackson Turner's frontier thesis, declared that immigrant group settlements were an aberrant departure from the "normal" type of settlement in which a pioneer individualist breaks away from well-worn paths and seeks freedom on the open frontier.[23] This book puts Mackintosh's interpretation of colonization reserves to the test. How did the reserves relate to the homestead system based on individualized freehold tenure? Were they islands of social, economic, cultural, and political difference, far removed from the mainstream of Anglo-Canadian settler society?

The argument presented here is that, far from being exceptional, immigrant colonization reserves were an integral part of the creation of a new liberal colonial order in the Canadian Northwest. As a state policy, they reflected the various "systematic" approaches to colonization that liberal thinkers developed during the nineteenth century and that were applied in diverse contexts across the British Empire and in the United States.

The spatial practice of reservation helped ensure peaceful relations between Indigenous peoples, the dominion government, and migrant settlers in Manitoba and the North-West Territories during the 1870s. Canadian officials aspired to both replicate and improve upon the experience of the western United States. They hoped to duplicate US success in attracting thousands of European agricultural settlers, but they also wanted to avoid the costly Indian wars that had accompanied American westward expansion. Attenuated lines of communication, a tiny settler population, and the Canadian state's limited financial, military, and administrative capacities guaranteed that using force to acquire Indigenous land would be a hazardous gambit. Treaties and Indian reserves helped ensure that Indigenous people did not militarily resist colonization, and immigrant reserves were an incentive to encourage agricultural settlers to apply their labour and capital to the development of the West. For both Indigenous people and settlers, reserved land held the promise of securing collective interests against the claims of other competing groups and of ensuring relative autonomy from centralized authority. Reserves seemed to offer a stable base of land and resources that would allow for a syncretic adaptation to the new order. For example, in the 1870s and 1880s, farmers on Indian reserves in the Treaty 4 area and Mennonites on reserves in southern

Manitoba both demonstrated that traditional modes of life, culture, and religion could coexist with new patterns of economic activity.[24] It was precisely this promise of being able to re-establish kin, community, and culture in a resource-rich environment, closely tied to local and continent-wide markets by the railway, that led the Icelandic Deputation to choose the reserve site on Lake Winnipeg in 1875.

The paradox of such reserves was that though they promised their residents autonomy within a limited sphere, they also created opportunities for regimes of surveillance and projects of social engineering. Reserves were tutelary spaces, where, under the watchful eye of state administrators, citizens could be made. The fact that the Canadian government saw Indian reserves as "social laboratories where the Indian could be 'civilized' and prepared for coping with the European" is well known.[25] However, many of the same discourses about civilization and assimilation were applied to the non-English-speaking European immigrants who settled in reserved spaces. Federal officials envisioned the day that, like Indian reserves, immigrant reserves would cease to exist, and their residents would be fully assimilated members of Canadian society.[26] The expected timelines for the two types of reserve were dramatically different, as were the levels of coercion and interference deemed necessary to achieve the desired ends. These differences were encoded in the unique legal and administrative regimes that governed the various types of reserves. In the case of Indigenous people, certain pieces of legislation, beginning with the 1857 Gradual Civilization Act, defined "Indians" as a distinct category of non-citizens. The "enfranchisement" provisions of these laws laid out a complex process by which individuals could renounce their Indian status and attain Canadian citizenship, but in ways that made it difficult or undesirable for them to exercise this option. Indeed, few ultimately did.[27] Immigrant reserves were governed by the 1872 Dominion Lands Act, which laid out a far simpler path to citizenship: as part of the process of obtaining title to a 160-acre homestead, immigrant aliens were required to become naturalized British subjects. In this sense, the act was a compact between immigrant settlers and the Canadian state in which political and civil rights were granted in exchange for adopting practices in relation to landed property that were consistent with notions of improvement.[28]

Although the settlers on colonization reserves were granted many more advantages than their Indian reserve neighbours, their path to landownership and full citizenship was not always straightforward. Much to their chagrin, Canadian authorities often treated the inhabitants of the Icelandic reserve as in need of tutelage before they could be entrusted with liberal rights and freedoms. The colony's problems during its first years tended to reinforce this image of the Icelanders as a backward race, remnants of the ancient European past, whose fitness for the business of colonization in the modern world was suspect at best.[29]

However, from the 1880s until the end of mass migration from Iceland in the first decades of the twentieth century, most assessments of the Icelanders as settlers were extremely positive. Federal officials praised them as model immigrants because of their ability to learn English and their willingness to integrate into the Anglo-Canadian community.[30] In the space of a generation, the Icelandic immigrants, although still forming a distinct ethnic community in western Canada, became tightly integrated with the dominant Anglo-Canadian mainstream and shared many of its basic goals and assumptions.[31]

Their dramatic transformation from impoverished, backward colonists to model citizens of the new dominion was the result of the interplay between their strategies for adaptation and Canadian perceptions about their racial identity. Contemporary European racial theories posited that Icelanders *should* be part of the dominant race. Canadian elites typically believed that "northern peoples" were ideally suited to become colonists and future citizens, and thus the Icelanders were recruited and settled in the Northwest.[32] For their part, many Icelanders were anxious to avoid being slotted into the exclusionary category of immigrant alien. Through the process of naturalization, they sought to claim the full civil and political rights enjoyed by the white British subjects of the dominion. This process began in New Iceland, whose inhabitants contrasted themselves with the region's Indigenous peoples. When they demanded changes in the administration of their reserve, they did so by distinguishing themselves from their mostly "Half-breed" neighbours, arguing that they should be treated in the same manner as other "civilized" communities.[33] This study therefore offers insights into the legal and cultural processes through which European immigrants in the Canadian Northwest acquired white racial identities.[34]

The case of New Iceland provides an opportunity to rethink the place of non-anglophone, non-francophone European immigrants in the development of a liberal white settler-dominated colonial society in the Canadian Northwest. The Icelandic immigrants came from a society that was itself undergoing dramatic social, economic, and political changes in which liberal discourses were central.[35] As reserve colonists, they generally demonstrated a strong desire to escape restrictions built into the "reserve-as-reformatory" structure by establishing a community and a set of institutions based on liberal principles. At the same time, they did not always agree about how to achieve this or whether it was even possible in their particular location on Lake Winnipeg. For the disaffected, Ottawa's slowness in extending individual property and political rights to the reserve, and the paternalistic tendencies of the federal colonization agent John Taylor, were among their principal grievances. As they challenged their exclusion from the promises of the liberal order, they simultaneously helped extend its concepts and practices over a new terrain.

In analyzing the Icelandic reserve as a project, or to use John Lowe's terminology, an "experiment" in liberal colonization, this study employs theoretical insights from the literature on the linkages between space, race, and power in colonial societies.[36] Colonization reserves such as New Iceland were part of a process that brought territories and people in northwest North America into the administrative orbit of the Canadian state. Reservation was a tactic of spatial organization that, when bundled together with other tactics – such as the systematic survey, land registration, and periodic censuses – produced specialized knowledge that enabled Ottawa to govern the region. People and places were linked to one another, and the particular characteristics of each could be quantified and compared in the statistical languages of state administration.[37] How many Icelanders lived in the reserve? What were their birth and death rates? On average, how many acres did they have under cultivation? After 1877, answers to these questions were at the fingertips of politicians and bureaucrats in Ottawa. Officials tasked with assessing the progress of the Icelandic colonization experiment could use these statistics to compare it to other colonization projects, and to form judgments about its success or failure. Significantly, it was the Icelanders themselves who collected, aggregated, and transmitted much of this information through their own system of representative local government.

This type of government is the essence of Michel Foucault's concept of governmentality. Foucault argued that in the eighteenth and nineteenth centuries, a new mode of government developed that differed from those of the past. Rather than simply imposing laws or using coercive means to induce compliance, governance became a question of employing "tactics rather than laws, and even of using laws themselves as tactics – to arrange things in such a way that ... such and such ends may be achieved."[38] The periodic census is a prime example of such tactics. It helped produce "population" as a category, which in turn created new possibilities for the articulation of various administrative projects for improvement.[39] In using this mode of government, the state hoped to shape the behaviour of its subjects in ways that served its larger purposes. If these were to be accomplished, the people themselves needed to share those ambitions, or at least a set of assumptions about the proper social, political, and economic organization of society. In the Canadian state's late-nineteenth-century colonizing project in the Northwest, those assumptions were derived primarily from liberalism.

Any study that places liberalism and colonialism at the centre of analysis must inevitably grapple with the problem of defining these notoriously capacious terms. Extracting a workable definition of either word from an existing body of political, economic, or social theory is easy enough: the difficulty comes in attempting to apply that abstract formula to an idiosyncratic historical context that inevitably deviates from any clear and stable precepts one can muster. The approach adopted here is to avoid rigid definitions in favour of a flexible set of parameters that delimit the field of inquiry in substantive ways but that also leave scope for engaging the localized and historically contingent formations.

There is little disagreement about the salient features of European overseas expansion from the fifteenth century onward – the development of global networks of trade and commerce, the appropriation of land and resources from Indigenous peoples, and the creation of various settler societies through free and forced migration. However, the question of whether these various endeavours amount to a uniform system whose broad global patterns definitively shape events in a multitude of local contexts has been the subject of considerable debate. Nicholas Thomas maintains that global theories of colonialism – whether of the liberal or Marxist variety – obscure the incredible diversity of "colonial projects," both in differing locations and among the colonizers themselves. He calls for a reading of colonialism not as a "unitary project but a fractured one, riddled with contradictions and exhausted as much by its own internal debates as by the resistance of the colonized."[40] Robert J.C. Young, by contrast, is not willing to abandon general patterns for specific locales. He attempts to find a balance between the competing pulls of the global and the local by distinguishing between imperialism and colonialism as distinct but interconnected manifestations of "empire." For Young, empire-as-imperialism relates to the top-down exercise of bureaucratic control, the assertion and expansion of state power within a global political and economic system. By contrast, empire-as-colonialism relates to the more localized phenomena of settlement colonies or the activities of chartered trading companies. Whereas imperialism lends itself more readily to study as a concept, colonialism is best studied as a set of practices that, though they might be employed across multiple sites of empire, often took on a form specific to their locale.⁴¹

To more precisely reflect this notion of colonialism as a process or set of practices, as well as the role of the state in shaping them, this book generally employs the word "colonization." This was the term – rather than the more benign "settlement," which serves to erase the presence of Indigenous peoples – that Canadian officials commonly used to describe their efforts to radically transform northwestern North America during the late nineteenth and early twentieth centuries. Their methods were in large measure derived from the philosophical tenets and administrative practices of nineteenth-century liberalism.⁴²

Ian McKay's definition of liberalism – drawn from the work of Fernande Roy and C.B. Macpherson – also attempts to balance general principles with shifting contexts and time-dependent formations.⁴³ At base, McKay argues, liberalism is predicated on the "epistemological and ontological primacy of the category 'individual'... whose freedom should be limited only by voluntary obligations to others or to God, and by the rules necessary to obtain the equal freedom of other individuals."⁴⁴ The rules and institutions that allow liberal individuals to live in community with each other are derived from three core principles: liberty, equality, and property. The importance accorded to each one changes over time, which makes it possible to distinguish between the different historical forms of liberalism. McKay suggests that the dominant form of "actually existing liberalism" in nineteenth-century Canada entailed "the formal equality of adult male individuals before the law, the liberty of some individuals to certain carefully delimited rights and freedoms, and ... their freedom to acquire and defend private property."⁴⁵ According to McKay, property rights occupied the paramount position in this triad, as one of several preconditions for the actualization of other liberal rights and freedoms. The primary strength of McKay's definition is its flexibility and emphasis on historical contingency. Conceptualizing liberalism as a set of principles that are constantly being rearranged into unique formulations across space and time enables us to see "liberal order" as a dialectical process, in which the goals and tactics of the liberal state intersect with a plurality of hybrid, vernacular liberalisms, as well as "aliberal" ways of thinking about personhood and community.

Although *White Settler Reserve* uses McKay's definition, it also incorporates some of the ways in which the contributors to *Liberalism and Hegemony: Debating the Canadian Liberal Revolution* have suggested it might usefully be reconfigured.⁴⁶ The most important for this study relate to the tension between the universal capacities that liberal theory attributes to the category of "individual" and the exclusionary practices that restrict many people, notably women and racialized minorities, from exercising the rights of liberal individuals.[47] Several commentators draw on Uday Singh Mehta's influential argument that such exclusions were essential to the very definition of the liberal individual. Mehta details how British theorists defined the liberal subject through a process of comparison that invoked developmental hierarchies of race and culture, and that made the actualization of universal capacities conditional upon colonial subjects becoming civilized in distinctly liberal ways. This sort of ordering of peoples was integral to meshing liberalism and empire by constructing an intellectual architecture that rationalized the subordinate status of colonized peoples.[48] In his more recent reflections on this issue, McKay too has followed Mehta's lead to contend that instances of exclusion and subjugation that apparently betray liberal principles, such as the coercive practices of Indian residential schools, can be viewed as consistent with the revolutionary ambition of instilling liberal principles in people who are imagined as backward and uncivilized.[49] This tutelary impulse was present in the Canadian state's approach to colonization, not only with regard to Aboriginal people but also in its relations with immigrant aliens such as the Icelanders. The Northwest was a vast laboratory of liberalism, inclusive of a variety of experiments, in which tactics of liberal government were mobilized in different measures among distinct collectivities within the colonial population.

McKay's call to view Canada as a "historically specific project of [liberal] rule" is one of the three historiographical currents that inform this study. His article "The Liberal Order Framework: A Prospectus for a Reconnaissance of Canadian History" outlines an analytic approach that is national in scope, but at the same time it departs from overtly nationalist historiographies of English and French Canada. McKay's ideas have been influential among historians of Canada working in both French and English in a wide range of subfields.[50] In this sense, the framework has largely fulfilled McKay's aim of building a bridge between traditional political and economic history with social history, as well as histories of state formation, law and order, and moral regulation informed by social and cultural theory, particularly the works of Antonio Gramsci and Michel Foucault.[51]

A similar perspective is at work in the recent literature on empire, sometimes called the "new imperial history" – the second historiographical current upon which this study draws. Scholars such as Christopher Bayly,

Ann Laura Stoler, Antoinette Burton, Catherine Hall, Tony Ballantyne, Alan Lester, and Elizabeth Elbourne have reconstructed the networks of production, communication, knowledge, and cultural exchange that bound various nodes of empire together and have investigated how shifting social categories have informed various colonial projects.[52] Adele Perry's influential work on race and gender in British Columbia has grown out of, and alongside, this literature.[53] I follow Perry's lead in attempting to move beyond the imagined economic, social, cultural, and geographic boundaries of the nation-state to reveal a wider set of connections that helped to shape colonial society in the Canadian Northwest.

Finally, this study owes much to the social and cultural histories of migration and Indigenous-immigrant interaction in Canada. Since the 1970s, these literatures have developed along parallel, but largely separate, tracks. Social historians of immigrant and Aboriginal communities have explored similar issues, including agency, class, racial, and gendered identities, family and household economy, and group relations with the Canadian state. They have generally shared an emphasis on the dialectical quality of cultural adaptation and change, and the admixture of accommodation and resistance.[54] Despite these similarities, these two literatures have had remarkably little to say to one another. As Adele Perry points out, the tendency to treat immigration and colonization as separate topics obscures the symbiotic relationship between the dispossession of Indigenous people and the building of a white settler population.[55] The challenge is not only to bring Indigenous people, immigrants, and the state into the same analytic frame, but also to reveal the internal complexity and the dynamics of their relationships with each other.

This sort of perspective has been lacking in the literature that deals with immigrant reserves. In state-focused studies of Dominion Lands administration and western settlement, the practice of reservation is addressed as one aspect of an overarching policy aimed at facilitating mass migration, railway construction, and agricultural development through a mix of public and private initiatives.[56] Attempts to analyze immigrant group settlement as a separate phenomenon tend to contrast reserves with an idealized "normal" pattern of "individual" settlement that oversimplifies the group and community aspects of British, Anglo-Canadian, or American settlement.[57] The Anglo-Canadian townships in Manitoba were just as much group settlements as their non-British counterparts in the sense that their inhabitants frequently came from the same area. Linked by ties of kinship, ethnicity, and religion, they had travelled west together as part of organized migrations. They also shared similar economic strategies that combined market-oriented production and consumption with family and household strategies for self-sufficiency and intergenerational transfer of wealth.[58] These parallels were lost to early-twentieth-century political economy and social research, which tended to associate group settlement with ethnic minorities who had gone west to "escape a world which pressed heavily upon them not as individuals but as groups."[59]

During the 1930s, the sociologist Carl Dawson went beyond the realm of policy to examine the actual social, economic, and cultural lives of ethnic group settlements. However, his conclusions resembled those of earlier studies: he argued that group settlement, or segregation as he called it, was the product of both the "natural desire of migrants to settle beside neighbours possessing the same language, religion and general culture" and state policies that permitted the practice. It left many of the groups in a condition of "arrested development" that delayed their "natural" process of assimilation into the Canadian social, economic, and political system, "whose outstanding characteristic was an experimental individualism."[60] However, it is far from clear that there was a simple communal/individual binary that separated reserve and non-reserve settler communities from one another. Anthony W. Rasporich draws attention to the utopian aspects of community settlements in western Canada during the late nineteenth and early twentieth centuries. Discussing British, Anglo-Canadian and American, and Continental European communities, he identifies a plurality of "abortive utopias" that sprang from diverse ideological currents ranging from the deeply conservative and religious to liberal-anarchist to socialist visions of a new order.[61]

Since the 1970s, the idea that there is a one-way trajectory from cultural distinctiveness to assimilation, and that traditional cultures are antithetical to participation in the market economy, has been challenged from a number of directions. Historical geographers have offered some important insights into the relationship between spatial organization and cultural change.[62] Social historians such as Royden Loewen and Kenneth Sylvester have turned Dawson's conclusions on their head by suggesting that, far from arresting development, economic and social patterns built on shared ties of language, religion, and culture were crucial to the successful adaptation of migrants. Older patterns of life intersected with new ones, a process that allowed the migrants to balance household and community-based economic strategies with growing participation in the market economy.[63] However, these social histories say relatively little about the role of the state in planning, sponsoring, and carrying out these group settlement projects. An interesting new perspective has been added by Rod Bantjes, who uses insights from Foucault to reinterpret group settlements. Bantjes sees reserves as largely the product of a relatively weak state acquiescing to the demands of subject populations for "asylums from the cruel forces of political economy."[64] He demonstrates how in practice, these reserves were less asylums than reformatories, where subordinate populations could be acclimatized to the demands of liberal political economy. Governmental apparatuses, particularly the survey grid, transport networks, individualized land tenure, and the state education system, slowly undermined the patterns of communal settlement and production.[65] This renewed focus on state power is important, but it runs the risk of resurrecting the false dichotomy between group settlement and its supposedly normal equivalent, with the former inherently communitarian and the latter competitive and individualistic, which does not hold up to micro-level analysis. Even when the intent is to demonstrate how government mechanisms internalized liberal principles of self-rule, this process can easily be reduced to a top-down exercise in social control. The challenge in studying land reservation and group settlement is to capture not only the relationship between the state and the people on the reserves, but also the internal debates within reserve communities. A microhistory approach is well suited to this task; the analysis presented here draws methodological insights from other studies of agricultural migrants that are often transnational in scope, while at the same time offering detailed examinations of particular local contexts in Canada and the United States.[66]

This approach has thus far been absent in the literature on Icelandic immigrants in North America. In comparison to work about other European ethnic groups, relatively little scholarship addresses their migration and resettlement experiences. Until recently, celebratory community histories from the 1950s and 1960s, emphasizing material progress and the personal achievements of Canadians or Americans of Icelandic descent, remained the standard general works on the subject.[67] Two more recent monographs are in large measure derived from these earlier histories and do not engage with the wider literature on migration and ethnicity.[68] Apart from a few articles and one master's thesis, the Icelanders were largely absent from the great upsurge in immigration and ethnic history in Canadian and American academic circles during the 1970s and 1980s.[69] One important exception is *Icelandic River Saga,* Nelson Gerrard's 1985 study of the Icelandic River district of New Iceland. Although presented in the format of a western Canadian community history book, its careful primary and secondary research has more in common with detailed microhistorical studies of rural communities.[70]

However, historians from Iceland have provided valuable insights into the background, processes, and demographic character of emigration from Iceland between 1870 and 1914. During the 1970s, Júníus H. Kristinsson and Helgi Skúli Kjartansson explored the general patterns and local manifestations of Iceland's short-lived but intense emigration movement. Prior to his untimely death in 1983, Kristinsson compiled a nominal record of 14,268 migrants, based on parish registers, passenger contracts, and emigrant reminiscences.[71] Kjartansson used these data to produce several articles on the demographic character of Icelandic emigration and has elaborated on the role of shipping in fostering the movement.[72] His recent monograph, co-authored by Steinþór Heiðarsson, compiles and expands on these contributions.[73] Although Kjartansson and Heiðarsson offer a comprehensive analysis of Icelandic emigration informed by the international literature on migration, they do not extend their analysis to the development of Icelandic communities in Canada and the United States. A few recent publications and graduate theses have begun to fill this void, but much more work remains to be done.[74]

This study offers insights into the establishment of the Icelandic immigrant community in the trans-border West but also seeks to situate it within a broader contextual frame of western colonization and liberal transformation. Chapter 1 examines the convergence of Icelandic mass migration and Canadian expansionism in the mid-1870s. It focuses on how the immigration policies and practices of the Canadian state reflected contemporary thinking about the relationship between race and nation building. Chapter 2 traces the roots of land reservation and group settlement in the history of British colonialism and explores how Ottawa used these practices in its efforts to colonize northwest North America after 1870. Influential thinkers on colonial questions believed that group settlements of white families were the most efficient method of colonization. The book then more closely scrutinizes the experience of the Icelandic colonists. Through an analysis of the first two contingents of settlers in 1875 and 1876, Chapter 3 provides a detailed picture of their origins, their demographic character, their reasons for leaving Iceland, and their settlement patterns in the reserve. Chapter 4 discusses the processes through which the New Icelanders displaced Indigenous people. It focuses on the smallpox epidemic of 1876-77 – the pivotal event in the colony's early history – in which the practices of public health and land administration served to reinforce each other. John Taylor, the Canadian government's Icelandic agent, is the subject of Chapter 5. Over the course of his long life, Taylor was, in succession, a convicted slave trader in Barbados, a Baptist missionary in Ontario, and a Canadian colonization agent in the Northwest. As Icelandic agent, he employed a paternalistic style of administration that won him both close friends and bitter enemies among the Icelanders. Chapter 6 deals with the efforts of the Icelanders to govern themselves through the creation of a unique municipal system. This local government was critical to their emergence as political subjects aligned with the norms and assumptions of the liberal state, although some Canadian legislators were unwilling to grant them political rights before they had become property owners and naturalized British subjects. The Icelanders' problems in converting their homestead claims into private property are the subject of the final chapter. It explores how Ottawa attempted to use the loan it had granted to the Icelanders as leverage in a futile attempt to hold the crumbling colony together. In this protracted dispute, the issues of indebtedness became entwined with personal liberty and citizenship.

This study of New Iceland offers an opportunity to draw linkages between two historiographies – immigration history and the history of colonialism – that often have little to say to each other, particularly in the Canadian context. The arrival of Icelanders in the Lake Winnipeg region was part of the profound changes experienced by its Cree, Ojibwe, and Metis inhabitants in the years after 1870. Economically, these changes included the restructuring of the fur-trade economy, the signing of the treaties, the creation of Indian reserves, and the development of new resource industries. At the same time, the legal and institutional framework of a new cultural order was being articulated through the efforts of Indian agents and missionaries tasked with bringing about Aboriginal compliance with the norms of white civilization.

This process has been well documented in many other contexts, but what has been less frequently explored is the way that racialized and gendered assumptions were used to extend control over non-English-speaking European immigrants who lived and worked within the policies of the colonial state. Lake Winnipeg provides an interesting case in which the lines separating Indigenous people and European colonizers were blurred. As the Icelanders struggled to survive a series of disasters, government officials and public commentators began to criticize their racial character, questioning their fitness for survival in the modern world. However, as the Icelandic colonists became more firmly established in their new home, they were drawn ever deeper into the local colonial project and were increasingly engaged in cultivating not only western lands, but also white racial identities.

I
Northern Dreamlands
Canadian Expansionism and Icelandic Migration

In May 1873, Department of Agriculture secretary John Lowe privately sought the advice of Lord Dufferin, Canada's governor general, on an important question of immigration policy. Lowe had received word from William Dixon, Canada's chief emigration agent in London, that a large migration from Iceland would probably occur that summer. Lowe's basic question to Dufferin was whether this migration should be directed to Canada. More specifically, he wanted to know "if the Icelanders were ... to come to the Prov. of Quebec, would they be adapted to the country? Or how would they be likely to consort with the Lower Canadians in the matter of religion?"[1] Dufferin was thought to be an authority on these questions because twenty years earlier he had travelled in Iceland for a few weeks. His rollicking account of the voyage, published in 1857 as *Letters from High Latitudes,* achieved some renown as a work of popular travel literature and was familiar to Lowe and other Canadian civil service mandarins engaged in the business of immigration and colonization. In 1864, Deputy Minister of the Interior Edmund Allen Meredith recorded in his diary that Dufferin's humorous narrative had made him laugh aloud in public.[2] Dufferin's book did not claim to be a scientific analysis of Iceland's people and society, but its author's pre-eminent social and political position gave his opinion considerable weight and made him a logical person to consult on the question of Icelandic immigration. In response to Lowe's query, Dufferin wrote, "I should say, the Icelanders would make good immigrants. They very much resemble the Norwegians. They are quiet peaceable folk, Lutheran in Religion but not fanatical."³ With this endorsement, Lowe set out to mobilize the financial resources and administrative machinery at his disposal to make Icelandic immigration to Canada a reality. He wrote to Dixon that "an immigration of Icelanders is much desired in Canada ... Facilities will be afforded to them to reach the Dominion lands in the North west where free grants of 160 acres would be made to each head of family or adult persons over 21 years of age."⁴ Two years later, this general offer had evolved into the Icelandic reserve colonization scheme.

THIS CHAPTER TRACES THE convergence of Icelandic mass migration and Canadian colonial expansion in the Northwest. Iceland's emigration movement coincided with Canada's aggressive new immigrant recruitment campaign focused on northern Europe. Stumbling upon the burgeoning emigration, agents of the Allan Steamship Line and the Canadian government successfully worked to redirect it from the Midwestern United States to Canada. The migration arose independently of Canadian recruitment efforts, but they were nonetheless important in facilitating it and directing its course. Icelandic migrants were a small component in the colonization of the Northwest, but an exploration of why Ottawa so vigorously recruited them offers a revealing window into the goals and assumptions of the larger project.

The main question addressed here is why Icelandic migration and Canadian colonial expansion became intertwined when, viewed from a distance, such an outcome seems unlikely. In 1966, the historian Norman Macdonald posed a similar question: "What particular obligation was the Dominion government under that it should discriminate between the Icelanders, who were a decided minority of the population and who brought little into the country" and other immigrants?⁵ What perplexed Macdonald was that the government's generosity toward the Icelanders seemed at variance with the liberal economic philosophy that underlay its policy during the period – a view of the world stressing individual self-sufficiency and personal initiative, and discouraging reliance on government. Canada's immigration policies in the 1870s were a dynamic mixture of material and cultural motivations; economic imperatives coexisted, not always harmoniously, with dreams about the future racial and cultural composition of the nation.⁶

The assumptions of Canadian immigration policy were often braided together under the concept of "desirability." Variations of the phrase "a desirable class of immigrants" frequently appeared in government reports and publications of the period. The first part of this chapter unpacks the meaning and significance of this concept. From there the chapter considers the question of why the Icelanders were seen as desirable immigrants in the early 1870s. At the time, there was little evidence to support such a conclusion and even some that contradicted it.

This chapter also recasts a familiar theme in both Canadian and Icelandic historiography – the emergence of colonial nationalism as the product of related transnational discourses about race and national belonging.[7] In both Canada and Iceland, the gradual political transition from colonial dependency to self-governing nation-state that occurred between the mid-nineteenth and mid-twentieth centuries was underwritten by a set of cultural projects whose purpose was to define and create boundaries around an imagined national community. These projects were distinct, but they shared a vocabulary drawn from the contemporary efforts of other European countries to fashion national genealogies and definitions of national character. Of particular importance was the idea that the political institutions and social organization of the ancient peoples of northern Europe were the basis for the national and imperial greatness of the western European nations and their colonial offspring. Thomas Jefferson believed that the representative institutions that he and his revolutionary colleagues created in the United States had their origins in the ancient assemblies of the German forests.[8] The European Romantic movement's fascination with the language, culture, and political traditions of the ancient Germanic tribes increased the interest in this idea and lent support to scientific theories about the racial superiority of the "northern races," which were variously labelled Caucasian, Teutonic, Nordic, or Aryan.[9] This interpretation of history offered both nationalists and imperialists a powerful justification for the legitimacy of their aspirations.

Visions of nation and empire in Iceland and Canada were very much derived from these larger currents. Iceland was a source of endless fascination to European Romanticism because of its presumed isolation from world history. Philologists claimed that the Icelandic language was the ancient Norse tongue, once common to all Scandinavia, and ethnologists argued that Icelandic people were a racial anachronism, a strand of the ancient northern race preserved on an isolated northern isle. Those who were interested in Iceland's medieval literature imagined contemporary Icelanders as modern equivalents of characters in the sagas. Icelanders helped to create and perpetuate many of these ideas, which became important to Icelandic nationalism. The island's nationalist project focused on a shared language and presumed ethnic and racial homogeneity, and aimed for greater domestic control over the homeland.

Many nationalists in Iceland saw the exodus of part of the population as a threat to the nation's well-being. In English-speaking Canada, by contrast, immigration underpinned visions of imperial destiny.[10] Anglo-Canadian dreamers looked forward to the reunion of the northern races in the Canadian Northwest, where they would build a transcontinental colonial empire destined to become a world power.[11] Knowledge of the Icelanders' racial character, largely derived from travel literature, seemed to presage their rapid material advancement as colonists and their aptitude to become nation builders. However, as became obvious when problems arose at New Iceland, ideas of racial fitness were not stable: positive valuations of racial character could easily be reversed.

Because race is associated with unstable meanings, it is difficult to define. It is best understood as a historically constructed category in which perceived physical differences are invested with meanings that can be mobilized as a basis for, and justification of, social hierarchy and asymmetries of power.[12] The articulations of race that this chapter addresses conform to the general picture of nineteenth-century racial thought, in which a mix of cultural characteristics, such as language, manners, and social organization, and perceived biological or physical difference, became increasingly more deterministic as the century progressed. As Christine Bolt succinctly states, after 1850, "something called 'race' came to be seen as the prime determinant of all the important traits of body and soul, character and personality, of human beings and nations."[13]

The relationship between race and nation is similarly a thorny topic. In Benedict Anderson's enduring definition of the nation as an "imagined political community," race is relegated to a supporting role. Anderson suggests that racial hierarchy did not originate in nationalist ideology but rather in aristocratic class distinctions that were interpolated into the "official nationalism" of the later nineteenth century.[14] In the context of imperial expansion, the general principle that the nobility was innately superior to other levels of society was broadened to conceptualize the relationship between colonizer and colonized; an English merchant might be inferior to an English lord, but both were superior to the Native population in any particular corner of the Empire.[15] Ann Laura Stoler highlights the ways in which the boundaries of race and other categories of inclusion/exclusion produced in colonial contexts circulated back through the metropole.[16] These exclusions were "not concerned solely with the visual markers of difference, but with the relationship between visible characteristics and invisible properties, outer form and inner essence."[17] In settler societies such as Canada, the question of inclusion/exclusion was of paramount importance. Government officials strongly believed that immigration was required for economic development, but it also produced a profound anxiety about the future character of the nation. In essence, this uneasiness was about the capacity of non-British immigrants to become liberal subjects, exercising economic and political rights, and observing various boundaries of class and gender order and moral propriety.

The hopes and fears about immigration were captured in the concept of "desirability." In the general parlance of the Department of Agriculture's Immigration Branch, the extent to which immigrants fit the category of "desirable" was an evaluation of their economic worth. Liberal economic theory saw immigration as essential to growth; immigrants brought both capital and labour that could be applied to the development of the dominion's vast natural resources. They added to the base of producers and consumers in the total economy and thus were vital in growing national wealth. In 1876, the Bureau of Statistics estimated the per capita value of healthy, productive immigrants to Canada at $800.[18] Although Canada's immigration policy gradually became more restrictive and included barriers to Chinese, Japanese, and South Asian migrants, the door was relatively open during the first decade after Confederation. The few formal restrictions that did exist were aimed at excluding people who were seen as unproductive and dependent – the disabled, the sick, and the indigent poor.[19]

Desirable immigrants could either step into vacant low-level niches in the labour market or augment it in areas where demand consistently outstripped supply, such as with female domestic servants.[20] The annual report of the Select Standing Committee on Immigration and Colonization for 1879 outlined the government's policy:

> No mechanics, artisans or professional men, who had simply their labour to offer, are invited to come to Canada, unless, it may be, for special situations requiring skill in certain areas of manufactures. Tenant farmers from the old countries with sufficient means to purchase lands ... are principally invited. Their immigration into Canada will very materially improve their circumstances and add to the wealth of the country. A limited number of female servants will easily find employment and receive much larger compensation for their labour than is offered in European countries.[21]

However, desirability was not simply about occupational criteria or the amount of capital that immigrants brought with them. It could also be an aspect of character, which was perceptible through appearance and demeanour. In 1876, J.J. Daley, agent at the Montreal Immigration Office, wrote that in addition to being "possessed of funds to aid them in their future success," the Mennonites and Icelanders who passed through his station "bore evident proofs of being a desirable class of immigrants and permanent settlers – they wore an aspect of cheerful, hale, resolute industry."[22] As this statement suggests, subjective assessments of intelligence, moral character, and work ethic were important to notions of desirability. The most prized immigrants were those who could contribute the maximum amount of productive and reproductive labour while at the same time being amenable to the assumptions about gender, race, class, and religion that policy makers took for granted as the hallmarks of modern, progressive civilization.

The line between desirable and undesirable immigration was often contested and could shift according to specific contexts and circumstances. In 1879, the BC MP Edgar Dewdney testified before the select committee on Chinese labour and immigration that the Chinese could be considered desirable in some respects, largely because of their high productivity as workers.[23] Another BC parliamentarian, Arthur Bunster, argued vociferously for the undesirability of the Chinese, insisting that their presence had "a very bad effect on the moral character of the white children."[24] Although the Icelanders were never subjected to the level of racist invective that the Chinese encountered in British Columbia, their status as desirable immigrants was not unassailable in Manitoba. In addition, they found themselves in an ambiguous position relative to the nationalist project of their home country.

During roughly the same time that the British North American colonies transitioned from oligarchic rule to responsible government to autonomous status within the British Empire as the Dominion of Canada, the relationship between Iceland and Denmark was transformed. However, unlike their Canadian counterparts, Icelandic nationalists could draw on their country's glorious medieval past as an independent nation to bolster their claims to nationhood. Settled by Norse farmers and their Celtic slaves in the ninth and tenth centuries, Iceland was initially governed by a federation of local chieftaincies who met at an annual assembly called the Alþingi to formulate laws and mete out justice. After 1262, Iceland became part of the Norwegian kingdom and later, as a result of some dynastic shuffling, passed under Danish control. A governing partnership between Icelandic elites and the Danish Crown persisted until the later 1830s, when a few Copenhagen-based Icelandic intellectuals, influenced by liberal reform movements in Europe, began to demand greater autonomy for Iceland. In 1845, a consultative assembly, named the Alþingi after its medieval predecessor, was established, and in 1851 a constituent assembly met for the first time in Reykjavík. The Danish parliament enacted a constitution for Iceland in 1874, giving the Alþingi some legislative powers over internal matters. Home rule was further expanded in 1904, and Iceland became a fully autonomous state in a personal union with the Danish king in 1918. Finally, the tie with the Danish monarchy was severed in 1944, when the Republic of Iceland came into being, albeit in the context of wartime occupation by the United States. Whereas traditional Icelandic historiography has labelled the century-long unwinding of the union with Denmark as a "struggle for freedom," historian Guðmundur Hálfdánarson suggests that it was more of a protracted negotiation about specific terms rather than a dispute over fundamental principles.[25] After mid-century, most Danish legislators adhered to the nationalist principle that ethnic and state borders should coincide and therefore did not generally dispute the legitimacy of Icelandic claims to national distinctiveness or the political aspirations of Icelandic leaders.[26]

Between 1870 and 1914, at least 16,408 people left Iceland, a figure that is estimated to represent a 20 percent net population loss.[27] During the late 1880s and early 1890s, the most intense period of emigration, Icelandic nationalists accused migrants of abandoning the country. Prominent journalists launched a campaign to discredit Icelandic Canadian emigration agents, and the Alþingi strengthened the laws that regulated their activities.[28] In 1893, when dominion and Manitoba emigration agents attempted to give a public lecture in Reykjavík, they were shouted down by a group of government officials, university professors and students, merchants, and "other members of the like class."[29] In the agents' opinion, this hostility did not reflect the attitude of the general population, which remained positively disposed to emigration. Despite the criticisms directed at them, many migrants sympathized with the aims of Icelandic political nationalism.

The preservation of Icelandic language and culture from foreign influences was central to Icelandic cultural nationalism, even for those who did not advocate severing ties with Denmark. Eggert Ólafsson, an eighteenth-century Icelandic poet, naturalist, and staunch defender of the Danish tie, argued that cultural purity and moral stature were fundamentally linked; Icelanders would prosper and the golden age would be revived if foreign influences were abandoned in favour of authentic Icelandic traditions.[30] Iceland's literary heritage was of particular significance in this regard. During the medieval period, its scribes had created compilations of mythic poetry, legal treatises, grammars, documentary histories, and prose sagas about both early Iceland and the kings and heroes of Europe. Some of these manuscripts, and later copies of them, survived and became the subject of great interest for European scholars. Some Icelanders could read these manuscripts without much difficulty, which led Danish philologist Rasmus Christian Rask to conclude that contemporary Icelandic had once been common to all of Viking Age Scandinavia.[31] Although his argument was exaggerated, Icelandic nationalists embraced it and made it a key component of their understanding of their nation as a homogeneous cultural community whose purity needed to be protected.

The themes, images, ideas, and texts that were important to Icelandic claims to cultural distinctiveness also made Icelanders a subject of fascination to outsiders, some of whom visited the island in person. This resulted in the production of a relatively large body of travel writing about Iceland by elite British and American visitors during the later nineteenth century.[32] In her 1882 travelogue *By Fell and Fjord*, Elizabeth Jane Oswald asserted that Iceland's increasing numbers of summer tourists were drawn by one of three things – the fishing, the geology, or the old literature. For her it was the literature, "the vivid Sagas which set men and women of the past before us as if we had known them ourselves."[33] She also noted the special attraction of the language, which gave the same thrill to Old Norse enthusiasts that classical scholars would derive from finding "some lonely island ... where the Greek of Pericles or the Latin of Augustus was still the common speech."[34] The English Romantic William Morris saw the Icelanders as a people forgotten by time – the authentic relics of Europe's medieval past.[35]

Most British and American travellers arrived in Iceland with the belief that "Anglo-Saxons" shared a genealogical connection with the Icelanders, stretching back to the ancient Germanic tribes of northern Europe, but that the islanders' isolation had stunted their racial development. The *New York Tribune* correspondent Bayard Taylor told the bishop of Iceland that he and his American countrymen "claimed kinship of the blood" with the Icelanders through the Goths, Saxons, and Normans.[36] Taylor viewed Iceland as a living ethnology exhibit: "To meet [its common people] was like being suddenly pushed back to the thirteenth century; for all the rich, complex, later developed life of the race has not touched them."[37] Lord Dufferin went much farther back into history, interpreting what he saw in Iceland as proof that Asia was the cradle of the northern races. As he watched the pack-horse caravans wind their way along the rough paths of the Icelandic interior, Dufferin found it easy "to believe that these remote islanders should be descended from Oriental forefathers."[38]

The Icelanders were not alone in being seen as living relics of the past or in being cited to support various theories of racial or linguistic development: western European scholarship and travel writing commonly advanced the same ideas about non-European people and places, as well as peripheral parts of Europe itself. Travel writing described Iceland, Africa, Asia, and the Middle East in strikingly similar terms, and comparisons were sometimes explicit: Bayard Taylor's 1875 travelogue was titled *Egypt and Iceland in the Year 1874*. Such texts served to legitimize imperial expansion by characterizing foreign peoples as inferior, backward, or otherwise outside the march of historical progress.[39] However, as Mary Louise Pratt argues, travel accounts were not simply the product of a monolithic dominant culture defining a subordinate periphery: the periphery was integral to the constant refashioning of the metropolitan self-image by reinforcing the hierarchies of civilization, nation, culture, and race that explained and legitimized empire.[40] In many instances, these discourses were co-productions in which subordinate peoples took an active part, incorporating elements of metropolitan discourse into their own self-representations.[41] This was particularly the case in Iceland, where British and American travellers almost invariably had elite Icelanders as their guides, hosts, informants, and interpreters. Thus, to some extent, the image that ended up in travelogues reflected stories that Icelanders told about themselves.[42] Travellers refracted this knowledge through their own prisms of understanding, incorporating Icelanders into genealogies of nation and empire that explicated past development and projected future destiny, often in racial terms.

The traveller who perhaps went the farthest in explicitly tying Iceland and its people into the currents of empire was the renowned British linguist, explorer, and diplomat Sir Richard Francis Burton. Sent to Iceland on a fact-finding mission for an English capitalist who was interested in developing its sulphur resources, Burton published an encyclopedic two-volume account of the trip in 1875. Titled *Ultima Thule; or a Summer in Iceland*, it joined Lord Dufferin's *Letters from High Latitudes* as the only works on Iceland that are known to have belonged to the Canadian Immigration Branch's reference library.[43] Burton accused previous authors of having "Iceland on the brain" and criticized their hyperbolic descriptions of the landscape as arising from their naivety as travellers.[44] He separated himself from the ranks of besotted tourists by projecting the image of a man of science and learning who had seen the wider world and could therefore cast a more discerning gaze on the island and its inhabitants.[45] His stated purpose was to advocate for the development of the island and its people, whom he believed still possessed the virtues of the ancient Norse but had become lost to history. As he put it, "The Icelander cannot be called degenerate. He is what he was. But whilst the world around, or rather beyond him, has progressed with giant strides, he has perforce remained stationary."[46] Burton saw emigration as a key method for pulling the Icelanders into modernity: it "will be beneficial to the islander, who, instead of dawdling away life at home, will learn to labour and to wait upon a more progressive race."[47] He compared the Icelanders to the Irish and the Basques, who, he asserted, were seeking a new "racial baptism" by moving to North America. He argued that because of their familiarity with toiling in a northern environment, "It might well be worth while for the Dominion [of Canada] to secure a number of these sturdy and strong-brained Northerners, who would form admirable advanced posts along the valley of the Saskatchewan."[48]

Around the same time as Burton made these statements, Canadians with dreams of building a transcontinental empire were voicing similar thoughts about the role of northern peoples in shaping the character of the nation.[49] One of the most passionate dreamers was the Montreal lawyer Alexander Morris, who, as lieutenant governor of Manitoba and Keewatin during the mid-1870s, played an important role in the history of New Iceland. Just as Burton had teased his British countrymen by saying they had Iceland on the brain, some of Alexander Morris's contemporaries alleged that he had "Canada on the brain."[50] In the late 1850s, Morris was among the growing number of young Canadian professional men who looked to the Hudson's Bay Company (HBC) territories as a frontier for colonial expansion. The British and Canadian scientific expeditions led by Captain John Palliser and Professor Henry Youle Hind in 1857–58 helped to overturn the notion of the HBC territory as a barren wilderness, replacing it with a vision of a fertile paradise that would one day be home to millions of agricultural settlers.[51] Morris's 1858 lecture "Nova Britannia; or, British North America, Its Extent and Future" advocated the incorporation of the Red River Colony into Canada and looked forward to the consolidation of all the colonies into a "British North American Colonial Empire."[52] Along with political and economic unification, Morris considered "the right development and formation of national character" to be of paramount importance. That national character was to be based primarily on the values and ideals of nineteenth-century liberalism:

> A widespread dissemination of a sound education – a steady maintenance of civil and religious liberty, and of freedom of speech and thought, in the possession and enjoyment of all classes of the community – a becoming national respect and reverence for the behests of the Great Ruler of events and his Word ... should be the preeminent characteristics of the British American people.

He imagined the day when British, French, and others would be fused into one people, "rendered more vigorous by our northern position."[53]

Morris and other believers in Canada's transcontinental destiny maintained that the country's geographical position would help shape the character of its people. The biggest perceived drawback of northern North America as a field for European colonization, its climate, was thus presented as the very factor that would guarantee its future greatness. This idea reflected the deterministic shift in mid-nineteenth-century racial thinking, part of which entailed an emphasis on the inherent compatibility or incompatibility of the races to particular environments. The success of European imperialism was often explained as a consequence of the northern climate: it had produced a strong, energetic, and virtuous conquering race.[54] In using the adjective "northern" to describe the character of the nation they hoped to build, Canada's imperial dreamers tied their aspirations into wider currents of British imperial thought.

The dreamer who most clearly articulated a vision of the Dominion of Canada as home to a vigorous northern race was Robert Grant Haliburton, an amateur ethnologist and founding member of the imperial-nationalist Canada First movement. His 1869 *Men of the North and Their Place in History* argued that history and geography proved that Canada "must ever be ... a Northern country inhabited by the descendants of Northern races."[55] Like the British race, the race of the new dominion would be a syncretic product, a mix of northern races – the Celtic, Teutonic, and Scandinavian – which were "here again meeting and mingling, and blending together to form a new nationality."[56] In a sweeping summation of human history, Haliburton claimed that the dead hand of ancient Greek and Roman civilization held the south in despotism and choked off liberty. Echoing the contemporary Anglo-American discourse regarding the Germanic roots of democratic government, he declared that modern liberty was an outgrowth of the dynamic political and legal traditions of the northern peoples.

Haliburton's writing explicitly connected Iceland with the destiny of Canada. He felt that the ancient Norsemen were the most interesting of the northern races, and he quoted from the Old Norse *Völuspá* (The seeress's prophecy), part of an ancient collection of poetry preserved in Icelandic manuscripts.[57] When the Icelandic immigrants arrived in the Northwest in 1875, they too drew on the *Völuspá:* they named their first village, Gimli, after the paradise in which the gods and heroes would happily retire following a cataclysmic battle at the end of the world, as a statement of their hopes about their future progress and happiness.[58] For Haliburton, the ancient prophecy of the "destruction and renovation of the earth" foretold a great future for Canada. In his racialized view of historical progress, the northern races were destined "to sweep away every vestige of a dead past, and build up a new world of life and hope in our race."[59] Implicit in Haliburton's vision was that the racially mixed society of the Red River Colony and the greater Northwest was part of the "dead past" to be swept away. After the Dominion of Canada completed the purchase of the Northwest from the HBC in 1869, Canadian expansionists anticipated that their hopes for a continent-wide empire of their own making would be realized. However, the organized resistance of the Red River Métis and their allies to undemocratic territorial rule in 1869–70 forced Ottawa to make a number of concessions that, at least temporarily, frustrated the ambitions of many Canadian dreamers.

Following the Red River resistance and the establishment of Manitoba, immigration became an important focus for Haliburton's associates in the Canada First movement. Through their North-West Emigration Aid Society, they hoped to assist in creating a deluge of immigrants that would shift the region's racial, linguistic, and religious balance against the French and Metis population, and assist in the founding of British institutions.[60] Although their ideal immigrants were British, they were also enthusiastic about the immigration of other northern peoples. The principal Canada First agitator at Red River, Dr. John Christian Schultz, whose father was Norwegian, expressed a keen interest in Icelandic immigration. In August 1875, Schultz assisted William C. Krieger, the dominion government's newly appointed Icelandic emigration agent, during his exploratory tour of Manitoba. Krieger later wrote to Schultz from Akureyri in northern Iceland, promising to forward him a copy of Richard Burton's *Ultima Thule*.[61]

The federal government's emigrant recruitment policies largely reflected the vision of Canada as composed of elements of the northern races. The Immigration Branch concentrated its human and material resources in the European countries, where the Teutons and Celts of contemporary racial theory resided. In 1872, the government greatly intensified its recruitment efforts to better compete with other potential emigrant destinations, particularly the United States, Australia, and New Zealand. An increased number of emigration agents were sent to the United Kingdom, France, Belgium, Germany, Switzerland, and the Scandinavian countries to disseminate propaganda, cultivate connections with local organizations interested in emigration, and supervise a system of commissions designed to give steamship booking agents an incentive to direct "desirable classes" of emigrants to Canada.[62] The man sent to establish this system in Scandinavia was William McDougall, whose ambitions of being the first lieutenant governor of the North-West Territories had been frustrated by Louis Riel and the Métis in 1869. In January 1873, McDougall was dispatched to Copenhagen as Canada's "Special Agent for the Scandinavian Kingdoms." Although such appointments were typically patronage plums that yielded few tangible results, McDougall took his mission very seriously. He considered mass migration from Scandinavia to be "one of the most important movements of modern times" and hoped that his exertions would facilitate the relocation of "the vigorous descendants of the 'Vikings' and 'Danes,' who conquered England and Scotland in ancient times, from their original home to the new and 'greater Britain' in the West."[63]

Scandinavian immigration and colonization was a cherished dream of Canadian expansionists and policy makers that, with a few exceptions, went largely unfulfilled until the early twentieth century, when the waning availability of land in the American West led Scandinavian migrants to move north into Canada. From the 1850s, thousands of Scandinavian migrants arrived annually at Quebec City, but the vast majority simply used Canada as a convenient transport corridor to destinations in the Midwestern United States. Canadian officials cast an envious eye on the success of US railway and colonization companies at attracting immigrants, particularly from Norway, and in the 1850s they commenced an active recruitment campaign in Norway that yielded limited success by creating a small colony in Gaspé.[64] In 1863, the engineer, inventor, and railway surveyor Sanford Fleming made an unsuccessful bid to convince a Norwegian farmer who was on an exploratory trip to assess potential colony sites in Canada and the American West that he should examine Red River, which "would shortly be opened up for Colonization." Fleming thought that Norwegians would be ideal colonists for northern North America. He told a friend, "The climate of Norway is so similar to that of the Red River country that people from the former could very easily adapt themselves to the latter than [sic] emigrants from more southern latitudes."[65]

Ten years later, efforts to recruit Scandinavian immigrants and to create colonies in the Northwest were renewed, first by McDougall and then by Colonel Hans Mattson, a Swedish American immigration promoter, politician, and Civil War veteran who was hired as dominion emigration agent for Scandinavia in September 1873. Despite their best efforts to elbow into an already crowded emigrant market with an energetic propaganda campaign, a system of commissions for agents, and assisted passage for certain groups of preferred migrants, they ultimately had limited success. Their main obstacle was an established pattern of migration to the United States, perpetuated by ties of kin and community and a well-articulated information and transportation network. McDougall and Mattson tried to overcome this problem by partnering with individuals to promote various group colonization schemes. The hope was that, once established, they would act as magnets for future immigration. However, McDougall's attempt to help Norwegian reverend J.H. Simonsen found a colony in Manitoba fell flat, and Mattson's success in establishing Swedish colonies in Minnesota was not repeated during his brief tenure as a Canadian agent.[66]

Although efforts in Scandinavia were a disappointment, they had the unintended consequence of helping bring the burgeoning emigration movement in Iceland to the attention of the federal government. At precisely this moment, Icelandic emigration changed from a few young people travelling to Wisconsin in response to favourable reports from Danish and Norwegian friends and relatives, to an organized mass movement of whole families. To this point, only one of the young Icelandic migrants, Sigtryggur Jónasson, had settled in Canada. Although the Canadian government had no evidence of Icelanders becoming successful immigrants in North America, the immigration officials classed Icelanders as "desirable immigrants" because of their assumed similarity to Scandinavians. Much of this is encapsulated in Lord Dufferin's May 1873 remark to John Lowe about the physical and cultural resemblance between Icelanders and Norwegians.[67] Others reinforced Dufferin's assessment: in noting the "great agitation among people of all classes on the subject of emigration" in Iceland, Hans Mattson commented that Icelanders "are a hardy, frugal, and industrious race – the oldest type of Scandinavian – they are well inured to a northerly climate, are excellent herdsmen and fishermen and I believe that the eastern coast of Canada would be well adapted for their future home."[68]

In the spring of 1873, the federal government began to extend the same assisted transportation incentives to the Icelanders that were available to agricultural labourers and domestic servants from Britain and northwestern Europe.[69] That summer, agents of the dominion and Ontario governments, working hand-in-glove with the Scottish Canadian Allan Steamship Line, arranged for the subsidized transport of 153 Icelanders to Quebec City via Scotland, the first large group migration from the island. The Ontario government settled approximately 115 of them at Rosseau in the Muskoka district, an area then being promoted as a settlement frontier. This experiment was repeated on a larger scale in 1874, when 351 Icelanders were settled at Kinmount in Victoria County; Ontario immigration authorities arranged for them to work as labourers on the Victoria Railway line being constructed to the Ottawa River, but the promised employment dried up by early 1875, and the Icelanders required assistance from the provincial government for basic survival.[70] Baptist missionary John Taylor's overtures to the dominion government on the Icelanders' behalf led to the creation of the Icelandic reserve and the removal of the majority of the 1873–74 migrants to the Northwest in the fall of 1875.

The failure of the Kinmount experiment prompted a fierce critique of the Icelandic character from Ontario's immigration commissioner Adam Crooks that tarnished the Icelanders' image as desirable immigrants. Crooks alleged that they did not have the necessary individual initiative to become independent settlers. He construed their poverty and dependence on the "paternal care" of the government as a sign that they lacked the spirit of liberal individualism: "Each individual must ... depend on his own exertion for his livelihood and success." Crooks somewhat disingenuously claimed that his government was not responsible for introducing "such a class of emigrants [sic] into Ontario," placing the blame squarely on the shoulders of federal authorities.[71] After learning that the Ontario government would no longer accept Icelandic immigrants, Edward Jenkins, the Canadian agent general in London, urged the dominion government not to follow suit; the Ontario episode did not overturn "all the information we have of that people," which generally indicated that they would eventually become "a very valuable class of settlers." As Jenkins explained,

> It is hardly to be expected that a people whose character, habits and modes of life are so wholly different from our own, should at once adapt themselves to the very great change to which their emigration to the colony subjects them, and as the question of Icelandic emigration has been well considered, and favourable results were expected to arise from it, it hardly seems politic to abandon it in its very first stage.[72]

Immigration officials in Ottawa generally shared this view; they tended to see the Icelanders' difficulties as temporary setbacks rather than chronic incapacities and were still firmly committed to promoting Icelandic immigration.

Their views were no doubt influenced by events in the United States, where the Icelandic journalist Jón Ólafsson was working to promote Alaska as a field for Icelandic settlement.[73] In August 1874, President Ulysses S. Grant received a petition authored by Ólafsson and signed by forty-three Icelanders residing in Milwaukee. It stated that a large migration from their country had just begun and that they were looking for a place to settle as a group. Upward of five hundred Icelanders were already in North America, and many more would soon come, once the location of a permanent colony was chosen. The petition even suggested that the Icelanders would willingly depopulate their barren island for a new homeland in the West. They had tried Wisconsin, Michigan, Minnesota, Iowa, Nebraska, and Canada, but those locations had proved unsuitable because their climates were too hot. As the petition asserted, "The heat of the summer is intolerable to our race."[74] Grant forwarded the petition to Secretary of State Hamilton Fish, expressing his approval: "It seems to me desirable to have Alaska settled, if it can be done, by an industrious hardy people, accustomed to a rigorous climate as the Icelanders are."[75] Ólafsson and two Icelandic delegates were granted passage on a naval ship bound for Alaska during the fall of 1874. Their expedition piqued the interest of the press, and the US government published Ólafsson's final report.[76] However, Congress did not pass legislation to fund the migration, effectively ending Ólafsson's dream of an Icelandic Alaska.[77]

The Canadian Privy Council, by contrast, did approve paying for the migration of the Icelanders from Ontario to the Northwest in September 1875. Since this constituted a break with established policy – assistance was not usually given to facilitate relocation within Canada – the government felt the need to justify its actions: "Continued suffering would seriously check immigration and render negatory the efforts now being made to attract as settlers to Canada a considerable portion of the inhabitants of Iceland, a very large part of which has been rendered uninhabitable by recent volcanic eruptions."[78]

The eruption of Mount Askja on Easter Monday 1875 raised the possibility that the relatively small emigration from Iceland would become a general exodus. Reports of damage to pasture and hay fields in the north and east of the island were widely circulated in Britain and North America.[79] The disaster received considerable attention in London, due largely to the efforts of the Cambridge professor Eiríkur Magnússon. He wrote to the *Times* that the eruption's "inevitable consequence will be famine and destruction on a large scale unless timely aid should be forthcoming."[80] In response to Magnússon's appeal, the mayor of London formed a committee to raise £1,000 in charitable donations for a shipload of relief supplies.[81] One *Times* correspondent thought the funds could be put to better use as an aid to emigration: "Immigrants are sorely needed in our more sparsely-peopled North American dependencies, where the thrifty and industrious islanders would make the very best of settlers."[82]

Well aware of the opportunity presented by the crisis, the dominion government accelerated its recruitment efforts in Iceland. William C. Krieger, a Danish American librarian who had worked in the Chicago offices of the Allan Line, offered his services as an emigration agent and was quickly hired by the Department of Agriculture.[83] John Lowe instructed Krieger to "induce such Icelandic emigrants to come to Canada as will have sufficient means after arrival to form a self-supporting colony."[84] Although Krieger found that reports of the devastation in Iceland were "most unconscientiously exaggerated," he nonetheless encountered considerable interest in emigration, particularly in the north of Iceland.[85] In September 1875, Sigtryggur Jónasson, the first Icelander to settle in Canada, who had recently returned from a federal-government-sponsored exploratory trip to Manitoba, was appointed as a second emigration agent for Iceland. Jónasson was authorized to have fifteen thousand copies of the report on the journey that he and the other members of the Icelandic Deputation had submitted to the government printed for distribution in Iceland.[86] In London, the report was published as a pamphlet titled *Nýa* [sic] *Ísland í Kanada* (New Iceland in Canada); its introduction, written by Agent General Jenkins, provided general information about Canada, outlined its relative advantages over the United States, and detailed the offer of assisted passage and free homesteads in New Iceland, the "splendid gift of the Canadian government." Jenkins warned that colonization was not an easy business. There would be hardships and difficulties, "but a strong and resolute man need fear nothing. The weak and thriftless and idle had better stay at home."[87]

During the winter of 1875–76, Krieger, Jónasson, and their sub-agents overcame a number of daunting logistical and financial hurdles to organize an emigration of two parties totalling 1,143 people, who arrived in Quebec City in July 1876.[88] Jónasson reported that the emigrants were farmers, farm labourers, and fishermen, primarily middle-aged men and their families, but there were also a significant number of single men and women.[89]

Dr. James Spencer Lynch (1841–94). *Archives of Manitoba, Personalities Collection, N12590.*

Except for a few, who went to join friends and relatives in Nova Scotia, the two groups travelled to New Iceland. During the journey, some were unwittingly exposed to the smallpox virus, which led to an epidemic that crippled the colony for almost a year and reduced its inhabitants to pariah status in Manitoba.

The troubles and failures of the Icelandic reserve during its first two years again brought the moral and racial character of the Icelanders into question. Lieutenant Governor Alexander Morris commissioned Dr. James Spencer Lynch, who had been chief medical officer at Gimli during the smallpox epidemic, to write a detailed report on the colony and its future prospects.[90] Prior to the transfer of the Northwest, Lynch had been a member of the Canadian annexationist party at Red River and was a close associate of John Christian Schultz. In December 1869, he was imprisoned along with Schultz and other Canadian agitators by Louis Riel's provisional government. By the mid-1870s, Lynch was working as the attending physician at the Winnipeg immigration sheds, where he treated the many cases of fever and dysentery among the Icelanders who arrived at Winnipeg in August 1876. On that occasion, Lynch observed that the Icelanders "are peculiar in their inaptitude for acclimatization here" and noted that "in spite of their fresh complexions and apparent sturdiness there is constitutionally a great want of vitality."[91] After spending the winter of 1876–77 at New Iceland, he was even less charitable: his report to Morris was a scathing critique of the colonists that highlighted their moral and physical weakness. Lynch ascribed the problems on the reserve – cramped and insufficient housing, poor sanitation, inadequate diet, slow progress in agriculture and fisheries, endemic and epidemic disease – to the "listless, dejected, apathetic natures" of its inhabitants. He saw their lack of material progress as a function of "their natural indolence, and a child-like faith in the providence of Government."[92]

The arrival of Lynch's report in Ottawa simply exacerbated the lingering doubts about the future of Icelandic immigration and colonization. In February 1877, William Krieger was summarily dropped as Icelandic emigration agent, for the reason that it was unwise to "make further propagandisation ... in view of the present condition of the Icelandic Colony in Keewatin."[93] After digesting the contents of Lynch's report, John Lowe wrote an exasperated private letter to Icelandic Agent John Taylor at Gimli: "The Government have been informed that the Icelanders don't work, that they have not the habits of thrift and industry, that they are not agriculturalists, and that they have even neglected to catch fish at their own doors."[94] Following Lynch's suggestion, Lowe threatened Taylor that all government support for the reserve would be cut off in hopes of encouraging a "self reliant spirit" among the colonists.

Lynch's report reveals that the notions of Icelanders as a people apart, a living fragment of the history and culture of the northern races, which had been used to portray them as desirable settlers, could be turned around to marginalize them as degenerates who were incapable of adjusting to colonial modernity. Lynch claimed that "centuries of isolation and intermarriage have had the effect of reducing their physical condition to a point below which they are likely to be successful in the rude contest with western pioneers, yet that contest is inevitable, and to the hardy settler should prove beneficial." He also linked their condition to the absence of warfare in the recent history of their country, which "had the effect of suppressing or obliterating whatever they possessed of ambition at an earlier period in their history."[95] The only bright spot in what Lynch conceded was a rather dark picture was another trope of Icelandic national identity – the "love of letters which seems to be innate to [the Icelander's] character." He speculated that this educational impulse would almost certainly lead to their quick absorption into the developing commercial towns of the Prairie West, a statement that was probably not meant as a compliment.[96] Lynch's pessimistic assessment of the Icelanders must have been widely disseminated in Winnipeg: the *Daily Free Press* reported that from the news circulating in the city, many people had the impression that the Icelanders were "an effete and unprogressive race, who were not equal to the struggle of life on this continent and must inevitably succumb to the fate of the 'least fit.'"[97]

However, Lynch's characterization of the Icelanders did not hold; though their backwardness was accepted as a fact, some people suggested that it could be reversed and that the race could be regenerated to Canada's benefit. Chief among them was Governor General Lord Dufferin, the one-time Iceland traveller. During an official visit to Gimli in September 1877, Dufferin told the assembled colonists that he had "pledged my personal credit to my Canadian friends on the successful development of your settlement" and that their future would undoubtedly be happy and prosperous.[98] Dufferin conceded that long-term isolation had largely left the "men and women of the grand old Norse race" outside the main currents of European civilization, but he believed that their intelligence and education would be the foundation of their racial renewal in the Canadian Northwest. He compared them to a seed found under an Egyptian pyramid, which needed only to be placed in fertile earth to burst into life: "Beneath the genial influences of the fresh young world to which you have come, the dormant capacities of your race, which adverse climatic and geographical conditions may have somewhat stunted and benumbed, will bud and burgeon forth in all their pristine exuberance."[99] Dufferin admonished them that even while "becoming Englishmen," they should not forget the ancient sagas of their nation that told of the "industry, energy, fortitude, perseverance, and stubborn endurance that have ever been characteristics of the noble Icelandic race."[100]

This strong endorsement was widely reproduced in the press, and it gave the government a renewed faith in the project, which was reinforced when the ministers of agriculture and the interior and their top administrators, including John Lowe, made their own visit to the colony a few weeks later. Lowe's account of this trip, published anonymously in the *Globe,* defended Ottawa's support for the project and speculated on its destiny:

Perhaps these Icelanders may make their mark in the history and on the face of this continent as men of their blood did in Europe. I don't mean in quite the same way, but with the means at their disposal. They are evidently a most prolific race. Every house swarms with children, and the pleasures of hope are plainly as great as those of memory.[101]

In this statement, Lowe brought together the ancient Norse past and the future of Canada. The supposedly remarkable fecundity of "the noble Icelandic race" would help transform the Northwest. This revivified faith in the Icelanders as colonists translated into the resumption of active emigrant recruitment in Iceland. John Lowe wrote to James Ennis of the Allan Line that Icelandic immigration was looking "up in the market; it did look very blue a few months ago but now it would be among the most favoured Immigrations ... I am very much inclined to believe that Iceland will in the immediate future be one of your best fields from which to obtain immigrants."[102] William Krieger was rehired for one final trip to Iceland, and Sigtryggur Jónasson was commissioned to produce a special edition of the Icelandic reserve's newspaper *Framfari* to be distributed to prospective emigrants.[103] Jónasson was also sent to Quebec City in the summers of 1878 and 1879 to meet arriving Icelanders and guide them to the Northwest.[104] In 1883, Jónasson's cousin Baldwin L. Baldwinson took over this function and was later appointed dominion Icelandic agent. Baldwinson held this position until 1896, which entailed travelling to Iceland to recruit emigrants, escorting them from Quebec City to Winnipeg, helping them to settle in the Northwest, and reporting on conditions in the various Icelandic colonies.[105]

John Lowe's 1877 prediction that Icelandic mass migration would become an important movement was borne out during the next several decades. Between 1873 and 1914, at least 13,958 Icelanders came to Canada, approximately 85 percent of the entire migration from the island during the period.[106] The vast majority of them travelled to the Canadian Northwest. In his 1901 address to the Historical and Scientific Society of Manitoba, Sigtryggur Jónasson estimated the number of Icelanders in Manitoba alone at 9,900. The most populous among the rural settlements was New Iceland, which, Jónasson wrote, "in spite of several misfortunes in its early days, now contains some 2,500 prosperous people."[107] Among those to commend Jónasson on his paper, and who voiced his "appreciation of the Icelanders as settlers," was the poet Charles Mair, who had been a member of the Canadian party that agitated for the annexation of the Northwest and a leading proponent of the dream of Canada as a nation peopled by the northern races.

By the time of Jónasson's address, the Icelanders' success as western colonists had firmly entrenched them among the ranks of the most desired immigrants to Canada. The doubts about their racial and cultural fitness, prompted by their early difficulties, were largely forgotten. However, the septuagenarian Irish Catholic senator Richard William Scott did remember. He believed that their story taught a useful lesson about toleration and patience toward newcomers. As secretary of state and frequent acting minister of agriculture and the interior in the administration of Alexander Mackenzie, Scott had played a key role in the creation of New Iceland and in the initial efforts to promote Icelandic immigration. In 1901, he used the Icelandic example to counter attacks against another group of recently arrived immigrants – the Doukhobors – by some of his colleagues. Scott pointed out that although the Icelanders had been extremely poor and had required considerable government assistance, they had become "a very valuable class of population" in the space of one generation: "So it will be with the Doukhobors. This prejudice will all pass away, and long before twenty-five years. I hope my Hon. friend from Monck will live to see it, and to admit that his statements about the Doukhobors are unjust."[108]

Canadian praise for the Icelanders in the first two decades of the twentieth century recapitulated the older themes about the characteristics of the northern race and combined them with anecdotal observations about the rapidity of Icelandic assimilation. J.S. Woodsworth's 1909 treatise on Canadian immigration *Strangers within Our Gates* again made the link between the medieval Norse and contemporary colonization: "It was the bold navigators of the isolated island who first set foot on the continent of America ... It is the descendants of these Viking sea-rovers who are making their way in the Canadian West, and who are becoming in their adopted land a potent influence."[109] Superintendent of Immigration William Duncan Scott's 1913 "Immigration by Races" asserted that their ability to learn English put the Icelanders in a class by themselves: "An Icelander who knows no word of English when the ground is being prepared for seed in the spring will speak the language with scarcely a trace of foreign accent by the time the harvest is being garnered in the fall."[110] Still, facility in English was no guarantee of being classed as a "desirable settler"; notions of whiteness, with their connotations of environmental suitability and inherent superiority, were too important to the boundaries placed around Canada's nation-building project. Scott's glowing description of Icelandic immigrants followed immediately after his discussion of African Americans; he noted that although their communities included many fine citizens, "It is to be hoped that climatic conditions will prove unsatisfactory to [them], and that the fertile lands of the West will be left to be cultivated by the white race only."[111]

THE ANSWER THAT HISTORIAN Norman Macdonald devised for his question about what "particular obligation" had led the Canadian government to expend such disproportionate resources on Icelandic immigration captured only part of the story. Macdonald argued that in their rush to attract mere numbers of settlers to the Northwest, government officials did not consider whether the Icelanders had the material resources to become independent farmers virtually overnight. When those hopes proved overly optimistic, it became necessary to intervene to prevent starvation.[112] Macdonald's analysis did correctly identify fundamental problems in the planning of the Icelandic reserve and their attendant consequences, but the answer to his question is actually more complex. The fact that the Icelanders were there at all was just as much a symptom of the government's "particular obligation" as its cause. They were recruited as immigrants because they could be slotted into a set of cultural understandings about the relationship between race and nation building. Ottawa desperately needed immigrant labour to fulfill the dreams of transcontinental empire that Canadian expansionists had entertained since the 1850s. Those dreams also entailed a racial order in which the "hardy northern races" would predominate in the new territories. Because they were believed to be the close racial kin of Britons, Icelanders fit neatly into the dreams of Anglo-Canadian expansionists who hoped to build an empire in the Northwest. They were seen as "desirable" and received substantial support from the state because they promised to realize both the material and cultural goals that undergirded the larger nation-building project.

2
Broken Townships
Colonization Reserves and the Dominion Lands System

IN JULY 1875, THE Icelandic Deputation, consisting of Baptist missionary John Taylor, Sigtryggur Jónasson, and four other Icelanders, arrived at the Winnipeg office of Dominion Lands Agent Donald Codd. They presented Codd with a letter of introduction from the surveyor general in Ottawa, which explained that the ministers of agriculture and the interior had sponsored their journey to Manitoba to locate a suitable site for an Icelandic colony. Codd showed them maps of the province, pointing out which areas were available for settlement and which had already been claimed or reserved for some other purpose.[1] It soon became apparent that the options in Manitoba were somewhat limited. The fertile land along the Red and Assiniboine Rivers to the north, south, and west was home to the long-established parishes of the Red River Colony. The northernmost parish, St. Peter's, was also an Indian reserve – one of several created under recently negotiated treaties. The townships immediately beyond the old parishes were the half-breed reserves – intended to fulfill the dominion government's obligation under the Manitoba Act to distribute 1.4 million acres to the children of Metis families. In the adjacent surveyed townships were numerous settlements of Anglo-Canadians, primarily from Ontario. Certain tracts were earmarked for other special group colonization projects: To the south and southeast of Winnipeg lay the reserves for French Canadians and Mennonites. To the north was a reserve for Germans, and farther to the west another for Danes. Finally, and overlapping with many of the other types of reserves and settlements, was the railway reserve – all the land for twenty-five miles on either side

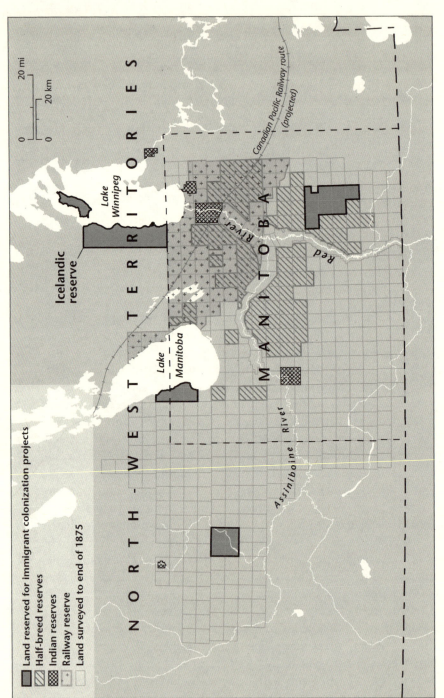

Reserves and surveyed land in Manitoba, 1875.

of the proposed route of the Canadian Pacific Railway was off-limits for homesteaders. A considerable amount of surveyed land remained available on the open prairie in the western part of the province, but it was generally unpopular, even among Canadian settlers, due to its lack of timber for building and fuel.[2]

Taylor and Jónasson's group concluded that there was "no land in the province ... suitable and attractive to the Icelanders."[3] They followed Codd's recommendation to visit the southwest shore of Lake Winnipeg, an area in the North-West Territories just north of the provincial boundary. The Hudson's Bay Company provided them with a boat, supplies, and two Metis navigators. Joseph Monkman, a man of Cree and Scottish ancestry who was a prominent member of St. Peter's parish community, acted as their guide. At Selkirk, dominion land surveyor A.H. Vaughn shared the insights that he had gained while conducting a coastal survey of the lake two years earlier. After a week's exploration, the members of the deputation returned to Winnipeg and wrote to the Department of the Interior, asking that the land along the lakeshore from the mouth of the Red River to Grindstone Point be set aside as a reserve for Icelandic immigrants.[4] They also informed Lieutenant Governor Alexander Morris of their choice and asked him to give their claim priority over a group of Cree from Norway House who wanted a reserve in the same location.[5] Just over a month later, as Morris was preparing to travel north to negotiate a treaty with the Indigenous people of the Lake Winnipeg region, he received definite instructions on the matter from Minister of the Interior David Laird: "In dealing with Norway House Indians, [you] must not promise them [a] reserve at Grassy Narrows, as Icelanders propose settling there."[6] An Order-in-Council of 8 October 1875 formally established the west shore of Lake Winnipeg as an exclusive Icelandic colonization reserve, the latest block of land to be outlined on Donald Codd's map of Manitoba and the North-West Territories.[7]

This chapter situates New Iceland within the framework of Dominion Lands policy. It also examines the origins of land reservation and group settlement in the history of British colonialism and how the Canadian state used them to further the colonization of the Northwest from 1870 to the early twentieth century. Land reservation and group settlement were spatial practices that reflected and helped enforce colonial categories of difference.[8] Reserves of various types were geographic expressions of legal and cultural distinctions that the colonial state employed to differentiate between its subjects. Those distinctions were inscribed onto the uniform survey grid, separating those who were deemed ready to assume full civil and political rights of liberal citizenship from those who needed further tutelage and supervision. Government officials saw reserves as reformatories, where subordinate populations could be prepared for the new order.[9]

Land reservation and group settlement generated tensions between individual and collective rights, integration and segregation, inclusion and exclusion. The analysis here explores these tensions and ambiguities by addressing four key questions, two relating to land reservation and group settlement in general, and two focusing on the Icelandic reserve in particular. First, where did these practices come from, and what was their purpose? Third, how did they fit within the wider framework for the alienation of land in the Northwest, as set out under the Dominion Lands Act? Finally, how, if at all, did the status of a reserve affect the types of spatial practices used within it?

During the early years of New Iceland, the federal government's failure to create the conditions necessary for a regime of private property was a source of continual frustration to the settlers. The official survey of the reserve remained incomplete for a long time, and the registration of land titles was neglected. It was the distance between the promise of acquiring private property, as held out in the Dominion Lands Act, and the reality of the reserve situation that prompted many Icelanders to demand they be treated in the same way as non-reserve settlers and even led some to assert that New Iceland itself was the problem.[10] Yet, the reserve persisted until 1897, and the colonists sometimes used its unique status to secure advantageous concessions from the Dominion Lands administration. The Canadian state's blueprint for a liberal order took on a new solidity as the immigrants internalized its assumptions, enforced its boundaries, and pushed at its limits.

Ottawa's overarching purpose in reserving tracts of land for particular individuals or for corporate or collective interests was to encourage private capital to help finance immigration and colonization. In this broad sense, reserves were a continuation of a practice that had deep roots in British colonialism. In the early seventeenth century, the British Crown began to make large land grants in North America to favoured elites, either individually or collectively as chartered companies. Recipients of these proprietary grants often aimed to generate income through plantation agriculture, rents, and later, land sales. These grants were large and imprecise, and the proprietors were given considerable autonomy in the exercise of local government. This led to the development of a diverse array of land allocation practices and types of land tenure in the various North American colonies.[11] The practice of elite land grants continued through the eighteenth century and was central to land allocation in the Canadas during the decades after the American Revolution. Over time, local administration became more regularized; land was distributed in clearly defined parcels and granted under certain conditions, usually involving settlement promotion. These conditions were frequently neglected as grantees held on to their unimproved property as a speculative asset.[12] Still, many did seek to increase the value of their holdings by actively developing them.

Group migration and settlement, organized under private auspices or with some level of state support, was an important method for promoting colonization in British North America. For their sponsors, these schemes often combined a speculative interest in land with humanitarian, ideological, or strategic motivations. The migrants recruited for these projects often came from the same part of Britain, Ireland, or Continental Europe and were connected with one another through kinship networks and by ties of language, religion, and culture. Lord Mount Cashel's holdings on Amherst Island in Upper Canada were intended to be an estate that replicated the landlord-tenant relationship among his Protestant Irish colonists.[13] The elite-sponsored group settlement schemes of the early nineteenth century also included philanthropic efforts to assist people who were adversely affected by structural changes in the economy of their home region. Lord Selkirk's colonies for dispossessed Scottish Highlanders in Prince Edward Island, Upper Canada, and Red River were shaped by an anti-modern and paternalistic sensibility that aimed to reconstitute relations of production and social hierarchy that were in the process of disintegrating in Britain.[14] Group settlement schemes sponsored directly by the state blended humanitarian and strategic motives; between 1750 and 1752, approximately two thousand German speakers from the Rhineland, purported to be the victims of religious persecution, received assistance from the imperial government to migrate to Nova Scotia. The purpose was to use these "foreign Protestants" to bolster British claims to the colony.[15]

During the 1830s and 1840s, colonial theorist Edward Gibbon Wakefield developed the highly influential concept of "systematic colonization." Wakefield argued that the state and private capital should work in tandem to promote the group migration of suitable settlers to compact colonies on designated tracts of land. He believed that colonization was the key to solving the demographic and economic problems of both Britain and its colonial empire; the metropole had an excess of labour and capital, whereas the colonies lacked both. Applying Britain's surplus human and material resources to the development of colonial land would help grow the overall economy by increasing the food supply and creating new markets for Britain's manufactured goods. Although he was a believer in free trade, Wakefield thought that the development of colonies whose economies were closely tied to Britain was an important form of insurance against protectionism and key to maintaining Britain's prestige on the international stage.[16]

Wakefield held that the alienation of Crown land in the colonies should be tightly regulated by the state. He argued that free grants and cheap land sales simply reduced the available supply of labour, which in turn discouraged investment and caused colonial development to stagnate. His alternative was to sell colonial land at a "sufficient price" so that ownership was initially, but not permanently, out of reach for most new immigrants. In the interim, they would become part of a labour pool that would help capitalists develop their colonial investments. Wakefield believed that manipulating the price of land in this way would create a social order like that of England, particularly if the immigrants were well chosen. He advocated the migration of couples or families rather than of single persons because this would help ensure a balanced gender order that did not challenge the norms of moral propriety. Wakefield's system was implemented in South Australia, New Zealand, and Vancouver Island, where it proved unworkable, either because the state had difficulty controlling access to land or because immigrants could not be attracted in sufficient numbers. But as Cole Harris notes, Wakefield "put his finger on a set of important relationships between society and land."[17]

The same sort of political and economic thinking underlay the Canadian push for the annexation of Rupert's Land from the Hudson's Bay Company (HBC) after mid-century. Deprived of both imperial trade preferences and reciprocity with the United States, Canadians looked to the Northwest as a field of investment and economic growth. Consumer goods and agricultural implements produced in the east would be sold to western farmers, who in turn would send grain and livestock east to feed the growing cities. Effective occupation of the Northwest by settlers would also solidify British sovereignty over the region and help defend against American designs on the territory.[18] Once the transfer of Rupert's Land was complete in 1870, that claim to sovereignty had to be asserted internally as well, and the practice of land reservation was integral to that process. The Canadian state used reserves for two broad purposes: to resolve pre-existing land claims and to encourage immigration and capital investment. In the former category were reserves for Indians, half-breeds, "original white settlers," and the HBC, whereas the latter were for the Canadian Pacific Railway, other railways, and various corporate colonization ventures.

At the core of the government's policies was the goal of transforming western lands into private property, with clear boundaries determined by a uniform survey and registered according to a centralized system of land titles. The practice of reservation was a crucial intermediate step in this dramatic reorganization of the human geography and the economic and social patterns of the region. In a piecemeal fashion, it established the new spatial and social distinctions between the Indigenous and European populations, between various groups of settlers, and between the rights of corporations, individuals, and communities. Reserves were a useful tool of colonization because their meaning was so capacious. For both Indigenous people and immigrants, they could be understood as a means to continue an old pattern of life, to manage the transition to a new one, or to guarantee a level of economic security and continued autonomy in religious and cultural matters. To an individual or corporate speculator in western lands, reserve grants represented an opportunity to translate government largesse into substantial capital gains. To the state, they were a way to effectively colonize a vast territory while at the same time avoiding costly wars with the Indigenous population.

The Dominion Lands Act was the central piece of legislation relating to the alienation of Crown land in the Canadian Northwest. From its inception in 1872 until its repeal in 1930, the act underwent many changes both large and small. Some addressed unforeseen circumstances that arose during the colonization process, and others claimed to be aimed at curbing the abuses of speculators. But in general, the key elements of the act, relating to survey and land administration, remained relatively constant. For the most part, these provisions were adapted from the US Homestead Act of 1862. The guiding principle of Dominion Lands policy after 1870 was to ensure that the Canadian Northwest emerged as a viable and competitive alternative to the United States in the fierce rivalry for agricultural settlers.[19] The Dominion Lands Survey system divided the land into square townships, each containing thirty-six sections of 640 acres, which were in turn subdivided into quarter sections of 160 acres.[20] This system established a uniform geometric pattern on the prairie landscape, but more importantly it enabled Ottawa to quantify and administer the vast land, timber, water, and mineral resources of the Northwest. The 160-acre quarter section was the basic unit of land that could be claimed as a free grant homestead by "any person, male or female, who is the sole head of a family" or a single adult male.[21] After paying a ten-dollar administrative fee and residing on and cultivating their homestead for three years, settlers could apply for a patent to their land, which, if granted, gave them full title to it. Applications for a homestead could be cancelled if the entrant did not meet the requirements, which frequently occurred. The Canadian system included innovations that were intended to be more generous than their US equivalent. For example, the quarter section adjoining a homestead could be claimed as a "pre-emption" that could later be purchased at the government price of a dollar per acre.[22] Between 1870 and 1928, approximately 62 million acres were permanently alienated through homestead and pre-emption. Securing individual title was far more difficult for Indigenous people who were defined as "Indians" under the 1876 Indian Act than for European immigrants. Indians were required to go through the onerous process of "enfranchisement" in which they had to prove that they were free of debt, able to read and write English, and of good moral standing. They also agreed to relinquish any claim to Indian status.[23] Apart from taking on homestead duties and fees, settlers had to pass a much lower bar to acquire civil and political rights. Becoming a naturalized British subject essentially involved simply swearing an oath to the Crown. The language skills and high moral standards expected of Indian applicants for enfranchisement were not applied to immigrants seeking the same rights.

Between 1870 and 1928, the volume of land alienated through land sales was roughly equal to that granted as homesteads. A portion of the lands that were sold, about 9 million acres, were school lands. The Dominion Lands Act set aside sections eleven and twenty-nine in every township as school land. Once the surrounding sections had been settled, the school lands were auctioned off to the highest bidder to build an endowment for public education. Somewhat smaller than the school lands, at 7 million acres, was the grant to the HBC. This translated to the reservation of section eight and three-quarters of section twenty-six in every township. By far the largest grants were to the Canadian Pacific and other railway lines, which amounted to more than 31 million acres by 1930.[24]

Over the same period, an unknown quantity of land was reserved for private colonization schemes.[25] Various forms of colonization reserves were used by both Conservative and Liberal administrations from 1872 until the first decade of the twentieth century. Their purpose was to encourage the movement of both capital and labour into the Northwest. Reserving land was believed to achieve this in two ways: First, it offered financial incentives to private investors for promoting the settlement of

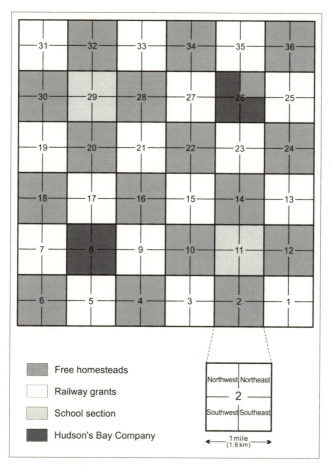

A generic township plan under the Dominion Lands Survey. Although the odd-numbered sections were reserved as railway lands after 1879, New Icelanders managed to secure an exemption from the Department of the Interior that allowed them to homestead odd-numbered sections in the reserve throughout the 1880s and 1890s. *From John C. Lehr,* Community and Frontier: A Ukrainian Settlement in the Canadian Parkland *(Winnipeg: University of Manitoba Press, 2011).*

agricultural migrants on specific tracts. Second, it appealed to the perceived tendency of migrants who shared linguistic and cultural backgrounds to settle in compact, homogeneous communities. In this way, the mammoth task of western colonization could be subdivided into smaller units that would be the building blocks of the overarching project. This practice underwent several changes, shifted in and out of favour, and yielded mixed results, since failure and settlement abandonment were relatively commonplace. As A.W. Rasporich points out, the possibility of group settlement in the Northwest inspired a wide array of short-lived experiments in pastoral utopianism, aimed at either reconstituting a vanishing way of life or projecting a new vision of an idealized society. Some were grounded in various forms of utopian socialism, but more frequently their ideological inspiration came from differing shades of liberalism.[26]

For many Icelandic immigrants, the utopian appeal of the reserve was its opportunity to fulfill the ethnic-nationalist ambition of creating a "United Icelandic colony" in North America. Between 1873 and 1875, Icelanders had founded small settlements in Wisconsin, Nebraska, Ontario, Nova Scotia, and Minnesota, and they had explored locations as far away as Alaska. Lively debates over the strengths and weaknesses of each location played out in Icelandic newspapers, at public meetings, and in private correspondence. Many of the Icelanders' intellectual and spiritual leaders framed the search for a colony in nationalistic terms and emphasized the goals of cultural autonomy and ethnic homogeneity.[27] Ottawa's offer of an exclusive colonization reserve found a receptive audience among those who shared this vision.[28] For migrants who were more concerned with material improvement than cultural autonomy, the proposed colony site on the southwest shore of Lake Winnipeg seemed to offer good land in a location near major transportation routes.

But whatever multiple meanings they may have had for the parties involved, the net effect of reservations was a deepening of the power of the state over the allocation of land and property rights. The promise of autonomy within a limited sphere was largely illusory, since other aspects of state power ensured that "reserved spaces" were what Henri Lefebvre calls "places of initiation within social space."[29] Whether for Indigenous people or immigrant settlers, reserves were laboratories whose purpose was to assimilate their communities into an Anglo-Canadian agrarian economic, political, and social order. The difference between Indian and immigrant reserves was more of degree than type, with the former being subjected to a much more highly coercive regime of economic, social, and cultural control and surveillance than the latter. In both cases, though, government officials assumed that these reserves would eventually cease to exist and that their inhabitants would assimilate into the mainstream. In this sense, colonization reserves in the Canadian Northwest represented an updated version of Wakefield's ideas about using access to land as a means to shape colonial society. The core principle of Wakefieldian systematic colonization – employing directed migration and land allocation to develop compact settlement colonies with desired socio-economic characteristics – endured even if Wakefield's preferred mechanism of social engineering, the sufficient price of land, had been superseded by the Dominion Lands Act's free homestead system.

The original 1872 version of the Dominion Lands Act did not include provisions for group settlement by corporate or collective entities, despite a plethora of applications from individuals and organizations promoting various schemes of systematic colonization after 1870.[30] However, in the fall of 1872 John A. Macdonald's Conservative government began experimenting with colonization reserves. In the mid-1870s, the Liberal administration of Alexander Mackenzie expanded the policy, and it continued in a modified form after Macdonald returned to power in 1878. Group settlement through the formal and informal reservation of land remained an aspect of Dominion Lands policy well into the Liberal administration of Sir Wilfrid Laurier. In spite of their importance, the genesis of colonization reserves has remained somewhat of a mystery.

An important and previously overlooked clue appears in a series of letters that BC immigration agent Gilbert Malcolm Sproat submitted to the minister of agriculture in the spring of 1872. In three characteristically long-winded epistles, Sproat, better known for his work on the Joint Indian Reserve Commission in British Columbia, laid out a comprehensive proposal for "farming colonies" in British Columbia and the Northwest.[31] His treatise was largely a warmed-over version of some central assumptions of Wakefieldian systematic colonization, combined with observations about contemporary railway and land policy in the United States. This is not surprising: Sproat had been involved in various schemes to bring white settlers to British Columbia since the period that Wakefield's ideas were at the height of their popularity. By 1871, Sproat had managed to turn his voluntary efforts into an official appointment as "Agent General" for British Columbia, doing his best to promote the province from an ill-funded London office.[32] During this time, he travelled widely through the United States, studying the progress of settlement in the Midwest and Pacific regions. He argued that the dominion government could learn important lessons from the US experience and was particularly enamoured of farm colonies organized by private colonization companies and backed by British and American capital.

Sproat thought that group settlement was preferable to individual settlement. He maintained that the beneficial effects of the former mitigated against the deleterious effects of the latter. Farm colonies could be a force for morality, progress, and nation building in frontier contexts, where the bonds of civilization were often tenuous and fragmented. In particular, he mentioned that individual settlers had "caused their government enormous trouble and expense by inconsiderate treatment of the aborigines." He advocated a humane and just Indian policy, which would also bring about greater separation between settler and Indigenous populations: "I would not recommend reservations for Indians to be placed ... in the probable direction of settlement." Sproat's vision was of a colonial landscape divided into compartments, ostensibly to prevent conflict but clearly also to avoid the mixing of populations, which could potentially disrupt the emergence of the "wholesome social system" that would produce the "ruling race of this continent."[33]

Sproat contended that group settlement could address the twin problems of isolation and disorganization: "Organized colonies, controlling large tracts seemed to have special facilities for keeping the houses together in small villages or hamlets." He believed that it would allow settler families to live in "society instead of solitude" and therefore contribute to their moral uplift and material progress. Individualistic settlement had undeniably been important in the United States and other colonial contexts, but in Sproat's opinion its disorganized character had impeded the larger colonization process: "These frontier men may assist in preparing wild lands for cultivation, but they do not add any moral force to a nation. Their children, if they have any, are very unfortunately situated. The isolation in which families are placed when settlers are thinly spread over a vast territory is decidedly a bar also to mere material progress." He also felt that group settlement would work best when old ties of kin, community, religion, and social beliefs were transplanted: "The colonies would be composed, sometimes of men of one religion or all pledged to temperance, or connected by some bond of that sort, but usually of families from the same locality, generally old neighbours and acquaintances, who, once they were located, would attract to their settlements annually a considerable number of recruits from their former homes."[34]

The wholesome social system that Sproat envisioned for the Canadian Northwest and British Columbia was not to be a communal one. The farm colonies along the route of the Kansas and Colorado railroad lines that he had studied were co-operative in only a very limited sense:

> The principal and almost the only co-operative feature about them, consists in the joint purchase by each party of colonists of one large tract of land, which is at once subdivided and deeded in fee simple in lots to the individual

members, the values of each lot being equalized in the apportionment. Community of profits is no part of the plan; after the apportionment each man works for himself, and he can sell his land, if he likes.[35]

In essence, Sproat's three letters to the minister of agriculture were about the process by which Ottawa could efficiently transfer its vast new territories into private hands in a way that promoted development rather than speculation. He hoped to convince the government to change pending legislation that reserved land twenty miles on each side of the proposed Canadian Pacific Railway line, with alternating sections being granted to the railway.[36] These terms were similar to railway grants in the United States, which Sproat considered to be "regrettable." The railways sold their land at much higher prices than the government did and thus diverted capital that the colonists could have used to develop their farms or reduced the number of settlers who could afford to purchase property, whether on their own or as part of a joint venture.[37]

Although Sproat was critical of US railway companies, he called for the federal government to follow the policies of the Northern Pacific Railroad: "Though I do not affirm that what is proper for a corporation is necessarily proper for a Government ... the Canadian gov't might safely follow in their steps."[38] This did not mean that Ottawa should undertake colonization projects itself. According to Sproat, experience had shown that large-scale group colonization ventures were best left in private hands; apart from adjudicating the merits of specific proposals, the government would enact and enforce regulations to protect immigrants from exploitation and neglect. Sproat believed that the government should mimic the Northern Pacific's practice of granting land to individuals or small companies who were paid either on a commission basis or through discounts on land purchases.

At the heart of Sproat's eighty-page dissertation was a request that Parliament reserve "a million acres between Manitobah [sic] and British Columbia" to be "settled systematically by degrees." Each parcel of 100,000 acres would be granted to a company that would co-ordinate the immigration and colonization process, receiving a commission for its efforts. Not surprisingly, Sproat offered to organize "the Central Canadian Land Co." to undertake the settlement of one such tract.[39] In this ambition, he was ultimately disappointed, but his ideas may have had a significant impact on government policy. Speaking before the House of Commons' Select Standing Committee on Immigration and Colonization in 1878,

Secretary John Lowe of the Department of Agriculture explained that the government's colonization reserve policy was modelled on the methods used by railway and land companies of the western United States.[40]

Although the impact of Sproat's letters is unknown, it is suggestive that Ottawa's first attempt to promote group colonization in the Northwest occurred a few months after he submitted them and largely conformed to his recommendations. A September 1872 Order-in-Council approved a grant of 100,000 acres in Manitoba for a Swiss immigration scheme spearheaded by a certain Dr. Foos.[41] Two more colonization projects were approved in October and November of the same year, one for Germans put forward by the German Society of Montreal and another for Scots under the direction of David Shaw, a former government emigration agent.[42] These initial plans were somewhat vague; the Orders-in-Council did not mention any specific locales, but rather approved the projects in principle and empowered the minister of agriculture to make further arrangements. Once the reserve was granted, it was incumbent upon the promoters to recruit settlers. This turned out to be a difficult task: the Swiss project never materialized, and the Scottish and German reserves were rescinded after their promoters failed to bring out any settlers. The approach proved more successful in attracting groups that were already searching for a settlement site, as in the case of the Mennonites from Russia. In March 1873, after visits by Mennonite delegations to Manitoba and successful negotiations with Ottawa over the terms of their resettlement, a reserve of nine townships in southeastern Manitoba was set aside "for the exclusive use by settlement, of Germans in Russia – Mennonites and others."[43]

In the spring of 1874, Alexander Mackenzie's Liberal government brought the previously ad hoc practices of land reservation for colonization purposes under the purview of the Dominion Lands Act. The act was amended to give the governor-in-council power to "withdraw any ... township from public sale or general settlement" that an individual or group undertook to settle "in the proportion of one family to each alternate quarter section." In return for bringing out settlers and establishing them on their land "free of expense to the government," the promoters of such schemes could purchase additional land in the same townships at a "reduced rate" – the standard government price for land in the Northwest being a dollar per acre.[44] What had been altered from Wakefield's scheme was not the principle but the mechanism. The price of land would not be manipulated to force migrants to improve the property of others – instead, they would work their own homesteads, but in doing so would indirectly increase the value of the nearby land, which the private promoters of the colonization schemes could purchase at a discount price.

Between 1874 and 1877, the Mackenzie government created nine colonization reserves encompassing approximately 1.3 million acres.[45] Some of these, such as Robert F. Rowan's plan to settle Danish immigrants west of Lake Manitoba, were undertaken by individual promoters.[46] Others were sponsored by organizations that had linguistic, religious, and cultural ties to the prospective settlers, such as the Saint-Boniface–based Société de Colonisation de Manitoba, which began in 1874 to work for the repatriation of French Canadians living in New England.[47] In 1876, seventeen townships west of the Red River were allocated as a second Mennonite reserve,[48] which, like the east reserve established in 1873, was sponsored by the long-established Mennonite community in Ontario. New Iceland was the sixth reserve created during this period, and it was unique in that no private organization was involved in its genesis. Officially, John Taylor was its promoter, but he did not possess the means to bankroll it. Instead, he and the Department of Agriculture tried unsuccessfully to enlist the HBC in this role to encourage it to take a more active part in promoting colonization.[49]

Most of the colonization reserves established under the 1874 regulations failed to attract settlers. By 1877, the Mackenzie government had lost faith in the policy and decided to open a number of reserves where no progress had been made. Minister of the Interior David Mills stated that though they had been intended to spur settlement, they had actually impeded its progress by locking up land.[50] Fortunately for the Icelandic reserve, it was among those that Surveyor General J.S. Dennis recommended be continued, since "the scheme still remains upon trial, the settlement so far, not having been marked by very much success."[51]

After their return to power in 1878, the Macdonald Conservatives initially shied away from privately sponsored group settlement projects, but by the early 1880s had returned to the idea and dramatically expanded its scope. The basic principle at the heart of the Liberals' 1874 amendment to the Dominion Lands Act remained the same, but a more detailed legal framework was developed to encompass the relationship between the government, private promoters of colonization, and migrant settlers. Between 1881 and 1887, this took the form of a short-lived experiment in bloc land sales to private colonization companies. From the mid-1880s onward, the more enduring practice of establishing nominal reserves for non-English-speaking European immigrants became common. Colonization companies and group settlements have often been considered as separate topics,[52] but in reality they were simply different aspects of the same approach to colonization, one that aimed to be systematic and highly profitable for individuals and groups with an interest in Northwest lands.

In the early 1880s, the prospect that the long-delayed Canadian Pacific Railway (CPR) would soon be completed set off a speculative land boom in Manitoba and the North-West Territories. The government looked to land sales as a way of recouping the massive cash and land subsidies it granted to the private CPR to undertake the task. The odd-numbered sections in the townships adjacent to the main railway line or any branch lines were granted to the railways. However, under regulations introduced in 1881, individuals and corporations could obtain the right to buy all the odd-numbered sections in tracts away from the railway belt for two dollars per acre. These colonization companies were required to locate at least two settlers on each section of the tract over a five-year period. If the company successfully fulfilled its obligations, it would receive a government rebate of $160 per bona fide settler, effectively reducing the purchase price of the land to a dollar per acre. The company could sell the land to settlers for between three and fifteen dollars an acre, thereby reaping a substantial profit on its initial investment.[53] At first, there was widespread enthusiasm for this plan; Conservative Party insiders and rank-and-file supporters were at the front of the line for land grants, and many managed to secure them. Other applications came from British and European capitalists, church and philanthropic organizations, and even fraternal and workingmen's associations. At New Iceland, Sigtryggur Jónasson, Friðjón Friðriksson, and their German Canadian partner Ferdinand Osenbrugge proposed the formation of a company that would pay off the colonists' debts to the government in return for title to the abandoned and undeveloped land in the reserve, which they would then resettle with Icelanders, Scandinavians, and Germans. The minister of agriculture was in favour of the plan, but the Department of the Interior rejected it for reasons that remain unclear.[54]

Many prospective colonization companies failed to win government endorsement. Of the 260 applications for company colonization grants received by the Department of the Interior between December 1881 and June 1882, only 106 were approved. For three-quarters of these, the companies were either unable to meet the initial financial requirements or unwilling to commit themselves to the terms of the contractual agreement with the Department of the Interior. In the end, only 26 colonization companies became operational. They were placed in possession of just over 1.3 million acres, far short of the 10 million acres that the government had hoped to sell to private capitalists.[55] The scheme was therefore considered a failure from the outset, and its prospects did not improve over time. Hopes of quick and easy profits soon evaporated into a cloud of debt, disappointment, and failure. Of the small number of migrants then heading to the Northwest, few could be convinced to buy company lands in isolated locations when ample homestead land was still available closer to the projected railway lines. For those who did come, the harsh realities of pioneering in the Northwest, including adverse climatic conditions, lack of infrastructure, and consequent poor access to markets, proved discouraging. In 1886–87, the government dissolved the surviving companies and abandoned the experiment. During their five years of operation, the companies brought only 1,080 settlers to the Northwest.[56] In the same period, tiny Iceland sent at least 3,819 migrants to Canada.[57]

In the mid-1880s, the federal government, the CPR, and the Manitoba and North West Railway began to partner with individuals and philanthropic organizations that had initiated schemes involving the settlement of Hungarians, Jews, Scandinavians, Scottish Highlanders, Germans, and Romanians in western Manitoba and the North-West Territories. The Dominion Lands Act allowed the railway companies to advance money to the settlers for the purchase of provisions, implements, building materials, and other supplies. This money, which amounted to a lien on the homestead, had to be repaid with interest before the patent was issued.[58] Thingvalla, the first Icelandic settlement in what became Saskatchewan, was begun under this sort of arrangement in 1886.[59]

Arthur Morton calls these group settlements "nominal reserves" because homesteading within them was technically not restricted to one ethno-religious group.[60] Whereas the colonization reserves of the 1870s were created through Orders-in-Council that granted members of an ethno-religious group the exclusive right to homestead in a prescribed space, the nominal reserves of the mid-1880s to the early twentieth century were more a matter of administrative prerogative on the part of the Department of the Interior.

Nominal reserves were used extensively during the frenetic period of immigration that coincided with Clifford Sifton's tenure as minister of the interior. Between 1896 and 1905, Sifton streamlined administrative practices and expanded recruitment efforts into Central and Eastern Europe at a time when the declining availability of land in the United States made the Canadian Northwest increasingly attractive for thousands of European immigrants.[61] Once they arrived at Winnipeg, colonization agents and land guides directed them to compact tracts in designated areas. At the same time as Sifton's administration was creating de facto reserves for new arrivals such as Ukrainians, Doukhobors, and others, old colonization reserves were being abolished. In July 1897, on Sifton's recommendation, New Iceland was opened to sale and homestead entry "by any class of settlers who may wish to locate in that vicinity" because "the purpose for which this Reserve was originally made has now been fully served."[62] Part of the reason for this change was that newly arrived Ukrainian settlers were being directed onto lands adjacent to New Iceland.[63] This decision to abolish a formal reserve while simultaneously creating a new informal one was consistent with Ottawa's perspective on colonization reserves since the 1870s. Spatial segregation of various ethno-religious groups was considered a temporary evil that had to be tolerated to realize the larger goal of extensive western colonization.

During the fifty-odd years of their existence, Ottawa was often roundly criticized for its use of colonization reserves. This opposition coalesced around two broad issues: reserves as barriers to land acquisition and group settlement as a threat to the future racial, political, and social composition of western Canada. In the 1870s, opponents of so-called land-lock alleged that reserves of all types frustrated the legitimate aspirations of bona fide Anglo-Canadian farmers who wished to acquire dominion land in the Northwest.[64] In 1876, the editor of the *Free Press* claimed that Manitoba had been "reserved to death by Acts of Parliament" and recounted the supposedly representative story of a Canadian migrant with a young family who had tried repeatedly to acquire a homestead, only to learn that he had chosen a quarter section reserved for half-breeds, the HBC, the Pacific Railway, or some special colonization project.[65] Opponents of land reservation often complained that though Ottawa made reserves for Indians, half-breeds, French Canadian Catholics, and foreigners, none were set aside for anglophones from Ontario or the British Isles.[66] This was not only inaccurate – there were formal reserves for British settlers and cases of rule bending by Dominion Lands administrators that allowed for compact settlement of Ontario migrants[67] – but it also ignored the privileged position of Anglo-Canadian settlers in the overall Dominion Lands system. For all intents and purposes, townships that were "open" for homestead and sale were closed to Indigenous people. In selecting the best available land, settlers from Ontario also had the edge over non-English-speaking immigrants, who had to learn to operate within a new legal and institutional framework.

Half-breed and railway reserves were the main targets of Anglo-Canadian settler enmity because they hindered the acquisition of choice agricultural land in the vicinity of Winnipeg. Whereas altering government policy would solve the problem of the railway reserves, the issue of Metis land was bound up with the deeply rooted racial and sectarian antagonisms of 1870s Manitoba. Alleging that Half-breed reserves were part of a conspiracy by the Roman Catholic Church to gain control of the province's best land for its own people, the *Free Press* asserted that the French-speaking Metis were not interested in agriculture and that at the earliest opportunity, they would gladly dispose of their rights to land for cash payments.[68] Other commentators, such as MP James Trow, chair of the Select Standing Committee on Immigration and Colonization, noted the widespread subterfuge practised by speculators and settlers in obtaining title to Metis land. Nonetheless, Trow believed the Half-breed reserves impeded progress and that bringing them into the market was "a step in the right direction."[69] The immigrant Icelanders soon came to share the Anglo-Canadian perspective: in 1879, disaffected New Icelanders sent a petition to the dominion government, complaining that the Half-breed and railway reserves to the south of them created "difficulty in communicating with other civilised people."[70]

The colonies of Mennonites and Icelanders were only rarely swept up in the general condemnation of reserves. Reverend George Bryce called the Mennonite and Icelandic reserves "real benefits" because they colonized land that Canadians had either bypassed or not yet begun to settle.[71] However, many Anglo-Canadians saw the lack of interaction between the "foreign colonies" and the English-speaking settler community as problematic because it delayed assimilation. In 1876, the *Free Press* questioned the wisdom of appropriating "large blocks for exclusive settlement by alien people of foreign customs, language, and institutions." The editor argued that interspersing them with English-speaking colonists would be much better, "to produce homogeneity of nationality in the near future."[72] Nonetheless, other Canadians viewed bloc reserves more positively. In his 1879 immigration pamphlet *The Prairie Lands of Canada,* Thomas Spence recommended the "colony system" as an advantageous and economical method of colonization: "Neighbors in the old land may be neighbours in the new; friends may settle near each other, form communities and the nucleus of new settlements and towns, establish schools and, in short, avoid many of the traditional hardships which have usually attended pioneer life."[73]

The same sorts of debates about colonization reserves continued over the ensuing decades. In the 1880s, Liberals denounced the Conservative government for handing over vast stretches of public land in the Northwest to railways and colonization companies with an eye for profit rather than serving the interests of agrarian settlers. At the end of the century, bipartisan critics of Sifton's policies objected to what they perceived as the special treatment afforded to Ukrainians and Doukhobors, and lamented the deleterious impact of foreign colonies on the racial, social, and cultural fabric of Anglo-Canadian settler society. These critics echoed the earlier calls for integrated settlement, since "the colony system tends to perpetuate their own language and peculiar customs."[74]

This debate was in essence about assimilation, specifically about the potential and appropriate methods for turning European immigrants into British subjects who spoke English, wholeheartedly accepted British institutions, and observed the same social customs and standards of moral propriety. Sifton's conception of who was fit to become a Canadian citizen was marginally more inclusive than that of many of his contemporaries. His judgments about the various races were based on perceptions about which ones possessed the necessary characteristics to become successful farmers in the Canadian West. For Sifton, this excluded African Americans, Italians, Jews, East and South Asians, and even English urbanites.[75] In encouraging group settlement, Sifton's ambition was to foster internally resilient immigrant communities that had the required skills and drive to contribute to the agricultural development of the West. He anticipated that these distinctive European ethno-religious communities would eventually be drawn into the Anglo-Canadian mainstream through their commercial and institutional contacts with the wider society.[76]

An important part of this process was turning the immigrants into property holders. Although the colonization reserve land was available only to members of the collectivity, they were still subject to the Dominion Lands Act in relation to both the system of survey and regulations governing the acquisition of free grant homesteads. In this sense, the reserves did not so much deviate from the homestead system as provide a means for its rapid implementation. Still, rules were sometimes bent to accommodate the wishes of ethno-religious communities. The Mennonites, as a condition of their settlement in Manitoba, negotiated special group rights that afforded their communities considerable autonomy in matters of political and spatial organization on their reserve.[77] They imported from Russia their practice of living in villages called *strassendoerfer,* which were divided into five- and six-acre *fiastaeden* on which they had their residence. The surrounding land was worked as open fields, which were held in common by the village.[78]

John Taylor's settlement plans for New Iceland led Canadian officials to believe that, like the Mennonites, the Icelanders would follow a communal pattern of land use.[79] Prior to leaving for the reserve with the first group of colonists, Taylor presented a plan of village settlement to the Canadian surveyor general, Colonel J.S. Dennis. Families would not be situated on 160-acre homesteads: instead, the Icelanders would be "congregated in long narrow villages close to and parallel with the [lake] shore for convenience of fishing, boating, &c."[80] The villages would consist of lots, approximately one acre in size, arranged in double rows, with north-south streets running in front and behind and intersected by cross-streets at regular intervals. The land to the rear of the villages would be developed for agricultural use, but no houses would be built there.[81] Taylor claimed that this replicated the way in which "communities exist in Iceland,"[82] by which he undoubtedly meant Iceland's small coastal fishing villages and trading centres – the only tiny pockets of urban life in what was otherwise a completely rural society. Dennis instructed Dominion Lands surveyor George McPhillips to accompany the Icelanders to the reserve and help Taylor put his plans into effect.

On 22 October 1875, McPhillips and Taylor travelled north along the coast to locate the site for "a village or Town which [the Icelanders] named Gimli."[83] A few days later, some of the Icelanders who had been exploring the region suggested that the village be moved farther north, but the surveyor overruled them. For the next month, McPhillips and his crew, which by this time included the Icelanders Páll Jóhannesson and Árni Þorláksson, worked at laying out a plan for Gimli and its township to connect it to the larger survey grid, while the Icelanders hurriedly erected shelters before the onset of winter. The new village's settlement pattern was far less systematic than either Taylor or McPhillips had hoped. McPhillips recorded, "As it was impossible for me to have their lots surveyed for them in time to build on them they commenced to build promiscuously on the Beach where they landed."[84]

In commenting on Taylor's plan, Dennis told the minister of the interior that it represented a "departure from the mode of settlement now provided in the Dominion Lands Act" and that this would probably require legalization by the Privy Council.[85] This recommendation was acted upon through a clause in the 1876 amendment to the Dominion Lands Act, which stated, "In the case of settlements being formed of immigrants in communities (such for instance as Mennonites or Icelanders) the Minister of the Interior may vary or waive, in his discretion, the foregoing requirements as to residence and cultivation on each separate quarter section entered as a

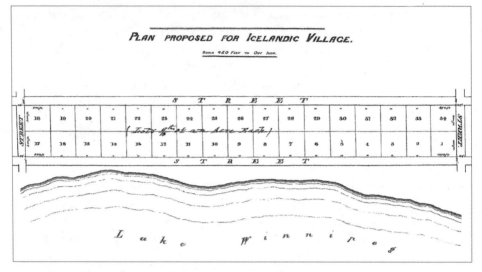

Surveyor General John Stoughton Dennis included this "Plan Proposed for Icelandic Village" in a November 1875 report to the minister of the interior after speaking to John Taylor in Winnipeg. *Library and Archives Canada, RG 15, D II 1, reel T-12183, vol. 235, file 5088.*

homestead."[86] In 1883, the status of village settlements with respect to homestead regulations was further clarified through a provision of the consolidated Dominion Lands Act that became known as the "Hamlet Clause":

> In case a certain number of homestead settlers embracing not less than twenty families, with a view to greater convenience in the establishment of schools and churches, and to the attainment of social advantages of life character, ask to be allowed to settle together in a hamlet or village, the Minister of the Interior may, in his discretion, vary or dispense with the foregoing requirements as to residence, but not as to the cultivation of each separate quarter section entered as a homestead.[87]

Prime Minister John A. Macdonald did not prefer this method of settlement, but he considered it necessary to meet the special demands of some settlers. As he explained, "It is not the desire of the Government to encourage settlement in hamlets, by which people lose half their time going to and from their farms, but this clause is necessary to meet the habits of some of the European settlements, as for instance, the Mennonites."[88]

However, on the whole this exception did not obviate the general rule that homesteads must be registered to an individual. Over time, Mennonite villages broke down as individuals decided to leave the voluntary communal system and become the sole proprietors of the farms registered in their names.[89]

At New Iceland, this occurred almost immediately after the colonists arrived. Contrary to the assumptions of Surveyor General Dennis and others, neither Taylor nor the Icelanders intended that reserve lands be held or worked communally. Although one or two families often initially pooled resources, and neighbours assisted each other with major tasks, individual ownership appears to have been the goal from the beginning. According to colonist Símon Símonarson, there was a scramble for both village lots and homesteads, and the people who were "on the most intimate terms with Taylor" received choice land along the waterfront.[90] In January 1876, Taylor reported to the minister of agriculture, "Forty [village] lots have been sold at $5 plot, a reserved lot being attached to each lot sold. A similar number of houses have been erected, and a village store is in active operation."[91] Many colonists also built houses on their homestead claims and moved out of the village once spring arrived.

The issue in New Iceland was not the willingness of the Icelanders to adapt to the individualistic homestead system, but rather the slowness of the Department of the Interior to fulfill the two preconditions necessary for the system to function: the cadastral survey and the central registration of land. Colonization in the reserve occurred either prior to the survey or while it was in progress. When the first Icelanders arrived in October 1875, only the southernmost township had been surveyed.[92] George McPhillips partially surveyed Gimli and its township in November 1875, but major survey work was not resumed until late August 1876. McPhillips surveyed Townships 19, 20, 21, and 22, Range 4 East, as well as the townsites for Lundi (Icelandic River/Riverton) and Sandy Bar.[93] A second surveying crew under the direction of Joseph Doupe laid out the section lines in advance of McPhillips and surveyed Township 23. A third survey and construction crew under the direction of Walter Beatty was engaged in building a colonization road from Red River to Gimli and later north to Icelander's River. By the spring of 1877, the townships closest to the lakeshore had been surveyed, but Big Island remained unsurveyed. John Taylor and the Big Island settlers sent several letters and petitions to Ottawa to have this done but without success.[94] Surveyor General Dennis refused these requests because the land was of poor quality and the other surveys in the reserve had proved overly expensive. He suggested that until the government was prepared to complete the survey, the settlers should subdivide the land themselves into waterfront lots measuring ten chains (approximately twenty metres) in width.[95] The settlers bickered among themselves over how best to do this, but it was ultimately achieved.[96] This pattern of settlement was later confirmed when the survey was completed in 1883.[97]

The geographical setting, absence of a comprehensive survey ahead of settlement, and the cultural traditions of the immigrants resulted in the development of a distinctive set of spatial practices at the reserve. In the first instance, this meant that in choosing lands the colonists had to deal with just one "government" authority, John Taylor, who does not seem to have maintained full control of the situation. In July 1876, Taylor informed John Lowe that "the people are squatting at random on the accessible localities."[98] In general, accessible localities meant along the lakeshore and the banks of rivers and creeks. In a place where there were many swamps and few roads, residing next to the water allowed for easier travel and transportation of goods. Símon Símonarson, who was not fortunate enough to be situated on the lake, noted that owners of lakefront homesteads were spared the inconvenience of carrying "all their necessities some distance inland, and over muddy and difficult trails."[99] Once the surveyors arrived, they confirmed this pattern by laying out river lots along Icelander's River and long lakefront lots on the east coast of Big Island and at some points along the mainland lakeshore. In this sense, New Iceland represented a northward extension of the old river-lot system of the Red River Colony, which was permitted under the Dominion Lands Survey system until 1884.[100]

Without the survey grid, the Icelandic tradition of naming farms took on a practical significance. From one end of the reserve to the other, colonists named their homesteads after local topographical features, places in Iceland, or even themselves. For example, in Víðirnesbyggð (Willow Point Settlement) Jón Jónsson from Múnkaþverá in northern Iceland homesteaded the farm Akur (Field) south of Gimli. In the local context, he might be known as "Jón á Akri" to differentiate him from the many other settlers with the same name. Letters could be addressed to the farm and the particular settlement in which it was located, and the Gimli Post Office would direct them to the intended recipient. In some instances, the Icelandic names became officially recognized geographical designations, as in the case of Húsavík (House Cove). But more often they existed alongside official names and the conventional section, township, and range descriptions of the Dominion Lands system as an internal geographical code that helped situate and connect people and places in the reserve.[101]

The absence of a survey prior to settlement left homesteaders uncertain as to whether the official boundaries would coincide with the ones they themselves had created. In February 1877, Sigtryggur Jónasson informed John Lowe that "quite a number of disputes [have] arisen amongst those who settled on unsurveyed lands, more than one being found to be on the same quarter section."[102] Shortly thereafter, the colony council passed a resolution stating that it was "absolutely necessary that some arrangements are made as soon as possible to have the settlers legally entered for their lots." John Taylor asked the government for instructions on how this might be done, and an informal arrangement was made whereby he was directed to act as a "quasi Dominion land Agent" to "make a record of the entries of the Icelanders on their homesteads."[103] Unfortunately, the entries that Taylor made in his own books were never transferred to the Lands Office, with the result that the homestead claims remained mired in uncertainty for a decade.

The Icelanders were keen to familiarize themselves with the Dominion Lands system. In March 1877, the colony council requested that the government publish extracts of the Dominion Lands Act and other relevant laws in Icelandic. The leadership group eventually did this itself by publishing sections of the act in the reserve newspaper, *Framfari* (Progressive).[104] The colonists appear to have been quick studies of the system: a sketch of Víðirnesbyggð that Benedikt Arason sent to a friend in Iceland in January 1879 demonstrates his clear understanding of the Dominion Lands system and its relationship to the local topography. Arason's map accurately depicts the physical features of the lakeshore and their relationship to the township and section lines; it also includes many of the Icelandic farm names and those of their occupants.[105] Colonists such as Arason closely followed Ottawa's periodic changes to the land regulations and worked to ensure that their individual and collective rights to the land – as they understood them – were not impinged upon.

The most contentious issue that arose between Ottawa and the Icelanders was the status of odd-numbered sections in the reserve. In June 1879, the Macdonald government passed an Order-in-Council that reserved all odd-numbered sections from homestead or pre-emption. They were to be sold by the government to finance the construction of the Canadian Pacific Railway, the price being determined by their distance from the tracks. As originally envisioned, the CPR line was to pass through the Interlake region

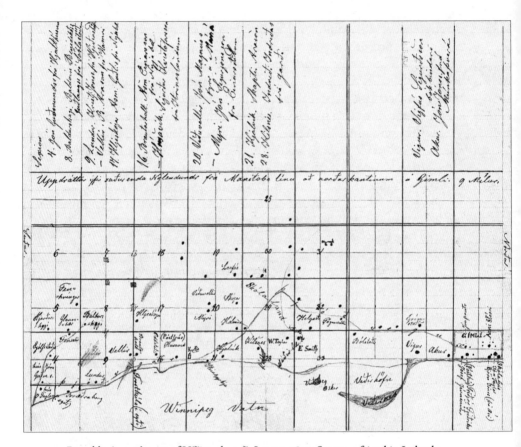

Benedikt Arason's map of Víðirnesbyggð, January 1879. Sent to a friend in Iceland, the map combines the Dominion Lands Survey grid with place names assigned by the Icelanders. It shows Township 18, Range 4 East, and part of Township 19, Range 4 East, as well as some of the Icelandic farm names, such as Benedikt's farm Vellir (Fields), and the names of some of the settlers. The southern boundary of the reserve is on the left of the map, and Lake Winnipeg (Winnipeg vatn) is at the bottom. *Landsbókasafn Íslands (National and University Library of Iceland), Lbs. 4415, 4to.*

within a few miles of New Iceland, but the plan had since been changed, and now the line extended straight west across the prairies, leaving the reserve between 40 and 110 miles from the railway. Prices for its odd-numbered sections were accordingly set at the low end of $3.50 per acre for the southern townships and $1.00 per acre for the more northerly ones.[106] The Icelanders, however, were already settled on many of these sections. After news of the changes was published in *Framfari,* including an opinion from an official in the Winnipeg Dominion Lands Office that there would be no exemption for the reserve, the colonists became deeply concerned over the status of their homestead claims. The editor stated that they were divided into three camps: those who were so incensed with what they perceived as the government's arbitrary alteration of the rules that they planned to leave the colony, those who intended to stay and "hold onto the colony as firmly as possible," and those who adopted a wait-and-see approach.

At a meeting on 8 November 1879, Friðjón Friðriksson informed the colony council that he had received assurances from the land agent at Winnipeg that the rights of the Icelanders to already settled sections would be respected, regardless of whether the sections were even- or odd-numbered. Still, many were also concerned about how the new rules would affect future Icelandic immigrants.[107] The widespread out-migration that followed the flooding in 1880–81 caused the matter to be left in abeyance. It resurfaced in 1883–84, when the remaining settlers attempted to secure their homestead patents and as newly arrived Icelanders resettled vacated farms. In both cases, the Dominion Lands Office in Winnipeg rejected claims to odd-numbered sections, but the Icelanders persisted in settling them.

In 1885, the colonists sent a petition to Ottawa, asking that the odd-numbered sections be made available for homestead and pre-emption. They argued that when New Iceland was granted to them, it was understood that only the HBC and school sections were to be withheld from settlement. Exempting the odd-numbered sections was therefore in violation of the original 1875 agreement they had made with the government. In responding to the petition, Deputy Minister of the Interior A.M. Burgess contended that the government had not broken faith with the Icelanders, because "the arrangement made in 1875 could not be supposed to last forever." He nonetheless recommended to cabinet that the petitioners' request be granted for a period of two years, since no one but Icelanders had expressed interest in the land in question. An Order-in-Council to this effect was passed in May 1885, and the privileges contained in it were renewed by subsequent orders over the next twelve years.[108] In some instances, the provisions of the orders were not automatically applied, and the colonists and their representatives were obliged to prod the government. In 1893, Icelandic Agent Baldwin L. Baldwinson advocated on behalf of an Icelander whose homestead application for an odd-numbered section had been rejected:

> The very word "Reserve" indicates and it was at that time understood that the reserve as originally granted should continue to be a reserve for these people. I claim therefore that the Government has no moral right to now withhold that which their predecessors granted to those people some 20 years [ago], and the undisputed right to which they have held ever since.[109]

Despite this vigorous defence of the sanctity of the reserve, Baldwinson sometimes argued that exclusivity was not in the interests of his people. In 1884, he and two other leading Winnipeg Icelanders sent a letter to the government, asking that assistance for Icelandic colonization be continued and offering their suggestions about why New Iceland had failed to achieve notable progress. They maintained that the exclusion of non-Icelanders had been detrimental to the colony and recommended that in the future "no Icelandic colonies should hereafter be closed, and thus excluded from the English element whose knowledge and practical experience is invaluable to the Icelandic settler."[110]

In general, the New Icelanders accepted the Dominion Lands system as the mechanism through which they could acquire land and develop the resources of the Northwest for their individual and collective benefit. The question was whether an exclusive reserve helped or hindered them in achieving that goal. Proponents of opening the reserve to other settlers saw the debate as a struggle to overcome some of the inherited legacies of their national culture, and they envisioned forging a "New Icelander" infused with the spirit of liberal progress. In 1881, Friðjón Friðriksson, who had earlier championed the idea of an exclusive colony, told Reverend Jón Bjarnason, "All hope of an exclusively Icelandic nationality in America is gone. Icelandic nationalistic arrogance and egotism are on the decline. Foolishness, dogmatism, superstition, and narrow mindedness are dwindling, while healthy common sense and liberalism - both in spiritual and worldly matters - are on the increase."[111]

3
The First New Icelanders
Family Migration and the Formation of a Reserve Community

ON 21 OCTOBER 1875, Icelandic Agent John Taylor wrote a hurried letter to Secretary John Lowe of the Department of Agriculture, announcing the safe arrival of the first party of Icelandic colonists in their reserve. Taylor noted that though a few had become ill, no one had died, and that the group had been augmented the previous night by the birth of a baby boy, "our first native born citizen."[1] This party of approximately 250 people was composed primarily of families with young children. For the next several years, their fate, both as individuals and as a collectivity, was bound up with the success or failure of this experiment in colonization. The outcome for many was ultimately disappointing: hardship, personal tragedy, slow material progress, and internal dissension convinced most of the initial settlers that there was no future in New Iceland. Within the first two years, upward of 30 had died of scurvy, smallpox, scarlet fever, and other diseases. In 1878 and 1879, more than 50 percent of the original settlers left for Winnipeg or Dakota Territory. Most of the remainder joined the exodus in 1880 and 1881, when floodwaters from Lake Winnipeg destroyed hay crops, washed out roads, and swept away fences and buildings. In 1897, when New Iceland's reserve status was rescinded, only twelve members of the original group still resided in what had finally become a growing, although not extremely prosperous, rural community. The rest were scattered across the Canadian West and the northern United States, many in predominantly Icelandic settlements that they had helped found after leaving the Icelandic reserve.

In the fall of 1875, the first colonists were hopeful about their future in New Iceland. A month after arrival, one of them wrote to a Canadian friend in Parry Sound, Ontario, expressing his cautious optimism: "There seems to be good prospects before us if only we can get through the winter. The land seems to be very excellent, and if we can get in plenty of seed in the spring besides what we make fishing, we will be sure to succeed. Our people are all in good spirits."[2] The dominion authorities also seemed pleased. The report of the Select Standing Committee on Immigration and Colonization stated, "The site chosen appears to be favourable for Icelandic settlement, and the Committee are of the opinion that colonization of this nature should be encouraged."[3] Given that the project had only just begun, this opinion was based on perceptions rather than hard evidence. To the members of the committee, the Icelanders represented an ideal type of colonist – northern Europeans whose racial characteristics made them well suited to life in the Northwest. The method of colonization – group settlement of families in compact colonies – was also then at the height of fashion. It seemed to offer the best prospects for building up an orderly and prosperous white settler society in the Northwest, one organized around the liberal principles of private property rights and market-oriented production. Politicians and civil servants in Ottawa had little direct knowledge of Iceland or Icelanders. Most of what they did know came from the travelogues of Lord Dufferin, Richard Burton, and others. The backgrounds, motivations, hopes, and dreams of the people who made up the first group would have been entirely opaque to them, save what the Icelanders' leaders had transmitted in petitions and reports to the Department of Agriculture.

This chapter looks in detail at the Icelanders who came to the Northwest in 1875 and 1876: the original 285 migrants from Ontario and Wisconsin, and the almost 1,200 members of Stóri Hópurinn (the Large Group), who arrived from Iceland the following year. This chapter asks, why did these people agree to relocate to the Icelandic reserve? What sort of economy and society did they hope to build there? Did their ambitions align with or diverge from those of the Canadian government? These questions are answered in two ways: first, through a demographic analysis of the colonists based on church and emigration records, census data, and biographical information; and second, by considering what the immigrants' own life-writings – contemporary letters and diaries as well as retrospective memoirs – have to say about their experiences in the reserve. The chapter locates the migrants within the social and economic structures of Iceland and considers the circumstances that made emigration a possible and desirable option. It then looks at how the migrants became involved with Ottawa's attempts at group colonization and examines how settlement patterns and household structure in the reserve related to their backgrounds in Iceland.

The picture that emerges is of a group that shared two broad characteristics with other nineteenth-century agricultural migrants to North America. First, its members clustered together with people of the same background.[4] The colonists shared ties of language, culture, and religion, common economic circumstances, and migration experiences. But more importantly, many were linked to one another through relatively large groups consisting of parents, siblings, cousins, or neighbours from the same districts in Iceland. In general, the closer they were connected in these ways, the closer they clustered geographically in the reserve. Second, their decisions about migration and resettlement were based not only on their present conditions and prospects, but also on the need to establish a future for the next generation.[5] Their primary reason for coming to New Iceland was to better the material circumstances of themselves and their kin, including those still in Iceland who might join them at some point in the future.

These similarities have not been explored in the historiography on New Iceland, which has instead been focused on the themes of isolation and cultural self-determination. Jónas Thor argues that the Icelanders chose the Lake Winnipeg site because it offered "the required isolation" to realize their ambition of preserving their language and cultural traditions.[6] Although many did aspire to establish a distinctive Icelandic ethnic community in North America, they did not consider geographical and cultural isolation to be a precondition for achieving that goal. In this respect, the Icelandic reserve colonists were similar to the Mennonites in southeastern Manitoba; though isolation has also been an important theme in their traditional historiography, Royden Loewen disputes this emphasis, suggesting that social boundaries, which "defined the community and ordered external and internal relationships," were more important than remoteness in shaping transplanted Mennonite communities.[7] The first New Iceland colonists envisioned a community that continued to use their language and to observe the religious and cultural traditions of their homeland but was also integrated with the larger economic and political structures of Anglo-Canadian settler society.

No contemporary document listing all of the 285 Icelanders who travelled to Winnipeg in September 1875 is known to have survived.[8] However, combining multiple sources from both Iceland and Canada enables us to determine the names, ages, sexes, places of origin, migration patterns, and familial relationships for 260 of them. This migration was predominantly a movement of families with young children. As a result, the group was fairly evenly split between the sexes. Females accounted for 47 percent of the known members of the first group, but many of the unknown individuals were probably girls and women who stayed in Winnipeg to work in domestic service. The true proportion of females was probably closer to 49 percent, which was the same as the overall sex distribution for Icelandic migrants during the 1870s.[9] There were at least fifty couples in the group, whose average age was thirty-seven for males and thirty-five for females. All but seven were married in Iceland; four married in Ontario prior to the move west; and three couples were unwed. Seven of the youngest couples arrived without children, although at least three of the young brides were pregnant. The remaining forty-three couples brought at least 114 children under the age of eighteen. There were five instances of blended families, and two couples who were accompanied by foster children. In two cases, a widower emigrated with a single female housekeeper and her children. Páll Bjarnason's wife, Ragnheiður Halldórsdóttir, died in August 1874 while waiting to leave for Canada. Páll continued the journey with their five children, the family's domestic servant Sigríður Jónsdóttir and her daughter Gíslína Gísladóttir. Páll and Sigríður, who was a widow, had at least one child together and later married in 1878.[10] The average number of children per couple upon arrival in 1875 was 2.2, and the largest families had 5 children. Most were young: only a quarter were twelve or older; 45 percent were between six and eleven; and 30 percent were five or less. At least five women arrived in Winnipeg with infants of younger than six months, and upward of nine women were more than six months pregnant when they landed at Willow Point on 21 October 1875. The presence of so many young children was a serious challenge for the colonists. For nineteenth-century North American settlers, family labour was crucial to establishing a farm on homestead land.[11] At New Iceland, the fact that most children were too young to contribute to the household meant that many families were caught in the "life cycle squeeze," when the need to care for small children stretched their resources.[12]

To some extent, this disadvantage could be offset by the presence of other adult relatives in the household. Many of the reserve's young families belonged to kin groups that also included older adults and younger unmarried persons. There were twenty-nine unmarried men and six unmarried women in the first group. The unmarried older adults were predominantly widows or widowers, frequently the parents or relatives of male or female family heads, whereas the younger single adults included many siblings of married settlers. Forty-three-year-old widow Helga Jónasdóttir arrived in New Iceland with her sons Jósef and Jónas Guðmundsson, aged nineteen and fifteen, and her twenty-two-year-old daughter Elín, who was married to Sigurður Jósúa Björnsson. Sigurður's father, widower Björn Jósúason, and half-brother Björn Jósúa Björnsson were also part of the first group. Fifty-five-year-old widower Bjarni Sigurðsson headed another group. He arrived in the reserve with his sons Samson and Friðrik, and daughter Sigurbjörg, their spouses, and at least two grandchildren. With them came Bjarni's thirty-nine-year-old housekeeper, Kristín Jóhannesdóttir, and her two teenage children, Hjörtur Jóhannsson and Ingibjörg Jóhannsdóttir. These large kin groups were exceptional examples of a common pattern of kinship-based migration; of the approximately 120 adults in the first group, at least 1 in 3 had a sibling in the group, and several had multiple siblings.

In addition, the first colonists had shared geographical origins in Iceland. Virtually all of them came from the northern districts of Eyjafjarðarsýsla (30 percent), Húnavatnssýla (22 percent), North and South Þingeyjarsýsla (20 percent), and Skagafjarðarsýsla (16 percent). The rest came from the adjacent counties of Dalasýsla (6 percent) and Strandasýsla (2 percent) in the west and North and South Múlasýsla (4 percent) in the east.[13] Most Icelandic emigrants during this period were from the north, but this trend was even more pronounced in the case of New Iceland. The four northern districts that accounted for 72 percent of Icelandic emigrants between 1873 and 1875 provided the reserve with 88 percent of its first settlers.[14] In many cases, people were not only from the same district, but also from the same commune *(hreppur)* – the smallest administrative unit in Iceland. For example, all of the first group colonists from Dalasýsla came from Miðdalahreppur.

The colonists also had a shared migration experience. Most had been recruited by the Ontario government in 1873 and 1874. In August 1873, 115 of the 153 Icelandic passengers on the Allan Line steamship *Manitoban* accepted an offer to settle in that province. In September 1874, the Allan Line and the dominion and Ontario governments arranged for a special direct sailing from Iceland to Quebec. The 351 passengers aboard the *St. Patrick* pledged to settle in Ontario in return for subsidized ocean passage.[15] The 1873 *Manitoban* and the 1874 *St. Patrick* contingents were settled on the southern fringes of the Canadian Shield, where the Ontario government was encouraging the colonization of "free grant" lands. Most of the 1873 group was transported to Rosseau in the Muskoka district, where its members either claimed land or sought out employment. Several

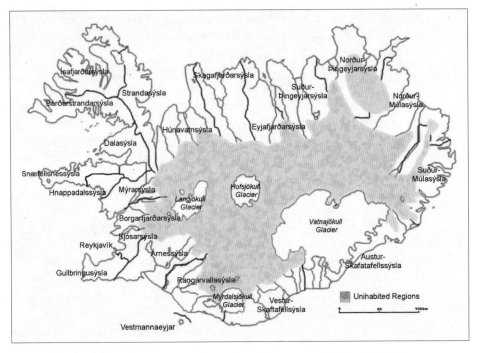

Sýsla (district) divisions in Iceland during the emigration period. *Adapted from Gunnar Karlsson,* The History of Iceland *(Minneapolis: University of Minnesota Press, 2000).*

who were dissatisfied with Ontario crossed the border and joined Icelanders settled in Wisconsin. The 1874 party was transported to Kinmount in Victoria County, where the men were employed as navvies for a railway then under construction.[16] When the railway ran into financial difficulties and work was halted, many of the Icelanders left Kinmount. Some claimed free grant land nearby, whereas others fanned out across the province in search of employment as labourers or domestic servants.[17] About eighty people followed one of their countrymen to Nova Scotia, where the provincial government provided them with cleared land and houses at a colony site fifty miles northeast of Halifax.[18] Most who stayed at Kinmount and vicinity took up Ottawa's offer of resettlement in the Northwest. They accounted for 143 of the 180 *St. Patrick* Icelanders who assembled at Toronto for the journey west in September 1875. The remainder of the group consisted of 44 people from the *Manitoban* and 28 who had come to Ontario in smaller groups over the previous three years. Eight more Icelanders from Wisconsin joined the party at Duluth, Minnesota.[19]

The Icelandic population of the reserve expanded fourfold with the arrival of approximately 1,000 settlers in the late summer of 1876. The Large Group, as it became known, originally included 1,169 people who travelled in three contingents in July 1876, first to Scotland and then to Quebec City on the Allan Line steamships *Austrian, Phoenician,* and *Canadian.* The *Austrian* party was the largest, numbering 752, followed by the *Phoenician* (391), and finally the much smaller *Canadian* (26). The three groups represented different parts of Iceland. All the passengers on the *Canadian* were from the south, whereas 93 percent of those on the *Phoenician* came from the eastern districts of North and South Múlasýsla, the areas most adversely affected by the 1875 Mount Askja eruption. Upward of 83 percent of the *Austrian* passengers departed from the districts that stretched across the northern half of the island, and a minority (13 percent) hailed from the west.[20] Approximately 11 people joined friends and relatives who were already in Nova Scotia or Ontario. At the same time, at least one Icelandic family living in Toronto joined the party. This family, which had come to Canada on the *St. Patrick* in 1874, was headed by Elísabet Þorláksdóttir, a forty-four-year-old widow, and included her adult daughter Björg and twelve-year-old son Ari.[21]

Elísabet was one of at least twenty women listed in the government loan records who emigrated with children but without a male partner. Twelve of these women were widows, five were separated from their husbands, and three were unwed mothers. Although all were single mothers, most were not entirely on their own, as they were travelling with or rejoining larger family groups. Forty-eight-year-old Margrét Guðmundsdóttir and her twelve-year-old daughter Ingibjörg were going to join her son, 1875 colonist Jón Gottvíl Palmason, at New Iceland. Margrét's unmarried daughter María and her one-year-old son Pálmi were also part of the *Austrian* contingent. Margrét's estranged husband, Pálmi Jónsson, was also with the group, but he fell overboard and drowned in the Red River on the way to New Iceland.[22] Fifty-three-year-old widow Guðný Einarsdóttir's son Einar Jónasson was part of the group that had selected the reserve site in 1875. She and her teenage daughter Jóna, along with her twenty-year-old son Jóhannes, joined Einar and his sister Kristín, who had also come to Manitoba the previous year. As might be expected, older widowed women like Guðný tended to be accompanied by their adult children, who could help provide for the family. However, this was not the case for many younger colonists: children aged fourteen years or younger accounted for 42 percent of the Large Group, and at least 233 children under the age of five left Iceland for North America with their parents in the summer of 1876.[23]

At least four single women with children homesteaded in the reserve. Under the Dominion Lands Act, a woman was eligible to claim a homestead if she were the sole head of a household that included minor children.[24] It appears that only women in their mid-forties, the median age for widowed or separated women with children among the Icelanders, pursued this option. Most of the younger women remarried, and the older ones, such as Guðný Einarsdóttir, settled in the household of one of their adult children. All but one of the female homesteaders abandoned their claims around the same time and for the same reasons as their male counterparts. The only woman to remain in New Iceland and acquire a patent for her homestead was forty-five-year-old Oddný Hannesdóttir, who left her husband and emigrated with eight of her nine children, ranging in age from twenty-four to eight, in the summer of 1876. Her eldest son, Jón Sigurðsson Voger, claimed a homestead adjacent to his mother. The older boys helped her on the farm, and the girls entered domestic service in Winnipeg, possibly sending home remittances to the family.[25]

The Large Group also included single adults. There were sixty men, whose average age was 28.1, and twenty women, with an average age of 33.1. The names of at least eighty other single adults in the Large Group, forty men and forty women, appear in emigration records but not the government loan register. This was either because they did not need to borrow money to cover the cost of getting to Winnipeg or because a relative, friend, or employer assumed responsibility for their portion of the loan, as was the case for some domestic servants who migrated with the farmer who had employed them in Iceland. Young, single people were encouraged to remain in Manitoba to work for wages, the men in construction or farm labour and the women in domestic service. When the *Austrian* contingent reached Winnipeg, Friðjón Friðriksson, one of the leaders in the 1875 group, recorded the names and skills of the single adults and attempted to place them with suitable employers. Nineteen-year-old Bjarni Guðmundsson Dalsteð was hired for fifteen dollars per month by a farmer who lived west of Winnipeg.[26] People in poor health also remained behind in Winnipeg and were temporarily housed in the dominion immigration sheds.

The vast majority of the more than 1,140 Icelandic migrants who arrived in Winnipeg between 8 August and 10 September 1876 were couples with children. On average, they were two years older than those who had arrived the year before: thirty-seven for the women and thirty-nine for the men. They and their children accounted for approximately 830 individuals, or over 70 percent of the Large Group migrants. Only 5 of the approximately 160 married couples in the Large Group were not accompanied by children. Of the married couples, 129 headed nuclear families in which the children were the acknowledged biological offspring of both the husband and the wife or had been adopted by them. The remaining couples had blended families consisting of children from previous marriages, children born out of wedlock before or between marriages, and some stepchildren and adopted children. There were also fifteen unmarried couples, nine of whom emigrated with children. In nineteenth-century Iceland, the birth of a child sometimes preceded the marriage of the parents, especially among the poorer classes.[27] This seems to have been the case in the Icelandic reserve; eight of the fifteen unwed couples were married by 1881. In the four remaining cases, two partners died and two older couples appear to have continued cohabiting without marriage.

Separating out individuals, couples, and families, and organizing them into categories obscures what is perhaps the most important characteristic of the Large Group: the presence of relatively large multigenerational family clusters. For example, twenty-five-year-old Pálína Sveinsdóttir emigrated with her husband, Sigurður Jónsson, and their three-year-old son, Þorsteinn. Pálína's parents, sixty-one-year-old Sveinn Þorsteinsson and his forty-nine-year-old wife, Sigurbjörg Jónsdóttir, were also part of the Large Group. They headed a large blended family that was the result of their very complex personal histories. Sveinn had married Sigurbjörg in 1868, seventeen years after Pálína's birth. At the time of the marriage, Sigurbjörg had four children, all of whom had different fathers. When Pálína was born, Sveinn was already a widower twice over. Before marrying and having another child with Sigurbjörg in 1871, Sveinn fathered three children with a widow named Anna Hallsdóttir. Ultimately, the family that Sveinn and Sigurbjörg brought to the Icelandic reserve in 1876 consisted of their five-year-old daughter Katrín Elísabet, Sigurbjörg's three sons, aged twenty-one, ten, and eight, Sveinn's son and daughter from his relationship with Anna Hallsdóttir, and a stepchild, Anna's daughter Kristín.[28]

Reconstructing the family networks among the Icelandic settlers in this way requires more than analyzing the emigration records or government loan registers. Without a detailed analysis of individual and family biographies, many connections can remain hidden. This is particularly true for adult female siblings. For instance, the government loan records list the names of male settlers Sigurgeir Björnsson, Björn Einarsson, and Magnús Jónsson as heads of families. These three men claimed homesteads in close proximity to one another in Township 19, Range 4 East. The biographical sources reveal the reason for this: the men were married to three sisters – Guðfinna, Jóhanna, and Oddný – whose father, Jóhannes Oddsson, also came to the reserve in 1876 and lived with Guðfinna.[29]

Regardless of which district or commune they had lived in before they emigrated or how closely related they were, the colonists had shared roots in the traditional agricultural society of Iceland. More than 95 percent of the first group emigrated from farms. This could hardly have been otherwise, since Iceland was overwhelmingly rural during this period; in 1880, only about 5 percent of the population lived in places that had three hundred or more inhabitants.[30] The few New Iceland colonists who came from an urban location were from the northern village of Akureyri. However, even they had spent most of their lives in the countryside. Jónas Jónasson, the brother of Assistant Icelandic Agent Sigtryggur Jónasson, had moved to Akureyri only in 1871 at the age of twenty-one to apprentice as a printer. Except for one year working as a farm labourer, Jónas spent his childhood and adolescence with his parents on several farms near the village.[31]

The first colonists left one farming society to help build another in the Canadian Northwest. But in establishing a "New Iceland," did they intend to re-create the familiar patterns of rural life, or did they hope to build a *new* society based on the principles of nineteenth-century liberalism? To answer this question, it is necessary first to sketch out the broad contours of the society they left, their place within its social and economic hierarchies, and the complicated relationship between liberalism and Icelandic nationalism during the late nineteenth century. The reasons for the Icelandic Deputation's choice of reserve location and the decisions of individual colonists to participate in the project can then be placed in context.

Farming in Iceland was synonymous with pastoral agriculture. Sheep, cattle, and horses were grazed whenever possible and otherwise fed with hay cut from home fields. Except for a small but growing number of people who lived by the sea as cottars, fishing was a secondary activity conducted on a seasonal basis. There were two major categories of farms, independent farms *(heimajörð)* and outlying farms *(hjáleigur)*. Outlying farms were typically marginal upland holdings that could sustain a household only during favourable climatic cycles. The countryside was thinly populated, and farms were geographically dispersed.

The vast majority of Icelandic farmers were tenants or sub-tenants. In 1850, only 17 percent of farmers were freeholders.[32] Landownership was concentrated in the hands of the Danish Crown, the Lutheran Church, and a few large proprietors. Under these circumstances, moveable goods and chattels, particularly livestock, formed the bulk of people's assets. Independent farms and one or more outlying farms were grouped together as a taxation unit called a legally assessed farm *(lögbýli)*. Farms were valued according to the number of cattle that they could support, and the tenant was obliged to pay the taxes due on the holding. A commune was composed of at least twenty legally assessed farms. Its two main functions were to organize the fall roundup of sheep from the highland pastures and to coordinate poor relief. The latter involved supporting paupers, typically but not exclusively children and the elderly, who were housed on farms in the commune (for more on local government in Iceland and how it shaped municipal institutions at New Iceland, see page 150).

As well as being the primary unit of production, reproduction, and consumption, the farm household was also the major social institution of the countryside. At its core was a nuclear family, headed by the farmer *(bóndi)* and his wife. It was not uncommon for households to include an elderly widowed parent as well as collateral relatives of the farming couple. The farmer and his wife exercised wide-ranging paternal authority over not only their own children and younger relatives, but also other household members who were not necessarily blood relations. This included a rotating pool of male and female servants *(vinnuhjú)*. It could also encompass boarders *(lausamenn)* who worked on a seasonal basis and paupers *(þurfamenn)* placed in the household by the commune. Lodgers *(húsmenn)* also worked on the farm and lived in the farmer's house but were often married and had more independence than other members of the household. They usually had a few animals among the farmer's herd and were allotted a share of the hayfield. According to the emigrant register *Vesturfaraskrá,* New Iceland's first settlers were farmers or farmers' sons (52 percent), servants (26 percent), and lodgers or cottars (20 percent).[33] The proportion of servants was representative of the broader Icelandic population. In the second half of the nineteenth century, servants accounted for at least a quarter of the total population and 35 to 40 percent of people over fifteen years of age.[34]

Each of these social distinctions could represent a different phase in a person's life cycle.[35] Children, both those of the farming couple and others in the household, received a rudimentary education at home that usually helped them attain at least basic literacy. Around age fifteen, they left home and went to work as servants on another farm. Time spent in service away from immediate family was considered an important part of a young person's education and socialization. The average age of marriage was about thirty for men and slightly lower for women. After a period of living as lodgers, the couple would form their own farming household. Elderly parents often resided with one of their children.

The first New Icelanders were broadly representative of these patterns in Icelandic rural society. Most of the children under 15 had lived with their parents prior to emigration. The servants in the group were predominantly young adults, aged about 24. Among those who had been married in Iceland, their average ages at first marriage were 27.2 for men and 25.0 for women. The farmers and lodgers were typically about 34 years old. The average age of farm wives was 38.0 and for lodgers' wives was 32.2.

Although movement between social categories was conceivable, family circumstances often limited an individual's possibilities. If a child's parents were unmarried, had died, or were too poor, the communal authorities could place it in another household as a pauper. A woman who did not marry spent most of her life in service. If she had no relatives to look after her, she was susceptible to becoming a pauper later in life. When no land was available for a couple to establish an independent farm household, they might spend a longer period in the intermediate social and economic position of lodger or cottar.

Internal migration was a common feature of life in nineteenth-century rural Iceland. Since tenancy and service contracts generally lasted for just one or two years, farmers, lodgers, and servants moved on a fairly regular basis. Young couples who wished to establish a household were often obliged to travel far from their home region to gain access to land.[36] Approximately 35 percent of adult male settlers in the 1875 group emigrated from a district in which they had not been born. Many who did emigrate from their birth district had moved around during the interim. Jakob Sigurðsson Eyfjörð was born in and emigrated from Eyjafjarðarsýsla but had spent five years working in North Múlasýsla as a young adult.[37] Frequent moves within a district were also common; from their marriage in 1862 to emigration in 1874, New Icelanders Indriði Indriðason and his wife, Sigurlaug Jóhannesdóttir, moved three times within Þingeyjarsýsla.[38]

A system of labour bondage underpinned Iceland's traditional rural society. Unmarried persons were required by law to hire themselves out to farmers as servants for a term of one year. Servants could legally marry, but if they lacked the means to be self-sufficient they risked having their family broken up and their children dealt with as paupers by the communal authorities. Landowners required the permission of the commune to have lodgers or cottars settled on their property. The implications of this social system were twofold: First, it ensured that farmers had an adequate supply of relatively cheap labour. Second, it served as a system of social discipline and a check on population growth by delaying marriage or placing it beyond the reach of many servants. Marriage and procreation were treated as privileges that were endorsed by the broader community only if the couple had attained the appropriate social position.[39]

In the second half of the nineteenth century, demographic pressures, environmental conditions, and economic developments undermined the stability of the social structure. In the first half of the century, warmer weather helped increase agricultural productivity. Favourable climatic conditions meant that farming on marginal lands became possible, which opened new opportunities for family and household formation. The population had grown from 47,230 in 1801 to 69,763 by 1870.[40] By mid-century, a large cohort of people was approaching marriageable age. Between 1845 and 1860, the twenty-five to thirty-four age group grew by 45 percent, whereas the population as a whole increased by only 13 percent.[41] At the same time, the conditions that had permitted this population expansion receded. The agricultural economy underwent a series of shocks brought on as the climate cooled, which reduced the hay-growing season, and an epizootic that decimated the sheep flocks during the 1850s.[42] There were now more people pursuing fewer opportunities in the agricultural economy. Wages fell, unemployment rose, and the number of paupers expanded by 264 percent between 1851 and 1871. Less land was available for young people who wished to marry and form their own farming households, which resulted in division and subdivision of holdings and larger households; the mean household size grew from 6.7 members in 1860 to 7.6 in 1870.[43] In these circumstances, many people began to look farther afield in hopes of improving the prospects for themselves and their children.

The traditional mobility of the rural population found new outlets as the economy was slowly transformed by the development of the fishery and the country became better integrated into the circuits of world trade. In 1855, mercantilist trade restrictions favouring Danish firms were replaced by a free trade regime. The fishery, which grew from a small seasonal activity conducted from rowboats to a large-scale industrial enterprise involving decked vessels, gradually superseded agriculture as Iceland's main source of wealth. In response to this new opportunity, the rural population moved into coastal villages. Gunnar Karlsson estimates that more than fourteen thousand people did so between 1870 and 1914, which was roughly equivalent to the number that migrated to North America during the same period.⁴⁴ Helgi Skúli Kjartansson and Steinþór Heiðarsson argue that levels of overseas emigration were lower in areas that were closest to fishing regions and urban centres.⁴⁵

Growth in the livestock trade with Great Britain during the 1870s was essential to the development of a mass emigration movement in Iceland. It allowed prospective migrants to convert their primary asset – their livestock – into cash that could finance their journey and resettlement in North America. Other factors included an increase in information about overseas destinations and the integration of Iceland into the networks of transatlantic migrant transport. In 1860, a prominent farmer in Þingeyjarsýsla recommended Brazil as the best possible destination for prospective Icelandic migrants. A few sojourners made the long trip and sent back encouraging reports that prompted 550 people to sign up to join them in 1873. Problems in arranging transportation for such a large group prevented all but a handful from following through with their plans. Many decided to join other prospective emigrants who intended to go to Wisconsin. A few young Icelanders had gone to Wisconsin after 1870, and when their letters were published in the newspaper *Norðanfari,* people became aware of the opportunities in the Midwestern United States. During the winter and spring of 1872–73, meetings were held in Akureyri to plan for a large migration to North America. They enlisted the help of Reykjavík merchant Guðmundur Lambertsen, shipping agent for the Scottish Canadian Allan Line.⁴⁶ The Allans contacted Canadian immigration authorities in hopes that they would offer subsidies to help boost this new source of transatlantic passengers.⁴⁷ As discussed in Chapter 1, Dominion officials took up this offer, ushering in a system of Canadian state intervention in the Icelandic emigrant market that would persist until the first decades of the twentieth century. As the migration movement intensified during the 1880s and 1890s, Icelandic nationalists accused emigrants of abandoning the nation just when it was struggling to gain greater autonomy from Denmark. Emigrant leaders countered that misrule and backwardness in the homeland were largely responsible for the decision to leave. They suggested that North America presented new opportunities to expand the economic and cultural horizons of the Icelandic nation.⁴⁸

The anxiety over emigration reflected broader concerns about how Iceland's social and economic transformation had affected its national character. Many farmers and government officials believed that the traditional structures of rural society were not only the stable core of the economy, but also the moral centre of national life. Through their representatives in the Icelandic parliament, farmers attempted to shore up the crumbling social system through increasingly restrictive legislation that aimed to constrain labour mobility and diminish the fertility of servants and paupers by limiting marriage rights. Guðmundur Hálfdánarson contends that these efforts were symptomatic of a deeply conservative streak in nineteenth-century Icelandic nationalism. Although the nationalist movement has traditionally been associated with a group of liberal intellectuals, many nationalists wanted greater freedom from metropolitan control, not to implement liberal reforms, but to curtail individual freedom and protect the old regime from the influences of Continental liberalism. As a cultural construction, the Icelandic nation included all people who spoke the Icelandic language and were united by shared history and literary traditions. But membership in the political project of the nation was far more circumscribed and hierarchical; political rights were dependent on social distinctions.[49]

This raises several questions about the New Iceland colonists. Were they attempting to transplant a vanishing way of life to the Canadian Northwest, or did they intend to leave it behind and build a "New Iceland" in economic and social terms as well as in name? How did their conception of themselves as a distinct linguistic and cultural community in North America relate to their economic goals? Was physical separation from the broader settler society an important consideration in their choice of the Lake Winnipeg site and their decision to migrate to the Northwest? These questions are important because the goals, ambitions, and economic strategies of the individuals who established New Iceland were as central to its creation as the cultural concerns that have received so much attention in the literature.[50]

It is clear that many of the migrants wished to settle in a homogeneous rural community alongside fellow Icelanders. This was expressed in the 31 May 1875 meeting at Kinmount that endorsed the Canadian government's proposal of sending a delegation to Manitoba. As John Taylor explained in a letter to the minister of agriculture,

> The Icelanders have been trying to find a suitable place both in the United States and eastern provinces of Canada, where they could get a quantity of good land set apart for the exclusive settlement of Icelanders, who are now in America and those who will immigrate in future, but not yet found anything they thought would answer the purpose, and whereas they have preserved their language and nationality for more than One Thousand years unchanged and wish to do so in the future, but this can't be done without them uniting and forming a settlement by themselves.[51]

This resolution was in keeping with the general outpouring of nationalist sentiment that accompanied the 1874 millennial anniversary of Iceland's settlement. It also echoed the rhetoric of the charismatic editor and poet Jón Ólafsson, the architect of the ambitious scheme to move Iceland's entire population to Alaska.[52] Ólafsson himself had nothing to do with the Canadian Icelandic reserve project, but the secretary of the Kinmount meeting, twenty-four-year-old Friðjón Friðriksson, had been a signatory to Ólafsson's petition to the US government.[53] Friðriksson believed that though the location at Kinmount could probably support a colony, it was far from ideal: "The amount of land is insufficient, and we would probably mix with the locals too much to be able to maintain into the future those useful aspects of our nationality – our language and religion."[54] Friðriksson did not elaborate on which national characteristics were dispensable, but on other occasions he criticized his fellow immigrants for clinging to the past or dreaming of the future instead of seizing present opportunities.[55]

The chairman of the Kinmount meeting, Sigtryggur Jónasson, had never been a supporter of Ólafsson's Alaska plan. He thought it impractical and believed that the Icelanders would be just as isolated from modern civilization in Alaska as they had been in their homeland.[56] The Kinmount meeting selected Sigtryggur and Einar Jónasson as delegates to examine land in Manitoba along with Baptist missionary John Taylor.[57] Whereas Sigtryggur was the established leader of the Kinmount Icelanders, Einar was probably chosen in part to make the delegation reflect their regional distribution: Sigtryggur was from Eyjafjarðarsýsla, and Einar was from Dalasýsla. Kinmount settlers Kristján Jónsson and Skapti Arason also joined what Taylor dubbed the "Icelandic Deputation." A sixth member, Sigurður Kristófersson (anglicized as "Christopherson"), joined the party in Milwaukee. These three men were from Þingeyjarsýsla. Except for the sixty-two-year-old Taylor, all were unmarried and in their early to mid-twenties.

As the previous chapter explained, their choice of land was limited by existing settlements and by the various tracts that were set aside for other purposes. They were also constrained by their mandate to find a site large enough to accommodate not only the current group of immigrants, but also those who were expected to arrive in the coming years, and the practical need to match a potential location with the skills and material resources of their countrymen. Skapti Arason later recalled that they did not think it advantageous to go too far west, since the Icelanders were unfamiliar with the methods of prairie farming and lacked the resources to purchase the animals and implements required.[58] There were in fact few European agricultural settlements on the prairies at the time. With no railways and few roads, the need for ready access to fuel and transportation, as well as the perception that the prairies were less fertile than forested land, kept settlement largely confined to partly wooded tracts in close proximity to waterways.[59] The damage done to farms in the Red River Valley by swarms of grasshoppers in recent years was also apparent to the Icelandic Deputation. Finding a site where the pests were not as troublesome was also important. Dominion Lands Agent Donald Codd directed them to the west shore of Lake Winnipeg as the location most likely to satisfy requirements.[60]

The Icelandic Deputation emphasized economic considerations in its choice of colony site. It noted that it had been tasked with finding a location for a "United Icelandic Colony," but the goal of preserving language and religion, as mentioned during the Kinmount meeting, is otherwise completely absent from its final report. Later published in the Canadian government immigration pamphlet *Nýa* [sic] *Ísland í Kanada* (New Iceland in Canada), the report contains a careful assessment of the resources and future prospects of the southwest shore of Lake Winnipeg as they appeared in the summer of 1875. The presence of marshes and fields, where hay for livestock could be obtained, and of abundant timber for building and fuel, was important. The Icelanders described the soil as a "rich black mould over a white clay" and asserted that "the land is excellent for raising grain, and that it is better than the very best land we have seen in Ontario."[61] Their claims about the soil were supported by the observable success of Indigenous people's agriculture around Lake Winnipeg:

> We did see with our own eyes good potatoes which the Indians had planted in June, and also what is termed Red river corn, both growing at Icelanders' [White Mud] river. And at the south end of the Lake Winnipeg, good wheat, potatoes, oats, peas and barley, as well as Red River corn just mentioned were all cultivated with success, the grasshoppers not yet having extended so far to the north as that.[62]

The Aboriginal fishery was also cited as evidence of another resource that could be developed. The Icelanders focused on whitefish, which they believed "would no doubt become a valuable article of commerce."[63] Furthermore, this promising environment and its resources came with good access to markets. Proximity to the proposed CPR line was of particular significance:

> [The colony site] lies on a Lake which abounds with fish. The people can go there the whole distance from Ontario and Quebec by railway and steamboats. Easy transportation along the coast by boats in the summer, and on the ice in the winter. The south east end of the reserve is only about twenty eight miles by water from the point where the Canadian Pacific Railway is to cross the Red River, and farther west it is not so far as that ... There are now about three hundred men employed on the work of this road, about six miles east of Red River. And it is possible that the road will in two years be completed from this point to the head of Lake Superior. There is plenty of wood on the reserve, both for building purposes and fuel, yet ... it is easy to clear the land, as the Poplar trees are not heavy, and their roots run near the surface of the ground, so that the stumps can be taken out and the land plowed in two years after they are cut. There is abundance of hay to be had at once.[64]

The deputation had no trouble securing this tract as a reserve. The Department of the Interior immediately approved its request, and Minister David Laird later instructed Lieutenant Governor Alexander Morris that in his treaty negotiations with the Lake Winnipeg Indians, the claims of the Icelanders would take precedence over any Indian reserves that would be created in the same region.[65] Taylor and Sigtryggur Jónasson returned east to inform the Icelanders in Wisconsin and Ontario of the results of their mission. Meetings were held in Milwaukee on 15 August and at Kinmount and Gravenhurst, Ontario, a few days later. The report of the deputation was favourably received at all three meetings, and resolutions were passed asking the Canadian government for financial aid to allow the settlers to move west that fall.[66] On 13 September, the dominion government passed an Order-in-Council allotting $5,000 to remove "200 adult Icelandic immigrants" from Ontario and resettle them in the reserve on Lake Winnipeg.[67] Seven days later, more than 250 Icelanders had gathered at Toronto in preparation for the journey west.

Despite the enthusiasm expressed at the Wisconsin and Ontario meetings, and the government's offer of subsidized transport, New Iceland turned out to be a relatively weak magnet for Icelandic migrants in North America. The first party to arrive there was the single largest concentration of Icelanders on the continent, but it represented just 33 percent of emigration since 1870.[68] There were several hundred Icelanders in Wisconsin, but only eight joined the trek west in the fall of 1875, perhaps because they did not receive support from Ottawa.[69] Even people who took a leading role in the Ontario meetings remained behind. This included Albert

Gíslason, who made the motion endorsing the Icelandic Deputation's mission to Manitoba.[70] He apparently wasn't pleased with its results, since he and his family moved to Milwaukee instead, where they settled permanently.[71] Sigurður Jóhannesson, chairman of the Gravenhurst meeting and member of the committee that drew up a plan for the migration west, chose to go to Nova Scotia.[72] Some who eventually did go west were at first hesitant. Jakob Sigurðsson Eyfjörð, who was settled in Parry Sound, Ontario, didn't believe it was feasible for him to travel west that fall. He thought he would eventually go to New Iceland, but he worried that he would not manage to sell the house that had cost him four hundred dollars to build and would therefore have little money with which to commence farming.[73] Although the vast majority of the 1876 Large Group did go to Manitoba, approximately 37 percent initially intended to settle in Nova Scotia. They were dissuaded from this plan in Quebec, where a settler from Markland, Nova Scotia, delivered an unfavourable report on both the economic conditions in the province and the prospects for the Markland Icelandic colony.[74]

After the founding of New Iceland, most pre-1876 Icelandic immigrants remained fairly widely dispersed throughout North America. They lived in small clusters of family farms in Ontario, Wisconsin, and Nebraska, and at the provincial-government-sponsored colony in Nova Scotia. They even included a few converts to Mormonism who had journeyed to Utah to join co-religionists who had left Iceland in the 1850s. In May 1875, Gunnlaugur Pétursson and his family moved from Wisconsin to southwest Minnesota, which soon became an important locus of Icelandic settlement in the United States. Many young Icelanders decided to continue working as agricultural labourers and domestic servants in Ontario or Wisconsin rather than going west to Manitoba. Most did eventually move west but not necessarily to New Iceland. By the late 1870s and early 1880s, Minnesota and Dakota Territory were attracting considerable numbers of Icelandic migrants. In some cases, the people who stayed away from New Iceland were close relatives of its first settlers. Nine members of the first group had siblings elsewhere in North America. For example, whereas Skapti Arason, his sister Guðný, and brother Benedikt were in New Iceland, their sister Guðfinna was in Toronto and another sister, Guðrún, was in Milwaukee. Family and kinship networks, common origins in Iceland, and migration experiences in Canada were therefore important in shaping people's decisions to move to the Icelandic reserve, but they do not tell the whole story.

The main factor that prompted people to accept Ottawa's offer of resettlement in the Northwest was the hope of improving their material circumstances. Despite initial assistance from the Ontario government, the groups that arrived in 1873 and 1874 aboard the *Manitoban* and the *St. Patrick* encountered numerous hardships. There were twenty-nine deaths in the Icelandic shanties at Kinmount between October 1874 and May 1875.[75] The unemployment and general suffering at Kinmount were what prompted John Taylor to ask the dominion government to help the Icelanders and were the main reason that the government sponsored the Icelandic Deputation's trip to Manitoba. Individuals with families who had little money and poor employment prospects saw the government offer as a chance for a fresh start. Símon Símonarson noted that although he, his wife, Valdís Guðmundsdóttir, and their son Guðmundur had been treated kindly in Lindsay, Ontario, "there was little work, the pay was low, and the future prospects poor."[76] Stefán Eyjólfsson, who was a young, single man living in Milwaukee, decided to go to New Iceland to stake a claim for the rest of his family, who were still in Iceland. In the summer of 1874, his father had sent him to scout opportunities in North America, and, from the Icelandic Deputation's report, New Iceland appeared to be the best choice thus far: "It was clear to me that my father would likely follow through on his intention of moving west when he heard about this opportunity. I therefore thought to give this place a try."[77] Once in New Iceland, Stefán claimed four lots along White Mud/Icelander's River for himself, his father, and two brothers, who arrived as part of the Large Group the following year.[78]

The Icelanders readily adapted themselves to the Dominion Lands homestead system. A major reason for this relatively seamless transition was that apart from its rigid geometry, the system did not differ radically from the familiar settlement patterns of rural Iceland. Farms in both contexts were dispersed over a relatively large area. The blending of the two systems was symbolized by the coexistence of Icelandic farm names with Dominion Lands Act legal descriptions. Thus, the map that Benedikt Arason sent to a friend in Iceland was derived from the survey grid but could still be understood within Icelandic conceptions of space and place. However, there were also important differences, particularly in the size and composition of households at the reserve. Smaller households containing a nuclear family replaced the large households of traditional Icelandic farming society, with their rotating pool of labourers. Some households consisted of unmarried individuals who had claimed their own 160-acre homestead. In New Iceland, the barriers to family and household formation that existed in Iceland – lack of access to land and restrictive social legislation – were

Símon Símonarson (1839–1927) and Valdís Guðmundsdóttir (1834–1923) with their daughter, Jóhanna Guðrún (b. 16 March 1878 in New Iceland), c. 1890. *Photo courtesy of Johanna Wilson.*

removed. This resulted in a proliferation of many relatively small households. According to the colony statistics for 1877, there were 264 "Heads of Families," as compared with 223 households, and the average household size was just 4.5 persons.[79]

However, households often consisted of more than a nuclear family. Early, informal social welfare arrangements in the reserve also resembled the traditional patterns of Icelandic rural society in that settler couples sometimes fostered the children of needy families. Símon Símonarson and his wife, Valdís Guðmundsdóttir, took in five-year-old Guðrún Jóhannsdóttir after her father died of smallpox in October 1876. Símon recalled that Guðrún's mother, Jóhanna Þorbergsdóttir, was hard pressed to care for her four surviving children and elderly mother. In the spring of 1877, Símon and Valdís took in a single mother and her daughter, who stayed with them through the following winter.[80]

Arrangements such as these illustrate how the reserve community was built on webs of relationships among the settlers. Household formation and settlement patterns were shaped by kinship and regional affiliation, particularly during the crucial first year. Kin groups frequently formed multi-family households or clusters of contiguous homesteads. North of Gimli, the brothers Friðbjörn and Þorlákur Björnsson, who were married to the sisters Anna Sigríður and Þórdís Árnadóttir, claimed adjacent quarter sections, which they called Nýhagi (New Pasture). The two couples initially lived together in a single log cabin along with ten children, five from each family, but later built an additional dwelling.[81] South of Gimli, Guðný Aradóttir, her husband, Sigurbjörn Jóhannesson, and their three daughters settled at Kjalvík (Keel Cove), along with Guðný's married brother Benedikt and unmarried brother Skapti. The claimants of the adjacent homestead, Kilsnes (Creek Point), were Indriði Indriðason and Sigurlaug Jóhannesdóttir, the sister of Guðný's husband, Sigurbjörn. These sorts of living arrangements were a source of mutual support, particularly in times of crisis, such as when Guðný's husband died in January 1877.[82] However, too many deaths, particularly among the adult women, could result in the dissolution of the household. Sigurður Jósúa Björnsson, one of the first settlers to abandon his homestead and leave the colony, lost his twenty-three-year-old wife, Elín Guðmundsdóttir, and his mother-in-law, Helga Jónasdóttir, in the spring of 1876.[83]

Migrants from the same districts in Iceland also tended to claim land near each other even if they were not closely related. Although people from Þingeyjarsýsla represented only 20 percent of the first group, they accounted for 32 percent of the residents of Víðirnesbyggð (Willow Point Settlement) and were concentrated primarily in Township 18 and the southern end of Township 19. People from Húnavatnssýsla settled north of Gimli, but especially in Townships 20 and 21, which later became Árnesbyggð (River Point Settlement). In the case of people from Eyjafjarðarsýsla, who formed the majority of the first group and who settled throughout New Iceland, being neighbours in a particular commune prior to emigration seems to have helped shape decisions about where to settle. The claimants of three adjacent quarter sections south of Gimli all came from Saurbæjarhreppur in Eyjafjarðarsýsla.[84] For those colonists who did not travel as part of extended family groups, friends from the same region could be an important source of support and mutual aid. This was the case for Símon Símonarson and Erlendur Ólafsson, who emigrated from the same commune in Skagafjarðarsýsla and claimed adjacent homesteads. During the first year, their families shared a house, and later they frequently assisted each other as they attempted to establish farms in the reserve.[85]

This proved to be a difficult task. Over the next several years, many of the first settlers endured numerous tragedies and setbacks as they worked to adapt their old rural pattern of life to their new home. For most, New Iceland did not live up to expectations and they eventually moved elsewhere. An important source of dissatisfaction fuelling out-migration was the colony's isolation. In taking up the Canadian government's offer of resettlement, neither the Icelandic Deputation nor the migrants themselves were seeking geographical isolation from settler society. Rather, they hoped to build a large, homogeneous Icelandic colony consisting of family, friends, and former neighbours, while at the same time enjoying links with networks of economic, social, and cultural exchange that would allow their community to achieve material progress. The importance that the Icelandic Deputation placed on the closeness of the reserve to the proposed CPR route highlights this motivation. Ottawa's decision to move the railway route to the south and west in the late 1870s shifted ease of transportation and access to markets from being a main attraction of New Iceland to one of its greatest weaknesses. Gimli took its place with Battleford, Prince Albert, and Edmonton as a disappointed population centre along the rejected Lake Manitoba–north Saskatchewan railway route.[86]

In building their lives in the reserve, the Icelanders had to navigate the uncertain waters of state immigration and colonization policies that were unevenly implemented, subject to change, and not amenable to their control. They also had to carve out a niche for themselves in an unfamiliar environment alongside an Aboriginal population that sometimes rendered assistance but also resented their presence and feared its consequences for its own competing claim to the region. All these issues were in play during the single greatest crisis to afflict the Icelandic reserve – the smallpox epidemic of 1876–77.

4

Quarantined within a New Order

Smallpox and the Spatial Practices of Colonization

O N 24 SEPTEMBER 1876, the Reverend James Settee conducted Sunday services at Sandy Bar in the northern portion of New Iceland. In his capacity as a Church of England missionary, Settee was a regular visitor to the Indigenous settlements around the lake, and he counted several converts among the Indigenous people who lived within the area now designated an Icelandic reserve. That day, the congregation included not only the Indigenous Christians Settee knew well, but also Icelandic immigrants from the Large Group who had recently settled among them. Settee said prayers in Cree, Ojibwe, and English, and one of the colonists provided an Icelandic translation. Settee's sermon was drawn from the First Epistle of John, a passage emphasizing God's infinite love and the duty of God's children to love one another.[1] The missionary probably chose this particular passage as part of an effort to diffuse tensions between the Indigenous residents and the settlers; the arrival of the Icelanders earlier that summer had triggered a tense confrontation over land that almost became violent.[2] Still, their joint attendance at Reverend Settee's service suggests that the two groups had a complex relationship; fear, suspicion, and resentment did not preclude co-operation and friendly interaction in specific circumstances. However, in this context, as in many others, the mixing of Indigenous and immigrant populations had unanticipated consequences. Smallpox broke out in the fall 1876 and within two months had decimated the Indigenous residents of the reserve. A doctor sent by the Canadian government reported that their numbers had been reduced from fifty or sixty to only seventeen. He found the scarred survivors huddled in tents

Church of England missionary James Settee (c. 1810–1902) was of Omushkego (Swampy) Cree and British ancestry. Settee was one of several Indigenous boys who attended the Church Missionary Society (CMS) school in the Red River Colony during the 1820s. The CMS hoped the boys would become Native catechists. This hope was realized in Settee; he was the second Indigenous person to be ordained into the Anglican priesthood (1856), and he served as a CMS missionary until 1884. *Archives of Manitoba, Cowley Collection, N80.*

surrounded by newly dug graves.[3] To prevent further infection, their homes and possessions were burned, and shortly thereafter dominion land surveyors arrived to plant posts marking the boundaries of the proposed Icelandic town of Sandy Bar.[4]

This chapter examines the role of the 1876–77 smallpox epidemic in drawing boundaries between Indigenous and immigrant land in the south basin of Lake Winnipeg. At first glance, this case seems to confirm general understandings about the relationship between disease and colonialism: the arrival of a group of Europeans on a colonial frontier precipitated an epidemic that devastated the Indigenous population and cleared the way for the appropriation of its land and resources. This generalized story, at best, serves only to highlight the tragic outcome of a complex set of events. At worst, it obscures that complexity by casting Aboriginal demographic decline primarily as a biologically driven process. What happened at Lake Winnipeg in 1876–77 was not inevitable: it was the product of a historically contingent set of circumstances. Historical geographers of medicine Jody Decker and Paul Hackett have demonstrated that the impact of disease on Aboriginal populations in northwest North America varied greatly over time and changed with shifting patterns of trade, migration, and settlement.[5] From the onset of European contact, epidemics stimulated migrations, shifted balances of power, and altered boundaries between peoples.[6] More recently, James Daschuk has drawn attention to the interplay of environmental conditions and disease epidemics in transforming the human geography of the northern Plains while also vividly revealing how, after 1870, Canadian government policies worked to exacerbate demographic decline among the region's Aboriginal peoples.[7]

The 1876–77 smallpox epidemic demonstrates how Aboriginal dispossession and immigrant resettlement were linked through the overlapping government apparatuses of land administration and public health. The measures taken in response to the epidemic allowed the Canadian state to exercise new forms of power over spaces and people where its influence had previously been quite limited. This occurred both through coercive means and – perhaps more significantly in a context where the state's presence was relatively light – the self-regulation of individuals and groups acting in their perceived best interests. Ultimately, however, quarantine and sanitation measures helped to reify a new spatial order mandating the compartmentalization of land and people into the system of racially segregated reserves that was integral to the Canadian colonization of the Northwest during the late nineteenth century.

New Iceland's official status as an exclusive immigrant colony did not mean that the colonists were isolated from the other inhabitants of the region. From the time of their arrival, they were engaged in a web of economic, social, and cultural interactions with the local Indigenous population, the established non-Indigenous settler community, and federal officials. Lake Winnipeg had long been a vital transportation corridor linking the Red River Colony in the south with the fur-trading centres of the north. By the early 1870s, it was regularly travelled by Anglo-Canadian speculators, journalists, and government officials. In addition, a handful of settlers had arrived, attracted by the area's fish, timber, and mineral resources.[8] The lands around the lake, including the site designated as the Icelandic reserve, were home to a substantial Cree, Ojibwe, and Metis population.⁹ These people continued to occupy their homes, even as treaty negotiators, surveyors, and immigrants disregarded their claims and moved to impose a new order. In short, the reserve was a dynamic contact zone in which frequent and sustained interaction across ethno-cultural boundaries was the norm and was fundamentally shaped by the asymmetrical power relations of colonialism.¹⁰

Strangely, a contact perspective emphasizing co-presence and interaction has been largely absent from the historical writing about New Iceland. Instead, the notion of its separateness and isolation has dominated historians' interpretations. Recent monographs by the Icelandic writers Guðjón Arngrímsson and Jónas Thor construct New Iceland as a *terra nullius*, where the immigrants attempted to replicate their Old World networks of kin and community, and fulfill previously frustrated national aspirations.¹¹ Their brief mentions of Aboriginal people simply repeat well-worn racial and cultural stereotypes about Indigenous passivity in the face of white encroachment that have long ago been exposed as convenient fictions of colonialism.¹² One important exception is anthropologist Anne Brydon's analysis of Icelandic Canadian mythic narratives about contact with Aboriginal people. Brydon reveals how stories stressing co-operation, friendly interaction, and mutual respect, especially involving John Ramsay, a leading resident of the Sandy Bar village, have obscured a more contentious history involving protracted disputes over land and bitterness about the tragedy of the smallpox epidemic. She argues that this refashioning of history is part of an Icelandic Canadian narrative strategy to diminish the painful legacy of colonialism.¹³ Although this chapter also recognizes and explores the role of the Icelanders as colonizers, its primary concern is with identifying how both they and the Indigenous people whom they displaced were caught up in the same project of colonial governance. It therefore seeks to draw connections between immigration and colonization, two topics that are frequently treated as historiographically distinct.¹⁴

The discourses of race, progress, and civilization, typically used to legitimate rule over Indigenous people, could also mark certain Europeans as racially and culturally degenerate.¹⁵ The 1876-77 smallpox epidemic exposed the ambiguous position of the Icelandic immigrants in the emerging colonial order of the Canadian Northwest. Although they were unquestionably the agents of European colonization at the local level, actively displacing the Indigenous population with the backing of the Canadian state, they were also impoverished non-English-speaking immigrants who were unfamiliar with local conditions and dependent on government rations for survival, and thus they were also clearly subordinate within settler society. Their susceptibility to smallpox was interpreted by some Anglo-Canadians as a function of their inherent racial characteristics as well as their specific material circumstances. In a report commissioned by Lieutenant Governor Alexander Morris, Dr. James Spencer Lynch provided a detailed description of the Icelanders' colony and an evaluation of their future prospects as settlers and as citizens of Canada. Lynch's experience as medical officer at Gimli during the epidemic led him to a mainly negative evaluation: "Centuries of isolation and intermarriage have had the effect of reducing their physical condition to a point below which they are likely to be successful in the rude contest with western pioneers." According to Lynch, contact with more vigorous peoples was the principal way for the Icelanders to survive and thrive in their new home. He also prescribed modifications in diet, hygiene, and housing, which he believed would ameliorate the worst defects of their character.[16] The essential problem that Lynch addressed was the Icelanders' ability to participate successfully in western colonization. The smallpox epidemic had brought this into question, and as a physician, Lynch was called upon to translate his knowledge of medicine and health into recommendations that would serve the prerogatives of state policy. In his view, the improvement of the Icelanders' health and their ultimate success as colonists were inextricably linked to their adoption of new modes of behaviour and integration with Anglo-Canadian settlers.

Lynch's assessment of the situation illustrates Michel Foucault's insights on the importance of public health and medicine as instruments of governmental power.[17] The literature on public health in colonial contexts that has followed from Foucault's work has demonstrated how medicine functioned not simply as a means of relieving human suffering, but also as a key instrument of governance. Public health was part of the matrix of governing power that rendered subject populations knowable in the statistical languages of state bureaucratic administration.[18] As Nayan Shah notes in connection with nineteenth-century San Francisco, public health was one of the most powerful mechanisms used by the civic government to regulate the property and conduct of the city's immigrant population.[19] During the late nineteenth century, migrants were subject to coercive public health measures such as quarantine, forced hospital confinement, and destruction of personal property to a far greater degree than more established sections of society.[20] In the Canadian context, Mary-Ellen Kelm and Maureen Lux have demonstrated that Aboriginal people were subject to even more intense and sustained regimes of public health and sanitation that reinforced ideas about their inferiority and served as a powerful justification for the policy of assimilation.[21] Placing migrant and Indigenous experiences with colonial medicine in the same frame enables us to analyze their mutual constitution as colonial subjects through what Nicholas Thomas calls the project of *sanitizing-colonizing*, in which there was "a constant slippage ... between interests in reducing mortality and other agendas; political, moral, and cultural impositions were justified by their association and conflation with the programme of sanitation."[22]

In the case of New Iceland's smallpox epidemic, the other agenda at work was the creation of a new system of racially segregated reserves in which the land available for whites was distinguished from Indian reserves that were established through the treaty process. Australian historian of medicine Alison Bashford notes that both race and public health were segregative discourses: "Spatial segregation on public health grounds often dovetailed with already existing spatial management of people through racial rationales: indigenous people in various systems of reserves and mission stations."[23] At New Iceland, the spatial management of people had, prior to the epidemic, been implemented only partially and unevenly. It was the disruption created by the emergency that allowed the new order to be translated into a more concrete form. During the entire period of the smallpox epidemic, two teams of surveyors travelled throughout the reserve, marking out the sections, quarter sections, and townsites with iron stakes. A third surveying and construction crew worked on a colonization road connecting the three Icelandic townsites of Gimli, Sandy Bar, and Lundi to the road network in Manitoba.[24]

During the 1870s, three key terms were used for communities that surveyors traversed: settlement, reserve, and colony. They were often employed interchangeably, but each had specific meanings that illuminate some of the transformations taking place in the Canadian Northwest during this period. "Settlement" described both a particular place and a process: the taking possession of a space that was often constructed as empty or inadequately used. It is therefore associated, quite correctly, with the ideas and practices of acquisitive European settler colonialism.[25] Yet in the Northwest of the mid- to late nineteenth century, "settlement" also applied to Indigenous communities that had adopted some modes of living that were traditionally associated with Europeans, such as permanent houses and cultivating plots of land. Examples include the Swampy Cree and Ojibwe villages that developed near Christian missions and HBC posts around Lake Winnipeg. Many of these, such as Norway House and Fort Alexander, later became Indian reserves.[26]

The word "reserve" is, of course, most commonly associated with Indigenous people, particularly with their dispossession and marginalization within their own homelands. Extinguishing Aboriginal title and creating Indian reserves through the treaty process were integral parts of the nascent Canadian state's efforts to assert control over its newly acquired lands in the early 1870s. However, as Chapter 2 explained, "reserve" could also mean the land grants made to a wide variety of corporate entities and ethnocultural collectivities. In this case, the term essentially denoted the legal relationship of these groups to the land distribution policies of the state. As a means of encouraging immigration to Manitoba and the North-West Territories, reserves were set aside for the exclusive use of particular ethnocultural or religious communities after the Aboriginal title had been "extinguished" through the treaty process.

These settlement reserves were sometimes called colonies, a word that emphasized their status as collective arrangements based on shared ethnic, religious, or ideological characteristics.[27] In the case of subordinate ethnocultural groups, "colony" could also indicate – in a more precise way than "settlement" or "reserve" – their dual status as the local agents of empire and the subjects of its civilizing mission.[28] Naturally, these groups had their own names for their communities and often rechristened local physical features to underline their possession of the land. Hence, the Icelandic colonists renamed the White Mud River Íslendingafljót (Icelander's River). They knew the various districts of New Iceland as *byggðir* (settlements). Immigrant Friðrik Sveinsson also applied this word to the Indigenous settlement that occupied the same territory as the Icelanders' Fljótsbyggð (River Settlement).[29]

According to James Settee, an Indigenous village at Sandy Bar was established in the autumn of 1871. He reported to the Church Missionary Society that "some of the Indians who are still wandering about had agreed amongst themselves ... that they wanted to take the example of the Whites and follow a civilized life." Settee stated that many had been born in the region and considered it their home. They chose the site for permanent settlement because its abundant fisheries and game offered many advantages for "new settlers."[30] When Settee visited the village in 1875, he found twenty-four families and a few widows residing there. He expected that the community would soon be a large one, and he reported that a schoolhouse was under construction and that the people had asked for a teacher.[31]

Although the records are fragmentary, it is clear that Indigenous settlement at Sandy Bar and the White Mud River reflected the general pattern of many pre-treaty communities around Lake Winnipeg, in that there was no sharp distinction between Indians and "half-breeds."[32] They were not racially, ethnically, or religiously homogeneous; they were Cree and Ojibwe speakers, some of whom were of partial European ancestry. They were mostly Christian converts, but adherents of traditional Indigenous beliefs were also present. They were linked to one another, and to other communities through the region, especially St. Peter's and Netley Creek to the south, by ties of kinship and by involvement in the fur trade economy. Some members of the community, such as John Ramsay, had been born on the nearby islands in Lake Winnipeg.[33] Others, such as Elizabeth Fiddler, had come from Norway House prior to the commencement of Icelandic colonization. According to a claim for compensation that she initiated in 1877, Fiddler and her husband were invited to settle with the "White Mud River band" by the "Old Chief" in the fall of 1875. They built a house and "had improvements done – 5 acres which I had grubbed and cleared with hard labour." Fiddler claimed that Icelanders had occupied her property while she was visiting the St. Peter's Indian Reserve in the summer of 1876.[34]

The Fiddlers were part of a group migration of Cree people from Norway House to the White Mud River, which began before the land was designated as an Icelandic reserve. In April 1875, Reverend John H. Ruttan, head of the Rossville Methodist mission at Norway House, informed Lieutenant Governor Alexander Morris that "thirty families or more will leave Norway House to settle at Grassy Narrows or perhaps better known as White Mud River, for the purpose of beginning farming."[35] He characterized these prospective agricultural settlers as "industrious able bodied men nearly all middle aged with small families."[36] His fellow Methodist missionary Egerton Ryerson Young met some of these Norway House people when he spent just over a week at White Mud River in December 1875. He recorded that the settlement contained "about a dozen little houses, in addition to a large number of wigwams."[37] During his stay, Young organized "a class or society of thirty-five members, ten of whom for the first time now decided for Christ, and resolved henceforth to be His loyal followers."[38]

This migration from Norway House was first contemplated in 1874 as a result of widespread unemployment caused by changes to the HBC transportation system: the company had begun to use lake steamships, which meant that many men who freighted goods on York boats or who worked in other seasonal employment related to freighting or provisioning quickly found themselves out of work and in difficult circumstances. In June 1874, the "Christian Indians of Rossville and Nelson River" petitioned Alexander Morris, asking whether they had the "same privilege as any other of her Majesty's subjects" to move to "lands wherein we may find good farming country, to form a settlement, in order to help our children from suffering hunger."[39] By February 1875, this general plan had evolved into a specific request for land at Grassy Narrows.[40] Initially, both Morris and Indian Affairs officials looked favourably upon this proposal, but it was opposed by James Settee, who told Morris that a settlement at Grassy Narrows might expose the Christian converts to unspecified "temptations which they as Indians could never resist."[41] Settee instead suggested Fisher River, which lay about twenty miles north of Grassy Narrows, as an alternative site. When the prospect of an Icelandic reserve materialized during the summer of 1875, Morris adopted Settee's suggestion. While he was negotiating Treaty 5 at Norway House in 1875, he told the prospective settlers that the land at Grassy Narrows had already been given to the Icelanders, but he "offered to allot them a reserve at Fisher River ... and this they accepted."[42] The Icelandic Deputation received assurances from Morris that any Indians who already lived in the chosen reserve would be "located elsewhere" as soon as the Icelanders began to arrive.[43] This promised removal did not occur, and thus the Icelanders had to learn to live with their new Indigenous neighbours, both inside and outside their reserve.

Relations with those new neighbours got off to an inauspicious start. In October 1875, the flatboats carrying the first group of colonists down the Red River became entangled with fishing nets belonging to people from the St. Peter's Indian Reserve. The nets were broken and destroyed, much to the consternation of their owners, who stood along the riverbank and glared angrily as the peculiar flotilla passed by. One colonist remembered an old woman who was particularly angry at the loss of her nets: "She waved her hands in the direction of the Icelanders, and spewed out an astonishingly awful tirade. She of course could not make herself understood, but it was clear to our countrymen that she was not giving her blessing, nor bidding them welcome."[44]

Most of the Indigenous people who lived along the southwest shore of Lake Winnipeg in 1875 were related of those St. Peter's residents. They resisted the Icelandic encroachment, persevering despite aggressive behaviour by the Icelanders, including the occupation of their log cabins. But when their numbers were decimated by smallpox and most of their homes were destroyed by public health officials, their ability to resist was greatly diminished.[45] The Sandy Bar and Big Island bands,[46] as the Canadian government referred to them, attempted to assert their claims to land in the reserve at negotiations with treaty commissioners during the summer of 1876. The land in question was technically included in Treaty 2 (1871), but neither band had participated in its negotiation. Ka-tuk-e-pin-ais (whose English name was Hardisty), chief of the Big Island band, wrote to the minister of the interior, insisting that his band be included in a treaty. Plans were duly made for a meeting at Dog Head in late July 1876 to bring his and several bands that lived around the narrows of Lake Winnipeg under the provisions of Treaty 5 (1875).[47]

The ensuing negotiations were a profound disappointment for the Sandy Bar and Big Island bands. Through a combination of open threats and ultimatums, the treaty commissioners forced a uniform template of Indian administration onto several resistant groups that held dissimilar ideas about their formal relationship with the Crown. First, the commissioners demanded that the five bands – Big Island, Blood Vein, Jack Fish, Dog Head, and Sandy Bar – elect a single chief and four councillors. The bands protested, saying that they were distinct from each other and did not wish to unite. Ka-tuk-e-pin-ais was especially vocal in his opposition to the plan; he foretold that his band would be split into factions if he signed under the conditions outlined by the commissioners. Commissioners Thomas Howard and J. Lestock Reid told him either to sign or go home with nothing. Ultimately, he acceded to their demands and signed, with the result that 40 percent of his band renounced both his leadership and the treaty.[48] Part of the reason for the split was Ka-tuk-e-pin-ais's failure to secure Big Island as a reserve; the band was directed to remove to the Bad Throat River on the east side of the lake, which some members apparently did.[49] The treaty was even more of a disappointment for the Sandy Bar band. The commissioners denied that the band was distinct, arguing that it should properly be considered part of the St. Peter's band because its members had previously received annuities under Treaty 1 at St. Peter's.[50] The Sandy Bar band attempted to have the White Mud River set aside as a reserve, but the commissioners firmly rejected that request. In the end, only twenty-seven of the approximately sixty Indigenous people living at White Mud River received annuities under Treaty 5 at Dog Head.[51] The Big Island and Sandy Bar bands were the only bands at the Treaty 5 adhesion meeting to be denied their chosen reserve sites; all the small reserve locales suggested by the other bands were accepted. Clearly, the reason for this was that the land had been granted to the Icelanders. However, in defiance of the treaty settlement, even among those who signed, many members of the Sandy Bar and Big Island bands returned to their homes for the remainder of the summer of 1876. By this time, the Icelanders were beginning to move north from Gimli to claim homesteads at White Mud River, Sandy Bar, and on Big Island. In August 1876, John Taylor reported that the Indians living in the reserve had refused to leave the area and predicted that their continued presence would be a source of problems.[52]

The Icelanders' northward migration resulted in a dispute between the two groups that almost became violent. The only record of this encounter is Friðrik Sveinsson's 1919 reminiscence "Fyrsta viðkynning við Rauðskinna" (First acquaintance with the redskins). Sveinsson, who was ten at the time, accompanied the three families who were the first Icelanders to settle at White Mud River in the summer of 1876. According to his account, there were a few *fjölskyldur villimanna* (families of savages) living in tents by the river when they arrived. Friðrik's foster father, Ólafur Ólafsson from Espihóll, became embroiled in a dispute with John Ramsay. When Ramsay attempted to stop Ólafur from building on a piece of land that he claimed, the Icelander threatened him with an axe. Ramsay retreated but returned a few days later, supported by several armed men and a translator. He told the Icelanders that they were building illegally because their chosen site, on the north side of the river, was not part of their reserve. Ólafur agreed to consult with the authorities, which satisfied Ramsay. After Ólafur's right to build had been confirmed by a dominion Indian agent, he and Ramsay worked out an agreement whereby Ramsay could continue to cultivate a garden and camp on Ólafur's homestead.[53] Once smallpox broke out, friendly exchanges between the two groups appear to have ended. Ramsay later reported to Dr. James Spencer Lynch that the Icelanders had refused to offer assistance to his people when they became ill and even demanded payment for helping to bury the dead.[54] In forwarding this report to Ottawa, Acting Indian Commissioner J.A.N. Provencher stated that he had previously received similar reports of the Icelanders' behaviour.[55]

It was in this fractious contact zone in the northern part of the Icelandic reserve that the smallpox epidemic began. It appears to have been part of the world-wide outbreak of 1876, which was reported in major ports such as Liverpool, Halifax, Quebec City, Montreal, and San Francisco.[56] All the Icelanders who arrived in the colony during the late summer of 1876 had recently passed through several of the Atlantic ports where the disease was circulating, and at least one became infected. On 22 September 1876, John Taylor, who was responsible for administering the reserve, reported to the Department of Agriculture that a small group of Icelanders had arrived at Winnipeg twelve days earlier. Among them was a boy, "just recovering from the small-pox," who had been left behind in hospital at Quebec City by an earlier contingent of settlers. Taylor was concerned: "As some danger may exist of this loathsome disease breaking out among the Icelanders, I would desire to be prepared against such an emergency. I would therefore request that a small supply of the best vaccine matter be speedily obtained, so that all the children may be at once vaccinated before winter."[57] The government does not appear to have forwarded the requested vaccine. In the meantime, the boy accompanied the group to the reserve and rejoined his family, possibly igniting the outbreak.

According to the journal of immigrant Þorgrímur Jónsson, smallpox was carried to the colony in clothing purchased in Quebec City by a man named Jón Jónsson.[58] Þorgrímur, Jón, and their families were part of a small group that sailed north from Gimli to claim land along the White Mud River in early September 1876. Too weak to help with the rowing, Jón developed a fever shortly after their arrival. It is likely that he was among the group that occupied Elizabeth Fiddler's house.[59] In the cramped quarters of the 23' x 14' cabin, the disease soon spread to other members of the group, including Þorgrímur's family. On 5 October, his two-year-old son became its first confirmed Icelandic fatality.[60] Fiddler's house became known among the Icelanders as Bóla (Pox) because of its association with the beginning of the epidemic.[61]

Although they believed that the sickness was related to their recent migration experience, there was confusion and disagreement over what disease it was. John Taylor stated that the "Icelandic doctors" – referring to several individuals who possessed various kinds of formal and informal medical training – were convinced that it was not smallpox. Taylor reassured his superiors in Ottawa that there was no need for alarm and again proposed vaccinating the settlers as a precautionary measure.[62] He did manage to procure some vaccine, but it proved ineffective and the disease spread through the colony unchecked. When three Icelanders and seven Indigenous people died at White Mud River in early November, Sigtryggur Jónasson, who by this time was the assistant Icelandic agent, requested that Taylor immediately send for medical help: "I think it is necessary to have a skilled physician from Manitoba to come down here to examine some of the patients, provide medicine and prescribe the proper treatment of the disease, of which the Icelanders, if it be the small-pox, are totally ignorant, that disease not being prevalent in Iceland."[63]

In 1876, neither the Icelanders nor their Cree and Ojibwe neighbours had much first-hand knowledge of the physical effects of the smallpox virus. However, the devastating results of past epidemics were preserved in their oral and written historical traditions. When recording the epidemic in their respective journals, Þorgrímur Jónsson and James Settee both referred to previous epidemics that had afflicted their people.[64] Over the long term, these two groups had remarkably similar histories with the disease. Both had been affected by disastrous smallpox epidemics in the eighteenth century. In 1707–09, the disease killed 26 percent of Iceland's population.[65] Iceland was affected by the global epidemic of the early 1780s, which also devastated a village of Cree, Assiniboine, and Ojibwe at the mouth of the Red River around 1780.[66] The impact of smallpox was mitigated after 1800, with the introduction of vaccination as a preventative measure. In the late 1830s, HBC vaccination campaigns in northwest North America and by the Danish colonial authorities in Iceland helped stop another epidemic in its tracks.[67] But by 1876, neither the Icelanders nor the Indigenous people in the Icelandic reserve had been subject to a comprehensive vaccination campaign, and therefore the generations born since 1840 were susceptible to smallpox. In his 1877 report on the epidemic, Sigtryggur Jónasson blamed the authorities in Iceland for becoming lax in their duty to vaccinate every person in the country. He asserted that the settlers who had been properly inoculated in the previous five to seven years did not contract the disease.[68]

By the time John Taylor wrote to Dr. David Young at Lower Fort Garry to ask for medical help, rumours of smallpox among the Icelanders and Indians at Sandy Bar had been circulating in the south for some time. News had been carried to St. Peter's by friends of the Sandy Bar band and relayed from there to Winnipeg. Local government officials began to take these rumours seriously only after 15 November 1876, when the *Daily Free Press* published a letter from one of the surveyors who was working at Sandy Bar. In light of his report, the editor asserted, "there can be no doubt that it is the small-pox that is raging, and that too of a most virulent type."[69] Acting Indian Superintendent J.A.N. Provencher sent Dr. James Spencer Lynch to New Iceland to assist Dr. Young and to treat the Indians of the district. On 22 November, Young and Lynch reported from Gimli that "the disease here is smallpox of a mild variety varioloid but very fatal owing to unfavourable circumstances[,] bad food[, and] want of ventilation. About twenty persons had died in this immediate neighbourhood within the past ten days; it is reported that only two Indians are left living at Sandy Bar out of twenty."[70] With this official pronouncement, the federal government began to formulate its response, but it was too late; the disease had already spread throughout the Icelandic colony and its immediate environs. By the time it ran its course, it had killed 103 of the approximately 1,200 settlers in the reserve. According to a list compiled by Sigtyggur Jónasson, the vast majority were children: only 25 were older than twelve.[71] The level of mortality among the Indigenous population is somewhat uncertain. The *Free Press* reporter who attended the Treaty 5 negotiations in July 1876 wrote that the Big Island band consisted of a hundred people and the Sandy Bar band of forty. In January 1877, Lieutenant Governor Morris stated that the number of ascertained Indian deaths was fifty-two but that information received from Dr. Lynch had led him to believe that it could be as high as two hundred.[72] A rudimentary analysis of treaty annuity records for before and after the epidemic suggests that the lower estimate was probably more accurate.[73]

The disease was identified as a problem of public health and governance only when officially pronounced upon by two white physicians working as agents of the state. However, at least one person had correctly identified it two months earlier. On 25 September, Sarah Settee, the Cree English wife of James Settee, told members of the Sandy Bar band that the Icelanders had contracted smallpox and that they themselves should leave Sandy Bar if they valued their lives. This advice was apparently ignored by all except one man who fled with his family, possibly spreading the virus to the other side of Lake Winnipeg. James Settee also disregarded his wife's claims, even though he admitted that she had first-hand knowledge of the disease.[74] Sarah's medical knowledge was discounted because of her race, gender, and lack of professional credentials. The same can be said for the Icelandic immigrant Rebekka Guðmundsdóttir, who had been trained as a nurse and midwife in northern Iceland. Rebekka's role in distributing helpful medicines to smallpox victims was noted in community histories, but her name does not appear on the list of Icelanders employed by the Keewatin Board of Health or in the official documentation.[75]

Epidemics are not merely the naturally occurring result of discrete biological processes – they are also events produced by public health authorities as they assess the situation and take particular courses of action. As an epidemic is pronounced upon and dealt with, new forms of knowledge about a population are generated, and new modes of governance are created.[76] The response to the 1876 smallpox epidemic was, quite literally, the creation of a new government that served as both a board of health and a territorial authority for Keewatin, the region north and east of Manitoba, which included New Iceland. This territory was created in October 1876, largely at the behest of Lieutenant Governor Alexander Morris, to respond to the planned transfer of the government of the North-West Territories from Winnipeg to a point farther west. Morris argued that because transport and communication networks were so limited to the north and east of Manitoba, governing the area would be utterly impossible. The Keewatin Act stipulated that the region was to be administered by a council of five to ten men, headed by the lieutenant governor of Manitoba. The dominion government did not appoint this council until the smallpox emergency forced its hand.[77] Morris recommended a council of six senior civil servants from various departments and agencies of the federal and Manitoba governments. The constant slippage between the council's role as a territorial government and as an instrument of public health enforcement was manifested in the official documents, whose references to it alternated between the "Council of Keewatin" and the "Keewatin Board of Health."[78]

The board of health directed a massive mobilization of state resources to stem the spread of smallpox. In the first instance, this focused on treating the disease at the Icelandic reserve and adjacent locations. Dr. William Augustus Baldwin was sent to assist Young and Lynch in this task. Indigenous guides and assistants, including John Ramsay, transported the doctors and relief supplies through the district, buried the dead, and burned infected property. The doctors centralized the treatment of the sick at a hospital at Gimli and employed several young Icelanders as nurses, orderlies, and translators. Toward the end of the epidemic, a former HBC physician, Dr. Henry Beddome, oversaw the disinfection of the Icelanders' property.

The second part of the response was the attempt to contain the disease geographically. Doctors were sent out to vaccinate the residents of the nearby Indigenous communities of St. Peter's, Brokenhead, Fort Alexander, and Fairford. New Iceland was put under quarantine and a cordon sanitaire was established at Netley Creek, about sixteen miles from the northern border of Manitoba at Boundary Creek. This quarantine line was enforced by a thirteen-member military garrison, which was part of a larger quarantine station that also included a hospital. The health officers at the Netley Creek station regulated the movement of people and goods from north to south.[79] Before being allowed to pass, individuals were forced to remain at the quarantine station for a certain time and to discard their clothes and other possessions, which were often destroyed. Those who were deemed infected were confined to hospital. This quarantine remained in effect until late July 1877.[80] The final goal of the board of health's activities was to protect the northern fur trade to avert the institution of an American blockade. The board sent health officers to Dog Head, Beren's River, and Norway House to inspect and tag furs bound for the south.[81]

This summary accurately describes the board's activities during the epidemic, but it does not convey the often fractious and contested process by which the measures were adopted and implemented. The official response was devised on an ad hoc basis through often acrimonious negotiations between Morris and the cabinet in distant Ottawa, which were frequently punctuated by fundamental disagreements over jurisdiction and practice, as well as bickering over money.[82] Yet the board managed to carry out its policies in a way that not only contained the epidemic but also furthered the Canadian state's goal of segregating Indigenous and European space. Because the number of government officials on the ground remained limited, implementation of the board's directives depended on the compliance of local people, secured both through coercion and the self-regulation of individuals and groups who acted in their perceived best interests.

Following from the work of Foucault, historians and sociologists of medicine have traced the process, beginning in the eighteenth century, by which brute force public health measures such as the cordon sanitaire were increasingly abandoned in favour of regimes of hygiene.[83] A central aspect of this new public health was fostering internalized self-discipline, particularly the desire for good health among a subject population.[84] Alison Bashford argues that in colonial contexts, the practice of public health encompassed both the exercise of coercive, sovereign power and new disciplinary modes of governance.[85] In settler societies such as Australia, New Zealand, and Canada, migrants and Indigenous people continued to be subjected to rigidly enforced regimes of quarantine. By quarantine, Bashford means not only a specific public health measure, but also a wider network of cultural practices involving isolation, containment, and the policing of spaces. In the Lake Winnipeg region, the public health practices of quarantine and sanitation operated hand in hand with the spatial practices of treaty, survey, and colonization reserves as apparatuses of governmental power.[86] The quarantine and sanitation measures used by the Keewatin Board of Health during the smallpox epidemic belong within Bashford's model. The dynamic interaction between the state's coercive force and disciplinary modes of governance allowed the new colonial organization of space to take hold around Lake Winnipeg.

The tension between coercion and self-discipline was evident in the debate over the use of a cordon sanitaire to prevent travel between Manitoba and the "infected district" of Lake Winnipeg. Lieutenant Governor Morris and Manitoba premier R.A. Davis insisted that a rigid quarantine, enforced

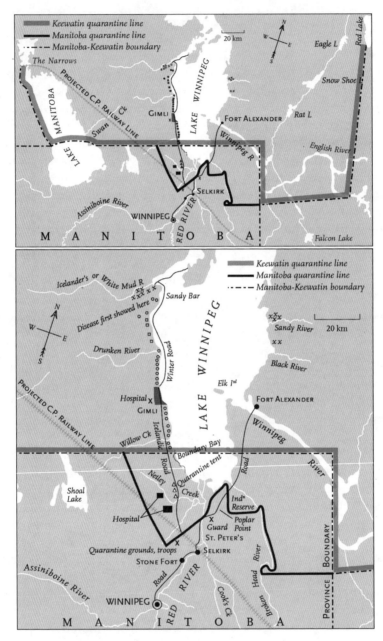

Quarantine map of Manitoba and Keewatin, 1877. The circles and squares indicate the location of Icelandic homesteads. The "x"s show places where smallpox fatalities occurred. *Adapted from a hand-drawn original in Library and Archives Canada, RG 15, D II 1, reel T-13868, vol. 576, file 178767.*

by the military, was essential to prevent the spread of the disease throughout the Northwest and the death of thousands of Indians. Dominion government officials, by contrast, believed that the quarantine was unnecessary. Prime Minister Alexander Mackenzie asserted that responsibility for the maintenance of health rested with the individual. In an encrypted telegram to Morris, Mackenzie stated bluntly, "People themselves must avoid contagion decline expenditure for Quarantine."[87]

Disagreement over the use of a quarantine was also voiced in public discussion. The editor of the *Daily Free Press* strongly favoured it:

> The Dominion has a grave responsibility. Let them keep watch and guard over their colonists in Keewatin. Let the Indians be confined to their reserves and vaccinated. Let the public give the authorities their moral support. What has already been accomplished at Gimli proves that the disease can, humanely speaking, be controlled. Let us all bear in mind that "an ounce of prevention is worth a pound of cure."[88]

On the other side, the *Manitoba Herald* opined that "the quarantine line is distinctly announced as being made of red tape."[89] A letter to the editor proclaimed, "Small Pox!! Bah! All we have to do is keep ourselves clean, live well, observing the laws by which God governs the world and allow science (medical men) to do the rest and none of us will die from that loathsome disease."[90] After the crisis ended, a letter to the *Free Press* complained that the destruction of clothes and property at the quarantine station had been useless. The editor saw fit to rebut this claim and congratulated the people of Manitoba for adopting and enforcing the quarantine regulations.[91]

The editor was correct in recognizing that the quarantine was successful only because local people chose to apply it. The area that it covered was simply too large for effective policing by the few soldiers and health officers that the board of health employed. Prominent among those whom Morris recognized for helping to stop the spread of the disease through strict adherence to the rules were the Ojibwe communities at St. Peter's, Fort Alexander, and Brokenhead.[92] In 1869–70, these people had been spared from an epidemic that killed more than 2,600 Blood, Peigan, Blackfoot, Cree, and Assiniboines on the Plains.[93] They therefore perceived the danger posed by smallpox, cut off their communication with people who had been to New Iceland, and voluntarily confined themselves to their reserves. Keeping the Lake Winnipeg Indians on their reserves was a policy goal of the dominion government that the emergency itself enabled. Although it protected them from smallpox, it nonetheless had a negative impact on their health because it prevented them from venturing farther out when their local resources failed, as happened with the fishery in the fall of 1876. The chief and councillors of the Fort Alexander reserve wrote to Morris, stating that they required provisions from the government if they were to survive the winter and that the local Indian agents and Superintendent J.A.N. Provencher had turned a deaf ear to them.[94] They also noted that Dr. Willoughby Clark, who was sent to vaccinate them, was doing nothing because he had run out of vaccine matter.[95] Clark confirmed that the band's poor health was caused by deprivation, not smallpox: "I found a great deal of sickness at this place caused principally by want of proper food and clothing – scrofula and pulmonary complaints predominantly." He recommended that assistance to the band be increased, but it is unclear if this occurred.[96]

The Icelanders also conformed to the quarantine, though the longer the regime continued, the more their resentment grew. They increasingly saw the quarantine as a key source of their continued poverty and ill health. It restricted the flow of supplies into the colony and therefore contributed to hunger and malnourishment. It also strained available resources by preventing the able-bodied from leaving the reserve to find work in Manitoba. To help alleviate this situation, Gimli storekeeper Friðjón Friðriksson went to Winnipeg to obtain supplies. During the journey, he had an encounter with two Indigenous women from St. Peter's that probably did little to improve their opinion of the Icelanders:

> There was no one [at Netley Creek] except two old Indian women in their boat. When they realized that [Friðjón] was an Icelander coming from the colony, they became terrified for fear of the disease. They moved with their boat out in the middle of the creek, and flatly refused to ferry Friðjón over. He called out to them in a very stern manner and said that if they did not immediately ferry him over the creek then all the colonists would return in war-like mood, and that in that case the Indians would be killed both by weapons and the disease. He ordered them in the name of their great mother, the Queen, to ferry him over without delay. This frightened them, and they rowed him not only over to the other side of the creek, but also a short distance up the river.[97]

At the end of the epidemic in April 1877, Dr. Henry Beddome reported that the colonists were suffering from scurvy and diarrhea.[98] In early July,

John Taylor wrote to Ottawa, complaining that the quarantine was maintained even though no fresh cases of smallpox had appeared for five months and the colony had been thoroughly disinfected. On 1 August, Minister of Agriculture C.A.P. Pelletier wrote to Morris, saying that the quarantine should be removed at once as it was "extremely cruel and unnecessary."[99] The military garrison was finally recalled on 21 July, but the colonists were not informed of this development. According to Taylor, they discovered it by chance when a hundred young Icelanders, both male and female, set out to force their way through the quarantine barriers.[100] In a later report, Taylor made a scathing attack on the administration of the Keewatin Board of Health: "The oppressive quarantine, so unnecessarily prolonged, has done more serious injury to the colony than can be repaired easily ... No quarantine procedures of a like character would have been submitted to for half the time by Canadians."[101]

The quarantine was lifted only when officials were certain that New Iceland and its residents had been completely sanitized. This was a protracted process that began with the arrival of the doctors in November 1876 and did not conclude until the following July. Dr. Lynch wrote a series of letters and reports that provided the board of health and the federal cabinet with information about the Icelanders' racial characteristics and modes of living, which he linked to disease. Lynch believed that centuries of inbreeding had made them racially degenerate but thought that they were ultimately redeemable through intermarriage with more vigorous races.[102] He claimed that their degeneracy was manifested in their indifference to material advancement and their habit of living in overcrowded, dirty, and poorly ventilated houses. Many of Lynch's official statements were echoed in a private letter from Dr. William Augustus Baldwin to his sister in Toronto. Baldwin said that the Icelanders were in poor health because they lived "like pigs." The letter conveys his general revulsion at conditions in the colony and includes specific references to the unsanitary behaviour of his patients:

> In one house a woman asked me if I would have a cup of coffee. I said yes, as the day was cold, so while I was making up some medicine for a poor sick boy – What do you think I saw the woman do – She no doubt thought that the cup was not clean enough for me, so she licked the cup all around with hir [sic] tongue and then took a towel as balck [sic] as could be – without it being a bit of black coth [sic] and dryed with it, and then gave it to me to drink. A nice sight to see for a man who wanted a drink to warm him.[103]

When expressing sympathy for the suffering of the Icelanders, Baldwin cast himself in the role of the man of science and reason, attempting to bring order to a disordered set of people who were badly in need of reform.

The Icelanders both accommodated and resisted the colonizing/sanitizing mission of the Canadian doctors. At least nineteen of them worked as nurses, attendants, and translators in the Gimli hospital, and others assisted the medical officers on their travels through the reserve.[104] Dr. Lynch complained that many smallpox patients refused to relocate to the hospital and that they complied only when attendants entered their homes and threatened to remove them by force.[105] While the Icelanders employed these strategies to meet both the disease emergency and the demands of the government, Sigtryggur Jónasson attempted to present federal officials with an alternative picture of their character. In words tailored to the government's hope of building an orderly settler population, he wrote that the Icelanders "have kept up a remarkably good spirit during this great calamity, which many who don't know their general disposition nor understand their language call indifference."[106] In sharp contrast to Lynch, Jónasson saw the Icelanders as hard working and deeply committed to progress. By the end of the epidemic, the leaders of the colony adopted some of the institutional mechanisms of public health as practised in Canada. One of the first actions of the colony's municipal council was to disinfect everything with soap and boiling water.[107] Each *byggð* (settlement) formed a board of health to co-ordinate these efforts.[108]

For the New Icelanders, disinfection did not involve the wholesale destruction of bodies and property. This was not the case at the Aboriginal communities of Sandy Bar, Sandy River, Black River, Bad Throat River, and Punk Island, where bodies, houses, and possessions were burnt. Sometimes, the survivors allowed this; at other times, they resisted fiercely. William Drever, one of the doctors' assistants, travelled to Bad Throat River on the east side of the lake to burn or bury the remains of several members of the Big Island band. He was permitted to bury the body of the chief, Kat-tuk-e-pin-ais, but was chased away when he attempted to burn two others.[109] John Ramsay, one of the few survivors of the Sandy Bar band, helped Dr. Baldwin and Magnús Stefánsson burn the Indian village of Sandy River on the east side of Lake Winnipeg.[110] However, Ramsay deeply resented the burning of his own village at Sandy Bar, conducted on the orders of Dr. Lynch.[111] With most of the band members dead, this act erased an important physical vestige of their presence in the Icelandic reserve. It cleared the way for the land to be settled according to the survey that had been completed near the end of 1876. Lynch apparently felt some remorse over this act and advised the government to compensate the surviving members of the band, although this does not appear to have been done. In June 1877, Ramsay travelled to Winnipeg to personally express his aggravation to Alexander Morris, but he received no guarantees. Morris suggested that he and the other Sandy Bar survivors should leave New Iceland and settle at Fisher River.[112]

In the summer of 1876, exactly how Ramsay's people and the Icelanders would resolve their joint claim to the southwest coast of Lake Winnipeg remained an open question. The Sandy Bar and Big Island bands repeatedly protested the appropriation of their land and refused to abandon their settlement even after their request to form an Indian reserve was denied. The smallpox epidemic resulted in their dispossession and in the appropriation of their land and resources by the Icelanders. This outcome was due not only to the devastation of smallpox, but also to the public health measures implemented by the Keewatin Board of Health. The quarantine boundaries, which the board enforced and local people observed, mirrored the boundaries of land distribution that the Canadian state wished to impose on the region. The crisis gave a new reality to the system of racially defined reserves and the separation of Indigenous and European settler populations. What had once been a dynamic zone of Icelandic-Indigenous contact became a far more homogeneous, though by no means exclusive, Icelandic space.

At the same time, the epidemic also dealt a serious blow to the Icelanders and their settlement. For many families that had hoped for a new beginning in North America, it was a terrible personal tragedy. Many settlers emerged from quarantine impoverished and disillusioned with the government's handling of the crisis. This disenchantment was an important factor in the out-migration that depopulated the colony during the early 1880s. Smallpox also accentuated the distance of the Icelanders, both literally and symbolically, from the wider settler community. In ways similar to those applied to Indigenous people in later decades, their poverty and sickness were interpreted as functions of their racial and cultural inferiority, rather than their specific material circumstances. The smallpox epidemic is an example of the linkages between discourses used to justify Indigenous dispossession and marginalization, and those that sought to bring migrant populations into line with the norms and values of the dominant settler society. It is a reminder of the need to consider European migrants and Indigenous people together as constituents of the related

St. Peter's resident Joseph Monkman (1810–99) was the son of a Cree mother and an English father. During the 1869–70 Red River resistance, he supported the Canadian party's opposition to Louis Riel's provisional government. He helped Canadian leader John Christian Schultz escape from Red River and travelled with him to Ottawa. In May 1870, Monkman testified before a Senate committee where he stressed the desire of the Indians to sign a treaty with Canada. *Archives of Manitoba, Personalities Collection, N30376.*

projects of governance and administration that helped create distinctions between various groups in the colonial population.

DESPITE ALL THE DIFFICULTIES that the arrival of the Icelanders had caused them, several Indigenous people went out of their way to help the colonists, both individually and as a group. John Ramsay is the Indigenous person most associated with assisting the Icelanders, but the contributions of his close friend Joseph Monkman of St. Peter's were perhaps even more significant. Monkman guided the Icelandic Deputation in the summer of 1875 and aided the physicians during the smallpox epidemic. In the fall of 1877, he again visited Gimli, where he spoke to eleven-year-old Gestur Oddleifsson, whose father had died of smallpox the previous winter. Gestur told Monkman that the coming winter would probably be difficult for him, his widowed mother, Una, and his ten-year-old sister Ingibjörg. Monkman invited Gestur to travel with him, Ramsay, and others from St. Peter's reserve north to their fall fishing grounds. In his absence, Gestur's mother and sister would stay in Monkman's house, where they would be provided room and board at no charge.[113] Gestur accepted this offer and spent the fall and early winter of 1877–78 gaining valuable knowledge about the land and the lake from two men who had been born and raised in the region. This experience undoubtedly helped Gestur become one of New Iceland's most successful settlers.

Monkman also helped the Icelanders to establish themselves as skilled fishers on the lake. During his fall trip of 1877, he stopped at Sandy Bar, where he told former Icelandic parliamentarian Björn Pétursson how to set nets in the lake. Björn wrote a letter on the subject for the colony's newspaper, *Framfari*, crediting Monkman as "a clever man and, of course, an extremely knowledgeable and experienced fisherman."[114] Monkman may have been among the "five half-breeds who live along the Red River" who reported to the Icelanders at Lundi that they had caught 2,300 whitefish in four days at Dauphin River.[115] Such accounts were undoubtedly important in encouraging the Icelanders to venture out from their reserve in search of the rich fishing grounds in the north basin of the lake. This was a crucial step, since it was the successful development of an export-oriented fishery that ultimately became the mainstay of New Iceland's economy by the turn of the century.

5
"Principal Projector of the Colony"
The Turbulent Career of John Taylor, Icelandic Agent

THE COLONIZATION OF THE Canadian Northwest after 1870 is not usually linked with the end of slavery in the West Indies during the 1830s. Although both occurred under the broad aegis of British imperial power and each entailed a profound shift in economic, social, and cultural relations built up over centuries, the two societies and their respective transformations seem to share few other characteristics. Whereas a system of plantation agriculture powered by enslaved African labour and tightly controlled by a small planter and mercantile elite predominated in the West Indies, the fur trade in northwest North America was directed by a tiny and geographically dispersed cadre of European traders working in partnership with effectively autonomous Indigenous nations.[1] And whereas the end of slavery challenged white minority rule, the waning of the fur trade signalled the advent of a white majority rule through mass migration and the marginalization of the Indigenous population. Nonetheless, these two places and events are linked through the life story of Barbados-born John Taylor, Canada's first Icelandic agent. An examination of his career makes it possible to connect some central processes in the Canadian colonization of the Northwest – migration, resettlement, and assimilation – with discourses around race, freedom, and citizenship that were integral to the emancipation era in the West Indies.

John Taylor was, in succession, a Texas settler, a convicted slave trader, Baptist missionary, and Canadian civil servant. In 1835, he moved to Texas along with a group of former slaves whom he had signed to indenture contracts. Once there, he sold the contracts to other white settlers in

John Taylor, Icelandic agent (1813–84), c. 1882. *Archives of Manitoba, New Iceland collection, N11297.*

exchange for cash. This transaction eventually resulted in Taylor's 1840 trial and conviction for violating the law for the abolition of the slave trade.[2] Although he was originally sentenced to fourteen years' transportation, Taylor was ultimately imprisoned in Barbados for just three years; his connections to the planter and mercantile elite helped to have his sentence commuted and later worked to secure his early release. He then ventured to England, where he petitioned the Colonial Office in an unsuccessful quest to clear his name. During the same period, he underwent a profound religious transformation that altered the course of his life. In the late 1840s, he moved to Canada West and joined a Baptist congregation in Kingston. By 1874, he was working as a missionary among the lumbermen in Ontario's Haliburton County, where he met some recently arrived

Icelandic immigrants. In the spring of 1875, he advocated on behalf of the destitute migrants to the Canadian government, and that summer he led the Icelandic Deputation to Manitoba to select a site for the Icelandic colony. In the autumn, he moved with the immigrants to New Iceland. From that point until his death in 1884, he was employed by the federal Department of Agriculture as the Icelandic agent responsible for the re-settlement of immigrant Icelanders in Manitoba and the North-West Territories.[3]

Taylor's story has never before been fully reconstructed. In the regional and national histories of several places where he lived, he made enough of an impact to receive at least passing mention. In Barbados, he is noted for being the subject of "a very important and remarkable trial."[4] In east Texas, stories about "Captain John Taylor" have been passed down in local lore about the illicit African slave trade.[5] In Manitoba, "Reverend John Taylor" is mentioned as the "missionary from Muskoka" who helped start a large migration of Icelanders to the region.[6] Icelandic Canadian historians have produced the most thorough treatments of Taylor's life, but his conviction for slave trading was previously either unknown or intentionally omitted.[7] The purpose of this chapter is to examine the full scope of Taylor's life to better understand his actions as Icelandic agent in New Iceland.

The fact that a man with such a common name was, over the course of the nineteenth century, able to leave behind a troubled past and reinvent himself in a new context is not particularly surprising.[8] What is significant about Taylor's career is the opportunity it provides for reinterpreting an idiosyncratic aspect of western Canadian history – the existence of an Icelandic immigrant reserve – as having been shaped by ideas, practices, and debates originating in unexpected places outside the formal boundaries of nation and ethnic community.[9] However, reconciling the John Taylor of Barbados with the John Taylor of New Iceland is not at first glance an easy task. The sources from these two locales paint dramatically different pictures of him. According to the testimony of the people he was convicted of selling into slavery, Taylor was a cruel and deceitful man who callously used them for his own personal gain.[10] According to the Icelanders, he was a flawed but fundamentally good man, whose deeply held religious views and humanitarianism impressed them.[11] How was this transition possible? What continuity, if any, was there between the old and new guises of John Taylor?

As he moved from master to missionary to agent, Taylor maintained a hierarchical understanding of race and culture in which he, along with other educated white British men, occupied the pinnacle position. Over time he incorporated a liberal faith in the potential of subordinate peoples to be remade in his own image as devout, loyal, and productive subjects that mirrored the paternalistic discourses of Baptist anti-slavery missionaries.[12] Taylor saw the Icelanders as struggling to escape centuries of poverty and backwardness, and he believed that his mission in New Iceland was to develop "a Canadian population" who spoke English, observed British customs, and were imbued with a commitment to the liberal ideals of material progress, market production, and self-government.[13] However, his inclusionary view of the Icelanders was contingent on both their whiteness and their obedience to his authority.[14] Unlike the Baptists of earlier in the century, Taylor does not appear to have believed that racial equality was possible. His exclusionary tactics with the Indigenous residents of New Iceland were symptomatic of the hardening of racial categories in the British Empire after mid-century. He had more faith in the Icelanders, but his ambivalent view of personal liberty exposed his roots as the product of a slave society. When his authority was challenged, he attempted to limit the Icelanders' individual freedom, prompting some of them to wonder whether they were to become bonded labourers in their new home.[15] Taylor's unusual career thus connects key themes in the histories of the West Indies and the Canadian Northwest.

John Taylor was born on 9 March 1813, the fourth of at least fifteen children of Richard Taylor, a deputy in the Commissariat Office, and Elizabeth Mehetabel Jones.[16] The office in which Taylor's father worked was responsible for the provisioning of the armed forces. His mother came from a prominent Barbados family that owned several plantations in the parish of St. John's. The Taylors lived at Enmore Cottage, a sixteen-acre property in St. Michael's parish on the outskirts of Bridgetown, the capital city. Slave registers from 1817 to 1833 show that Richard Taylor was slowly increasing the family's slave holdings. On the eve of emancipation in 1833, he owned twenty-eight slaves, most of whom were involved in domestic service and household provisioning.[17] In March 1836, as part of the imperial government's scheme for compensating former slave-owners for the loss of their human property, he was awarded £604.[18]

The Taylors were not among the upper echelon of the island's planter elite, but they were considered respectable members of white society. Abel Clinckett, editor of the conservative newspaper the *Barbadian*, described Richard Taylor as a family man of "unreproachable character" who had served the Crown "with exemplary fidelity and honour" for thirty years.[19] Taylor's work in the Commissariat Office, which involved supplying the navy's ships, entailed close business dealings with island merchants.[20] These connections helped John secure positions as a clerk with various merchant houses and in the Commissariat Office as a young man.[21] Apart from this, very little is known about John Taylor's early life in Barbados. According to his friend Sigtryggur Jónasson, Taylor was educated at the island's "Latin School" before attending university in Halifax, where he studied theology and briefly considered ordination in the Anglican priesthood.[22]

As Taylor grew to adulthood, the anti-slavery movement and Afro-Barbadian resistance were slowly eroding the slave society in which he had been born. The Act for the Abolition of the Slave Trade, under which he would later be convicted, was passed in 1807. In 1816, a month after his third birthday, a major slave rebellion convulsed the island and terrified the white population. By his tenth birthday, Barbadian whites had found a scapegoat for Afro-Barbadian resistance: the Methodist chapel of William Shrewsbury was torched by an angry mob in 1823.[23] However, by this time the anti-slavery forces in London had gained a decisive advantage, and the imperial government formally adopted a policy of amelioration. The end of slavery in 1834 came on the heels of Taylor's twenty-first birthday. Full emancipation for the formerly enslaved Barbadians had to wait until 1 August 1838, when the quasi-slavery apprenticeship system ended. On that historic day, the eight Afro-Barbadians who had left the island under John Taylor's leadership (one of his nine servants was white) remained enslaved in Texas.

Taylor made the fateful decision to move to Texas in 1835, "for the purpose of engaging there in mercantile as well as other pursuits."[24] According to his attorney, he had heard glowing accounts of Texas while doing business in the United States.[25] In the mid-1830s, Texas, then a province of Mexico, was attracting considerable numbers of American settlers. Many of them came from the southern states, bringing their slaves with them, even though chattel slavery had been abolished in Mexico in 1829.[26] Americans managed to perpetuate the slave system by manipulating Mexican laws concerning indentured servitude and debt peonage. They drew up indenture contracts for their ostensibly free servants to sign, the terms of which effectively reduced the servants to the condition of slavery. Contracts could span many years, and though they could be bought out, achieving this was typically far beyond the reach of most servants. Mexican authorities attempted to end this practice but to little effect; black indentured servants were treated as slaves – they were bought and sold, hired out, and bequeathed in wills.[27] Contemporary settler guides gave advice on how to "evade the general law of abolition" through indenture contracts.[28] Prior to leaving Barbados, Taylor and his partner Thomas Ames signed a number of their servants to indenture contracts. One of these, shoemaker Edward Whittaker, testified that Taylor had given him the money to buy out his apprenticeship in Barbados.[29] In return, Whittaker signed a four-year indenture to serve Taylor and Ames "in this and other places" for forty dollars a year.[30]

There is some indication that even if Taylor didn't set out from Barbados with the intention of selling his servants as slaves, he had not received government permission to take them to Texas and would have known that doing so was of questionable legality. In his April 1837 petition to the secretary of state for the colonies, Taylor asserted that his servants had received permission to travel from the Secretary's Office in Barbados "as the law directs."[31] However, he neglected to mention where they had received permission to travel to. One of his servants, William Gunsell, testified that Taylor instructed him not to mention where they were going, and if asked was to reply that their destination was the Leeward Islands.[32] Gunsell also testified that he and the other black people were hidden below deck during a stop in Grenada and at sea when they encountered a United States Navy ship.[33] The pattern of Taylor's 1835 journey precisely replicated that of other slave traders in the region. Fast, ocean-going cargo vessels arrived in Galveston Bay, Texas, where slaves were transferred to smaller vessels that carried them up through the river system to places where they could be sold.[34] Taylor's party landed at Bolivar Point, at the entrance to Galveston Bay, and camped there before travelling east along the coast to the Sabine Pass, a place at which slaves were often sold to buyers from nearby Louisiana.[35]

Taylor could hardly have picked a more turbulent time to relocate to Texas. He arrived during the revolutionary war between the Mexican government and American settlers, known as Texians, that ultimately resulted in the creation of the Republic of Texas in March 1836. The Texas Revolution had important consequences for the legal status of the black servants whom Taylor brought with him. On 2 December 1835, just days before their arrival, the Beaumont Committee of Safety wrote to the Texian leadership, expressing its concern that the presence of free blacks in Texas could potentially inflame the slave population and help ignite a revolt.[36] In response, the revolutionary council adopted an ordinance making it illegal "for any free negro or mulatto to come within the limits of Texas."[37] In February 1836, Taylor and his party were arrested by Samuel Rogers, collector of customs at Beaumont, which was near the Sabine Pass, and were detained for over a month.[38] In a sworn deposition, April Lashley, one of Taylor's servants, stated that Rogers told Taylor the Texian government "did not allow free colored men to stay in the place." As a result, Taylor asked Lashley and the others to sign on as his slaves, but they refused.[39] In the meantime, the Texian government had formally reintroduced slavery: "All persons of color who were slaves for life, previous to their emigration to Texas, and who are now held as bonded servants or otherwise, shall remain in the like state of servitude in which they would have been held in the country from which they came."[40] After his release from custody, Taylor transferred the indenture contracts of his nine servants to several Texians in return for cash. He asserted that he had done so at his servants' request, but they themselves either contradicted or qualified his claim. Edward Whittaker testified that he had asked Taylor to transfer his contract to a man named William Moore but only because Moore had given him fifty lashes and then threatened to "blow his brains out" if he refused to do so.[41]

Taylor's case first came to the attention of the British government in April 1837. After consulting with Sir Evan MacGregor, governor general of the Windward Islands, Taylor sent a petition to Lord Glenelg, secretary of state for the colonies, asking that the eight black and coloured persons be restored to liberty "to which [they] are justly entitled, as British subjects" and that the government reimburse him for his financial losses.[42] The Colonial Office referred the case to the foreign secretary, Lord Palmerston, who took a skeptical view of the truthfulness of Taylor's account.[43] Over a year passed without any action from London, and Taylor became increasingly anxious. In November 1838, he approached the prominent coloured Barbadian abolitionist Samuel Jackman Prescod to help him with his case.[44] In January 1839, he wrote to MacGregor that, because the Texas affair had become widely known on Barbados, he was "scandalized in the community & injured in the opinion of many of my friends."[45] By this time, the Crown was beginning to consider prosecuting Taylor for the crime of selling free British subjects into slavery. The attorney general of Barbados informed the Colonial Office that "doubt exists whether he has not in these transactions rendered himself liable to a prosecution for a breach of the Act of Parliament for the Abolition of the Slave Trade."[46] In October 1839, April Lashley arrived back in Bridgetown after a harrowing escape from Texas. According to his mother, April confronted Taylor, demanding, "Mass John, what did you sell me for?" Taylor answered, "Couldn't do better, April; I had the schooner expenses to pay."[47] On the strength of April's deposition, Taylor was arrested and committed to jail.[48] Early in 1840, the British government sent Captain Hamilton, one of the special magistrates appointed to adjudicate disputes between freed slaves and their former masters, to Texas to recover Taylor's ex-servants and gather evidence for the case against him.[49] Hamilton managed to recover only five of the eight missing people; the others, Samuel McIntosh, Thomasin Ann, and Taylor's white servant Henry Foderingham, were believed to be dead.[50]

The trial at the end of June 1840 was a sensational event that attracted considerable attention in Barbados and was noted in the anti-slavery press in England. The white population of Barbados evinced little enthusiasm for prosecuting Taylor. The editor of the *Barbadian,* a planter newspaper, opined that he was reluctant to report on the trial of the "unfortunate young man," owing both to the respectability of his parents and because the trial would be "eagerly seized upon by the Anti-Colonial faction in England who take advantage of any isolated case to fulminate their cruel and sweeping charges against West Indians who are not so fortunate to be of African descent."[51] Taylor's defence focused on the fact that he had voluntarily approached the government to secure the release of his ex-servants. His lawyer attempted to portray him as a respectable young man and even "a perfect martyr in the cause of liberty."[52] The white community of Barbados was virtually united in its support of Taylor. Even Samuel Jackman Prescod, a champion of the rights of the black and coloured population, defended him: "Although Mr. Taylor acted imprudently, was ill advised, and exposed himself to a good deal of suspicion ... it was impossible for him to have acted the part he did if he had believed his conduct to have been criminal – or had he been conscious of a guilty intention."[53]

Despite this broad-based support for Taylor, the jury had little choice but to convict him; the imperial government was watching, and both the documentary evidence and the testimony of the survivors left little doubt that Taylor had sold his servants into what was essentially slavery: they had received no wages from their new masters, some had been tortured and threatened with death, and all had been worked and kept in conditions that were consistent with bondage. Taylor was convicted and sentenced to transportation for a term of fourteen years. Shortly afterward, a petition for clemency was sent to the colonial secretary, bearing the signatures of several members of the Barbados Assembly, Anglican rectors and other clergymen, prominent planters, barristers, justices of the peace, and even the jury that convicted him.[54] As a result of this and other representations, the sentence was eventually commuted from transportation to New South Wales to three years' imprisonment in Barbados.[55] In 1841, Taylor was one of only three white prisoners in Bridgetown's common jail, whose total population was 172.[56] In March 1843, after he had served three years and three months in prison, he was released by Governor Sir Charles Grey.[57]

He left Barbados for England early in 1844, and while there he repeatedly lobbied the imperial government to "interfere on behalf" of the remaining Afro-Barbadians he had taken to Texas, "with the view of recovering them from their present miserable condition." Taylor readily acknowledged that his efforts were motivated in part by a self-interested desire to clear his name, but he stressed that even if that were not the case, his sense of duty and responsibility for his servants would have prompted him to advocate for them.[58] The Colonial Office and the Foreign Office brushed aside his petitions as unimportant and ultimately did nothing to help free the rest of his party.

Taylor had grown up and been educated in the Church of England, but his difficulties led him to rethink his relationship with God, first through reading Non-conformist teachings and finally, after emigration to Canada, conversion to the Baptist faith. Two documents that he wrote during the 1840s describe this evolution in his religious thinking. The first recounts an episode from his time in Texas: in "December in the year 1837, I, ... pondering on my misfortunes and perplexed with my business, thought I saw mentally a vision which showed me the way to Heaven and the abode of men in this world. It has given me great comfort and I therefore write it down to assist my memory in future days."[59] In Taylor's vision, there was a pool of water representing the earth, encased in a round tent. At the top of the tent was an opening through which glowed an exquisite light: "To this light men who loved God looked constantly whilst men who sought after wealth dived below ... to where the greatest wealth was and soon got so entangled with the weirs below that they could not regain the light of Heaven."[60] Taylor believed that through this vision, God had shown him that the search for wealth was not compatible with the search for personal salvation.

His stint in jail undoubtedly gave him ample opportunity for further religious reflection; in 1840, the prison chaplain petitioned for his release, noting his regular attendance at church services.[61] However, it wasn't until he sailed for England and had a near-death experience during a terrible storm at sea that Taylor made a commitment to spend the rest of his days as a servant of God. A statement of faith, signed in the Seymour Street chapel-of-ease, London, in June 1844, details his personal religious awakening. He was inspired to take this step after reading *The Rise and Progress of Religion in the Soul* (1745), a highly influential book by the English Non-conformist Philip Doddridge.[62] Taylor recounted his personal struggle to become "one of God's people" by overcoming the cycle of sin and repentance that had characterized his life. Due to his own moral weakness, he had steadily abandoned attempts to resist temptation, until "it pleased the all wise God to lay his afflicting hand upon me." However, Taylor did not simply believe that he had suffered the wrath of a vengeful God – he had also been given a chance to escape his old ways and be reborn, stronger and fortified by God's love:

> In the midst of all my troubles ... the Almighty kept me from falling into the utmost extremity of despair, although he would not remove his heavy hand from off me for several long years, during which I received very gradually small portions of that strength which I had formerly besought him to give me, until at length I found myself enabled by a power not mine own, to resist and to overcome those sins which I had been accustomed to fall almost as often as spoiled by their temptation.[63]

This document does not refer to specific sins or to the events that led Taylor to these conclusions. However, it provides a personal view into his moral universe and an understanding of his relationship with God. Neither it nor the account of his 1837 vision were meant for public consumption: they were private records that he kept with him, hidden in a secret compartment of his travelling writing desk, for the rest of his life. As a result of his 1844 commitment to become God's servant, Taylor's life moved in a new direction, one that would ultimately lead to his appointment as Icelandic agent in 1875.

Around 1847, Taylor and his younger brother William moved to Kingston, Canada West, and were later joined by their parents and three of their siblings. Comparatively little is known about Taylor's life after his arrival in Canada. He and his family initially settled near Kingston, in the vicinity of Ernestown in Lennox and Addington County. According to the 1851 federal census, John Taylor had a small farm and taught in a grammar school. By that time, he was married to Elizabeth Mary Haines, a member of a prominent Baptist family.[64] He had also formally adopted the Baptist faith. Sometime after 1850, the couple moved to Peterborough, where Taylor operated a store in partnership with his brother-in-law. Although they had no children of their own, after 1864 they raised Jane and Susanna, the two youngest daughters of Taylor's brother William.[65]

At about this time, Taylor renewed his commitment to place himself in God's service. For a period, he was a "colporteur" – a travelling Bible salesman – and was probably affiliated with the Upper Canada branch of the British and Foreign Bible Society.[66] Between 1870 and 1875, he devoted most of his time to missionary work for the Baptist Church. He relocated his family north from Peterborough to Dysart Township, part of a new settlement promoted by the Canadian Land and Emigration Company in Haliburton County.[67] His mission field was the region's lumber camps, and he aimed to win converts from among the rough-and-tumble "shantymen" who toiled in the forests. It was in this capacity that he first encountered some of the Icelandic immigrants who had arrived in Ontario in 1874, after learning of their plight from his niece Caroline.[68]

Taylor's original purpose in approaching the government on behalf of the Icelanders was not to found a colony in the Northwest, but rather to establish an "industrial farm" in the centre of the Ontario region where the provincial government had encouraged Icelandic settlement. In letters to the *Montreal Daily Witness* and to Governor General Lord Dufferin, Taylor asserted that the main barrier to the Icelanders becoming "independent and self-supporting" citizens was their ignorance of the language and culture of the host society. His remedy was to further isolate them in an agrarian institution, where they would be placed under the supervision of "some knowledgeable person" whose instruction would transform them from backward foreigners into prosperous Canadians. As he explained, "Employment and useful education could there be given to all who require it, and general information and assistance rendered in the selection of their lots and mode of procedure in clearing and cultivating them."[69] This plan got a cool reception in Ottawa, but government officials were nonetheless interested in promoting Icelandic immigration and settlement. The ministers of agriculture and the interior directed Taylor to form a delegation of Icelanders to search out a colony site in Manitoba or the North-West Territories.[70]

Thus, in July 1875, Taylor led what he called the Icelandic Deputation to Manitoba and selected the colony site on Lake Winnipeg. He received an eight-month appointment as Icelandic agent that ultimately stretched into nine years. Like many civil service appointees of this period, he secured his position largely because he had friends in government.[71] As a result of his new job, Taylor, then in his early sixties, was given broad responsibility for a colony that contained upward of 1,500 people at its peak. Although the land was reserved exclusively for Icelanders, an exception was made in the case of Taylor's own extended family. John and Elizabeth Taylor's household in the village of Gimli included their teenage nieces Caroline (Carrie), Jane, and Susanna (Susie). The girls' father, William Stewart Taylor, along with their stepmother and three half-siblings, settled at

Foresthome, a homestead south of Gimli. Later, William Taylor Hearn and John Hearn, two sons of Taylor's sister Jane Hearn, also settled at New Iceland.[72] In short, "Uncle John" was building not only a colony of Icelanders but also a colony of Taylors. Símon Símonarson perceived that distinctions were made between the majority of the settlers and the "better-class" of people – Taylor's family and the few Icelanders who could speak English. Símon alleged that those who were "on the most intimate terms with Taylor" received preferential treatment, particularly when it came to selecting land.[73] Whether this was true or not, Taylor clearly intended to place himself at the centre of life in the colony. Shortly after arrival, he hired the Icelanders to build him a two-storey house with double walls in the centre of Gimli, from which he conducted the business of his "agency."[74]

Although he was a political appointee, John Taylor's position was no sinecure. Officials in the Department of Agriculture probably expected him to work as hard as the inland agents who provided logistical and material support to new immigrants and reported to the government on the conditions in newly settled districts.[75] Taylor was instructed to "assist the Icelanders in their first settlement," primarily by distributing various forms of government aid.[76] However, in the context of the new and relatively isolated colony, that basic directive came to encompass an extensive list of duties. Taylor arranged for the purchase, transport, and distribution of food, seed, implements, livestock, and other necessities. Since most of this was funded by a government loan that had to be repaid, he was required to keep detailed accounts of what each family owed. When new immigrants arrived, he arranged for their transport from Winnipeg and ensured that their immediate needs were met after they reached New Iceland. In the absence of a Dominion Lands Office in the region, he was instructed to register the settlers' homesteads, and when the government agreed to construct a road to connect the reserve with Manitoba in 1876, Taylor was given the additional task of jointly overseeing the project and paying the workers. He also looked out for the health of the colonists and arranged for medical assistance during frequent disease outbreaks, including the disastrous smallpox epidemic. The position required Taylor to carry out a voluminous correspondence with government officials in both Ottawa and Winnipeg that was often frustratingly slow, due to poor communications. He delegated work to his assistant agent, Sigtryggur Jónasson, and relied heavily on his friend Friðjón Friðriksson as his interpreter, since he could not speak Icelandic. However, ultimate responsibility for the colony's welfare and material progress rested squarely on Taylor's shoulders.

That responsibility was a heavy one; during the first five years of its existence, New Iceland was almost perpetually in crisis. Malnutrition and near starvation in the first winter were followed by the devastating smallpox epidemic in the second that put the colony under quarantine for eight months.[77] Chronic wet weather and flooding over several summers ruined crops and dashed hopes of agricultural progress. A divisive religious controversy between two competing Lutheran pastors – which was as much about the colony's future as it was about articles of faith – caused a profound split among the colonists.[78] Throughout New Iceland's manifold crises, Taylor set priorities for the settlement – such as the formation of a militia company – that seem strangely out of touch with its reality. Even when the situation was at its blackest, he used his position as agent to work toward the goal of assimilating the Icelanders. He did this because he considered assimilation and material progress to be inextricably linked. In his view, the ultimate success of the project hinged on building a settler community that adhered to his notions of the proper class, gender, and racial order. Over time, he was confident that this would occur: "A perfect identification in all respects with our people will eventually take place, so that whether by birth or assimilation, a Canadian population is being rapidly developed here."[79] In this way, he believed that the experiment would meet both the larger goals of Ottawa's colonial project in the Northwest and the Icelanders' desire to build a prosperous settler community.

Taylor thus interpreted his role as agent in much more expansive terms than did his superiors in the Department of Agriculture. He sought to exercise wide-ranging paternal authority over the settlement and the lives of its inhabitants. In addition to acting as a conduit of government assistance, he aspired to religious, moral, and even legal authority. Although he had formally exchanged the role of Baptist missionary for that of civil servant, his deeply held religious views led him to interpret events as having been guided by Providence. In July 1875, he wrote in his exploration journal, later published in the *Daily Free Press,* that "if the Lord shall plant the colony of Icelanders here, may there never be wanting among them true and devoted hearts to serve the living God."[80] On the journey to the Northwest in the fall of 1875, Taylor preached a sermon drawn from the Book of Exodus: "Behold I send an angel before thee to keep thee in the way, and to bring thee into the place which I have prepared."[81] One of the Icelanders listening to the sermon wondered if Taylor saw himself as a Moses figure, destined to guide the Icelanders to their promised land.[82] Taylor clearly aspired to be a religious leader to the Icelanders. During the first winter, when there was no Icelandic pastor in the colony, Taylor conducted Sunday services with the assistance of his translator Friðriksson.[83] Ólafur Ólafsson from Espihóll wrote to his friend Reverend Jón Bjarnason that although Taylor fervently wanted to become the Icelanders' pastor, the people largely rejected him because of differences between his Baptist beliefs and their own Lutheranism. Of particular importance to them was infant baptism, a rite that Taylor refused to perform.[84] Still, Taylor long retained the dream of being a spiritual leader to the Icelanders. In 1883, he told his niece's husband, the Icelandic pastor Halldór Briem, "how greatly I long to preach the Gospel of Christ to them without any interpreter! Perhaps the Lord may yet permit me to see this before I die."[85]

But though Taylor shied away from infant baptism, he was generally willing to play a role in regulating gender and family relations among the colonists. Shortly after arriving at New Iceland, he sought out an appointment as justice of the peace to ensure that unions between couples observed the bounds of legality and moral propriety.[86] He also used his powers as justice of the peace to arrange informal adoptions. He and his wife were themselves part of this process: they adopted two baby girls born to Sigurlaug Björnsdóttir and Kristmundur Benjamínsson – a poor couple who already had a large family.[87] One of the two girls, Rannveig Sigríður Kristmundsdóttir, whom the Taylors renamed Rose, survived and was raised to adulthood as their own daughter.[88] In general, the Taylor family presented itself as a model of properly ordered English middle-class family life for the Icelanders to emulate.

With its religious underpinnings and emphasis on performing proper gender roles, the Icelandic reserve was in essence a type of mission community in which the paternalistic missionary/agent oversaw a wide-ranging civilizing mission. In this respect, it was not entirely unlike the free villages that Baptist missionaries established for former slaves in Jamaica and other West Indian islands after emancipation.[89] Taylor's plan for the Icelanders echoed the abolitionists' dreams for the future of the freed slaves: they would become thrifty, industrious, and independent commodity producers, exercising the full rights, privileges, and obligations of British subjects. Taylor saw himself as taking the "hardy and able bodied people of Iceland," whom he conceded were "rather deficient on their first arrival," and demonstrating "their fitness for becoming good settlers and peaceable citizens."[90]

To this end, he worked to establish the basic structures of governance and civil society with which he was familiar: a school, a post office, a rudimentary judicial system, a police force, a militia unit, a system of municipal government, and a newspaper. Before the first settlers had even set foot in the reserve, Taylor wrote to Lieutenant Governor Alexander Morris requesting that he and Ólafur Ólafsson from Espihóll be appointed as justices of the peace, that Páll Jóhannesson be made constable, and that the Icelanders be allowed to form a volunteer militia unit.[91] Nine days after settling at Gimli, Taylor again wrote to Morris, this time asking for the creation of a "national school ... connected with the regular educational system of Canada."[92] Although government support for the school never arrived, it was nonetheless established, with Carrie Taylor as its teacher. The introduction of basic structures of representative local government began in January 1876, with the election of the five-man *bæjarnefnd* (village committee), of which Taylor was himself a member.[93] In the colony's second year, Taylor pushed for an expanded system of municipal government (discussed in the next chapter). He argued that these structures were vitally necessary in "bringing the Icelanders to a practical knowledge and possession of our civil and political privileges, so that they may acquire and make use of the position of naturalized British subjects at as early a period as possible."[94]

However, though Taylor's rhetoric resembled that of his Baptist co-religionists earlier in the century, his mission was quite different with regards to race. New Iceland was founded during a period when the earlier faith in the basic equality and perfectibility of humanity was being replaced by a more rigid biological determinism that drew sharp distinctions between the capabilities of various races. In actuality, Taylor was working to demonstrate that the Icelanders could claim the full privileges of whiteness. His mission represents the unification of the abolitionist's civilizing endeavour with the planter's understanding of a hierarchical racial order. In this respect, Taylor was essentially the settler counterpart to another paternalistic functionary of the Canadian colonial state – the Indian agent. Like the agents who worked on Indian reserves around Lake Winnipeg, Taylor was an outsider, seeking to encourage the values of thrift, industry, and self-sufficiency in people who were constructed as backward and dependent; both types of agents relied on similar assimilative rhetoric to describe the future relationship of their charges to Anglo-Canadians.[95] But whereas Taylor's activities paralleled those of Indian agents and drew on the same discourses of civilization and citizenship, they were not identical in either practice or expected outcome. Race-based exclusionary practices trumped the inclusionary pretensions of the civilizing mission.

Whatever deficiencies Taylor ascribed to the colonists on first arrival, he believed that they could eventually be overcome and that the Icelanders would fully assimilate with Anglo-Canadians and lay claim to the full privileges of whiteness. He was convinced that for the Icelanders, assimilation and achievement of material progress went hand in hand. In confidential letters to Secretary John Lowe of the Department of Agriculture, he frequently proposed altering the exclusive character of the reserve to allow Canadian farmers to settle among the new immigrants "to show the people what can be done here."[96] Contact with Anglo-Canadians outside the reserve was just as important. Taylor acted as an employment agent, arranging for children, women, and men to be hired out to farmers and city residents as manual labourers. This sort of contact was, he felt, essential to the process of becoming Canadian. He was encouraged by the eagerness of the Icelanders to learn English and by changes in their dress and behaviour that brought them more closely into line with Anglo-Canadian norms. As he happily reported to the agriculture minister, "I would state that as characteristic of the Icelandic immigrant to this country, a gradual change is taking place with reference to those especially who live with Canadian families, so that I am often misled by their appearance, their dress, and their speech, so much and so closely resembling our own."[97] Over time, the Taylor family itself became intertwined with the Icelanders. In addition to John and Elizabeth's adoption of Rannveig Sigríður Kristmundsdóttir, two of their nieces married leading Icelanders: Carrie Taylor married Sigurður Christopherson, a member of the Icelandic Deputation. Susie Taylor married Halldór Briem, editor of *Framfari*, the colony's newspaper. In 1882, Susie and Halldór moved to Iceland, where they spent the rest of their lives. After the death of his second wife, John's brother William Taylor married Sigríður Jónsdóttir, mother of the renowned children's author Jón Sveinsson (Nonni) and the artist Friðrik Sveinsson (Fred Swanson).[98]

Whereas Taylor sought to bring the Icelanders into as close contact as possible with Anglo-Canadians, he worked to separate them from local Indigenous people. In informing Lieutenant Governor Morris of the Icelandic Deputation's choice of reserve site, he reported on the plan of the Norway House Indians to settle in the same place and asked that something be done to prevent it: "This is the very spot which we have selected as the nucleus of our settlement, and therefore it would be of the very greatest advantage both to these Indians and to ourselves, if some very distinct and clearly defined line of division could be adopted and enforced."[99] Elizabeth Fiddler, one of the Norway House people who did settle at the White Mud River, claimed that Taylor had ordered her to leave the area.[100] When she sought compensation for land, improvements, and building materials that the Icelanders had seized, he dismissed her case as having little to no merit.

He did the same for a similar claim by John Ramsay, downplaying the scale of Ramsay's improvements and stating that before the treaty, Ramsay had only "a small cultivated plot of less than one acre, not fenced." He also declared that the Icelanders at White Mud River had already compensated Ramsay for his land, though he provided no evidence of this. Furthermore, Taylor asserted that he had received assurances from both Morris and Acting Indian Commissioner J.A.N. Provencher that the Indians "had no claim whatever to the lands at Sandy Bar, and White-mud River on the West Shores of Lake Winnipeg, and that they were about signing a Treaty under the terms of which they would remove to a Reserve at Doghead, further north."[101] Taylor greatly admired the vision of the reserve system, with its compartmentalized world. Many Icelanders shared this view but felt that Taylor and the government had not gone far enough: an 1879 petition to Ottawa, spearheaded by district council foreman Ólafur Ólafsson from Espihóll and Lutheran pastor Páll Thorlaksson, expressed this dissatisfaction, complaining that New Iceland was "situated far from the settlements of all civilised people" and surrounded by Indian and half-breed reserves.[102]

This specific criticism from Ólafsson and Thorlaksson was part of a broader indictment of the colonization project generally and Taylor's administration in particular, one of many instances in which his judgment and leadership were questioned during his tenure as Icelandic agent. Was it wise to move young families onto the reserve at the beginning of winter? Had the site been poorly chosen? Did the Icelanders have the capacity to become self-supporting settlers in the Northwest? Had the government loan been distributed equitably? During the smallpox crisis of 1876–77, Lieutenant Governor Morris had called Taylor irresponsible and chastised Ottawa for advancing the considerable sum of $25,000 to his credit.[103] The government became deeply concerned that this money had been spent for naught; John Lowe implored Taylor to do everything in his power to ensure that the Icelanders became self-supporting. He threatened that if Taylor did not succeed, relations with the government would be cut off, "throwing to the ground your Castle in Spain."[104]

Taylor's listing and drafty house in the muddy village of Gimli was hardly a castle, and the climate of the Interlake region bore little resemblance to that of the Iberian Peninsula. Nonetheless, Lowe's comment accurately reflected Taylor's ambiguous position as an intermediary between the government and the immigrant Icelanders. The reserve was in large measure his private fiefdom; he was afforded considerable latitude in his decision making, and Ottawa provided him with generous resources to build the colony. But, as Lowe reminded him, he was also a mere functionary whose position was wholly dependent on the good graces of his superiors in Ottawa. To the Icelanders, however, Taylor was the everyday face of government power. He was the conduit through which vital aid flowed, and he exercised paternal authority over them, a fact that was not universally appreciated on the reserve. Even those who were on good terms with Taylor felt a general frustration at their seemingly endless series of reverses. Many were looking for a way out, and Ólafsson and Thorlaksson became their champions. Whereas Taylor's solution to the problems was to push the government to encourage Anglo-Canadians to settle vacant lands in and around the reserve, thereby helping to abate its isolation and encouraging agricultural progress, his critics called for the breakup of the colony and forgiveness of the government loan.[105]

The 1879 petition, circulated in secret and sent directly to Ottawa without his knowledge, infuriated Taylor. He assured the government that it was the work of a group of lazy malcontents who had done nothing to build New Iceland but everything to destroy it.[106] Of course, he could not possibly have supported its stated goals, as the dissolution of the colony would disgrace him and prove that his critics had been correct. Less than a year into the colonization experiment, its struggles led the government to put forward a confidential offer to relocate it to another part of the Northwest.[107] Taylor, however, declined the offer.[108] With so much on the line, he lashed out at his enemies in a bitter public announcement in the pages of *Framfari*. He rebuked those who dared to leave the colony without repaying their debt to the government: "Such treacherous conduct is both wanting in gratitude and dishonourable, and likely to abase the reputation and honour of the entire Icelandic people, it becomes particularly degrading for the settlers of New Iceland."[109]

As he struggled to salvage both the colony and his own reputation, Taylor revealed that he had carried over more than his understanding of race from his earlier life in Barbados – he had also retained his ideas about the relationship between work, debt, and mobility. He had never entirely abandoned the idea of bonded labour. When he left Ontario for the Northwest in 1875, he signed a servant to an indenture contract, just as he had done forty years earlier when he set off for Texas. The young English immigrant Everett Parsonage agreed to work for Taylor for eight months.[110] As well, Taylor's attempt to control the situation in New Iceland bears a resemblance to the labour regime that followed emancipation in Barbados.

The Master and Servants Act provided for relations between former slave-owners and the newly free labour force. Workers could live on the plantation, where they could occupy houses and provision grounds, but if they broke their contract they would forfeit almost all the fruits of their labour. The purpose of the act was to ensure that the estates had a sufficient supply of labour, and its effect was to curtail freedom of movement.[111] Taylor appears to have believed that the Icelanders' acceptance of government support constituted a form of indenture contract that required their continued residence on the reserve and their sustained labour toward its development. He therefore tried to use their indebtedness as a lever to ensure that they would not abandon New Iceland. To this end, he asked Ottawa to appoint him stipendiary magistrate so that he could seize individuals' property, principally livestock, to hold them accountable for their debts to the government. Anyone who left New Iceland would be forced to start over from scratch.[112] Although he was eventually appointed magistrate, the chief justice of Manitoba, the lieutenant governor, and the federal Department of Justice all doubted the legality of seizing the Icelanders' property. Thus, he was instructed to use the threat of his legal power as a deterrent against out-migration but to stop short of actually exercising it.[113] As a result of this, many of the disgruntled Icelanders realized that Taylor was a toothless tiger.

Taylor's opponents were keenly aware of the implications of tying indebtedness and work to freedom of movement. The former Icelandic parliamentarian Björn Pétursson astutely observed that it was an infringement on their personal liberty: "It never occurred to the government, I dare say, to establish the Icelanders (as beneficiaries of the loan) as a kind of serfs [sic] on the land here."[114] The idea that they were to be kept on the reserve in a form of debt-slavery must have circulated widely, as Sigtryggur Jónasson was forced to clarify the issue in *Framfari:* "It was never intended to institute a form of slavery in this colony; it was intended only as a colony of free and honourable men."[115] Nonetheless, Taylor does appear to have been attempting to create a system of debt peonage to ensure that the project would not end in failure. The crisis demonstrated that he was capable of reverting from optimistic and encouraging Baptist missionary to his earlier incarnation as the product of West Indian slave society, a man who used coercive measures toward those placed under his authority.

However, the situation in New Iceland had changed by 1880. Consecutive years of flooding caused further hardships, and Taylor was forced to entertain the prospect of vacating the reserve. In a letter to John Lowe, he wrote,

I am making arrangements for my family to remove for a season to Red River. It will be a heavy loss if I have to abandon the place entirely. I have taken great pleasure in improving my house and garden and have everything now so comfortable that it is very trying to give it up ... I can well understand the feelings of a young fellow who got married and settled here 5 years ago and who after working like a slave to make a comfortable home, is now forced to leave and says that it made him cry like a child when he first realized that he had to abandon everything.[116]

With Taylor's blessing, his brother William, his former servant Everett Parsonage, his niece's husband Sigurður Christopherson, and several other Icelanders from in and around Gimli took steps to found a new colony in southwestern Manitoba. In 1881, Taylor and his family left Gimli permanently, moving first to St. Andrews on the Red River and then to Carberry in southwestern Manitoba. He continued to work as Icelandic agent by assisting the new settlement, attempting to resolve the issue of the government debt, and making proposals to found Icelandic colonies on the Bow River in Alberta and in British Columbia.[117] He also continued, as his friend Friðjón Friðriksson put it, "to build castles in the air."[118] This included a reformulation of his industrial farm plan of 1875, which he now termed an "Emigrants refuge." The plan called for new immigrants to be temporarily settled in well-organized villages on reserved sections, to mitigate some of the hardships of the colonization experience: "In a thousand ways the sorrows, the sufferings and the anxieties of newly arrived settlers might be relieved. How great these troubles are at times, few can conceive. How many are crushed by them and die helplessly at their lonely farms, no one knows."[119] He even attempted to move beyond his association with the Icelanders. In 1882, he petitioned Governor General Lord Lorne to assist Jewish refugees fleeing pogroms in Russia by establishing a block settlement somewhere in the Northwest that could be "placed in hands of trustees to carry out the benevolent design of providing new homes far removed from the cruelties and atrocities so shamefully perpetrated on these people in the name of religion."[120]

By this time, however, the septuagenarian had grown tired of the climate in the Canadian Northwest, and he devised a final, deeply revealing dream that if successful, would have brought his life full circle. In December 1883, Taylor explained to Halldór Briem that he had "been considering for several months past whether some other part of the world might not be better for the poor emigrants from Iceland. To my mind there is no place more desirable than in the mountainous parts of the large islands in the tropics, such as Trinidad and Jamaica in the West Indies."[121] Taylor went so far as to propose the scheme to the governor of Jamaica, who replied that though the Icelanders were a fine people, he doubted that they could survive the tropical heat.[122] With his Jamaica plan soundly rejected, Taylor decided to move to Florida along with several members of his extended family.[123] He was granted a leave of absence from his position as Icelandic agent but was ordered back to Manitoba in July 1884 to assist in settling an unexpected influx of new Icelandic immigrants.[124] On the return journey, he took ill and died in Milwaukee at the age of seventy-one.[125] Elizabeth Taylor returned to Manitoba for a time before settling in Trenton, Ontario, with her brother and foster daughter Rose. She died at Rose's home in Toronto in 1920, her ninety-fourth year.[126]

Despite the terrible difficulties of the first years in New Iceland, many of its residents had a profound respect for John and Elizabeth Taylor. Kristmundur Benjamínsson, father of Rose Taylor, wrote, "I lack the means to pay my benefactors for what they have done for me and, what is more, they do not want any repayment; but I wish in this manner to declare my gratitude publicly and wish God's blessing on Mr. Taylor and his wife."[127] Símon Símonarson, who was generally critical of Taylor's lack of forethought, nonetheless described him as "a good and God-fearing man."[128] Friðjón Friðriksson, one of Taylor's closest allies, wrote of him, "Poor soul! I do respect him highly in spite of his shortcomings. He is such a good, loyal, and well-intentioned person."[129] Taylor's friend Sigtryggur Jónasson later reflected that though he had done a wonderful service for the Icelanders by leading them into the Northwest, he received decidedly less gratitude from many settlers than Moses did from the Israelites.[130] Taylor's eventual successor as Icelandic agent, Baldwin L. Baldwinson, was less generous:

> Mr. Taylor never brought an Immigrant to this country and was in short of no earthly use to our people. This is not said as a reflection on his memory for he meant well but his great age and inability to converse or associate with the people for whose interest his position was rightly created made him of much less use than he should have been had he been one of them.[131]

In the work of later Icelandic Canadian historians, the controversies over Taylor's term as Icelandic agent faded to the background, and his contribution to the founding of their community was highlighted. In 1975, New Iceland's centenary, Wilhelm Kristjanson wrote, "John Taylor was God-fearing and devout. His family ties were close. He was kind-hearted and generous and there was love in his heart. He was a strong humanitarian whose active concern was for the distressed individual as well as humanity in general."[132]

This remark illustrates that, despite the disappointments and failures of his term as Icelandic agent, Taylor was able to leave his past behind and reinvent himself as God's servant in the Canadian Northwest – to some degree at least. Still, his new guise was not entirely cut from fresh cloth: it was a patchwork of old elements recombined or turned inside out. Its common thread was a paternalistic relationship with those who came under his authority. As he made the transition from slave-owner to missionary and colonization agent, he came to sound like the evangelical humanitarians who had campaigned to abolish slavery, protect Indigenous people from settlers, and forge a new Christian community based on virtue and personal salvation. However, faith in the inherent perfectibility of mankind had been replaced by a more rigid vision of hierarchical racial order, one with a marked resemblance to the world in which Taylor was born. He was thus ideally suited to help build a new settler order in the Canadian Northwest in which European agriculturalists predominated and Indigenous people were pushed to the margins.

6
Becoming British Subjects
Municipal Government and Citizenship

ONE OF THE MOST persistent myths about the Icelandic reserve is that during its first twelve years, it was a semi-autonomous state called "the Republic of New Iceland."[1] This myth is derived from the fact that, in 1877, the colonists began to manage their local affairs according to a unique form of representative municipal government of their own making. Under this system, each of their four settlements annually elected committees of five men to deal with matters such as road construction and maintenance, public sanitation, and poor relief. A district council, composed of the foremen of each settlement committee plus a chairman and vice-chairman elected by a majority of the twenty settlement councillors, was responsible for matters that affected the entire colony, for resolving disputes between settlements, and for liaising with higher levels of government.[2] The original settlers did not refer to this system as a republic or claim that it had any special constitutional status within Canada.[3] Sigtryggur Jónasson, the first foreman of the district council, referred to it as a municipal system.[4]

New Iceland's government has figured prominently in Icelandic ethnic histories. Icelandic community historians Þorsteinn Þ. Þorsteinsson, Wilhelm Kristjanson, Walter Lindal, and Nelson Gerrard, as well as Icelandic historians Guðjón Arngrímsson and Jónas Thor, never call New Iceland a republic or use the proper name "Republic of New Iceland."[5] Yet since the 1940s, the myth of the republic has figured consistently in popular history and the public memory of the Icelandic community in North America. Its origins can be traced to the writings of Steina Jónasina Sommerville, a women's suffrage activist, *Free Press* journalist, and daughter of original New Iceland pioneers Jónas Stefánsson and Steinunn Grímsdóttir. During the 1940s, Sommerville wrote a series of historical articles in which she claimed that during its early years, New Iceland functioned "virtually as a republic" and was a "sovereign" or "independent" state.[6] One of Sommerville's articles was published in the 1945 transactions of the Historical and Scientific Society of Manitoba. A few years later, the society's secretary, W.L. Morton, referred to the "Republic of New Iceland" in his *Manitoba: A History*.[7] This was probably the first instance in which that proper noun was used, and it has become the authoritative source for later writers.[8]

Even though New Iceland was not a republic, and did not possess the sweeping formal autonomy that has sometimes been claimed, the colonists' attempt to create and operate a system of local government in the Canadian Northwest during the 1870s was unique and deserves closer examination. By focusing on the separateness of this system, Icelandic ethnic historians have missed a parallel story – the way in which local government contributed to the integration of the colony and its people into the institutional and political framework of Canada. This chapter addresses two main questions about local government at New Iceland: First, how did it compare with contemporary equivalents in Iceland and Canada? Second, how were local government and citizenship related to the process of colonization in the Canadian Northwest?

It is important to recognize that this system was not imposed on the Icelanders from the outside. The initiative came from within the reserve and, in part, reflected grassroots demands for better local organization in the District of Keewatin.[9] The Icelanders therefore improvised, creating an institution that was grounded in both their own experience from Iceland and the information about Canadian practices that government agents John Taylor and Sigtryggur Jónasson provided. Taylor and Jónasson, in fact, were instrumental in the process and worked to shape it to meet the goals and expectations of Ottawa. They oversaw the drafting of a set of regulations, which was approved at public meetings in the reserve and then forwarded to the government. Minister of the Interior David Mills was sympathetic to their purpose and used their regulations to draft the Keewatin Townships and Municipalities Bill, which was intended to allow for the establishment of municipal governments in the expansive Keewatin Territory. In the spring of 1878, the bill was the subject of a lively parliamentary debate about the relationship between property, citizenship, and municipal institutions as well as the capacities of Icelanders for self-government. However, the bill never became law. It was bogged down by partisan and sectional wrangling, and it aroused concerns that the proposed system was too complex for "ignorant Icelanders" to operate.[10] However, New Iceland's municipal system persevered without the legal sanction the settlers had sought. During its brief, tumultuous history, it was a key forum in which the central issues of the colony's early years – the viability of the Lake Winnipeg site and the settlers' relationship with the government and wider society – were debated and contested.

This chapter argues that New Iceland's municipal system played an important role in integrating the reserve into the project of liberal colonial rule in the Canadian Northwest. Local government was critical to the Icelanders' emergence as political subjects aligned with the norms and assumptions of the contemporary liberal state. Although the system had some unique features and a distinct terminology, its significance does not reside primarily in its institutional features. Its history is worth examining because it reveals the extension of liberal rule as a dynamic process of interaction and contestation between centre and margin. The colony leadership saw the municipal system as a means to weave the reserve into the political and administrative architecture of the Canadian state and to educate the immigrant Icelanders about the rights and responsibilities of liberal citizenship, a goal that was shared by David Mills. Though the government's efforts at legalization through the Keewatin Townships and Municipalities Bill failed, New Iceland's municipal system helped to extend the project of liberal rule by tying the reserve and its people into the same kind of governmental apparatuses that operated in other places and at other levels of state power.

Canadian historians have generally paid little attention to municipal government. According to Michèle Dagenais, most of the literature on the subject tends to take one of two approaches: either as part of a triumphal narrative about the march of democracy or through a somewhat mechanical understanding of local government as an instrument of social control.[11] The brief mentions of New Iceland's government that appear outside the narrow confines of Icelandic Canadian ethnic history tend to fall in the former category. Historian Lewis H. Thomas saw it as an aspect of the "struggle for responsible government" in the North-West Territories. Echoing Fredrick Jackson Turner's famous frontier thesis, Thomas presented the Icelanders' initiative as an example of the democratic tendencies of frontier communities.[12] The push for democratic rights was unquestionably germane in the genesis of New Iceland's government, but it can also be seen as an instance of local state formation in the sense used by Allan Greer and Ian Radforth – it involved the creation of an institutional framework and the employment of administrative practices that served to increase the level of state surveillance.[13] In this regard, it was part of the "revolution of government" that had led to the expansion of representative institutions and bureaucratic administration in Canada since the 1840s.[14] In a colonial context where distances were great and communication was often problematic, local government could play an invaluable role as a semi-autonomous node of state power, dealing effectively with local issues and providing the central authorities with intelligence about conditions in distant regions.[15] In his post-rebellion report on the affairs of the Canadas, Lord Durham cited the lack of effective local government as a factor that had contributed to unrest in the colonies. Durham's successor as governor general, Charles Poulett Thomson, later Lord Sydenham, also believed in the importance of local government in stabilizing the colonial state, and thus he instigated important reforms.[16]

Durham and Sydenham saw local government as more than a mere administrative convenience: by training individuals in the rights and responsibilities of citizenship, it was a foundation on which the pillars of the liberal state could be constructed. Liberal theorists such as John Stuart Mill argued that the local council was an appropriate field for the "nourishment of public spirit and development of intelligence" by men from the lower classes who had no previous experience in politics or administration.[17] Radicals such as Mill were prepared to challenge the exclusion of women from political participation, but in general, local government reinforced and perpetuated inequalities of gender and race. As Bruce Curtis nicely puts it, "Having served a political apprenticeship under the careful gaze of a tutelar state, men of the lower classes might act as political guardians in their turn, guardians of the inequitable distribution of property, of women's subordination, and of the dominance of the 'white' races."[18]

The analysis in this chapter builds from recent work on municipal government that has explored the role of spatial practices in extending state surveillance and liberal governance. Drawing inspiration from Foucault, Michèle Dagenais suggests that municipal government was a "territorialization of state power at the local level," one that integrated regions where state power had previously been limited.[19] Rod Bantjes makes a similar argument in exploring the connection between the cadastral survey and local government in rural Saskatchewan.[20] He maintains that though spatial organization was intended to shape community and serve the interests of panoptic governmentality, it could also be a base for class formation and political mobilization against the predominant political and economic order.[21] In New Iceland, the municipal system deepened the spatial practices of colonization and surveillance that had developed during the smallpox crisis. The geographical units established by the Dominion Lands Survey and enforced by the public health measures taken during the quarantine were carried over into the local administration system.

Protest and resistance were also part of local government in the reserve during the 1870s. Residents used the municipal system to voice their frustrations with the federal government and to demand that their situation be improved. However, local resistance did not entail rejecting the liberal principles of private property, market production, and individual rights in favour of some communitarian alternative. Despite their many grievances, the Icelanders were fundamentally agents of the new order, and their experiment in governance confirmed their acceptance of representative local government on the Ontario model, shaped as it was by liberal political economy and the accompanying hierarchies of class, race, and gender. The Icelanders' protest was framed as a demand for the full set of rights accorded to white, male, British subjects. If, as Bantjes suggests, government immigrant reserves were reformatories where the character of migrants could be refashioned to suit the demands of liberal modernity,[22] it seems that, in New Iceland at least, it was the inmates who were actively pushing for their own reformation. Still, we must resist the temptation to simplify this case into a story of grassroots democratic mobilization versus unresponsive and autocratic centralized rule. The competing factions and ideological disagreements that were on parade in Ottawa had their counterparts among the Icelanders.

During the smallpox quarantine, John Taylor and Sigtryggur Jónasson were desperate to prove that the colony was not a failure, but rather was turning the corner toward progress, even under the most difficult of circumstances. The formation of a municipal government was one way to accomplish this goal. In this task, the two men received very little direction from Ottawa.[23] Officials in the Departments of Agriculture and the Interior were sometimes sympathetic with their efforts but did not generally share their enthusiasm for institution building. This was largely because their main concern was ensuring that the colony could feed itself without government assistance. However, as John Lowe explained to Taylor, jurisdictional issues came into play as well: "Most of all that you ask for pertains to the Local and not to the Federal Government."[24] The Icelanders' problem was that their local jurisdiction, Keewatin, had no rules regarding the creation of elective municipal institutions. Given this, Lowe was wrong:

provision for municipal government in the reserve *was* a matter of federal responsibility.

This situation developed because the reserve was part of the North-West Territories when it was established in October 1875. At that time, the territorial government consisted of a lieutenant governor and an appointed council that had virtually no independent legislative powers. Governor and council served, often unhappily, in an advisory role to centralized rule from Ottawa.[25] Justices of the peace appointed by the lieutenant governor, and the North-West Mounted Police, comprised the territory's rudimentary justice system.[26] It appears that John Taylor was aware of this situation and attempted to bring the Icelandic reserve into line with practices elsewhere in the Northwest. Before leaving Winnipeg with the first party of settlers, Taylor asked Lieutenant Governor Alexander Morris that he and Ólafur Ólafsson be named justices of the peace and that Páll Jóhannesson be appointed the colony's constable.[27] As the previous chapter detailed, Taylor believed that institution building was essential to the growth and stability of New Iceland. He thought that involving its residents in its administration was imperative. In January 1876, he established an elected council "for the management of [the Icelanders'] affairs, and for regulating generally all matters among them."[28] This five-man council, called the bæjarnefnd (village committee), dealt with issues such as the distribution of government supplies and the recording of the settlers' homestead claims. Taylor was a member of this body, as were his right-hand man and translator Friðjón Friðriksson and his fellow justice of the peace Ólafur Ólafsson, who served as its chairman.[29] As conditions worsened during the winter of 1875–76, the bæjarnefnd became the target of the settlers' frustration.[30] It dissolved in the spring, as the colonists dispersed from the area around Gimli to claim land in other parts of the reserve or to find waged work in Manitoba.[31] Local government was not discussed again until the fall of 1876 and was further delayed by the smallpox crisis.[32]

By this time, Alexander Mackenzie's government had brought a new North-West Territories Act into effect that provided for elective institutions at both the territorial and municipal level. The franchise was restricted to "*bona fide* male residents and householders of adult age, not being aliens, or unenfranchised Indians."[33] Under these rules, only 5 of New Iceland's approximately 1,200 residents would have been eligible to vote.[34] However, even they could not vote in the District of Keewatin, because there was no one to vote for. The Keewatin Act recapitulated most of the provisions of the North-West Territories Act of 1875, but the sections related to elective and representative institutions were intentionally excluded.[35] The Mackenzie government's reasoning was that the legislation was a temporary measure that anticipated the incorporation of the new territory into Manitoba or its re-annexation to the North-West Territories after the boundary between Manitoba and Ontario was settled. Once that occurred, the laws respecting municipal and educational organization in those jurisdictions would be applied to Keewatin, but until then, the "few people" in the new territory would be subject to a "primitive system of government" that concentrated authority in the hands of the lieutenant governor.[36] What was left implicit was that the vast majority of the people who lived in Keewatin were in any case excluded from political rights because they were either immigrant aliens or unenfranchised Indians.

This did not prevent John Taylor and Sigtryggur Jónasson from again trying to forge ahead with a colony government, which they thought would help quell unrest and educate the Icelanders about their civic responsibilities in Canada. As Jónasson explained to John Lowe, "Some sort of organization was necessary to encourage the people to work together and each individual to take interest in the welfare and progress of the whole colony" and to "train them for citizins [sic] under the Government of this country."[37] In January 1877, public meetings were held at Gimli and Icelander's River to draft a set of regulations for the colony government. The various proposals that emerged were combined and adopted by majority vote at a meeting in Gimli on 5 February 1877.[38] These regulations were later published in *Framfari*, as *Sampykktir til bráðabirgðar stjórnarfyrirkomulags í Nýja Íslandi* (Decisions reached on a temporary form of government for New Iceland).[39] The same issue of the paper included an "exhortation" in which Jónasson urged the settlers to aspire to and push for full citizenship rights: "We must not think of ourselves as strangers here, but as an integral part of the society in which we are now living ... We must make certain that we enjoy equal rights with other subjects of this country."[40] After further public discussion, the temporary rules were revised and published as the *Stjórnarlög Nýja Íslands* (The governmental regulations of New Iceland), which came into effect on 14 January 1878.[41]

The *Stjórnarlög Nýja Íslands* is a key document in the colony's history. It is often called a constitution and has been central to the claim that New Iceland was a republic.[42] However, neither the word *stjónarskrá* (constitution) nor *lýðveldi* (republic) appear in its pages. Sigtryggur Jónasson's correspondence with the dominion government clearly shows that stjórnarlög meant "constitution" in the sense of "by-laws or regulations" *(lög)*, under which the colony would be governed/administered *(stjórna)*.⁴³ Although New Iceland's local government was not a republic in either name or function, it was technically a contravention of Canadian law. By creating municipalities and making rules about their functioning, the colonists had assumed powers that belonged to the provinces under section 92 of the British North America Act.⁴⁴

The first Manitoba municipal act in 1873 authorized cabinet to establish municipalities when there were more than thirty male householders in an area and when two-thirds of them petitioned for the municipality's formation.⁴⁵ The North-West Territories Act of 1875 placed this authority in the hands of the lieutenant-governor-in-council, after they had ascertained that a given district had reached a population of a thousand.⁴⁶ The *Stjórnarlög Nýja Íslands* presumed the same authority. Article I constituted the Icelandic reserve as a political and administrative unit called Vatnsþing (Lake District) and further divided it into four municipalities.⁴⁷ The *Stjórnarlög Nýja Íslands* also dealt with the frequency and timing of elections and the procedures governing them (article II), eligibility for the franchise and holding public office (article III), taxation and statute labour (article IV), and the composition and function of municipal councils (articles V and VI), all of which were normally the purview of provincial statute.⁴⁸

In the case of the franchise, New Iceland's rules represented a substantive liberalization of practices in both Iceland and Canada. In Iceland, the electorate consisted of males over the age of twenty-five who were farmers or householders and who paid taxes; this represented only about 9 percent of the population.⁴⁹ In Canada, until the Franchise Bill of 1885, the provinces determined who could vote in municipal, provincial, *and* federal elections. The vote was restricted to male British subjects who had reached the age of twenty-one. All provinces, except British Columbia, also had property and income qualifications. Three provinces had qualifications that amounted to race-based restrictions. Ontario and Manitoba excluded Indians who received treaty annuities from the Crown, and British Columbia excluded all Indians as well as Chinese immigrants whether they were naturalized subjects or not.⁵⁰ New Iceland's rules expanded the franchise in three ways: first, by allowing immigrant aliens who had not become naturalized British subjects to vote; second, by lowering the minimum age to eighteen; and finally, by essentially eliminating property qualifications. Voting was open to the permanent resident who "possesses real estate, or who is a householder, or has permanent employment in the district" and, somewhat ambiguously, "who has an unblemished reputation."⁵¹ The regulations may also have partially overcome gender-based exclusion by extending the franchise to unmarried or widowed women. They described a qualified elector as a *maður,* which has typically been translated as "man." However, this word is not gender-specific. It is a generic term more correctly translated as "person" or "individual."[52] Elsewhere in the regulations, the gender-specific *karlmaður* (man) is applied to individuals who were obliged to perform statute labour on the colony's roads.[53] Not enough is known about the elections in the colony to determine whether women voted, although it is clear that no woman ever served on any of its committees or councils.[54] Still, a comparison with the situation in Iceland suggests that women could potentially vote there as well, at the local level. The 1872 law that instituted elective local government in Iceland also used "maður" to describe qualified voters. Icelandic jurists soon recognized that the law did not technically disqualify women from voting, so Parliament was forced to address the issue. In 1881, the Icelandic legislators confirmed that unmarried women and widows who headed independent households and otherwise met the property and tax payment qualifications could vote in local elections.[55] In the same year, the Ontario legislature extended municipal voting rights to unmarried women on similar terms.[56]

The Icelandic system of local government unquestionably influenced the colonists. From the mid-nineteenth century, a series of reforms slowly shifted political power from appointed officials to elected ones. As the issues regarding the franchise indicate, this was less a radical democratization than a limited accommodation of the aspirations of the farming class.[57] The eligible voters in each Icelandic commune selected a *hreppstjóri* (communal overseer). The hreppstjóri functioned as the deputy of the *sýslumaður* (sheriff), who wielded judicial and administrative power over the larger territorial unit called a *sýsla* (district). The *amt* (region) was composed of several districts and was headed by the *amtmaður* (regional governor), who was a royal appointee. In 1872, just as the emigration movement was beginning, a democratic element was added to this system when elected committees were created at each of the commune, district, and regional levels of local administration. The farmers of each commune elected a committee of three to seven men called the *hreppsnefnd* (communal committee). A representative of this committee sat on the *sýslunefnd* (district committee). These district committees elected representatives from among themselves to sit on the *amtsráð* (regional council).[58] Many of the settlers who played a prominent part in New Iceland's local government had first-hand experience with this system or came from families who did.

Ólafur Ólafsson from Espihóll, who held several important positions in the colony, had been the communal overseer of the Grýtubakkahreppur in northern Iceland.[59] In New Iceland, the settlers abandoned the terminology of their homeland in favour of older territorial designations that had been used during the settlement of Iceland in the ninth and tenth centuries. For example, the basic unit in New Iceland was byggð (settlement) rather than hreppur, and the *þing* (district) replaced sýsla.

Even if the colonists had replicated Iceland's system of local government in its entirety, its structure and division of responsibilities would have been recognizable to Canadians. There were strong parallels between the commune-district-region system of Iceland and its township-county-province equivalent in Canada West/Ontario. Sigtryggur Jónasson explicitly stated that the Ontario municipal system was the model for New Iceland; he told John Lowe that he and Taylor had "tried as far as possible to organize everything in conformity with what is customary under the municipal act."[60] By this, Jónasson meant that the reserve's government had been modelled primarily on the Municipal Corporations Act of 1849 and subsequent amendments. This legislation, largely the work of constitutional reformer Robert Baldwin, provided the structures of local government for Ontario that continue in a similar form to this day.[61] But exactly how was New Iceland's government modelled on the Ontario system? What were the similarities, and what were the differences?

The most obvious parallel between the two systems was the way in which territorial divisions were structured. From the beginning of colonization in Upper Canada during the eighteenth century, the basic unit of local administration was the township, which consisted, on average, of fifty thousand acres. As new areas were opened up for colonization, the provincial government surveyed new townships. This practice was continued in the Northwest in the form of the standardized Dominion Lands Survey system. The *Stjórnarlög Nýja Íslands* subdivided the colony into four byggðir (settlements); these coincided with the territorial divisions created by the survey and were approximately the same size as Ontario townships. Víðirnesbyggð (Willow Point Settlement) comprised Townships 18 and 19, Árnesbyggð (River Point Settlement) encompassed Townships 20 and 21, Fljótsbyggð (River Settlement) Townships 22 and 23, and Mikleyjarbyggð (Big Island Settlement) consisted of the entire island.[62] The reserve as a whole, called Vatnsþing (Lake District), was analogous to a county in Ontario – a collection of adjoining townships and villages in a given region.[63] Manitoba also adopted a municipal system based on the Ontario county model in 1877.[64]

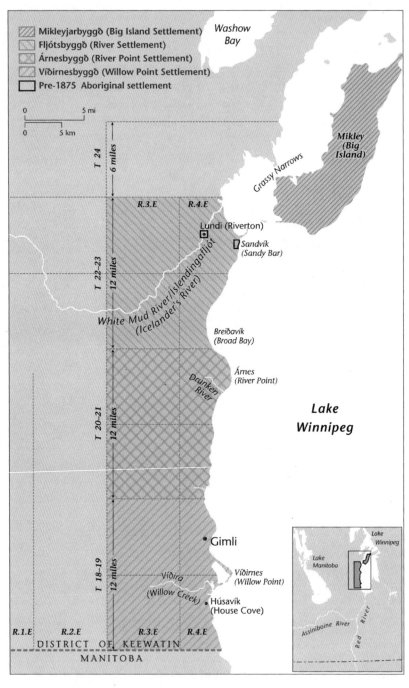

The four *byggðir* (settlements) of New Iceland.

The organizational structure of the Ontario and New Iceland systems was also virtually the same. In Ontario, every year on the first Monday in January, the electors of each township chose a council of five men. The township council chose a reeve and one or more deputy reeves from among its number, depending on the population in the township. The county council was made up of the reeves and deputy reeves from the various townships that comprised the county. Its members elected a warden to serve as their chairman.[65] In New Iceland, each settlement held a public meeting on the seventh of January to elect a *byggðarnefnd* (settlement committee) consisting of five councillors.[66] From among their ranks, the councillors elected a *byggðarstjóri* (settlement foreman), a *varabyggðarstjóri* (deputy settlement foreman), a secretary, and a treasurer. The foremen of the four settlements comprised the *þingráð* (district council), which was headed by a *þingráðsstjóri* (district council foreman). Unlike in the Ontario system, the district council foreman and his deputy, the *varaþingráðsstjóri*, were elected by a majority of the twenty settlement councillors, rather than the district council itself.[67] When John Taylor corresponded with Ottawa about the district council, he simply used the Ontario cognates in place of the distinctive Icelandic terms. For example, in 1879 he referred to þingráðsstjóri Ólafur Ólafsson as "holding the office of Warden for this County."[68]

The duties and responsibilities of a New Iceland settlement committee were in large measure the same as those of a township council in Ontario, but the district council exercised virtually none of the county council's functions. Like their Ontario equivalents, settlement committees dealt with road making and repair, public health and sanitation, care of the poor, assessment of property, and the collection of taxes; they could also pass by-laws that came under their area of responsibility.[69] In Ontario, county councils built and maintained a courthouse and jail, provided for policing, high schools, and the payment of officials such as school inspectors.[70] The *Stjórnarlög Nýja Íslands* said nothing about either school organization or the administration of justice – two crucial components of local government. The former appears to have been left out because the colonists felt they would need assistance to establish a school system. John Taylor asked repeatedly that one be set up, but it never materialized. Education was the constitutional responsibility of the provinces, so New Iceland's ambiguous jurisdictional position again worked to its disadvantage. Early in 1876, the colonists sent a petition to Ottawa, asking that the government provide funding for a school. It was rejected by Minister of the Interior David Laird, on the grounds that his department was "not charged with the education of any but Indian children."⁷¹ The Icelanders nevertheless persisted in asking Ottawa to take responsibility for the matter. In its first meeting, the district council produced a resolution, applying to the government for a grant to establish common schools.⁷²

Although the Keewatin Act did not cover municipal government or school organization, it was fairly clear on the administration of justice. All stipendiary magistrates in the North-West Territories continued to have jurisdiction in Keewatin, and matters that went beyond a magistrate's authority were to be referred to the Manitoba courts. As well, the lieutenant governor could call on the North-West Mounted Police to enforce the law in the district.⁷³ This probably explains why this topic was excluded from the *Stjórnarlög Nýja Íslands*. The settlers understood that their colony was subject to Canadian civil and criminal law, although they weren't always certain what the laws were. At the first district council meeting, River Settlement foreman Jóhann Briem moved that the statute labour system of Ontario be implemented in the colony to open up east-west roads along township lines. The only problem was that the council did not have copies of the relevant statutes, so it asked the council foreman to relay its request to Ottawa.⁷⁴

To navigate these uncertain legal waters, New Iceland's regulations included a unique conflict resolution mechanism aimed at preventing clashes and civil litigation. At the settlement committee elections, two conciliators and one deputy conciliator were chosen for each settlement. Their task was to bring about agreement in private disputes. If they failed, a committee of arbitration consisting of two men appointed by each of the disputants, plus one agreed on by both, or, in the absence of that agreement, the foreman or deputy foreman of the district council, decided the issue by majority vote.⁷⁵ This process was also intended to resolve disputes between the settlements if the district council's efforts at mediation failed.⁷⁶

The main function of the district council was regulating relations between the colony and the outside world. On the administrative level, this entailed maintaining the colonization road that connected New Iceland to Manitoba. On the legislative side, the *Stjórnarlög Nýja Íslands* gave the council power to enact by-laws to enlarge the boundaries of the Lake District, to admit non-Icelandic settlers into the reserve, and to make "arrangements" with individuals who were "launching productive and beneficial undertakings."⁷⁷ The district council foreman had the responsibility of liaising with the *yfirstjórn* (superior government) on all matters affecting the colony. This could mean either the Keewatin government, which consisted solely of the lieutenant governor, or the dominion government. In practice, however, the district council foreman did not communicate directly with either, but rather through John Taylor, as the federal official who was responsible for the colony. This appears to have happened very infrequently: only two sets of resolutions passed by the council, those from its first two meetings, are contained in the records of the Department of Agriculture.[78]

New Iceland's municipal system differed from the county system of Ontario in one other important way: elected officials performed both legislative and administrative duties. In Ontario townships, the council members had little in the way of administrative responsibility, with the important exception of superintending road construction. The township employed a number of permanent and seasonal officials, such as clerks and assessors. The clerks kept the township records and drew up the tax rolls and the lists for statute labour. The assessor compiled statistical information about the holdings of township residents, which was used to generate the voting and taxation rolls.[79] In New Iceland, the elected members of the settlement committees – the same people who drafted by-laws – performed these administrative tasks. The check against abuse in the system was the radically democratic practice of requiring all proposed by-laws to be approved by a majority of the electorate at the annual public meetings held in each settlement.[80] The choice to unify legislative and administrative functions was undoubtedly made because of the colony's poverty and relatively small population; it simply did not have the resources to employ permanent officials. In fact, all participation in the municipal system was on a voluntary basis; elected officials received no remuneration for their services, except being reimbursed for the stationery that they needed to carry out their official duties.[81]

A main administrative chore of a settlement foreman was compiling statistical information about each colonist in his settlement. The head of every household was required to provide him with a detailed account of the homestead on an annual basis. These data, which included information about population, agricultural production, and the amount of capital goods owned by each household, were aggregated for each settlement and for the colony as a whole. This material served several purposes. John Taylor submitted the aggregate data from these statistical accounts to the Department of Agriculture to provide detailed information on the condition of the colony.[82] River Settlement foreman Jóhann Briem claimed that the purpose of gathering and tabulating the data was to inform would-be emigrants in Iceland about conditions in the reserve. Upon introducing the statistical form to his fellow colonists in *Framfari,* he sought to assure them that the information would not be used to tax them, as it had been in Iceland.[83] The only taxation provision in the *Stjórnarlög Nýja Íslands* was that each householder would pay an annual flat-tax of twenty-five cents into the settlement committee's coffers.[84] Still, progressive property taxation may have been planned for the future; the gathered information was precisely the same as that compiled by the township assessor under the Ontario system, and council also realized that more substantive taxation would eventually be necessary to pay for public expenditures.

The architects of New Iceland's government clearly understood that their organization was operating outside of Canadian law. They saw this not as an advantage, but rather as a hindrance to effective governance and progress in their colony. Björn Jónsson, foreman for the Willow Point Settlement, suspected that his countrymen would not pay even a small tax for the care of widows and orphans unless it were mandated by Canadian law.[85] It was partly for this reason that, in the spring 1877, the district council formally requested the dominion government to legally recognize New Iceland's system.[86]

After several months, the council found its champion in Minister of the Interior David Mills. Mills visited the reserve in the autumn of 1877 and was impressed with the Icelanders' intelligence and education. Upon returning to Ottawa, he wrote to Taylor, asking for details on the "voluntary organization ... for municipal purposes, which you desired should be superseded by a system having the sanction of law."[87] On the basis of Taylor's reply and documents forwarded from the Department of Agriculture, Mills drafted the Keewatin Townships and Municipalities Bill, which was introduced into the House of Commons in February 1878.[88]

In many ways, Mills was the ideal person to put forward the required legislation. He was one of Canada's foremost experts on constitutional law and the British North America Act, and during the debates over the acquisition of Rupert's Land, he had advocated extending the rights of local self-government and parliamentary representation to settlers in the Northwest.[89] His efforts on behalf of the Icelanders with the Keewatin bill reflected his ideological commitment to the liberal values of self-government and local autonomy. Mills subscribed to the standard nineteenth-century liberal view of municipal government as a useful educational device for training lower classes in the rights and duties of citizenship, and believed that the institutions created by his bill would achieve the same end

David Mills (1831–1903), minister of the interior, 1876–78. *Library and Archives Canada, Topley Studio, PA-025349.*

among the Icelanders: "There is no better way to prepare the people for becoming British subjects and appreciating British institutions than to permit them to act as this Bill provides."[90]

However, the bill's opponents in Parliament argued that the Icelanders must attain the formal citizenship rights of British subjects through the process of naturalization before they could undergo this type of tutelage. Conservative members correctly pointed out that granting the municipal franchise to unnaturalized aliens would set a precedent. Mills responded that the peculiar situation of the Northwest necessitated this new principle: "We want the country settled, and aliens can hold property. In municipal institutions you represent property and the rights of property."[91] To counter objections about the openness of the franchise, Mills stated that property qualifications would eventually be instituted, but for now it was best to leave the franchise relatively open. In fact, citizenship and property rights were bound together through a stipulation added to the Dominion Lands Act in 1874 – to receive a patent to a homestead, a claimant must be "a subject of Her Majesty by birth or naturalization."[92] None of the Icelanders in the reserve had gone through this process, so their status as property holders remained in limbo. In fact, their situation as assisted immigrants living on a government-sponsored reserve made patenting their homesteads extremely difficult for reasons that are detailed in the next chapter.

Although there is no known surviving copy of the original draft of the Keewatin Townships and Municipalities Bill, a published copy of the amended version does exist.[93] There were five main differences between New Iceland's constitution and the bill that David Mills presented in the House of Commons. First, Mills retained the division of the colony into four municipalities, but he jettisoned the district council. The four municipalities were to function as separate legal entities, and the lieutenant-governor-in-council or the Manitoba Court of Queen's Bench would settle disputes between them. Second, the formal mechanism of arbitration and dispute resolution was discarded. The bill made no provision for settling disagreements between individuals, probably because this was not considered to lie within the purview of municipal government. Third, the more radically democratic aspects of New Iceland's constitution were reined in. The requirement that all by-laws be approved at an annual plebiscite was dropped, the voting age was raised from eighteen to twenty-one, and eligible voters were defined as "any male freeholder or householder in the municipality" (section 8), which removed any ambiguity about their gender. Sheriffs and sheriffs' officers, convicted felons, and anyone who held the office of clerk, treasurer, or collector were also excluded from the franchise (section 5). If these rules had been part of the New Iceland system, members of the settlement committees would have been barred from voting since they were the ones who carried out the functions of these officers. Mills's system assigned those duties to officers who were appointed by the elected officials, a fourth difference between the Keewatin bill and the New Iceland system. A fifth discrepancy was the level of detail accorded to election procedures, the powers of municipal councils, and the system of taxation and assessment. The New Iceland regulations allotted one or two brief sections to each of these matters. In fact, it is unclear whether reserve elections used the secret ballot or the practice of voting *viva voce*. Mills's bill required that the secret ballot be used, and it laid out election procedures in such detail that the bulk of it (sections 9–50) is devoted to that topic. The bill also specified thirty different powers of municipal councils (section 55), whereas New Iceland's regulations were far less precise. The taxation and assessment regimes were spelled out in much greater detail, as were the procedures for seizing property in the event of taxes going unpaid (sections 56–58, 75–82). The final difference was that the Keewatin bill made provision for the creation of school districts and for a school levy to fund their operation (sections 83–100).

Why Mills made these changes is unknown. He probably wanted a system that generally conformed to Canadian practices, would work efficiently, and would meet the needs of the Icelanders. In the House of Commons, he stated that the legislation had been framed on the Ontario municipal system at the settlers' request. However, he also noted that the sections related to municipal taxation had been drawn from the Manitoba legislation.[94] It is unknown whether the Icelanders ever saw a copy of his bill, but it is highly probable that at least the upper echelon of their leadership did see it. John Lowe sent the original draft to John Taylor, who provided commentary and suggestions that were passed on to Mills.[95] Unfortunately, this train of correspondence has been lost along with most of the other documents regarding the reserve's municipal government.[96]

However, the reaction of Mills's parliamentary colleagues is available. The Keewatin bill produced an animated debate in the House of Commons in March 1878, near the end of the parliamentary session. The combative Opposition members, already in election mode, took issue with several of its provisions and used them to expound on general issues around local governance, such as the relative merits of the Ontario municipal system and those of other provinces, particularly Quebec. Much of the discussion focused on the value of the secret ballot, prompting one excited Conservative MP to assert, "If a man had not sufficient manliness to come and vote openly for whom he pleased, he was not fit to possess the franchise."[97] The final blow came when Peter Mitchell, an independent MP from Ontario who was distrusted by both parties and known for delaying the business of the House on petty matters, launched into a tirade that denounced the legislation as a useless expense: "The attempt of the Government to place a measure of that kind at work for 1,500 ignorant Icelanders, who never had the opportunity of understanding municipal affairs or exercising the powers to be vested in them was the most preposterous piece of legislation which had ever been submitted during his experience as a public man."[98] As a result of this harangue and the more substantive concerns raised by Opposition MPs, the bill died on the order paper at the end of the session. In the general election of a few months later, the Conservatives defeated the governing Liberals. Prime Minister John A. Macdonald, who also succeeded Mills as minister of the interior, made no attempt to revive the bill.

Even in the absence of legal sanction from the federal government, the Icelanders continued to operate their system until at least 1880.[99] Nonetheless, it turned out not to be the unifying force that Sigtryggur Jónasson had hoped. Sectarian religious conflict, chronic flooding, lack of material progress, and disputes over dominion government policies precipitated a succession of crises, all of which were played out in the settlement committees and the district council. The political situation became increasingly polarized; those opposed to Jónasson, Taylor, and their allies began to leave for Dakota Territory in the United States. Catastrophic flooding in 1880–81 turned the migration into a general exodus of even the most committed settlers; it is at this point that the district council may have ceased to operate. However, improved conditions and new immigration from Iceland led to the revival of local government in 1883, this time as the County of Gimli under the Manitoba municipal law of 1883.[100] Under the 1883 statute, the County of Gimli was the junior partner in a union with two more populous counties to the south and east, as the United Counties of Lisgar, Plessis and Gimli. However, Manitoba's experimentation with the Ontario model was short-lived; poor road conditions and sparse populations made the counties unworkable. In 1886, a new system was instituted that created smaller units called rural municipalities. This system has continued, with some alterations, to the present.[101] The creation of the Rural Municipality of Gimli in 1887 was the end of the line for the institution established by the original colonists.

The municipal organization of New Iceland clearly pushed the boundaries of Canada's constitutional order. By presenting a local government to Ottawa as a *fait accompli,* the colonists inverted the top-down approach to the delegation of state power contained in the British North America Act. The point of this was not to create an independent republic, but rather to exercise the same forms of local autonomy that existed in both Iceland and Ontario. In some respects, such as the franchise, their system was more democratic than those of Iceland and elsewhere in Canada. Their efforts earned them the approval of David Mills, who unsuccessfully attempted to bring their system under the purview of Canadian law, albeit with his own substantive modifications.

By supporting the Icelanders, Mills and the Liberal government of Alexander Mackenzie were more willing than some of their parliamentary colleagues to expand the parameters of local self-government. However, neither Mills nor Mackenzie were radical democrats. Theirs was a hierarchical liberal order in which access to political rights was limited by class, gender, and race-based exclusions. Their support for New Iceland's efforts at local self-government was contingent on the fact that the reserve was a project of liberal colonial rule in progress; its inhabitants may not have been property-holding, English-speaking British subjects, but they were seen as moving toward that goal. As such, they were worthy builders of settler society in the Northwest. They did not disrupt the vision of the Northwest as a colonial frontier dominated by white, English-speaking Protestants and governed according to an Ontario vision of liberal democracy. Prime Minister Mackenzie believed that due to economic necessity, the Icelanders' cultural and linguistic distinctiveness would slowly fade away, and they themselves would become fully integrated into the Anglo-Canadian mainstream.[102] He and Mills were not so sanguine about other communities in the Northwest that seemed to challenge this new order. It was their government that passed the restrictive and paternal Indian Act, and failed to address petitions from the Métis for municipal and school organization and for representation on the North-West Territories Council.[103]

New Iceland's municipal government was an attempt by the colonists to integrate their reserve into the state system as a political and administrative unit. Its architects aspired to further cement their hold on the territory and its resources, as set aside for them by the Canadian government, over and above competing Aboriginal claims. Although Indigenous people continued to live in and around the reserve, they were excluded from participation in local government. In fact, one of the district council's first resolutions stated that it was "necessary to have the Indians removed from the Icelandic Reserve particularly as the Indians also spoil the fishing in Icelanders River by blocking the mouth of the river completely with their nets."[104] The Icelanders positioned themselves as agents of the new order and sought to align themselves with its vanguard element – Anglo-Canadian settlers from Ontario. Reverend Jón Bjarnason, who served as one of New Iceland's Lutheran pastors from 1877 to 1880, suggested that the reserve be opened to Anglo-Canadians on the grounds that they would advance agricultural and commercial progress and teach the Icelanders to be citizens of Canada. Bjarnason felt that this step was necessary because the colonists' current neighbours were "for the most part half-breeds, who have not yet made progress ... in those matters most essential for Icelanders to learn."[105] To some extent, excluding the Icelanders from certain civil and political rights until such time as they became naturalized British subjects paralleled the treatment of unenfranchised Indians. The same sorts of paternal metaphors about minority and tutelage were at play, although at different levels. Men such as David Mills felt that the Icelanders needed only a brief apprenticeship before they became full participants in the liberal order. The Icelanders themselves, or at least their leaders, were determined to overcome their political disabilities at the earliest possible moment. Sigtryggur Jónasson stated that they should not regard themselves "as underage children or helpless dependents" but rather as "full-grown men, capable of directing our own affairs."[106] Managing their local affairs according to a system that reinforced the principles of liberal governance was vital to this effort.

7
"Freemen Serving No Overlord"
Debt, Self-Reliance, and Liberty

IN SEPTEMBER 1877, GOVERNOR General Lord Dufferin made a special visit to the embattled Icelandic colony as part of his tour of the Northwest. Even though the quarantine had been lifted, and the Icelanders were free to leave their reserve in search of work, fears that it was contaminated by smallpox or some other disease persisted. The Manitoba government quietly attempted to dissuade Dufferin from his visit, and the Hudson's Bay Company only reluctantly transported him to Gimli aboard its steamer *Colville*. Dufferin walked through the village and then travelled a mile west along one of the rough-hewn roads that the settlers had cut through the forest. He visited three farms along the road, where he entered their houses, inspected their contents, and chatted with the inhabitants about their present conditions and hopes for the future. In his official address at Gimli, Dufferin urged the Icelanders to struggle on through the difficult times. If they persevered, he assured them, they would become "freemen serving no overlord, and being no man's men but your own; each master of his own farm."[1]

The inference of this remark was that, of itself, the act of migrating to Canada did not confer liberty. True liberty existed only in a possible future that had as its precondition the acquisition of property – the 160-acre homestead. In the case of the Icelandic reserve, those homesteads had to be carved out of the bush acre by agonizing acre and brought into agricultural production. According to the Dominion Lands Act regulations that governed western colonization, this land would be granted "free" to the settler, provided that basic conditions were met. But in reality, there was a heavy price to be paid in labour and time, and the final reward could remain elusive. Among the farms that Dufferin visited was Nýibær (New Farm), the home of Páll Jónsson, Ólöf Níelsdóttir, and their nine children, who came from Iceland in the summer of 1876. They had little capital with which to commence homesteading, so they relied heavily on the loan provided by the Canadian government. By 1879, the family's labour had resulted in the fulfillment of the basic conditions for acquiring a patent to their homestead. However, according to another section of the act, created specifically for group settlement schemes such as the Icelandic reserve, Páll was required to repay his $574.44 debt to the government before he could obtain the patent. This was well beyond the family's means, and when flooding forced him and many other colonists out of the Willow Point Settlement in 1880, Páll relinquished the dream of being "master of his own farm."[2]

Páll Jónsson's predicament was shared by hundreds of other Icelandic colonists who felt that, for a variety of reasons, their situation had become untenable. Because of the way in which the Dominion Lands rules were administered, leaving the reserve meant forfeiting almost everything they had worked for. Until 1883, obtaining a land patent at New Iceland was not possible simply by fulfilling one's homestead duties and faithfully paying the requisite fee: it also required repaying a debt owed to the government for material assistance during the first years of settlement. The Department of Agriculture referred to this arrangement as a "mortgage," but the loan functioned more like the indenture contracts that were characteristic of colonization schemes in earlier periods – complete with the limitations on personal freedom that such contracts had traditionally entailed. The repayment of the loan became one of the most divisive issues in the colony, particularly when some settlers began leaving for Dakota in 1878 and 1879. The debate, which was played out in the pages of *Framfari*, pitted the government agents John Taylor and Sigtryggur Jónasson against those who advocated abandoning the reserve. In essence, this conflict hinged on two related questions: First, could the Icelanders' freedom of movement be impaired by their debt? Second, did their de facto possession and improvement of land give them rights as property holders that helped to balance out their obligations as debtors? In time, virtually all the colonists came to share the view that their labour and improvements entitled them to equity in their homesteads that should be respected by the government, regardless of their indebtedness.

This chapter explores the link between the loan and the transfer of property rights from the dominion government to individual settlers at the reserve. Without the loan, it is unlikely that New Iceland would have become a reality. Government support was absolutely essential in launching the scheme and providing basic subsistence to the settlers during their first two years. Icelandic ethnic historians have repeatedly recounted their suffering, without fully interrogating its root causes. The suffering of the first New Iceland settlers is said to be part of a shared narrative of sacrifice and ultimate perseverance by a stalwart pioneer generation that has helped bind subsequent generations into a cohesive ethnic community.[3] However, some of the settlers themselves were not silent on the cause of their problems: 1875 pioneer Símon Símonarson blamed decisions made by the colony's leadership. As he put it, "The people suffered for years to come from the improvident way in which preparations were made for the settlement."[4] The aim of this chapter is to connect those dire conditions to policies and ideas emanating from Ottawa and circulating among the settlers themselves. Active government support for colonization schemes was considered at best a necessary and temporary evil; assistance should be granted in the interests of promoting immigration and colonization, but not to such an extent that it would discourage self-sufficiency. Officials in Ottawa intended to transform the Icelanders into independent citizens, possessed of property and imbued with liberal values of thrift, industry, and self-reliance. This was not simply an idea thrust onto the immigrants from above: the loan became a catalyst for an internal debate about the rights and obligations of the individual in a liberal society.

Nowhere was this more apparent than in the tensions generated by the fact that the government loan must be repaid before the transfer of property rights in reserve lands could occur. Repayment and landownership could not be disaggregated from one another: they were quite literally linked through a little-studied provision in the Dominion Lands Act of 1874 that related to group settlements.[5] The pressure became most acute when some settlers contemplated leaving New Iceland, and John Taylor imposed coercive measures to keep "government property" on the reserve. Those who left the colony would not be compensated for their improvements and would be obliged to surrender any goods and chattels obtained through the loan. Many among the disaffected had deep ideological commitments to liberalism and believed that, in establishing these conditions, the government was impinging on their individual liberty. One settler who ran afoul of Taylor, former Icelandic parliamentarian Björn Pétursson, mused whether the colonists' situation amounted to being "serfs on the land."[6] By invoking serfdom, Björn was pointing to the ambiguous position of himself and his fellow New Icelanders with respect to the Canadian state: On the one hand, they were encouraged to become liberal subjects, owners of property enjoying the full rights of citizenship. However, for the time being, their indebtedness excluded them from the promises of liberalism and seemed to lock them into a form of indentured apprenticeship on the reserve. The issues explored in this chapter thus provide a ringside view of the untidy process through which the Icelandic immigrant's place in the liberal order of Canada was negotiated and contested.

The colonization of New Iceland could not have occurred when it did without the support of Ottawa. Most of the approximately 1,500 immigrants who were brought to the reserve with assistance from the Department of Agriculture had very little capital. Few could afford the long and expensive journey to Winnipeg. Fewer still could pay for the necessary tools, implements, and livestock to begin homesteading, not to mention the necessary provisions to sustain them until the first harvest. After transport, outfitting, and provision, there was still the matter of freighting goods, chattels, and supplies to the reserve. This was an expensive proposition in 1875: New Iceland lay beyond the road network of Manitoba, and the water routes became impassable during the fall and spring, when the ice on the lake was forming or breaking up. Guðlaugur Magnússon, who was among the first settlers in 1875, stated that had the large government loan not been forthcoming, the colonization of New Iceland would not have happened when it did. He and the approximately 250 other settlers relied almost totally on provisions obtained through the loan to survive their first winter. But even with this assistance, life during the winter of 1875–76 was characterized by crowded accommodations, insufficient food, and numerous deaths from disease.[7]

Given these difficulties, it is fair to ask why Ottawa actively facilitated the relocation of the Icelanders in the fall of 1875. Prime Minister Alexander Mackenzie and his cabinet were not unaware of the danger of sending a relatively large group, consisting mainly of families with young children, into a new colony far from established settlements at the onset of winter. However, they felt that something must be done to assist the Icelanders in Ontario. They could not be left to winter in the province, because their chances of finding enough work seemed remote and because the provincial commissioner of immigration had renounced all responsibility for their welfare. The option of supporting immigrants settled in Ontario did not receive serious consideration in Ottawa, because of the potential jurisdictional conflict and the fear of setting a precedent. Transporting the Icelanders to Manitoba and the North-West Territories was therefore the only viable solution.[8] But at the same time, it was clear that they could not spend the winter in Winnipeg, since there was neither work nor suitable housing to accommodate a group of that size in a city of five thousand. The only remaining option was to send them to their chosen colony with enough provisions to last through the winter.

By granting assistance, the Mackenzie government felt that it could minimize the potential dangers of the scheme, while at the same time serving its own policy goals for immigration and colonization. The reserve advanced the project of resettling Indigenous land in the Northwest with white farmers. The government expected that once the colony was firmly established, it would attract further immigration from Iceland. However, assisting the colony also presented a policy problem. The policy of the Department of Agriculture was that after transporting immigrants to their final destination, the federal government had no further responsibility for them.[9] The provision of loans or other forms of aid to facilitate settlement was left to either the provinces or private entities that were interested in colonization for reasons of ethno-religious affinity or as a land speculation. As an example of the former, the French Canadian migrants from New England who came to Manitoba during the 1870s received some support from Ottawa, but most of their care after arrival was left in the hands of the Société de Colonisation de Manitoba, an organization headed by Archbishop Alexandre Antonin Taché and other prominent French Canadian Manitobans.[10] Some equivalent private group would have to be found to help shoulder the burden of Icelandic colonization.

The Mennonites from Russia provided an immediate precedent for the government's approach to the Icelandic project. They settled in southeastern Manitoba in 1874, with the assistance of the Canadian government and their long-established co-religionists in southern Ontario. Although they were relatively well-off, their Ontario friends recognized that colonization was an expensive and risky business that required contingency plans. The Department of Agriculture estimated that the cost of provisioning an immigrant family of five through the winter was $90. The addition of the basic outfit required to begin farming brought the cost per family up to $135.[11] In 1876, the 1,339 Mennonites who arrived in Toronto brought $119,000.00, or $88.87 per capita.[12] By comparison, the 1,162 Icelanders in the same year brought only $8,026.00, or $6.91 per capita.[13]

To help fund the Mennonite colonists, J.Y. Shantz, chairman of the Committee of Management of Mennonites in Ontario, arranged for a federal government loan, which the Mennonite communities of Ontario would guarantee. The committee signed a bond, according to the terms of which it was to be advanced up to $100,000 for distribution as needed among the Mennonite colonists in Manitoba. The loan was granted for ten years at an interest rate of 6 percent, with no payments for principal or interest demanded during the first four years. After four years, the principal and interest were to be capitalized, and interest would continue to be charged at an annual rate of 6 percent. The bond stipulated that during the last six years of the loan, annual payments would be made to the receiver general of Canada until the loan and all interest charges were paid off.[14] Because of crop failures due to grasshoppers and frosts during the first years, the Mennonites, particularly those with little means, had to draw heavily on the loan. However, they managed to pay it off by 1892, with the help of a 60 percent reduction in the principal and a complete waiving of the interest charges, negotiated in 1880.[15]

Through this bond process, the federal government hedged its bets on the success or failure of Mennonite colonization by involving a private third party. If everything went well, the new settlers would repay the loan. If it didn't, the Ontario Mennonites would absorb most of the losses. However, a sizable problem impeded the application of this method to the Icelandic reserve – there was no large, well-established community that would aid the Icelanders in the way that the Ontario Mennonites had helped the Manitoba settlers. In the absence of a third party that was motivated by ethnic or religious reasons, the government approached the Hudson's Bay Company (HBC), which had acquired a speculative interest in western lands as a result of the 1870 transfer of its territorial claims to Canada. John Taylor instigated the HBC's involvement in the scheme during the August 1875 visit of the Icelandic Deputation to Winnipeg. He claimed to have reached a verbal agreement with James A. Grahame, chief commissioner of the HBC at Fort Garry, to guarantee a loan up to $100,000 to the Icelandic immigrants on the same terms as the Mennonite bond.[16] When Taylor returned to Ottawa and reported this development to the Department of Agriculture, he was told that something more than a verbal arrangement would be required if the project were to go ahead. Written confirmation was not forthcoming from the HBC, so Taylor penned a detailed letter to Grahame in which he spelled out the terms of the agreement and stressed the need for prompt action, as winter was approaching and time was running out for moving people to the colony. Taylor implied that the Icelanders' homesteads would be security for the HBC – if the settlers defaulted on their repayment, the company would get their lands and all improvements.[17] In reply, Chief Factor J.H. McTavish, acting in

Grahame's absence, sent a telegram to Ottawa on 14 September 1875, stating that "the Hudson's Bay Company will receive & guarantee advances made to the Icelanders in the terms of the printed Mennonite bond."[18]

In a confidential department memo, John Lowe stated that the support of the HBC was the decisive factor in convincing the government to go ahead with the colonization scheme in the fall of 1875:

> This sanction of the Hudson Bay Company, really led to the formation of the Icelandic colony at Gimli, they being presumed to have intimate local knowledge of the proposed site and the means it possessed to support the Icelanders which the Department could not have. I may say, in fact, that the project of this Colony would not have been acted upon in the absence of such sanction.[19]

This statement seems to be borne out by the fact that, on the day after the McTavish telegram was received, Taylor was instructed to commence the removal of the Icelanders from Ontario.[20] On 20 September 1875, an Order-in-Council was passed, recommending that the HBC guarantee be accepted for the $2,500 already advanced to the Icelanders in Ontario and a further $5,000 for provisions until the first harvest. In choosing $5,000 as the amount of the loan, the government based its calculations on the assumption that there would be fifty families and that each of them would require $100 to finance a year's maintenance.[21]

This hastily crafted plan was soon thrown into disarray when the HBC reversed itself and refused to take on the role of guarantor of the loan. Commissioner Grahame later claimed that his initial conversations with Taylor included nothing about a bond. He had agreed to the plan in principle because he had imagined that, as the monopoly supplier to a new colony with access to government cash, the HBC would benefit. He added that the land in the reserve was of little use to the company as a security, because if the Icelanders could not succeed there, it was unlikely that any willing purchaser would be found. But despite his objections to the bond, Grahame agreed to advance $5,300 to Taylor's personal credit for transportation and supplies, with the expectation that this would be reimbursed by the government and that the HBC would not become financially liable if the settlement failed.[22] Throughout much of 1876, the government clung to the hope that it could persuade the HBC to sign the bond and accept responsibility for the Icelanders. At the same time, the company's man in Ottawa, MP for Selkirk Donald A. Smith, pushed for this reimbursement. Ultimately, the government relented: in August

1877, it reimbursed the $5,300 to the company, ending its hope of replicating the Mennonite colonization plan.[23] From this point on, Ottawa had sole responsibility for New Iceland, both financially and morally. Other than the government, the Icelanders had virtually no friends in Canada that were capable of assisting them. If the government wanted to recover the loans it had granted to them – which it did – repayment would have to come directly from them. Therefore, they had to be both given further assistance and encouraged to become self-supporting.

By the spring of 1877, John Lowe had testified before the Select Standing Committee on Immigration and Colonization that the failure of New Iceland had become a distinct possibility.[24] As bad weather, crop failure, poor fishing, a lack of employment, and consequent hunger and disease took their toll, Ottawa was forced to extend more and more money to prevent starvation and death. In large measure, it was the desire to keep costs down that ultimately prompted this larger expenditure. Officials in the Department of Agriculture were concerned by the Icelanders' lack of capital but did not take it seriously into consideration when calculating the amounts that they would require. In the case of the Mennonites, who did have some capital, the government loan was their insurance against adverse conditions. For the Icelanders, it was their sole means of support; they were operating without a net. None of the various memorandums that passed back and forth at the Department of Agriculture addressed the question of what would happen if the situation in the colony deteriorated due to circumstances that the settlers could not control. In consequence, the government responded in a largely ad hoc manner as various crises arose, such as the smallpox epidemic of 1876–77. This resulted in $25,000 being added to the loan amount, the single largest disbursement of all the monies granted to the colony.[25]

The Department of Agriculture based its estimates of the colony's needs almost entirely on its experience with the Mennonites. However, it sought greater efficiencies whenever possible. For example, John Lowe claimed that the Icelanders would require a smaller sum than the Mennonites because they lived next to a lake full of fish and because many of the men were believed to be earning good wages working on railway construction in Manitoba.[26] Authorization for the purchase of necessary provisions was sometimes delayed in hopes that other arrangements would be made, which would save the government money. Lowe hatched a scheme in which Manitoba farmers who had received a government loan due to grasshopper damage in 1874–75 could repay it in produce, which would then be redistributed to the Icelanders.[27] This plan caused considerable delays in transporting the necessary winter provisions to the colony.

The events of the winter of 1875–76 serve to illustrate how Ottawa's attempts to maintain "rigid economy" were ultimately self-defeating and led to considerable suffering among the settlers. The Department of Agriculture estimated that maintaining a family of five through the winter would cost about $90.[28] Assuming that only fifty families would come to the reserve during the fall of 1875, the government had approved a loan of $5,000, which awarded each family the apparently comfortable cushion of $100. This amount proved dangerously insufficient, however, as the number of families that actually went to the reserve in the fall of 1875 was eighty, therefore reducing the amount per family to just $62.50. Only fifteen days after arriving at Gimli, Taylor informed Lowe that "a larger amount of provision will be necessary to preserve the people from want and suffering through the winter."[29] Lowe replied that no further aid would be forthcoming: "There is good will to help your colony, but the difficulties of principle are very great, and in fact I have now a ministerial order to tell you, that nothing further can be done by the Government."[30] By January 1876, Taylor was making urgent appeals to the HBC and Lieutenant Governor Alexander Morris.[31] He also continued to press Ottawa for further assistance, underlining the seriousness of the situation. Taylor believed that the colonists were on the verge of revolt. As he explained to John Lowe, "The fear of suffering from starvation has become so great that I am necessitated to telegraph for further supplies in order to allay the feeling. Unless I do so, I feel assured that they will soon take matters in their own hands and speedily become disorganized."[32] Sufficiently convinced of the gravity of the situation, the government granted another $5,000 in provisions.[33] These supplies saved the Icelanders from starvation, but they did not prevent the onset of malnutrition-related diseases, particularly scurvy. Approximately thirty-five people are believed to have died during the winter and spring; the infirm, children, and nursing mothers were the most seriously affected. One couple lost seven of their nine children.[34]

With the arrival of the Large Group in the summer of 1876, Ottawa again sought to minimize winter maintenance costs but this time was more cognizant of the dangers. As Lowe privately told Taylor, "If any serious suffering takes place, & deaths occur from it the fort would be again on fire, and all our grand colonization projects will go by the board."[35] Nonetheless, the crisis of the smallpox epidemic again forced the government to advance more money to save the colonists from starvation. Because of the quarantine regulations, the Icelanders could not travel to Manitoba in search of work, and therefore they survived solely on government aid and whatever fish they caught in the lake. This helped swell the costs associated with the settlement to nearly $100,000 by the spring of 1877, far more money than the thrifty Mackenzie government had envisioned spending when the colonization scheme was launched in the fall of 1875.[36] Slightly more than half of this amount was classed as a loan; the portions for some transportation, feeding at immigration stations, and for the salaries and expenses of the Icelandic agents Taylor and Sigtryggur Jónasson were seen as normal costs of facilitating migration and settlement. Prime Minister Mackenzie had wanted to make the Icelanders repay the cost of building a colonization road to connect Gimli to Manitoba during the winter of 1876–77, but the road was ultimately categorized as a permanent public work.[37] The loan amount was the portion for supply and provision, which totalled more than $54,000 by the time government aid was formally cut off in May 1877.[38] News of the last installment of $25,000 was communicated to Taylor by Lowe in both official and private letters. The private letter contained the stern warning that the colony was "on its last trial, in as far as Government aid is concerned" and that there would be serious consequences for everyone involved if it failed:

> I do earnestly, both for my sake and your own, beseech you to make such exertions as will induce the people to make a supreme effort to establish themselves with this *last aid* seeing that no more can be had from the Government[.] I say for my sake, because if the Colony is not successful, the strong advice which I have given to the Ministers respecting it, and has been one reason for inducing the expenditure of about $100,000 would constitute one of the most serious official mistakes of my life. And I say for *your* sake, because it would probably involve the breaking up of Official relations, and throwing to the ground your Castle in Spain. Of the poor people themselves the case is also in the last degree serious, as if it does not actually involve the issues of life and death it does involve bitterness, disappointment, and misery.[39]

Given the suffering of the Icelanders during their first two winters, why did the government not simply grant money to them rather than charging the costs of their basic subsistence to them as a loan? In part, this decision was based on the desire of the government to minimize costs during a period of severe economic depression.[40] It was also a matter of policy and precedent: the Department of Agriculture was routinely bombarded with requests from various parties to support their migration and settlement in the west. The government's policy was to provide assistance only to new immigrants and not to British subjects currently residing in other parts of the dominion. Giving what was perceived as lavish support to the Icelanders opened the government and public servants to criticism, as John Lowe's comments above attest.[41] But underpinning the political and financial considerations was the fundamental liberal belief that individuals are responsible for their own well-being and must not look to government for their support. If Ottawa gave the Icelanders too much assistance, it would undermine their ability to become self-supporting citizens. This ideological perspective made it easy for the government to blame the Icelanders, or any other immigrants, for their own misfortune when the colony faltered.[42] As John Lowe told Taylor, "The Government have been informed that the Icelanders don't work, that they have not the habits of thrift and industry, that they are not agriculturalists, and that they have even neglected to catch fish at their own doors."[43] Taylor was instructed to withhold what government funds he still retained from all the able-bodied colonists to force them to get some kind of work. This would enable them not only to be self-supporting, but also to take steps toward repaying their portion of the loan.

The legal mechanism for the government to secure repayment consisted of two clauses added to the Dominion Lands Act in 1874 to encourage group settlement.[44] They were designed to break down a perceived barrier to settlement – lack of access to capital by incoming colonists – while at the same time encouraging capital investment in Dominion lands in the Northwest. The first new clause empowered the minister of the interior to reserve from general settlement any townships on which individuals and groups settled at least sixty-four families "free of expense to the Government." Such group settlements remained subject to the homestead regulations of the original 1872 act – household heads were entitled to receive a 160-acre quarter section free, as long as they resided on their claim for three years, fulfilled the essential requirements for improvement, and paid a ten-dollar administration fee. However, what the act aimed to do was encourage capital investment in colonization, by making homestead lands security against advances to settlers. The land might technically have been granted free, but settlers often required assistance to meet their basic needs for provision and supply. An individual or group that sponsored a settlement of two townships would need to loan settlers who lacked capital some funds to establish their homesteads. Sponsors could expect to lend approximately $17,280 to establish the required number of settlers.[45] In compensation for undertaking such an outlay, those who had put up the initial capital would have the special right to purchase additional land in the township for themselves at a reduced price.

The second new clause permitted the organizers to recoup money advanced to settlers for transport, supply, or provision during initial settlement, up to the amount of $200, with the 160 acres standing as security. The patent to the land could not be issued until the debt was cleared. If settlers vacated their homesteads in the reserve and took up other homesteads elsewhere, the debt would follow them, and the patent for the subsequent homestead would also be withheld until it was paid.[46] Although the act did not say so, colonization schemes such as those of the Mennonites and Icelanders were presumably classed as "free of expense to the Government" because repayment of the loans was supposed to be guaranteed by third parties. Together, third-party guarantors and securitized homestead lands were seen as a sensible and efficient way of off-loading the costs of potentially risky group colonization schemes on Dominion land in the Northwest.

The railway land grant policies of the United States were the inspiration for this addition to the Dominion Lands Act. In the United States, the federal government granted large tracts of land to railway companies, which then undertook to recruit, transport, and settle immigrants on the land. The companies sold the land to the immigrants, taking mortgages on improvements as security.[47] Department of Agriculture secretary John Lowe was a proponent of this form of colonization and formally recommended it to Secretary of State Richard William Scott: "Advances to assist Colonization secured by a lien on the Colonists improved land has been the general mode successfully pursued, for many years in settling the railway companies lands in the Western states. The Northern Pacific Railway Co. is now advertising free passage to families who will settle on their lands."[48] The railway companies aimed to recoup their initial outlay for recruiting and settling the immigrants, and sell the land they had received free from the government after their sponsored immigrants had increased its value by improving their own properties.

The 1874 Dominion Lands Act amendment acknowledged the start-up costs inherent in settling on "free" homestead lands. For settlers without capital, the cost of basic subsistence must somehow be met, and the loan provision supplied the means. However, if the settlement turned out to be a disappointment, settlers could amass debts that far outweighed the value of their land. This was the case for the majority of Icelanders who came to the reserve in 1875 and 1876. Most families accumulated debts of close to or more than the supposed maximum of $200. For example, Páll Jónsson of Nýibær owed the government $574.44. Although Páll and his family had substantially improved their homestead since arriving in 1876, they were faced with a difficult choice by 1880. To secure their patent to the land, they would have to pay off their government debt. This was a challenge for cash-poor settlers who still had few marketable commodities. However, even if discharging the debt and obtaining a patent were possible for Páll and his family, it was not necessarily in their best interests. The future of New Iceland – and therefore the future market value of their property – was in question. Would they be better off if they left the reserve and started again somewhere else? Between 1879 and 1881, many New Icelanders grappled with this question.

There was considerable confusion in the reserve regarding the precise meaning of these provisions in the Dominion Lands Act. First, although the act referred to the debt as "a charge against the homestead," many settlers believed that it was a mortgage. This confusion appears to have emanated largely from John Lowe: when he appeared before a parliamentary committee, he referred to the arrangement as the settlers giving "mortgages on their improvements."[49] This raised the question of whether improvements to the land gave the settlers equity that would be considered in the repayment of their debts. Second, the act did not answer the question of what happened to moveable property obtained through the government loan. Settlers used the loan to buy implements and livestock. If they chose to leave the reserve, could they legally take these goods and chattels with them? Both these issues became highly contentious, and the colonists were split into opposing factions. One side held out hope that conditions would eventually improve if a little more work were put in, whereas the other claimed that New Iceland had no future and that moving elsewhere at the first opportunity was the best course.

Two of the principal antagonists – Sigtryggur Jónasson and Ólafur Ólafsson from Espihóll – lived on adjacent lots along Icelander's River. Jónasson resided at Möðruvellir, named after the administrative hub in northern Iceland where he had been apprenticed as a secretary to the district governor.[50] Although he was only twenty-six in 1879, he was one of the most powerful and influential men in the reserve. He was the Canadian government's assistant Icelandic agent and official translator. As mentioned, John Taylor could not speak Icelandic and thus relied heavily on Sigtryggur to communicate the directives he received from Ottawa. Sigtryggur was also entrusted with the task of keeping the ledger books that recorded the indebtedness of each settler.[51] When the Icelanders held the first elections for their newly organized district council early in 1877, Sigtryggur became the first þingráðsstjóri (district council foreman, or county warden). At roughly the same time, he was instrumental in founding the New Iceland Printing Company, which began publishing *Framfari* in September 1877. In March 1878, Sigtryggur resigned his position as district council foreman over allegations of vote rigging and was succeeded by the varaþingráðsstjóri (deputy district council foreman), Ólafur Ólafsson, his next-door neighbour.[52]

A popular member of the colony's leadership, Ólafur was initially closely associated with John Taylor. He was among the first settlers to arrive at Gimli in 1875 and is credited with giving the place its name.[53] Ólafur had experience in local government, having been appointed overseer of his home commune in Iceland. In January 1876, he was elected to the five-man bæjarnefnd (village committee) and in March, at Taylor's suggestion, was appointed justice of the peace for the North-West Territories.[54] When talk of leaving New Iceland for Dakota began in 1878, Ólafur did not openly come out in favour of it. However, it is clear that he sympathized with the efforts of the Lutheran pastor Páll Thorlaksson to help the struggling settlers start over in the United States, and he himself made plans to leave. By the time of the colony elections in early 1879, many of the disaffected saw Ólafur as their spokesman. Ólafur was elected district council foreman despite the fact that he had declined the nomination. In the pages of *Framfari,* Sigtryggur Jónasson clung desperately to the belief that Ólafur was not working with Páll Thorlaksson to undermine the colony, despite his personal intentions to leave.[55] Almost immediately afterward came the explosive revelation that Ólafur and Páll had secretly co-authored and distributed a petition to the Canadian government that was signed by 130 colonists, expressing their dissatisfaction with the reserve. Feeling that their trust had been betrayed, Sigtryggur and his allies on the council accused Ólafur of having violated the principles of the colony's governing regulations and forced him to resign his position.[56] Shortly thereafter, Ólafur left for Dakota Territory, never to return to New Iceland. The petition was denounced in *Framfari,* where it was scathingly referred to as the "Secret Deal letter."[57] In a letter to John Lowe explaining the issue, Taylor claimed that Páll Thorlaksson had used Ólafur as his pawn, exploiting his popularity among the settlers to obtain signatures.[58]

The petition criticized the way in which Taylor and Sigtryggur had administered the government loan and accused them of a lack of transparency:

Reverend Jón Bjarnason, Sigtryggur Jónasson *(standing, left to right)*, Halldór Briem, and Reverend Páll Thorlaksson *(seated, left to right)*, Minneapolis, 1878. *Þjóðminjasafn Íslands (National Museum of Iceland)*, mms-4335.

It never came to [our] knowledge what rules and regulations have been prescribed by the Government as to the management and distribution of the loan therefore we can not say whether it has been used so as to suit [the] creditors purpose or not, especially as we have not yet been able to obtain any accounts of its distribution from the part of the Agents.[59]

When asked by John Lowe to respond to the allegations in the petition, Taylor attempted to portray its signatories as lazy malcontents who blindly followed the lead of their "disturbing priest" Páll Thorlaksson:

They have not labored industriously by any means, unless bringing ½ acre to one acre of land into cultivation in three years can be so considered. In fact many of them have burned their fences, or killed their cows during the last winter, and are now stealing away secretly and adopting every scheme to defraud the very Government, which they profess in the memorial [petition] to be so grateful to for supplying them so liberally.[60]

However, not all of the signatories were among Páll's followers, and a number had made quite substantial improvements to their land. Many did leave the colony, but others remained for the rest of their lives. Some were Taylor's bitterest enemies, but others were among his closest friends. Kristmundur Benjamínsson, who had signed the petition, publicly thanked Taylor for aiding him since his arrival in 1875, particularly in adopting two children that he and his wife could not care for.[61] Why would Kristmundur, who saw Taylor as a friend and benefactor, participate in an effort to reach a "secret deal" with Ottawa?

The petition probably had wide appeal because it was primarily a reasonable assessment of the problems that had plagued the colonization scheme from its inception and because it offered a sensible solution for them. It argued that despite good intentions on all sides, New Iceland had proved a disappointment to both the settlers and the government, and as a result, the losses should be distributed equally. The government had lost its investment, but the settlers had lost substantially as well, since their efforts seemed unlikely to produce a successful colony. The petition asserted that the site had been poorly chosen, not because of the land per se, but because it was too far from other settlements and prone to flooding. New Iceland could potentially become viable in the future, but only if roads and ditches were built to facilitate communication and drainage, projects that would demand substantially more capital than the Icelanders possessed. The main goal of the petition, however, was to revise the terms of the government loan and thus enable those who wished to leave to settle their accounts in an equitable manner.

The petition identified the central problems with immigrant colonization reserves in general, and with the government acting as their creditor. The petitioners knew that their homestead land was the security for the loan and therefore reasoned that their improvements should be taken into account. Even if they had not obtained legal title to their land, their labour had increased its value, and this entitled them to some consideration. They suggested that a five-person panel consisting of government agents and representatives from their own district council be charged with assessing the value of each settler's improvements. Those who had done enough to cover the amount of their loan would be free to leave the reserve with all their moveable property. Those who had not done enough would also be allowed to depart with all their property but would be required to sign a promissory note to repay the balance.[62] The settlers thus attempted to force a more expansive notion of property rights than that applied by the Canadian government. For its part, Ottawa insisted that, regardless of long-term residence or improvements made, the realization of property rights in Dominion Lands awaited the granting of the patent, which in turn depended on repayment of the loan. This rigid approach was at variance with the way in which many other colonization zones administered settler claims during this period.[63]

Many of the Icelanders believed that they had the right to compensation for improvement on their land as well as the right to sell it because by accepting their homesteads as security for the loan, they had entered into a form of mortgage contract with the federal government. A key pillar of mortgage law was the ability of debtors to redeem their mortgaged property.[64] John Lowe called the arrangement a "mortgage on improvements" when he appeared before the Select Standing Committee on Immigration and Colonization in February 1878.[65] But at the same time, he shied away from taking that position in his instructions to Taylor:

> It is perfectly true, as you state, that a mortgage was to be the form of security. But the debt is nevertheless a simple debt, quite apart from any form of security that was to be given for it, and of course if any of them think of going away there is nothing more clear than that you must demand payment.[66]

The result was the half-measure of the formal acknowledgment. In May 1877, Sigtryggur Jónasson had begun to require that the settlers sign a document in which they acknowledged their debt to the government and pledged to repay it.

The loan acknowledgment stated, "The lands ... that we have taken up in the settlement ... with all buildings and improvements shall become security to the Dominion Government of Canada until the repayment of that portion of the said loan."[67] In addition to this collective acknowledgment, Taylor and Jónasson drew up a form on which each recipient of a portion of the loan would acknowledge his share of it (see the loan acknowledgment on page 180). When it became apparent that some settlers had interpreted this arrangement as a mortgage, Sigtryggur clarified

Icelandic colony government loan acknowledgment. John Taylor and Sigtryggur Jónasson attempted to get all the settlers who had received a portion of the government loan to sign one of these documents. *John Taylor to John Lowe, 20 May 1879, Library and Archives Canada, RG 17, A I 1, vol. 250, docket 25759.*

that it had simply been an acknowledgment of the settlers' responsibility to repay their debts, in keeping with orders he had received from Ottawa.[68] As out-migration commenced, and whether sanctioned by the agents or not, the settlers began to sell their interests in the land they occupied – essentially squatter's rights – to other settlers for the amount of their outstanding loan. For example, Ólafur Ólafsson sold his homestead Ós for $260, which was roughly the amount of his indebtedness.[69]

Sigtryggur's acknowledgment form created a great deal of confusion. If it were not a legal mortgage, what was it? The "secret deal letter" asserted that Sigtryggur had intended the acknowledgment as an indenture contract, obliging the immigrants to stay in the reserve until they had paid off their debts. The petitioners noted that "it *was not mentioned at all* that we were bound to live in the reserve ... whether it proved bad or good, though we are told so now."[70] It is not known whether Taylor or Sigtryggur ever explicitly told any of the settlers that they were not free to leave the reserve as long as their debt remained on the books. For his part, Sigtryggur vigorously denied having said any such thing: "It was never intended to institute a form of slavery in this colony; it was intended only as a colony of free and honourable men."[71] For Taylor, the former slave-master and frequent user of indenture contracts, decreeing that the colonists were not at liberty to leave was certainly not impossible. However, if he did so he was acting without authority from his superiors in Ottawa. The Dominion Lands Act contained no such caveat, and Taylor never received any such directions. He was, however, instructed to collect all debts from departing settlers, including their animals and implements, which "were intended solely to assist in building up that colony."[72] The difference between being forced to remain on the reserve and being required to repay one's debts before leaving was a nuance that was lost on the petitioners. Because of their poverty, the latter virtually guaranteed the former. As the only Icelandic speaker connected with the government, Sigtryggur became the target of general dissatisfaction, even though he worked diligently to provide information about the loan and kept meticulous records of the accounts.[73] In large measure, he was criticized for faithfully carrying out the instructions he had received from Ottawa.

When migration to Dakota began in the spring of 1878, Taylor urged the government to take legal measures against any departing settlers who attempted to remove livestock and implements without first paying their share of the government loan.[74] Following the discovery of the secret deal letter a year later, Taylor became increasingly bellicose. In *Framfari,* he threatened those who were attempting to leave, asserting that "such treacherous conduct is both wanting in gratitude and dishonourable, and likely to abase the reputation and honour of the entire Icelandic people." Thus, he noted,

> it becomes particularly degrading for the settlers of New Iceland ... I therefore publicly declare herewith that all who make themselves guilty of moving out of this colony without my permission any livestock or objects provided by the government loan, or knowingly and maliciously harm or destroy the said animals or objects, will be prosecuted upon the order of the government, and should they be found guilty, will be punished in accordance with the law with the imposition of fines or imprisonment as ordered by the court.[75]

Although Taylor was subsequently appointed a stipendiary magistrate, he was discouraged from using his authority to seize property from the settlers. As John Lowe told him privately, "It is not certain whether there is any law by which the Icelanders could be prevented from removing away with cattle for which they are indebted to the Government or whether you could be justified in arresting them. It is not therefore, best to try doubtful experiments."⁷⁶ Edmund Burke Wood, the chief justice of Manitoba, also told Taylor that a policy of forced seizure was of questionable legality and was undesirable in any event.⁷⁷ However, Taylor and Sigtryggur had already taken this step, seizing an ox from Jakob J. Jónsson and Sveinn Björnsson as they vacated the reserve.⁷⁸ This act touched off a firestorm of allegations and counter-allegations in *Framfari* between Sigtryggur and former Icelandic parliamentarian Björn Pétursson, who owned a partial share in the disputed ox and still resided at New Iceland. He was incensed that the ox had not at least been returned to him and claimed that Sigtryggur and Taylor were acting in an unfair and arbitrary manner: "At home in old Iceland I was familiar with the circumstances of loans and acquainted with people who had borrowed from the National Treasury, public institutions and private individuals, but I have never encountered anything resembling this situation."⁷⁹ Björn challenged the agents to reveal which laws of the country supported their actions.

The protracted and bitter debate between Björn and Sigtryggur was not simply over "a single, wretched half worn out ox," as *Framfari* editor Halldór Briem put it in retrospect.⁸⁰ It recapitulated all the problems and ambiguities that had arisen from linking government aid for the colonization scheme to the transfer of landed property rights in the reserve. The repayment of the loan was cast as both a legal and a moral issue, which had consequences for the future of the Icelanders in Canada. Halldór Briem opined, "The Dominion Government and even Lord Dufferin have been reproved for having done so much for the Icelanders and extending to them so large a loan, on the grounds that Icelanders are not and never will become useful members of the national society. Is it proper to let experience prove the words of such men?"⁸¹ Björn Pétursson thought that the issue came down to one central question: "Is it dishonourable or unmanly to move out of the colony before first repaying one's share of the government loan, or has the government loan diminished people's personal liberty?"⁸² Björn, probably a co-author of the secret deal letter, reinforced the point that New Iceland had been a speculation based on the best intentions of all concerned, but for a variety of reasons it had not lived up to expectation. The losses for the speculation should thus be equally divided among all parties, not simply placed on the Icelanders to be repaid no matter what the consequences: "The Canadian Government undoubtedly ... intended the recipients [of the loan] to settle here and cultivate the land, but it never occurred to the government, I dare say, to establish the Icelanders (as beneficiaries of the loan) as a kind of serfs on the land."⁸³

Accusations and recriminations continued to fly between the antagonists, but ultimately Björn gave up the fight and departed for Dakota. Over the next few years, as the situation was finally resolved, Taylor and Sigtryggur changed their views, eventually espousing a position that did not differ radically from those they had so vigorously opposed.

Whatever difficulties the Icelanders faced in obtaining patents for their homesteads paled in comparison to what happened to the Indigenous residents who survived the smallpox epidemic. John Ramsay asked Dr. James Spencer Lynch to help him secure compensation for his land and improvements at both Sandy Bar and White Mud River, and he travelled to Winnipeg to personally make his case to Lieutenant Governor Morris.[84] Lynch and Morris both recommended that Ramsay be compensated for his losses, but there is no indication that this was done. However, one source indicates that Björn Pétursson, whose homestead was at Sandy Bar, personally paid Ramsay for his improvements.[85] Ramsay continued his claim to land and other assets at White Mud River, which had been occupied by Ólafur Ólafsson and named Ós in the summer of 1876, into at least 1880, but again does not seem to have received any compensation, possibly due to John Taylor's refutation of his claim: "No resident here knows anything of the said 40 acres of land claimed by Ramsay. A small cultivated plot of less than one acre, not fenced was formerly used by him before the Treaty."[86] Taylor also dismissed Elizabeth Fiddler's claim to what became Sigtryggur Jónasson's homestead Möðruvellir.[87]

The basic problem for both John Ramsay and Elizabeth Fiddler was that, as treaty Indians, they were not entitled to claim homesteads. Section 70 of the 1876 Indian Act stated, "No Indian or non-treaty Indian, resident in the province of Manitoba, the North-West Territories or the territory of Keewatin, shall be held capable of having acquired or acquiring a homestead or pre-emption right to a quarter section."[88] However, the section also specified that a treaty Indian "shall not be disturbed in the occupation of any plot on which he has or may have permanent improvements prior to his becoming a party to any treaty with the Crown" and that the government could, at its discretion, compensate treaty Indians for their improvements. These two clauses clearly applied to both Ramsay and Fiddler, but ultimately the claims of white settlers under the Dominion Lands Act trumped the claims of treaty Indians under the Indian Act; the land in question was among the first in the reserve for which Icelanders obtained patents.

These first patents were not issued until 1884, nine years after the founding of New Iceland.[89] By that time, most of the original settlers had gone, including John Taylor and his extended family. Widespread flooding in late 1879 and 1880 convinced even the deeply committed to give up and go elsewhere. "The Loyalists," as they were sometimes called, chose not to join their compatriots in Dakota Territory, but instead founded a new settlement in the Tiger Hills region of southwestern Manitoba. Nonetheless, they continued to petition the government through John Taylor to obtain the patents for their New Iceland farms. Both these settlers and those who remained in the reserve recognized their obligation to pay back the government loan but asserted that according to the general terms of the Dominion Lands Act, their real possession of the land and years of labour entitled them to their patents regardless of their indebtedness. If they received their patents, payment of the loan would follow.[90]

To resolve the situation, the Department of the Interior sent a lands agent, George Newcomb, to the reserve in the summer of 1883. The Department of Agriculture asked Newcomb to collect debts and to record entries or grant patents to land.[91] Newcomb initially encountered resistance from the settlers, who feared that they would be held responsible for the outstanding loans of people who had abandoned the reserve. When Newcomb told them that the question of indebtedness was entirely separate from the question of patents, they agreed to have their homesteads registered. In reporting back to Ottawa, he stated that the original settlers were still too poor to pay off their loan, but he noted that they were assisting newcomers from Iceland who would otherwise need government aid to survive. He believed that, in this way, they were discharging their debt to the government.[92] After Newcomb's report, the Department of Agriculture made some half-hearted efforts to get the Icelanders to repay their loan. In failing health and considered redundant by his superiors in Ottawa, seventy-year-old Icelandic agent John Taylor was given a new role as a "commission on the collection of the Icelandic arrearages."[93] However, the government realized that the loan was "for the most part bad" and was unlikely to be collected.[94] This proved largely true, as virtually none of it was ever repaid.[95]

The path to becoming "freemen serving no overlord, and being no man's men but your own; each master of his own farm," as Lord Dufferin had put it in 1877, was a difficult and winding one for New Iceland's settlers. Few who listened to Dufferin on that day would achieve this goal in the reserve, if at all. For some, the physical and mental challenge was simply too much, the setbacks too many. Others persisted and worked faithfully, but the goal remained elusive for years after their arrival at New Iceland. The colonists were generally thankful for the support they had received from the government, but they were not prepared to let it confine them in the reserve or delay their achievement of the status of property holders. They successfully turned the debt caveat in the 1874 Dominion Lands Act inside out by demanding that patents be issued before the loan was repaid. They thus turned an effective indenture restricting their freedom into a negotiated mortgage that facilitated their attainment of the rights and privileges of liberal citizenship in Canada. Even in the muddy village of Gimli, and in the unlikely context of a feud over "a single, wretched half worn out ox," the liberal order in the Canadian Northwest was being contested.

Conclusion

BETWEEN 1875 AND 1897, the Canadian government reserved land along the southwest shore of Lake Winnipeg for an experiment in colonization. Its initial goal was to establish a self-sufficient community of Icelanders that would attract further Icelandic immigration to the Northwest. The Icelandic reserve was one of several such projects launched by both Liberal and Conservative administrations in Manitoba and the North-West Territories during the 1870s and 1880s. Some were set aside for Continental Europeans, such as the Mennonites, whereas others were designed to attract settlers from Britain and Ireland or French Canadians from Quebec or New England. The goal of this policy was to rapidly augment the non-Aboriginal population of the Northwest with people who would help transform Indigenous lands into a settler-dominated agricultural empire. Indian and Half-breed reserves were created at the same time and often bordered on settler reserves. Together, they were part of a broader patchwork that also included railway and Hudson's Bay Company reserves, and areas that were "open" for homesteading but were in effect earmarked for Anglo-Canadian, British, and American migrants. The establishment and administration of these various spaces must be interpreted as a relational process. In the Canadian Northwest, Indigenous dispossession and the building of settler communities were fundamentally intertwined. Distinctions between categories of people in the colonial population were related to new regimes of spatial organization. The experience of a specific group of migrants such as the Icelanders cannot be understood without reference to the wider socio-economic and cultural frameworks into which it fit.

Conclusion

The Canadian state's recruitment of Icelandic migrants reflected ambitions and ideologies that were at the heart of its colonization efforts in the Northwest. European Romanticism and nineteenth-century racial science stressed the racial and historical connections between Icelanders and Anglo-Saxons. Icelanders were counted among the "hardy northern races" that imperial dreamers such as Richard Burton, Alexander Morris, and Robert Chandler Haliburton believed were ideally suited to building a great empire in the North American continent. This belief, combined with the powerful endorsement of Governor General Lord Dufferin, prompted Canadian immigration officials to class Icelanders as "desirable settlers" during the early 1870s. Almost continuously from 1875 until the First World War, special emigration agents armed with propaganda and offers of subsidies for transportation and resettlement travelled throughout Iceland, promoting the promise of a better life in Canada. Canadian officials were seeking to facilitate and direct a movement that had developed independently of their efforts. Mass emigration from Iceland was spurred primarily by the poor economic prospects for young people, by the increasing availability of information about overseas destinations, and by developing linkages of transportation and trade in the Atlantic economy. Between 1870 and 1914, the involvement of Ottawa and its corporate allies – most notably the Allan Steamship Line – was important in directing upward of 80 percent of the more than fifteen thousand Icelandic emigrants to Canada. Despite its many difficulties, New Iceland ultimately did become an important locus of Icelandic settlement that spawned other settlements elsewhere in the Canadian and American Wests.

The legal and institutional framework that undergirded the colonization of the Canadian Northwest during this period was derived from the principles of nineteenth-century liberalism. Group reserves for immigrant settlers, such as New Iceland, were integral to the process of colonial state formation and to spreading liberal ideas and practices in the region. Although the political economists and social scientists of the early twentieth century who studied the "problem" of ethno-religious group settlement would certainly have agreed with the former statement, they would just as certainly have disputed the latter. W.A. Mackintosh and Carl Dawson saw group settlements as deviations from the "normal" pattern of settlement, in which a pioneering individual – implicitly white, anglophone, and male – broke away from the herd to chart a new course in the West. As subsequent research into both English-speaking and Continental European settler enclaves has revealed, this pattern was possibly quite rare. Historians of settler communities have chronicled broadly similar forms of behaviour that seem to transcend ethnic boundaries, including chain migration and the desire to transfer wealth from one generation to another.[1]

Group settlements were neither inherently conservative nor liberal in orientation. In many cases, settlers chose a middle course between replicating old patterns and adapting to the new liberal conceptions of community. Such was the case with the New Icelanders. Although they wanted to live in a rural community with other Icelanders, especially kin and neighbours from their home districts, they did not desire geographic, economic, political, or cultural isolation from the wider settler society. The closeness of the reserve to the projected CPR line was a main reason why the Icelandic Deputation chose the site on Lake Winnipeg. The chief motivation of the families who made up the bulk of the first settlers was to better their material circumstances. Many colonists initially believed that because of its abundant natural resources and central location, New Iceland offered this possibility, not only for themselves, but also for friends and relatives who planned to emigrate from Iceland. When this possibility receded, they looked elsewhere to achieve their objectives.

Colonization reserves facilitated liberal transformation in the Canadian Northwest in three main ways. First, they enabled the Canadian state to assert its sovereign authority over the area. This was done according to legal and administrative mechanisms that blended older methods of colonization with more recent liberal theories and practices. The Orders-in-Council that created the reserves gave individual and corporate settlement promoters, including ethno-religious communities, the exclusive right to colonize specified territories. In this sense, they were distant cousins of the proprietary grants of the seventeenth-century European colonization of North America, in which rights to conquer, control, and administer large tracts were meted out to various aristocratic grantees. However, the reserves of the 1870s and 1880s were more closely related to the ideas and practices of systematic colonization developed by British and American liberal thinkers during the mid-nineteenth century. In these schemes, private initiative was constrained within a legal and administrative framework established by the centralized colonial state. In large measure, land in western Canadian colonization reserves was subdivided and granted to individuals according to procedures laid out in the Dominion Lands Act. Whereas provision for one alternative system of landholding, the Mennonite villages, was inserted into the act in 1876, its general provisions were applied in most colonization reserves, including New Iceland. Under the Dominion Lands system, individualized freehold land tenure, organized through the system of 160-acre homesteads, was the norm.

This new order had to be superimposed over existing patterns of Indigenous settlement and resource use. The subdivision of the south basin of Lake Winnipeg into Indigenous and settler spaces occurred in the context of the 1876–77 smallpox epidemic. In that crisis, the new regime of reserves and systematic survey dovetailed with the imperatives of public health. Although the disease was devastating for both the Indigenous and settler populations, the mortality rate was highest among the Cree and Ojibwe inhabitants. With many of their relatives, friends, and neighbours dead, their collective and individual claims to land in the Icelandic reserve were muted. At the same time, the physical vestiges of their presence were erased in the name of sanitation. This dramatic episode, which was only the beginning of interaction between Icelanders and Indigenous people, had far-reaching consequences. Several Indigenous survivors remained in the area, and a few, such as John Ramsay, continued to press their claims to land in the reserve. However, the epidemic and the administrative response it elicited irrevocably altered the human geography of the region and solidified the segregation of various components of the colonial population into distinct types of official or unofficial reserves. The status of the reserves in the Dominion Lands system mirrored their residents' status as citizens, non-citizens, or quasi-citizens of the Canadian colonial state.

The second way in which colonization reserves facilitated liberal transformation was by creating discrete territorial units where projects of social engineering could be carried out. Part of the reason that colonization promoters such as Gilbert Malcolm Sproat advocated "farm colonies" was that they would encourage the development of an orderly settler population. Compact colonies were presented as an alternative to the rough-and-tumble homosocial cultures and patterns of mixed-race sociability and intimacy that predominated in many corners of the British Empire. Sproat and others who shared his vision aimed to create nodes of agricultural settlement in which the proper order of race, gender, and class prevailed.[2]

For those whom Canadian officials considered unprepared to exercise the full rights and privileges of liberal citizenship, reserves could function as social laboratories to civilize and assimilate. In the racial hierarchy that predominated in the Canadian Northwest during the late nineteenth century, unnaturalized immigrant aliens such as the Icelanders occupied an intermediate position between white English-speaking British subjects at the top and unenfranchised Indians at the bottom. Whereas the Icelanders were generally seen as racially and culturally suited to the task of colonizing the Northwest, they were simultaneously thought to be a somewhat backward people in need of tutelage. Many contemporary North Americans believed that they represented a fragment of medieval culture; their supposed long isolation from the European mainstream had left them sadly behind in the march of history. Icelandic Agent John Taylor thought he had a God-given mission to help the Icelanders by fostering the spirit of liberal progress among them. Taylor aspired to administer the reserve as an edifying space, where its inhabitants would be trained to exercise the full rights and privileges of British subjects. Both critics and proponents of the reserve frequently expressed their admiration for the widespread literacy and emphasis on education that they observed among the colonists. However, apostles of liberalism who sought to shape the colony, such as Minister of the Interior David Mills, do not seem to have fully appreciated the degree to which the Icelanders were already deeply engaged with liberal ideas and practices. Although Canadian parliamentarians may have disparaged them during the debate over the Keewatin Townships and Municipalities Bill, many were hardly neophytes in the principles of liberal order; they came from a society that was in the process of redefining its economic, social, political, and cultural relationships in dialogue with notions of liberal freedom. The fact that the Icelanders readily adopted the Dominion Lands system and instituted a municipal government structure with broad affinities to Canadian practices reflected this reality. By contrast, Ottawa's failure to create the conditions necessary for private property relations – by completing the survey and instituting a formal system for registering land titles – was a source of continual frustration to them.

As conditions in the reserve deteriorated due to bad weather, crop failures, and flooding, the discrepancy between the hopeful rhetoric of Lord Dufferin and the reality of their situation became increasingly apparent to many. Although they were encouraged to become property owners, enjoying the full rights of liberal citizenship, and were invited to become one people with the Anglo-Canadians, real progress remained elusive. Many colonists worked diligently to establish productive farms, both through the conventional work of homesteading and by undertaking wage-labour on and off the reserve, but their indebtedness to the government seemed to lock them into a form of indentured apprenticeship. Whether progress were even possible at New Iceland became a fundamental point of disagreement, and the pages of *Framfari* chronicle an intense debate over whether the reserve had helped or hindered them. Favourable reports of a few Icelandic pioneers in Dakota Territory, and catastrophic flooding in the early 1880s, led most of the original colonists to give up on New Iceland. Nonetheless, some persevered and were joined by later waves of migrants from Iceland, both before and after the colony's reserve status was rescinded in 1897.

The case of the Icelandic reserve reveals how the process of liberal transformation in the Canadian Northwest was not simply a matter of the top-down exercise of state power or of the pioneer initiative of enterprising colonists. Instead, it was a dialectical process between the centre and the periphery, between government officials and people who were the objects of state power. The Icelandic colonists played a crucial role in extending the ideas and practices of liberal rule over a new terrain. They did so because they believed it would help their community achieve material progress and because they wanted to escape the limitations on their civil and political rights that their status as unnaturalized immigrants placed upon them. In the process, they drew a sharp distinction between themselves, as members of a civilized community, and their Indigenous neighbours in ways that were intended to bolster their claims to white racial privilege. As they challenged their exclusion from the promises of the liberal order, they helped extend its concepts and practices over a new area and worked to integrate themselves into the developing white settler society of the Canadian Northwest.

On the larger scale of global settler colonialism, the case of New Iceland serves as a reminder of the internal diversity of European settler populations in many British colonial contexts. The mass British migrations that helped produce an Anglo world were significantly augmented by people from outside the British Isles who became acculturated as they carried out the work of colonization. In relation to migration history, this study makes the argument for a reconfiguration of the "host society" encountered by non-British migrants to include not only the culturally dominant British population, but also the Indigenous peoples whom European migrants were recruited to displace. Those Indigenous peoples were themselves inclusive of considerable internal diversity, both in terms of traditional languages and cultures and in their responses to colonialism. In short, when we interrogate relations between Indigenous people and settlers, it is important not to reduce either to monolithic entities. It is much more productive to recognize the internal complexity on both sides of that oft-invoked binary and the webs of relationships that developed among individuals in the colonial population, Indigenous and European alike, even in the context of rapidly shifting power dynamics.

If we fail to think about colonial relations in this way, we are unlikely to comprehend the actions of John Ramsay. Although the arrival of the Icelanders had brought about almost unimaginable personal loss for him, he made many close friends among them in the years following the smallpox epidemic. In 1882, when his infant daughter died at Icelander's River, he went to one of those friends, Friðjón Friðriksson, to ask that the girl be buried alongside the young son that Friðjón and his wife, Guðný, had recently lost. Friðjón and Guðný thought this a beautiful idea, and the two children were laid to rest together, not far from the banks of the river.[3]

Notes

INTRODUCTION

1 *Globe*, 2 October 1877.
2 *Daily Free Press*, 25 September 1877. See also *Manitoba Herald*, 11 and 18 January 1877.
3 *Globe*, 2 October 1877.
4 A few days after the article's publication, Lowe sent a copy to William Annand, Canada's emigration agent in London, remarking, "I may tell you (this, however, quite privately) that I wrote the article in question." John Lowe to William Annand, 19 October 1877, Library and Archives Canada (LAC), Department of Agriculture fonds, RG 17 (hereafter RG 17), "English and Continental Letterbooks" series, reel T-158, vol. 1666, 126.
5 *Globe*, 2 October 1877.
6 I use "Indian" when quoting historical sources and when paraphrasing what non-Aboriginal people said about First Nations people. The word also refers to the legal Indian Act definition of an individual or a community (Indian reserve, Indian band). In some instances (especially Chapter 4), the more specific Indian Act term "treaty Indian" is used. However, in general this study uses "Indigenous" and "Aboriginal" to refer to the first peoples of northern North America, including Metis people. These terms are employed more or less interchangeably, although some preference is given to Indigenous in keeping with current usage in Canadian scholarship and civil society. For a more detailed discussion of terminology, see Robert J. Muckle, *Indigenous Peoples of North America: A Concise Anthropological Overview* (Toronto: University of Toronto Press, 2012), 4–8.
    My use of "Metis," capitalized and unaccented, follows that of Nicole St-Onge, Carolyn Podruchny, and Brenda Macdougall: "An unaccented *e* (rather than *é*) is our effort to show that Metis people should not be considered simply as the descendants of French Canadian voyageurs; we recognize the patrilineal diversity of heritages beyond French Canadian to embrace Orcadian, Scottish, English, and so on. The capitalization of the term points to the existence of a group identification, if not nationhood, that was diverse and not tied solely to the political expressions of nationhood reflected in the resistance to Canadian

annexation in the Red River settlement in present-day Manitoba and Batoche in present day Saskatchewan." See Nicole St-Onge, Carolyn Podruchny, and Brenda Macdougall, eds., *Contours of a People: Metis Family, Mobility and History* (Norman: University of Oklahoma Press, 2012), 6–7. This usage is particularly well suited to my study because one of the Metis people who was most important to the history of the Icelandic reserve, Joseph Monkman, self-identified as a Scottish "Half-Breed" and opposed the resistance movement led by Louis Riel. In the few references to that movement, and the sense of political nationhood connected to it, I use "Métis."

7 *An Act to Amend and Consolidate the Laws Respecting Indians*, 1876, 39 Vic., c. 18, s. 70. See Sarah Carter, "Erasing and Replacing: Property and Homestead Rights of First Nations Farmers of Manitoba and the Northwest, 1870s-1910s," in *Place and Replace: Essays on Western Canada*, ed. Adele Perry, Esyllt W. Jones, and Leah Morton (Winnipeg: University of Manitoba Press, 2013), 14–39.

8 J.R. Miller, *Compact, Contract, Covenant: Aboriginal Treaty-Making in Canada* (Toronto: University of Toronto Press, 2009), 152–56.

9 Order-in-Council, PC 1875–0987, 8 October 1875, LAC, Privy Council Office fonds, RG 2 (hereafter RG 2), "Orders-in-Council" series (hereafter A 1 a), reel C-3313, vol. 338.

10 Order-in-Council, PC 1897–2306, 7 July 1897, LAC, RG 2, A 1 a, reel C-3658, vol. 74.

11 Henry Youle Hind, *Narrative of the Canadian Red River Exploring Expedition of 1857 and of the Assiniboine and Saskatchewan Exploring Expedition of 1858* (London: Longman, Green, Longman, and Roberts, 1860), 10–11.

12 Helgi Skúli Kjartansson and Steinþór Heiðarsson, *Framtíð handan hafs: Vesturfarir frá Íslandi, 1870–1914* (Reykjavík: Háskólaútgáfan, 2003), 83–104.

13 Frank Tough, *'As Their Natural Resources Fail': Native Peoples and the Economic History of Northern Manitoba, 1870–1930* (Vancouver: UBC Press, 1996), 80–81.

14 See ibid., 14–43. For more on the pre-1870 history of the Cree and Ojibwe in the region, see Laura Lynn Peers, *The Ojibwa of Western Canada, 1780 to 1870* (Winnipeg: University of Manitoba Press, 1994); and Victor P. Lytwyn, *Muskekowuck Athinuwick: Original People of the Great Swampy Land* (Winnipeg: University of Manitoba Press, 2002).

15 James Settee, Annual Report, 23 November 1875, Birmingham University Library, Birmingham, UK, Church Missionary Society Archive (hereafter CMSA), Section V: Missions to the Americas, Part 3: North West Canada, 1822-1930, Original Letters and Papers, Original Letters and Papers of Rev. James Settee Senior, 1845-1846, 1852-1878, reel 55, CC1/O/57. I used a microfilm copy of the CMSA records held by the Elizabeth Dafoe Library, University of Manitoba.

16 Tough, *'As Their Natural Resources Fail*,' 91–97.

17 For more on the history of the St. Peter's Indian Reserve, see Sarah Carter, "'They Would Not Give Up One Inch of It': The Rise and Demise of St. Peter's Reserve, Manitoba," in *Indigenous Communities and Settler Colonialism*, ed. Zoë Laidlaw and Alan Lester (Basingstoke, UK: Palgrave Macmillan, 2015), 173–93.

18 "Norway House Agency – Correspondence regarding the Removal of Indians from Norway House to Grassy Narrows, 1875," LAC, Department of Indian Affairs and Northern Development fonds, RG 10 (hereafter RG 10), Black series, reel C-10107, vol. 3613, file 4060.

19 Icelandic Deputation to Alexander Morris, 3 August 1875, Archives of Manitoba (hereafter AM), Alexander Morris fonds, MG 12, Lieutenant Governor's collection (hereafter B1), Correspondence series, reel M136, no. 1066.

20 Tough, 'As Their Natural Resources Fail,' 80–81. John Taylor to the Minister of Agriculture, 31 August 1875, LAC, RG 17, "General Correspondence" series (hereafter A I 1) vol. 140, docket 14663.
21 Ian McKay, "The Liberal Order Framework: A Prospectus for a Reconnaissance of Canadian History," *Canadian Historical Review* 81, 4 (2000): 617–45. See also Jean-François Constant and Michel Ducharme, eds., *Liberalism and Hegemony: Debating the Canadian Liberal Revolution* (Toronto: University of Toronto Press, 2009).
22 McKay, "The Liberal Order Framework," 623 (emphasis in original).
23 W.A. Mackintosh, foreword to Carl A. Dawson, *Group Settlement: Ethnic Communities in Western Canada* (Toronto: Macmillan, 1936), ix.
24 See Sarah Carter, *Lost Harvests: Prairie Indian Reserve Farmers and Government Policy* (Montreal and Kingston: McGill-Queen's University Press, 1990); and Royden Loewen, *Family, Church and Market: A Mennonite Community in the Old and the New Worlds, 1850-1930* (Toronto: University of Toronto Press, 1993).
25 John L. Tobias, "Protection, Civilization, and Assimilation: An Outline History of Canada's Indian Policy," *Western Canadian Journal of Anthropology* 6, 2 (1976): 15.
26 Rod Bantjes, *Improved Earth: Prairie Space as Modern Artefact, 1869-1944* (Toronto: University of Toronto Press, 2005), 32.
27 For more on the enfranchisement policy, see John S. Milloy, "The Early Indian Acts: Developmental Strategy and Constitutional Change," in *As Long as the Sun Shines and the Water Flows: A Reader in Canadian Native Studies*, ed. I.A.L. Getty and A.S. Lussier (Vancouver: UBC Press, 1983), 56–64; and Robin Jarvis Brownlie, "'A Better Citizen Than Lots of White Men': First Nations Enfranchisement – an Ontario Case Study, 1918–1940," *Canadian Historical Review* 87, 1 (2006): 29–52.
28 On improvement as an ideology of landholding, see John C. Weaver, *The Great Land Rush and the Making of the Modern World, 1650-1900* (Montreal and Kingston: McGill-Queen's University Press, 2003).
29 "Lt. Governor of Manitoba Transmits Report by Dr. S.S. [sic] Lynch on Condition of the Icelandic Settlement, Lake Winnipeg, 1877," LAC, Department of Secretary of State fonds, RG 6 (hereafter RG 6), "General Correspondence" series (hereafter A 1), vol. 28, file 536.
30 William Duncan Scott, "Immigration and Population," in *Canada and Its Provinces: A History of the Canadian People and Their Institutions by One Hundred Associates*, vol. 7, ed. Adam Shortt and Arthur G. Doughty (Toronto: Glasgow, Brook, 1914), 526–27.
31 Anne Brydon, "Icelanders," in *Encyclopedia of Canada's Peoples*, ed. Paul Robert Magocsi (Toronto: Multicultural History Society of Ontario and University of Toronto Press, 1999), 697.
32 Carl Berger, *The Sense of Power: Studies in the Ideas of Canadian Imperialism, 1867-1914* (Toronto: University of Toronto Press, 1970), 129–30.
33 "Memorial from Icelanders Tendering Thanks for the Gov't Loan and Making Suggestions as to Their Future Movements," March 1879, LAC, RG 17, A I 1, vol. 247, docket 25445.
34 See Matthew Frye Jacobson, *Whiteness of a Different Color: European Immigrants and the Alchemy of Race* (Cambridge, MA: Harvard University Press, 1998); and David R. Roediger, *The Wages of Whiteness: Race and the Making of the American Working Class*, rev. ed. (London: Verso, 1999).
35 See, for example, Guðmundur Hálfdánarson, "Defining the Modern Citizen: Debates on Civil and Political Elements of Citizenship in Nineteenth-Century Iceland," *Scandinavian Journal of History* 24, 1 (1999): 103–16.

36 Some of the works that have shaped my thinking on the subject include Henri Lefebvre, *The Production of Space* (Oxford: Blackwell, 1991); R. Cole Harris, *The Resettlement of British Columbia: Essays on Colonialism and Geographical Change* (Vancouver: UBC Press, 1997); James C. Scott, *Seeing Like a State: How Certain Schemes to Improve the Human Condition Have Failed* (New Haven: Yale University Press, 1998); Kate Brown, "Gridded Lives: Why Kazakhstan and Montana Are Nearly the Same Place," *American Historical Review* 106, 1 (2001): 17–48; R. Cole Harris, *Making Native Space: Colonialism, Resistance, and Reserves in British Columbia* (Vancouver: UBC Press, 2002); and Bantjes, *Improved Earth*.
37 Bruce Curtis, *The Politics of Population: State Formation, Statistics, and the Census of Canada, 1840-1875* (Toronto: University of Toronto Press, 2001), 26.
38 Michel Foucault, "Governmentality," in *The Foucault Effect: Studies in Governmentality*, ed. Graham Burchell, Colin Gordon, and Peter Miller (Chicago: University of Chicago Press, 1991), 95.
39 Curtis, *The Politics of Population*, 3.
40 Nicholas Thomas, *Colonialism's Culture: Anthropology, Travel, and Government* (Princeton: Princeton University Press, 1994), 51.
41 Robert J.C. Young, *Postcolonialism: An Historical Introduction* (Oxford: Blackwell, 2001), 17–18.
42 For example, the title of the parliamentary committee that dealt with western settlement matters was the Select Standing Committee on Immigration and Colonization.
43 Fernande Roy, *Progrès, Harmonie, Liberté: Le libéralisme des milieux d'affaires francophones de Montréal au tournant du siècle* (Montreal: Boréal, 1988); C.B. Macpherson, *The Political Theory of Possessive Individualism: Hobbes to Locke* (Oxford: Clarendon Press, 1962).
44 McKay, "The Liberal Order Framework," 623–24.
45 Ian McKay, "Canada as a Long Liberal Revolution: On Writing the History of Actually Existing Canadian Liberalisms, 1840s-1940s," in Constant and Ducharme, *Liberalism and Hegemony*, 355.
46 Summarized in Jean-François Constant and Michel Ducharme, "Introduction: A Project of Rule Called Canada," in Constant and Ducharme, *Liberalism and Hegemony*, 12.
47 See especially Adele Perry, "Women, Racialized People, and the Making of the Liberal Order in Northern North America," in Constant and Ducharme, *Liberalism and Hegemony*, 275.
48 Uday Singh Mehta, *Liberalism and Empire: A Study in Nineteenth-Century British Liberal Thought* (Chicago: University of Chicago Press, 1999), 47–49.
49 McKay, "Canada as a Long Liberal Revolution," 387–88.
50 Constant and Ducharme, "Introduction: A Project of Rule Called Canada," 6.
51 A few prominent examples from the latter category include Mariana Valverde, *The Age of Light, Soap, and Water: Moral Reform in English Canada, 1885-1925* (Toronto: McClelland and Stewart, 1991); Allan Greer and Ian Radforth, eds., *Colonial Leviathan: State Formation in Mid-Nineteenth-Century Canada* (Toronto: University of Toronto Press, 1992); Bruce Curtis, *True Government by Choice Men? Inspection, Education, and State Formation in Canada West* (Toronto: University of Toronto Press, 1992); and Tina Loo, *Making Law, Order, and Authority in British Columbia, 1821-1871* (Toronto: University of Toronto Press, 1994).
52 C.A. Bayly, *Imperial Meridian: The British Empire and the World, 1780-1830* (London: Longman, 1989); Ann Laura Stoler, *Race and the Education of Desire: Foucault's History of Sexuality and the Colonial Order of Things* (Durham, NC: Duke University Press, 1995);

Antoinette M. Burton, *At the Heart of the Empire: Indians and the Colonial Encounter in Late-Victorian Britain* (Berkeley: University of California Press, 1998); Catherine Hall, *Civilising Subjects: Colony and Metropole in the English Imagination, 1830-1867* (Chicago: University of Chicago Press, 2002); Tony Ballantyne, *Orientalism and Race: Aryanism in the British Empire* (New York: Palgrave, 2002); Alan Lester, *Imperial Networks: Creating Identities in Nineteenth-Century South Africa and Britain* (London: Routledge, 2001); Elizabeth Elbourne, *Blood Ground: Colonialism, Missions, and the Contest for Christianity in the Cape Colony and Britain, 1799-1853* (Montreal and Kingston: McGill-Queen's University Press, 2002).

53 Adele Perry, *On the Edge of Empire: Gender, Race, and the Making of British Columbia, 1849-1871* (Toronto: University of Toronto Press, 2001). Perry's work has helped prompt a more generalized renewal of interest in Canada's place in the British Empire, a subject that has drawn the attention of a diverse collection of Canadian historians working from a variety of theoretical and methodological perspectives. See Phillip A. Buckner, ed., *Canada and the British Empire* (New York: Oxford University Press, 2008).

54 See, for example, Arthur J. Ray, *Indians in the Fur Trade: Their Role as Trappers, Hunters, and Middlemen in the Lands Southwest of Hudson Bay, 1660-1870* (Toronto: University of Toronto Press, 1974); J.R. Miller, *Skyscrapers Hide the Heavens: A History of Indian-White Relations in Canada* (Toronto: University of Toronto Press, 1989); Carter, *Lost Harvests;* Maureen K. Lux, *Medicine That Walks: Disease, Medicine and Canadian Plains Native People, 1880-1940* (Toronto: University of Toronto Press, 2001); Nicole J.M. St-Onge, *Saint-Laurent, Manitoba: Evolving Métis Identities, 1850-1914* (Regina: University of Regina, Canadian Plains Research Center, 2004); and Brenda Macdougall, *One of the Family: Metis Culture in Nineteenth-Century Northwestern Saskatchewan* (Vancouver: UBC Press, 2010). Some important examples of the social and cultural history of immigration and ethnicity from the Canadian context include Donald Harman Akenson, *The Irish in Ontario: A Study in Rural History* (Montreal and Kingston: McGill-Queen's University Press, 1984); Bruce S. Elliott, *Irish Migrants in the Canadas: A New Approach* (Montreal and Kingston: McGill-Queen's University Press, 1988); Bruno Ramirez, *On the Move: French-Canadian and Italian Migrants in the North Atlantic Economy, 1860-1914* (Toronto: McClelland and Stewart, 1991); Kay Anderson, *Vancouver's Chinatown: Racial Discourse in Canada, 1875-1980* (Montreal and Kingston: McGill-Queen's University Press, 1991); Franca Iacovetta, *Such Hardworking People: Italian Immigrants in Postwar Toronto* (Montreal and Kingston: McGill-Queen's University Press, 1992); Frances Swyripa, *Wedded to the Cause: Ukrainian-Canadian Women and Ethnic Identity, 1891-1991* (Toronto: University of Toronto Press, 1993); Dirk Hoerder, *Creating Societies: Immigrant Lives in Canada* (Montreal and Kingston: McGill-Queen's University Press, 1999); and Elizabeth Jane Errington, *Emigrant Worlds and Transatlantic Communities: Migration to Upper Canada in the First Half of the Nineteenth Century* (Montreal and Kingston: McGill-Queen's University Press, 2007).

55 Perry, *On the Edge of Empire*, 19.

56 See Arthur S. Morton and Chester Martin, *History of Prairie Settlement/"Dominion Lands" Policy* (Toronto: Macmillan, 1938); André Lalonde, "Settlement in the North-West Territories by Colonization Companies, 1881-1891" (PhD diss., Laval University, 1969); John Langton Tyman, "The Disposition of Farm Lands in Western Manitoba, 1870-1930: Studies in Prairie Settlement" (D. Phil. diss., Oxford University, 1970); James Morton Richtik, "Manitoba Settlement, 1870 to 1886" (PhD diss., University of Minnesota, 1971); John Langton Tyman, *By Section, Township and Range: Studies in Prairie Settlement*

(Brandon, MB: Assiniboine Historical Society, 1972); and James Morton Richtik, "The Policy Framework for Settling the Canadian West, 1870-1880," *Agricultural History* 49, 4 (1975): 613–28.
57 Norman P. Macdonald, *Canada: Immigration and Colonization, 1841-1903* (Aberdeen, UK: Aberdeen University Press, 1966), 197–256. For an important micro-study of an English-speaking settler community in Manitoba, see D.M. Loveridge, "The Garden of Manitoba: The Settlement and Agricultural Development of the Rock Lake District and the Municipality of Louise, 1878-1902" (PhD diss., University of Toronto, 1987).
58 See, for example, Bruce S. Elliott, *Irish Migrants in the Canadas: A New Approach,* 2nd ed. (Montreal and Kingston: McGill-Queen's University Press, 2004), 185–91.
59 Mackintosh, foreword to Dawson, *Group Settlement,* ix.
60 Dawson, *Group Settlement,* xiii.
61 A.W. Rasporich, "Utopian Ideals and Community Settlements in Western Canada, 1880-1914," in *The Prairie West: Historical Readings,* ed. R.D. Francis and Howard Palmer (Edmonton: Pica Pica Press, 1992), 352–77.
62 See Hansgeorg Schlichtmann, "Ethnic Themes in Geographical Research on Western Canada," *Canadian Ethnic Studies* 9, 2 (1977): 9-41; John C. Lehr, "The Government and the Immigrant: Perspectives on Ukrainian Block Settlement in the Canadian West," *Canadian Ethnic Studies* 9, 2 (1977): 42–52; Donald T. Gale and Paul M. Koroscil, "Doukhobor Settlements: Experiments in Idealism," *Canadian Ethnic Studies* 9, 2 (1977): 53-71; and Richard J. Friesen, "Saskatchewan Mennonite Settlements: The Modification of an Old World Settlement Pattern," *Canadian Ethnic Studies* 9, 2 (1977): 72–90.
63 See Loewen, *Family, Church and Market;* Kenneth Michael Sylvester, *The Limits of Rural Capitalism: Family, Culture, and Markets in Montcalm, Manitoba, 1870-1940* (Toronto: University of Toronto Press, 2001).
64 Bantjes, *Improved Earth,* 32.
65 Ibid.
66 Jon Gjerde, *From Peasants to Farmers: The Migration from Balestrand, Norway to the Upper Middle West* (Cambridge: Cambridge University Press, 1985); Robert Clifford Ostergren, *A Community Transplanted: The Trans-Atlantic Experience of a Swedish Immigrant Settlement in the Upper Middle West, 1835-1915* (Madison: University of Wisconsin Press, 1988); Lyle Dick, *Farmers "Making Good": The Development of Abernethy District, Saskatchewan, 1880-1920* (Ottawa: National Historic Parks and Sites, Canadian Parks Service, 1989); Jack I. Little, *Crofters and Habitants: Settler Society, Economy, and Culture in a Quebec Township, 1848-1881* (Montreal and Kingston: McGill-Queen's University Press, 1991); Loewen, *Family, Church and Market;* Catharine Anne Wilson, *A New Lease on Life: Landlords, Tenants and Immigrants in Ireland and Canada* (Montreal and Kingston: McGill-Queen's University Press, 1994); Sylvester, *The Limits of Rural Capitalism;* R.W. Sandwell, *Contesting Rural Space: Land Policy and Practices of Resettlement on Saltspring Island, 1859-1891* (Montreal and Kingston: McGill-Queen's University Press, 2005).
67 Þorsteinn Þ. Þorsteinsson and Tryggvi J. Oleson, *Saga Íslendinga í Vesturheimi,* 5 vols. (Winnipeg and Reykjavík: Þjóðræknisfélag Íslendinga í Vesturheimi, 1940–53). Þorsteinsson authored volumes 1 to 3, and Oleson is the author of volumes 4 and 5; Thorstina Walters, *Modern Sagas: The Story of the Icelanders in North America* (Fargo: North Dakota Institute for Regional Studies, 1953); Wilhelm Kristjanson, *The Icelandic People in Manitoba: A Manitoba Saga* (Winnipeg: Wallingford Press, 1965); Walter J. Lindal, *Canada Ethnica II: The Icelanders in Canada* (Winnipeg: Viking Press, 1967).

68 Guðjón Arngrímsson, *Nýja Ísland: Saga of the Journey to New Iceland,* trans. Robert Christie (Winnipeg: Turnstone Press, 2000); Jónas Thor, *Icelanders in North America: The First Settlers* (Winnipeg: University of Manitoba Press, 2002).
69 John S. Matthiasson, "Icelandic Canadians in Central Canada: One Experiment in Multiculturalism," *Western Canadian Journal of Anthropology* 4, 2 (1974): 49–61; John S. Matthiasson, "The Icelandic Canadians: The Paradox of an Assimilated Ethnic Group," in *Two Nations, Many Cultures: Ethnic Groups in Canada,* ed. Jean Elliott (Toronto: Prentice Hall, 1979), 331–41; Jónas Þór, "A Religious Controversy among Icelandic Immigrants in North America, 1874-1880" (master's thesis, University of Manitoba, 1980); Howard Palmer, "Escape from the Great Plains: The Icelanders in North Dakota and Alberta," *Great Plains Quarterly* 3, 4 (1983): 219–23; Jane McCracken, "Stephan G. Stephansson: Icelandic-Canadian Poet and Freethinker," *Canadian Ethnic Studies* 15, 1 (1983): 33–53; James Morton Richtik, "Chain Migration among Icelandic Settlers in Canada to 1891," *Scandinavian Canadian Studies* 2 (1986): 73–88; Mary Kinnear, "The Icelandic Connection: Freyja and the Manitoba Woman Suffrage Movement," *Canadian Woman Studies* 7, 4 (1986): 25–28.
70 Nelson Gerrard, *Icelandic River Saga* (Arborg, MB: Saga Publications, 1985). A three-volume follow-up, focusing on the Gimli district of New Iceland, *Gimlunga Saga,* is forthcoming.
71 Júníus Kristinsson, *Vesturfaraskrá, 1870-1914: A Record of Emigrants from Iceland to America, 1870-1914* (Reykjavík: Sagnfræðistofnun Háskóla Íslands, 1983).
72 Helgi Skúli Kjartansson, "The Onset of Emigration from Iceland," *American Studies in Scandinavia* 9, 1 (1977): 87–93; Helgi Skúli Kjartansson, "Emigrant Fares and Emigration from Iceland to North America, 1874-1893," *Scandinavian Economic History Review* 28, 1 (1980): 53–71; Helgi Skúli Kjartansson, "Icelandic Emigration," in *European Expansion and Migration: Essays on the Intercontinental Migration from Africa, Asia, and Europe,* ed. P.C. Emmer and Magnus Mörner (New York: Berg, 1992), 105–19.
73 See Kjartansson and Heiðarsson, *Framtíð handan hafs.*
74 Anne Brydon, "Dreams and Claims: Icelandic-Aboriginal Interactions in the Manitoba Interlake," *Journal of Canadian Studies/Revue d'Etudes Canadiennes* 36, 2 (2001): 164–90; Ryan C. Eyford, "Icelandic Migration to Canada, 1872-1875: New Perspectives on the 'Myth of Beginnings'" (master's thesis, Carleton University, 2003); Laurie K. Bertram, "'Fight Like Auður': Gender, Ethnicity, and Dissent in the Career of Salome Halldorson, Social Credit MLA, 1936–41" (master's cognate research paper, McMaster University, 2004); Ryan C. Eyford, "From Prairie Goolies to Canadian Cyclones: The Transformation of the 1920 Winnipeg Falcons," *Sport History Review* 37, 1 (2006): 5–18; Ryan C. Eyford, "Quarantined within a New Colonial Order: The 1876-1877 Lake Winnipeg Smallpox Epidemic," *Journal of the Canadian Historical Association* 17, 1 (2006): 55–78; C. Lesley Biggs and Stella Stephanson, "In Search of Gudrun Goodman: Reflections on Gender, 'Doing History' and Memory," *Canadian Historical Review* 87, 2 (2006): 293–316; Laurie K. Bertram, "Public Spectacles, Private Narratives: Canadian Heritage Campaigns, Maternal Trauma and the Rise of the Koffort (Trunk) in Icelandic-Canadian Popular Memory," *Material Culture Review* 71 (2010): 39–53; Laurie K. Bertram, "New Icelandic Ethnoscapes: Material, Visual, and Oral Terrains of Cultural Expression in Icelandic-Canadian History, 1875–Present" (PhD diss., University of Toronto, 2010). In addition to the English-language scholarship listed above, important new Icelandic-language histories of the Icelandic migrant experience in North America have been published in recent years by Viðar Hreinsson, Sigurður Gylfi Magnússon, Úlfar Bragason, Ólafur Arnar Sveinsson, and Vilhelm Vilhelmsson.

Chapter 1: Northern Dreamlands

1. John Lowe to Colonel Fletcher, 12 May 1873, LAC, Office of the Governor General of Canada fonds, RG 7 (hereafter RG 7), G 20, vol. 129, file 3066.
2. Sandra Gwyn, *The Private Capital: Ambition and Love in the Age of Macdonald and Laurier* (Toronto: McClelland and Stewart, 1984), 164.
3. Lord Dufferin to John Lowe, 13 May 1873, LAC, RG 7, G 20, vol. 129, file 3066.
4. John Lowe to William Dixon, 22 May 1873, LAC, RG 17, "General Letterbooks" series (hereafter A I 2), reel T-115, vol. 1507, 100.
5. Macdonald, *Canada: Immigration and Colonization*, 212.
6. See Donald Avery, *"Dangerous Foreigners": European Immigrant Workers and Labour Radicalism in Canada, 1896-1932* (Toronto: McClelland and Stewart, 1979); and Donald Avery, *Reluctant Host: Canada's Response to Immigrant Workers, 1896-1994* (Toronto: McClelland and Stewart, 1995).
7. I am guided here by Tony Ballantyne's work on Aryanism. See Ballantyne, *Orientalism and Race*, 6.
8. Reginald Horsman, *Race and Manifest Destiny: The Origins of American Racial Anglo-Saxonism* (Cambridge, MA: Harvard University Press, 1981), 20–24.
9. See ibid., 24–25.
10. See Doug Owram, *Promise of Eden: The Canadian Expansionist Movement and the Idea of the West, 1856-1900* (Toronto: University of Toronto Press, 1980).
11. Berger, *The Sense of Power*, 131.
12. My operational definition of race is derived from the work of David Roediger and Matthew Frye Jacobson. See Roediger, *The Wages of Whiteness*, 7; and Jacobson, *Whiteness of a Different Color*, 10.
13. Christine Bolt, *Victorian Attitudes to Race* (London: Routledge and Kegan Paul, 1971), 9.
14. Benedict Anderson, *Imagined Communities: Reflections on the Origin and Spread of Nationalism*, rev. ed. (London: Verso, 2006), 6–7, 150.
15. Ibid.
16. Stoler, *Race and the Education of Desire*, 8, 29–31.
17. Ibid., 8.
18. "Report of the Select Committee on Immigration and Colonization," Canada, *Journals of the House of Commons of the Dominion of Canada*, 3rd sess., 3rd Parliament, 1876, A8-2.
19. *An Act Respecting Immigration and Immigrants*, S.C. 1869, 32–33 Vic., c. 10.
20. See Marilyn Barber, *Immigrant Domestic Servants in Canada* (Ottawa: Canadian Historical Association, 1991); and Lisa Chilton, *Agents of Empire: British Female Migration to Canada and Australia, 1860s-1930* (Toronto: University of Toronto Press, 2007).
21. "Report of the Select Standing Committee on Immigration and Colonization," Canada, *Journals of the House of Commons of the Dominion of Canada*, 1st sess., 4th Parliament, 1879, A1-2.
22. "Report of the Montreal Immigration Agent (John J. Daley)," Canada, *Sessional Papers of the Dominion of Canada*, vol. 6, 4th sess., 3rd Parliament, 1877, no. 8, 10.
23. "Select Committee on Chinese Labor and Immigration," Canada, *Journals of the House of Commons of the Dominion of Canada*, 1st sess., 4th Parliament, 1879, A4-44.
24. Ibid., A4-2.
25. Guðmundur Hálfdánarson, "Severing the Ties: Iceland's Journey from a Union with Denmark to a Nation-State," *Scandinavian Journal of History* 31, 3 (2006): 245–46.

Notes to pages 28–32   201

26 They did, however, have their doubts about the economic viability of an Icelandic state. The revenues that the state collected did not cover expenditures, so Iceland relied on an annual contribution from the Danish treasury to balance its books. See Gunnar Karlsson, "The Emergence of Nationalism in Iceland," in *Ethnicity and Nation Building in the Nordic World*, ed. Sven Tägil (Carbondale: Southern Illinois University Press, 1995), 43.
27 Kjartansson and Heiðarsson, *Framtíð handan hafs*, 102–4.
28 Kjartansson, "Icelandic Emigration," 107.
29 "Report of Mr. B.L. Baldwinson (Icelandic Agent)," in Canada, *Sessional Papers of the Dominion of Canada*, vol. 10, 4th sess., 7th Parliament, 1894, no. 13, 128–29.
30 Hálfdánarson, "Severing the Ties," 240.
31 Karlsson, "The Emergence of Nationalism," 43.
32 For excerpts from some of the main British works, see Alan Boucher, *The Iceland Traveller: A Hundred Years of Adventure* (Reykjavík: Iceland Review, 1989).
33 Elizabeth Jane Oswald, *By Fell and Fjord; or, Scenes and Studies in Iceland* (London: Blackwood and Sons, 1882), 1.
34 Ibid.
35 Anne Brydon, "Inscriptions of Self: The Construction of Icelandic Landscape in Nineteenth Century British Travel Writings," *Ethnos* 60, 3 (1995): 248.
36 Bayard Taylor, *Egypt and Iceland in the Year 1874* (New York: G.P. Putnam's Sons, 1875), 204.
37 Ibid., 206, 49.
38 Frederick Temple Blackwood Dufferin and Ava, *Letters from High Latitudes: Being Some Account of a Voyage, in 1856, in the Schooner Yacht "Foam," to Iceland, Jan Mayen, and Spitzbergen*, 3rd ed. (London: John Murray, 1857), 141.
39 See Edward W. Said, *Orientalism* (London: Routledge and Kegan Paul, 1978).
40 Mary Louise Pratt, *Imperial Eyes: Travel Writing and Transculturation* (New York: Routledge, 1992), 6–7.
41 Ibid.
42 Brydon, "Inscriptions of Self," 248.
43 Edward Jenkins, the Canadian agent general in London, sent a copy of Burton's book to John Lowe in October 1875. See Edward Jenkins to John Lowe, 28 October 1875, LAC, RG 17, A 1 1, vol. 145, docket 15102.
44 Richard Francis Burton, *Ultima Thule; or a Summer in Iceland* (London: Nimmo, 1875), 1:x.
45 For a more detailed analysis of Burton's writing on Iceland, see Brydon, "Inscriptions of Self," 243–63.
46 Burton, *Ultima Thule*, 1:144.
47 Ibid., 1:xiii–xiv, 208.
48 Ibid., 1:209.
49 Owram, *Promise of Eden*, 5.
50 Alexander Morris, *Nova Britannia; or, Our New Canadian Dominion Foreshadowed; Being a Series of Lectures, Speeches and Addresses* (Toronto: Hunter, Rose, 1884), 187.
51 Owram, *Promise of Eden*, 72–77.
52 Morris, *Nova Britannia*, 6–7.
53 Ibid., 49, 50.
54 Mark Harrison, *Climates and Constitutions: Health, Race, Environment and British Imperialism in India, 1600-1850* (Oxford: Oxford University Press, 1999), 16–18; Berger, *The Sense of Power*, 129.

55 R.G. Haliburton, *The Men of the North and Their Place in History; A Lecture Delivered before the Montreal Literary Club, March 31st, 1869* (Montreal: Lovell, 1869), 2.
56 Ibid.
57 Ibid., 7.
58 David Arnason, "The Icelanders in Manitoba: The Myth of Beginnings," in *The New Icelanders: A North American Community*, ed. David Arnason and Vincent Arnason (Winnipeg: Turnstone Press, 1994), 4.
59 Haliburton, *The Men of the North*, 7.
60 Berger, *The Sense of Power*, 66–67.
61 W.C. Krieger to J.C. Schultz, 1 November 1875, AM, Sir John Christian Schultz fonds, MG 12, E1, vol. 15, no. 7594–7.
62 For a more detailed description of this system, see Macdonald, *Canada: Immigration and Colonization*, 39–46.
63 "Report of the Special Mission of Hon. W. McDougall, C.B.," Canada, *Sessional Papers of the Dominion of Canada*, vol. 6, 1st sess., 3rd Parliament, 1874, No. 9, 64.
64 Paul W. Gates, "Official Encouragement to Immigration by the Province of Canada," *Canadian Historical Review* 15, 1 (1934): 31–32.
65 Sanford Fleming to Edward Watkin, 30 July 1863, LAC, Sir Edward Watkin fonds, MG 24, E 17, reel A-519, vol. 1.
66 For a more in-depth analysis of Canada's campaign and the work of McDougall and Mattson, see Lars Ljungmark, "Canada's Campaign for Scandinavian Immigration, 1873-1876," *Swedish-American Historical Quarterly* 33, 1 (1982): 21–42.
67 Lord Dufferin to John Lowe, 13 May 1873, LAC, RG 7, G 20, vol. 129, file 3066.
68 "Annual Report of H. Mattson, Special Immigration Agent in Scandinavia," Canada, *Sessional Papers of the Dominion of Canada*, vol. 8, 2nd sess., 3rd Parliament, 1875 no. 40, 134–35.
69 John Lowe to William Dixon, 22 May 1873, LAC, RG 17, A I 2, T-115, vol. 1507, 100.
70 The first migrations to Canada and the Ontario colonization schemes are detailed in Eyford, "Icelandic Migration to Canada," 46–117.
71 Adam Crooks to John Lowe, 30 January 1875, LAC, RG 17, A I 1, vol. 126, docket 13297.
72 Edward Jenkins to the Minister of Agriculture, 18 February 1875, LAC, RG 17, A I 1, vol. 128, docket 13443.
73 See Hjörtur Pálsson, *Alaskaför Jóns Ólafssonar 1874* (Reykjavík: Menningarsjóður, 1975).
74 The Icelanders of Wisconsin to U.S. Grant, 2 August 1874, in Walters, *Modern Sagas*, 211.
75 U.S. Grant to Hamilton Fish, 17 August 1874, in Walters, *Modern Sagas*, 213.
76 *New York Times*, 9 December 1874; Jón Ólafsson, *Alaska: Lýsing á landi og lands-kostum, ásamt skýrslu innar íslenzku sendinefndar: um stofnun íslenzkrar nýlendu* (Washington, DC, 1875).
77 Pálsson, *Alaskaför Jóns Ólafssonar 1874*, 189–90.
78 Order-in-Council, PC 1875–0889, 13 September 1875, LAC, RG 2, A 1 a, reel C-3313, vol. 337.
79 Including in Winnipeg, where Sigtryggur Jónasson, then in Manitoba as part of the Icelandic Deputation, translated a piece on the eruption from the Icelandic newspaper *Norðanfari* that was published in the *Free Press*. See *Daily Free Press*, 10 August 1875.
80 *Times*, 1 July 1875.
81 Ibid., 11 August 1875.
82 Ibid., 14 August 1875.

83 W.C. Krieger to Luc Letellier de St. Just, 24 June 1875, LAC, RG 17, A I 1, vol. 136, docket 14235.
84 John Lowe to W.C. Krieger, 10 July 1875, LAC, RG 17, A I 2, vol. 1511, 263.
85 "Report of the Icelandic Immigration Agent (W.C. Krieger)," Canada, *Sessional Papers of the Dominion of Canada,* vol. 7, 3rd sess., 3rd Parliament, 1876, no. 8, 175–76.
86 John Lowe to Sigtryggur Jónasson, 15 September 1875, LAC, RG 17, A I 2, vol. 1513, 1–3. For the report, see "Report of the Icelandic Deputation," included in John Taylor to the Minister of Agriculture, 31 August 1875, LAC, RG 17, A I 1, vol. 140, docket 14663.
87 Edward Jenkins to the Minister of Agriculture, 29 October 1875, LAC, RG 17, A I 1, vol. 145, docket 15119. For the complete pamphlet, see Canada, Department of Agriculture, *Nýa Ísland í Kanada* (London: Gilbert and Rivington, 1875).
88 "Reports on Arrivals at Quebec," 1876, LAC, RG 17, Immigration Branch, A III 1, Department Correspondence, vol. 2395.
89 Sigtryggur Jónasson to the Minister of Agriculture, 7 July 1876, LAC, RG 17, A I 1, vol. 162, docket 16850.
90 "Lt. Governor of Manitoba Transmits Report by Dr. S.S. [sic] Lynch on Condition of the Icelandic Settlement, Lake Winnipeg, 1877," LAC, RG 6, A 1, vol. 28, file 536.
91 Dr. J.S. Lynch to William Hespeler, 30 October 1876, LAC, RG 17, A I 1, vol. 172, docket 17824.
92 Dr. J.S. Lynch to Alexander Morris, 17 April 1877, in "Lt. Governor of Manitoba Transmits Report by Dr. S.S. [sic] Lynch on Condition of the Icelandic Settlement, Lake Winnipeg, 1877," LAC, RG 6, A 1, vol. 28, file 536.
93 John Lowe to W.C. Krieger, 26 February 1877, LAC, RG 17, A I 2, reel T-117, vol. 1518, 12.
94 John Lowe to John Taylor, 2 May 1877, LAC, RG 17, "Semi-Official Letterbooks" series (hereafter A I 6), reel T-132, vol. 1633, 217.
95 Dr. J.S. Lynch to Alexander Morris, 17 April 1877, in "Lt. Governor of Manitoba Transmits Report by Dr. S.S. [sic] Lynch on Condition of the Icelandic Settlement, Lake Winnipeg, 1877," LAC, RG 6, A 1, vol. 28, file 536.
96 Ibid.
97 *Daily Free Press,* 25 September 1877.
98 Ibid., 17 September 1877.
99 Ibid.
100 Ibid.
101 *Globe,* 2 October 1877.
102 John Lowe to James Ennis, 19 October 1877, LAC, RG 17, "English and Continental Letterbooks" series, reel T-158, vol. 1666, 124.
103 John Lowe to W.C. Krieger, 27 February 1878, LAC, RG 17, A I 2, reel T-117, vol. 1520, 210; John Lowe to John Taylor, 1 April 1878, LAC, RG 17, A I 2, reel T-117, vol. 1520, 273. For the special edition, see *Framfari,* 22 March 1879.
104 Sigtryggur Jónasson to John Lowe, 3 September 1878, LAC, RG 17, A I 1, vol. 232, docket 23807; Sigtryggur Jónasson to John Lowe, 29 July 1879, LAC, RG 17, A I 1, vol. 255, docket 26247.
105 See "Baldwin L. Baldwinson, Icelandic Agent, 1892-1900," LAC, Department of Employment and Immigration fonds, RG 76 (hereafter RG 76), I A 1, reels C-4679 and C-4680, vol. 22, file 389, parts 1 and 2.
106 Based on the reports of the Quebec immigration agent and the Icelandic agents, contained in the Canadian *Sessional Papers;* and Scott, "Immigration and Population," 526–27.

107 Sigtryggur Jónasson, *The Early Icelandic Settlements in Canada,* Transaction 59 of the Historical and Scientific Society of Manitoba (Winnipeg: Manitoba Free Press, 1901), 15.
108 Canada, *Senate Debates* (29 March 1901), 171–72.
109 J.S. Woodsworth, *Strangers within Our Gates, or Coming Canadians* (Toronto: Frederick Clarke Stephenson, 1909), 92.
110 Scott, "Immigration and Population," 532.
111 Ibid., 531.
112 Macdonald, *Canada: Immigration and Colonization,* 212.

Chapter 2: Broken Townships

1 "Report of the Icelandic Deputation," included in John Taylor to the Minister of Agriculture, 31 August 1875, LAC, RG 17, A I 1, vol. 140, docket 14663.
2 On colonization in Manitoba before 1880, see Chapters 7 and 8 of W.L. Morton, *Manitoba: A History* (Toronto: University of Toronto Press, 1957). For a more comprehensive survey of land policy and administration in the same period, see Chapters 3 and 4 of Richtik, "Manitoba Settlement."
3 "Report of the Icelandic Deputation," included in John Taylor to the Minister of Agriculture, 31 August 1875, LAC, RG 17, A I 1, vol. 140, docket 14663.
4 John Taylor to the Minister of Agriculture, 11 and 31 August 1875, LAC, RG 17, A I 1, vol. 140, dockets 14644 and 14663; *Daily Free Press,* 8 and 11 August 1875; "Field Notes of Survey of Part of the Coast of Lake Winnipeg, from a Point East of Brokenhead River Near the Province Line Along the South and West Shore in Little Grindstone Point Including Adjacent Islands, Manitoba. Commenced March 1873, Ended April 1873, Surveyed by A.H. Vaughn, D.S.," Survey notebook no. 531; "Field Notes of Township 18 Range 4 E, N.W. Territory, Surveyed by A.H. Vaughn, D.S., Commenced 22 September 1873, Ended 2 October 1873"; Survey notebook no. 336, AM, Land Surveyors' Field Books, NR 0157 (hereafter NR 0157), GR 1601.
5 The Icelandic Deputation to Alexander Morris, 3 August 1875, AM, Alexander Morris fonds, MG 12, B1, Correspondence series, reel M136, no. 1066.
6 David Laird to Alexander Morris, 15 September 1875, LAC, David Laird fonds, MG 27, I D 10.
7 Order-in-Council, PC 1875–0987, 8 October 1875, LAC, RG 2, A 1 a, reel C-3313, vol. 338.
8 The perspective on space here is derived from Lefebvre, *The Production of Space;* Scott, *Seeing Like a State;* and Brown, "Gridded Lives," 17–48.
9 Bantjes, *Improved Earth,* 32.
10 See Reverend Jón Bjarnason's article "The Most Pressing Need," *Framfari,* 16 July 1878, 298–301. Page numbers cited for *Framfari* refer to George Houser's English translation of the newspaper. See George Houser, ed., *Framfari: 1877 to 1880* (Gimli, MB: Gimli Chapter Icelandic National League of North America, 1986).
11 Weaver, *The Great Land Rush,* 178–81.
12 Ibid., 202–4.
13 Wilson, *A New Lease on Life,* 5.
14 Weaver, *The Great Land Rush,* 202–8.
15 See Winthrop Pickard Bell, *The Foreign Protestants and the Settlement of Nova Scotia: The History of a Piece of Arrested British Colonial Policy in the Eighteenth Century* (Fredericton: Acadiensis Press, 1990).

16 See Edward Gibbon Wakefield, *A View of the Art of Colonization in Present Reference to the British Empire; in Letters between a Statesman and a Colonist* (1849; repr., New York: A.M. Kelley, 1969).
17 Harris, *Making Native Space*, 5.
18 Gerald Friesen, *The Canadian Prairies: A History* (Toronto: University of Toronto Press, 1987), 162–63.
19 For what is still the most thorough treatment of the subject, see Chester Martin, *"Dominion Lands" Policy* (Toronto: McClelland and Stewart, 1973). For an excellent summary of the first decade, see Richtik, "The Policy Framework," 613–28.
20 As Richtik points out, the core Dominion Lands policies were put into practice before the passage of the act, under a Privy Council Order of 25 April 1871. See Richtik, "The Policy Framework," 616. For a more detailed history of the Dominion Lands Survey, see Don W. Thomson, *Men and Meridians: The History of Surveying and Mapping in Canada*, 3 vols. (Ottawa: Queen's Printer, 1966).
21 *Dominion Lands Act*, S.C. 1872, 35 Vic., c. 23, s. 33. The original minimum age for claimants was twenty-one, but this was changed to eighteen in 1874.
22 Richtik, "The Policy Framework," 618–19.
23 Sarah Carter, "Aboriginal People of Canada and the British Empire," in Buckner, *Canada and the British Empire*, 208.
24 Martin, *"Dominion Lands" Policy*, 227–28. The amounts of acreage in this discussion are taken from Martin.
25 Martin's detailed accounting of land distribution under the Dominion Lands system did not include these reserves, possibly because he anticipated that they would be dealt with in the projected third volume of the Canadian Frontiers of Settlement series, D.A. McArthur and W.A. Carrothers, *History of Immigration Policy and Company Colonization*, which unfortunately never materialized.
26 Rasporich, "Utopian Ideals," 372–73.
27 See Eyford, "Icelandic Migration to Canada," 118–46.
28 Minutes of the Icelandic meeting at Kinmount, Ontario, 31 May 1875, LAC, RG 17, A I 1, vol. 315, docket 14103.
29 Lefebvre, *The Production of Space*, 35.
30 Macdonald, *Canada: Immigration and Colonization*, 235–36.
31 For more on the commission, see Harris, *Making Native Space*, 104–66.
32 Perry, *On the Edge of Empire*, 135.
33 G.M. Sproat to J.H. Pope, Letter 'A,' 27 March 1872, LAC, RG 17, "Immigration Branch" series (hereafter A III 2), vol. 2397.
34 Ibid.
35 Ibid.
36 *An Act respecting the Canadian Pacific Railway*, S.C. 1872, 35 Vic., c. 71; Richtik, "The Policy Framework," 623.
37 G.M. Sproat to J.H. Pope, Letter 'A,' 27 March 1872, LAC, RG 17, A III 2, vol. 2397.
38 G.M. Sproat to J.H. Pope, Letter 'C,' 1 April 1872, LAC, RG 17, A III 2, vol. 2397.
39 Ibid.
40 "Report of the Select Standing Committee on Immigration and Colonization," Canada, *Journals of the House of Commons of the Dominion of Canada*, 5th sess., 3rd Parliament, 1878, A2-20, A2–21.

41 Order-in-Council, PC 1872–0847, 18 September 1872, LAC, RG 2, A 1 a, reel C-3301, vol. 300.
42 Order-in-Council, PC 1872–0981, 16 October 1872, LAC, RG 2, A 1 a, reel C-3302, vol. 302; Order-in-Council, PC 1872–1079, 28 November 1872, LAC, RG 2, A 1 a, reel C-3302, vol. 303.
43 Order-in-Council, PC 1873–0226, 3 March 1873, LAC, RG 2, A 1 a, reel 3303, vol. 307.
44 *An Act to amend the Dominion Lands Act*, S.C. 1874, 37 Vic., c. 19, s. 14.
45 For a description of all the various colonization reserves granted in this period, see Richtik, "Manitoba Settlement," 160–69.
46 Order-in-Council, PC 1875–1052, 14 August 1874, LAC, RG 2, A 1 a, reel 3309, vol. 326.
47 Order-in-Council, PC 1875–0256, 19 March 1875, LAC, RG 2, A 1 a, reel 3311, vol. 331.
48 Order-in-Council, PC 1876–0397, 25 April 1876 LAC, RG 2, A 1 a, reel 3315, vol. 344.
49 John Lowe to R.W. Scott, Confidential Memorandum, 17 October 1876, LAC, RG 17, "Secret and Confidential Correspondence" series (hereafter A I 4), vol. 1629. For more on the efforts to recruit the HBC, see page 168.
50 "Report of the Department of the Interior for the Year Ended 30th June 1876," Canada, *Sessional Papers of the Dominion of Canada*, vol. 7, 4th sess., 3rd Parliament, 1877, no. 11, xx.
51 J.S. Dennis to the Minister of the Interior, 20 April 1877, LAC, Department of the Interior fonds, RG 15 (hereafter RG 15), "Dominion Lands Branch" series (hereafter D II 1), reel T-12320, vol. 239, file 13765.
52 See, for example, Macdonald, *Canada: Immigration and Colonization*, 197–256.
53 Lalonde, "Settlement in the North-West Territories," 43–45.
54 John Lowe to A.M. Burgess, 22 May 1882, LAC, RG 17, A I 2, reel T-119, vol. 1534, 191; John Taylor to the Minister of Agriculture, 1 January 1883, LAC, RG 17, A I 1, vol. 358, docket 38365.
55 Lalonde, "Settlement in the North-West Territories," 59–71.
56 Ibid., 258–59.
57 Reports of the Department of Agriculture, in Canada, *Sessional Papers of the Dominion of Canada*, 1883–88.
58 Morton, *History of Prairie Settlement*, 76. For more on this practice, see Chapter 7.
59 Ibid., 81.
60 Ibid., 80.
61 See D.J. Hall, "Clifford Sifton: Immigration and Settlement Policy," in *The Settlement of the West*, ed. Howard Palmer (Calgary: University of Calgary and Comprint, 1977), 60-85. For a more detailed account of Sifton's career, see D.J. Hall, *Clifford Sifton*, vol. 1, *The Young Napoleon, 1861-1900* (Vancouver: UBC Press, 1981); and D.J. Hall, *Clifford Sifton*, vol. 2, *A Lonely Eminence, 1901-1929* (Vancouver: UBC Press, 1985).
62 Order-in-Council, PC 1897–2306, 30 July 1897, LAC, RG 2, A 1 a, reel C-3658, vol. 741.
63 See Michael Ewanchuk, *Spruce, Swamp and Stone: A History of the Pioneer Ukrainian Settlements in the Gimli Area* (Winnipeg: privately printed, 1977).
64 Morton, *Manitoba: A History*, 178.
65 *Daily Free Press*, 13 June 1876.
66 Morton, *Manitoba: A History*, 159.
67 In 1876, four townships near Lake Manitoba were reserved for English and Welsh colonists, who were to be brought in by former Allan Line agent Spencer A. Jones. In 1878, land

west of the Pembina River was closed to sale and scrip application to allow close settlement by a group of Ontarians. See Richtik, "Manitoba Settlement," 160, 66; and Tyman, *By Section, Township and Range*, 85–103.
68 *Weekly Free Press*, 5 August 1876.
69 James Trow, *Manitoba and North West Territories: Letters ... Together with Information Relative to Acquiring Dominion Lands, Cost of Outfit, Etc.* (Ottawa: Department of Agriculture, 1878), 17–19.
70 "Memorial from Icelanders Tendering Thanks for the Government Loan and Making Suggestions as to Their Future Movements," March 1879, LAC, RG 17, A I 1, vol. 247, docket 25445.
71 *Weekly Free Press*, 12 August 1876.
72 *Weekly Free Press*, 29 July 1876.
73 Thomas Spence, *The Prairie Lands of Canada* (Montreal: Gazette Printing House, 1879), 47.
74 *Winnipeg Telegram*, 3 February 1899, quoted in Lehr, "The Government and the Immigrant," 45.
75 Hall, "Clifford Sifton," 77.
76 Ibid., 79–81.
77 Order-in-Council, PC 1873–0226, 3 March 1873, LAC, RG 2, A 1 a, reel 3303 vol. 307.
78 Loewen, *Family, Church and Market*, 76.
79 "Annual Report of the Surveyor General (J.S. Dennis)," Canada, *Sessional Papers of the Dominion of Canada*, vol. 7, 3rd sess., 3rd Parliament, 1876, no. 9, 5.
80 Ibid.
81 Ibid.; J.S. Dennis to the Minister of the Interior, 1 November 1875, LAC, RG 15, D II 1, reel T-12183, vol. 235, file 5088.
82 J.S. Dennis to the Minister of the Interior, 1 November 1875, LAC, RG 15, D II 1, reel T-12183, vol. 235, file 5088.
83 "Townsite of Gimli," Survey notebook, no. 607, AM, NR 0157, GR 1601.
84 Ibid.
85 "Annual Report of the Surveyor General (J.S. Dennis)," Canada, *Sessional Papers of the Dominion of Canada*, vol. 7, 3rd sess., 3rd Parliament, 1876, no. 9, 5; J.S. Dennis to the Minister of the Interior, 1 November 1875, LAC, RG 15, D II 1, reel T-12183, vol. 235, file 5088.
86 *An Act to amend the Dominion Lands Act*, S.C. 1876, 39 Vic., c. 19, s. 9.
87 *Dominion Lands Act*, S.C. 1883, 46 Vic., c. 17, s. 32.
88 Canada, *Official Debates of the House of Commons of the Dominion of Canada*, 1st sess., 5th Parliament, 1883, 880.
89 Friesen, "Saskatchewan Mennonite Settlements," 74–75.
90 University of Manitoba Archives and Special Collections (UMASC), Símon Símonarson fonds, Mss 34 (A. 80–04).
91 John Taylor to the Minister of Agriculture, 1 January 1876, LAC, RG 17, A I 1, vol. 149, docket 15525.
92 "Field Notes of Township 18 Range 4 E, N.W. Territory, Surveyed by A.H. Vaughn, D.S., Commenced 22 September 1873, Ended 2 October 1873," AM, NR 0157, GR 1601, Survey notebook no. 336.
93 AM, NR 0157, GR 1601, Survey notebooks nos. 651, 662, 663, 664. Under the Dominion Lands Survey system, townships were numbered north from the Canada-US border. The

ranges differentiated the long columns of numbered townships. Ranges were numbered east and west of the Principle Meridian, located just west of Winnipeg. Gimli is located in Township 19, Range 4 East of the Principle Meridian (abbreviated as 4E or 4EPM).
94 John Taylor to John Lowe, 8 February 1877, LAC, RG 17, A I 1, vol. 181, docket 18754.
95 J.S. Dennis to John Lowe, 25 March 1878, LAC, RG 17, A I 1, vol. 219, docket 22512.
96 For the protracted internal debate about the surveying of Big Island, see *Framfari*, 13 March 1878, 146.
97 AM, NR 0157, GR 1601, Survey notebooks nos. 4250 and 4251.
98 John Taylor to John Lowe, 19 July 1876, LAC, RG 17, A I 4, vol. 1629.
99 UMASC, Símon Símonarson fonds, Mss 34 (A. 80–04).
100 Morton, *History of Prairie Settlement*, 234.
101 For more on Icelandic naming practices, see Haraldur Bessason, "A Few Specimens of North American-Icelandic," *Scandinavian Studies* 39, 2 (1967): 115–46. Nelson Gerrard's unpublished manuscript "Örnefni í Nýja Íslandi" (1975) contains a detailed listing of all the farm names in New Iceland.
102 Sigtryggur Jónasson to John Lowe, 9 February 1877, LAC, RG 17, A I 1, vol. 178, docket 18408.
103 John Lowe to A.M. Burgess, 22 May 1882, LAC, RG 17, A I 2, reel T-119, vol. 1534, 191.
104 *Framfari*, 14 and 28 January 1878, 73–74, 83–84.
105 Böðvar Guðmundsson, *Bréf Vestur-Íslendinga* (Reykjavík: Mál og menning, 2001), 1:316.
106 Richtik, "The Policy Framework," 624–25.
107 *Framfari*, [? August], 23 September, and 14 October 1879, 30 January 1880, 648, 670–72, 690–91, 735.
108 Orders-in-Council, PC 1885–1103, 29 May 1885, reel C-3373, vol. 468; PC 1887–1072, 21 May 1887, reel C-3386, vol. 502; PC 1888–2150, 6 October 1888, reel C-3396, vol. 529; PC 1889–0007, 5 January 1889, reel C-3397, vol. 533; PC 1896–4314, 7 January 1897, reel C-3651, vol. 724, all in LAC, RG 2, A 1 a.
109 Baldwin L. Baldwinson to H.H. Smith, 11 December 1893, LAC, RG 15, D II 1, reel T-1443, vol. 698, file 344410.
110 B.L. Baldwinson, F.B. Anderson, and Jon Julius to John Lowe, 16 December 1884, LAC, RG 17, A I 1, vol. 425, docket 46378.
111 Friðjón Friðriksson to Jón Bjarnason, 11 August 1881, UMIC, Friðjón Friðriksson papers. My translation, edited by Nelson Gerrard.

CHAPTER 3: THE FIRST NEW ICELANDERS

1 John Taylor to John Lowe, 21 October 1875, LAC, RG 17, A I 1, vol. 144, docket 15091.
2 Anonymous letter, dated Gimli, 20 November 1875, reprinted in *Daily Free Press*, 17 January 1876.
3 "Report of the Select Standing Committee on Immigration and Colonization," Canada, *Journals of the House of Commons of the Dominion of Canada*, 3rd sess., 3rd Parliament, 1876, A8-3.
4 Dirk Hoerder, "From Migrants to Ethnics: Acculturation in a Societal Framework," in *European Migrants: Global and Local Perspectives*, ed. Dirk Hoerder and Leslie Page Moch (Boston: Northeastern University Press, 1996), 245.
5 See Elliott, *Irish Migrants in the Canadas*, 2nd ed.

6 Thor, *Icelanders in North America*, 80.
7 Loewen, *Family, Church and Market*, 79.
8 William Hespeler to John Lowe, 26 October 1875, LAC, RG 17, A I 1, vol. 151, docket 15749. John Taylor stated that "about thirty persons" stayed behind in Winnipeg for the winter, but from the available sources it is not possible to determine who most of them were. See John Taylor to John Lowe, 1 January 1876, LAC, RG 17, A I 1, vol. 149, docket 15525.
9 Kjartansson, "Icelandic Emigration," 113.
10 G.J. Oleson, "Gíslína Gísladóttir Olson," *Almanak Ólafur S. Thorgeirsson*, 1952, 80–85.
11 See Harriet Friedmann, "World Market, State, and Family Farm: Social Bases of Household Production in the Era of Wage Labor," *Comparative Studies in Society and History* 20, 4 (1978): 545–86; Gérard Bouchard, "Family Reproduction in New Rural Areas: Outline of a North American Model," *Canadian Historical Review* 75, 4 (1994): 475–510; and Sylvester, *The Limits of Rural Capitalism*.
12 Sandwell, *Contesting Rural Space*, 143–44.
13 There was also one individual from the western county of Snæfellsnessýsla, but he was born and raised in Dalasýsla.
14 See Table 1 in Kristinsson, *Vesturfaraskrá, 1870-1914*.
15 List Number 77, SS *St. Patrick*, 23 September, 1874, LAC, RG 76, C 1 a, reel C-4529.
16 See Eyford, "Icelandic Migration to Canada," 79–117.
17 Sigtryggur Jónasson to David Spence, 29 May 1875, Archives of Ontario (AO), Department of Immigration fonds, RG 11, 8-1, file 44476.
18 For more on the Nova Scotia settlement, see Thor, *Icelanders in North America*, 74–77.
19 These numbers account for 265 of the 285 people who travelled west in the fall of 1875. Information is lacking on the remaining 20. John Taylor to John Lowe, 18 December 1875, LAC, RG 17, A I 1, vol. 143, docket 15412. A total of thirteen people joined the party in Duluth, five of whom were probably John Taylor's brother William and his family.
20 *Austrian* passenger information is derived from Kristinsson, *Vesturfaraskrá, 1870-1914*. The numbers are North and South Þingeyjarsýsla (101), Eyjafjarðarsýsla (97), Skagafjarðarsýsla (246), Húnavatnssýsla (94), Strandasýsla (22), Barðastrandarsýsla (2), Dalasýsla (61), Snæfellsnessýsla (34), Hnappadalssýsla (16), Mýrasýsla (25), Borgarfjarðarsýsla (12), and Gullbringusýsla (12). The place of emigration is unknown for 34 of the *Austrian* group.
21 Letter from Large Group migrant Björn Andrésson to his father, 25 July 1876, translated and published in Gerrard, *Icelandic River Saga*, 30.
22 *Daily Free Press*, 6 September 1876.
23 Assistant Icelandic Agent Sigtryggur Jónasson counted individuals older than fourteen as adults. See Sigtryggur Jónasson to the Minister of Agriculture, 20 August 1876, LAC, RG 17, A I 1, vol. 166, docket 17252.
24 On women homesteaders in Canada, see Sarah Carter, "'Daughters of British Blood' or 'Hordes of Men of Alien Race': The Homesteads-for-Women Campaign in Western Canada," *Great Plains Quarterly* 29, 4 (2009): 267–86.
25 *Lögberg*, 19 July 1934.
26 "Bjarni Dalsted's [Auto]Biography," *Lögberg-Heimskringla*, 11 July 1997.
27 See Ólöf Garðarsdóttir, "The Implications of Illegitimacy in Late Nineteenth-Century Iceland: The Relationship between Infant Mortality and the Household Position of Mothers Giving Birth to Illegitimate Children," *Continuity and Change* 15, 3 (2000): 435–61.

28 Gerrard, *Icelandic River Saga,* 498–500.
29 Thorleifur Jóakimsson Jackson, *Framhald á Landnámssögu Nýja Íslands* (Winnipeg: Columbia Press, 1923), 60.
30 Magnús S. Magnússon, *Iceland in Transition: Labour and Socio-economic Change before 1940* (Lund: Ekonomisk-historiska föreningen i Lund, 1985), 57.
31 Gerrard, *Icelandic River Saga,* 346.
32 Guðmundur Jónsson, "Institutional Change in Icelandic Agriculture, 1780-1940," *Scandinavian Economic History Review* 41, 2 (1993): 109.
33 The remaining 2 percent were skilled tradesmen, paupers, and people with no specified occupation.
34 Jónsson, "Institutional Change," 103.
35 Gísli Ágúst Gunnlaugsson, *Family and Household in Iceland, 1801-1930: Studies in the Relationship between Demographic and Socio-economic Development, Social Legislation and Family and Household Structures* (Uppsala: S. Academiae Ubsaliensis, 1988), 63.
36 Ibid., 61.
37 *Heimskringla,* 15 February 1922.
38 Nelson Gerrard, *Gimlunga Saga: A History of Gimli and the Víðirnes Settlement,* vol. 1 (Arborg, MB: Saga, forthcoming).
39 Gunnlaugsson, *Family and Household in Iceland,* 36.
40 Guðmundur Jónsson and Magnús S. Magnússon, *Hagskinna: Sögulegar hagtölur um Ísland/ Icelandic Historical Statistics* (Reykjavík: Hagstofa Íslands, 1997), 49.
41 Jónsson, "Institutional Change," 103.
42 Gunnar Karlsson, *The History of Iceland* (Minneapolis: University of Minnesota Press, 2000), 277.
43 Jónsson and Magnússon, *Hagskinna,* 140.
44 Karlsson, *The History of Iceland,* 239–42.
45 Kjartansson and Heiðarsson, *Framtíð handan hafs,* 113–15.
46 *Norðanfari,* 19 April and 28 May 1873.
47 William Dixon to John Lowe, 26 April 1873, LAC, RG 17, A I 1, vol. 84, docket 8168.
48 Kjartansson, "Icelandic Emigration," 107.
49 Guðmundur Hálfdánarson, "Social Distinctions and National Unity: On Politics of Nationalism in Nineteenth-Century Iceland," *History of European Ideas* 21, 6 (1995): 774.
50 See Thor, *Icelanders in North America,* 78–94.
51 John Taylor to the Minister of Agriculture, 5 June 1875, LAC, RG 17, A I 1, vol. 315, docket 14103.
52 See Ólafsson, *Alaska;* and Pálsson, *Alaskaför Jóns Ólafssonar 1874.*
53 Walters, *Modern Sagas,* 213.
54 Friðjón Friðriksson to Jón Bjarnason, 15 June 1875, University of Manitoba Icelandic Collection (UMIC), Friðjón Friðriksson papers (my translation).
55 Friðjón Friðriksson to Jón Bjarnason, 26 July 1875, UMIC, Friðjón Friðriksson papers.
56 *Norðanfari,* 29 April 1875.
57 John Taylor to the Minister of Agriculture, 5 June 1875, LAC, RG 17, A I 1, vol. 315, docket 14103.
58 Thorleifur Jóakimsson Jackson, *Frá Austri til Vesturs: Framhald af Landnámssögu Nýja-Íslands* (Winnipeg: Columbia Press, 1921), 72.
59 See James Morton Richtik, "Mapping the Quality of Land for Agriculture in Western Canada," *Great Plains Quarterly* 5, 4 (1985): 236-48.

60 John Taylor to the Minister of Agriculture, 11 August 1875, LAC, RG 17, A I 1, vol. 140, docket 14644.
61 John Taylor to the Minister of Agriculture, 31 August 1875, LAC, RG 17, A I 1, vol. 140, docket 14663.
62 Ibid.
63 Ibid.
64 Ibid.
65 David Laird to Alexander Morris, 15 September 1875, LAC, MG 27, I D 10.
66 Minutes of the annual meeting of Icelanders' Society in America, Milwaukee, 15 August 1875, and minutes of a meeting of the Icelanders held at Gravenhurst, Ontario, 19 August 1875, included in John Taylor to John Lowe, 3 September 1875, LAC, RG 17, A I 1, vol. 140, docket 14679.
67 Order-in-Council, PC 1875–00889, 13 September 1875, LAC, RG 2, A 1 a, reel C-3313, vol. 337.
68 According to Kristinsson, *Vesturfaraskrá, 1870-1914*, there were 813 emigrants between 1870 and 1875. Among the 270 individuals in the Icelandic reserve's first group whose birthplace is known, at least 7 were infants born in North America.
69 The poor turnout in Wisconsin may have reflected a lack of means rather than a lack of enthusiasm for the project. On 15 August 1875, the Icelanders' Society in America held a meeting in Milwaukee at which it endorsed the Icelandic Deputation's report and requested that Ottawa provide subsidized transport from Milwaukee to Winnipeg. This support did not materialize. See minutes of the annual meeting of Icelanders' Society in America, Milwaukee, 15 August 1875, included in John Taylor to John Lowe, 3 September 1875, LAC, RG 17, A I 1, vol. 140, docket 14678.
70 John Taylor to the Minister of Agriculture, 5 June 1875, LAC, RG 17, A I 1, vol. 315, docket 14103.
71 See *Lögberg*, 17 January 1907.
72 Þorsteinsson, *Saga Íslendinga í Vesturheimi*, 2:166.
73 *Norðanfari*, 30 November 1875.
74 John Stafford to John Lowe, 27 July 1876, LAC, RG 17, A I 1, vol. 163, docket 16911.
75 Sigtryggur Jónasson to David Spence, 29 May 1875, AO, RG 11, 8–1, file 44476.
76 UMASC, Símon Símonarson fonds, Mss 34 (A. 80–04), translation by Wilhelm Kristjánsson.
77 Thorleifur Jóakimsson Jackson, *Brot af Landnámssögu Nýja Íslands* (Winnipeg: Columbia Press, 1919), 9.
78 Gerrard, *Icelandic River Saga*, 241.
79 John Taylor to John Lowe, 1 April 1878, LAC, RG 17, A I 1, vol. 220, docket 22684.
80 UMASC, Símon Símonarson fonds, Mss 34 (A. 80–04).
81 George Freeman, ed., *Pembina County Pioneer Daughter Biographies*, vol. 1, *Icelandic Settlements of Akra/Cavalier, Gardar, and Mountain North Dakota* (Grand Forks, ND: Laxa Press, 2007), 45.
82 Jackson, *Frá Austri til Vesturs*, 69–81.
83 Þorsteinsson, *Saga Íslendinga í Vesturheimi*, 3:255.
84 The three claimants were (with farm names and Dominion Lands legal land descriptions in parentheses) Helgi Sigurðsson (Helgasstaðir; SE 32–18–4E), Sigurður Jónsson (Fögruvellir; NE 32–18–4E), and Jóhann Vilhjalmur Jónsson (Bólstaður; SE 5–19–4E).
85 UMASC, Símon Símonarson fonds, Mss 34 (A. 80–04).
86 Friesen, *The Canadian Prairies*, 178.

CHAPTER 4: QUARANTINED WITHIN A NEW ORDER

1 James Settee's Journal, 8 September 1876 to 15 May 1877, CMSA, reel 55, CC1/O/57. The passage from 1 John 4:16 reads, "God is love; and he that dwelleth in love dwelleth in God, and God in him."
2 Jackson, *Brot af Landnámssögu Nýja Íslands*, 33.
3 Dr. J.S. Lynch to J.A.N. Provencher, 11 April 1877, in "Clandeboye Agency – Correspondence regarding an Outbreak of Smallpox among the Indians of Lake Winnipeg and the Subsequent Vaccination Campaign," LAC, RG 10, Black series, reel C-10112, vol. 3638, file 7213.
4 "Field Notes of the Village of Sandy Bar and Riverton, Township 23 Range 4 East, Keewatin, Surveyed in 1876 by George McPhillips, D.L.S.," AM, NR 0157, GR 1601, Survey notebook no. 664.
5 Jody F. Decker, "Depopulation of the Northern Plains Natives," *Social Science and Medicine* 33, 4 (1991): 381–93; Paul Hackett, *"A Very Remarkable Sickness": Epidemics in the Petit Nord, 1670-1846* (Winnipeg: University of Manitoba Press, 2002), 237–38.
6 Hackett, *"A Very Remarkable Sickness,"* 242.
7 James Daschuk, *Clearing the Plains: Disease, Politics of Starvation, and the Loss of Aboriginal Life* (Regina: University of Regina Press, 2013).
8 See Tough, *'As Their Natural Resources Fail.'*
9 See Alexander Morris, *The Treaties of Canada with the Indians of Manitoba and the North-West Territories, Including the Negotiations on Which They Were Based, and Other Information Relating Thereto* (Toronto: Belfords, Clarke, 1880), 155–57.
10 My use of the term "contact zone" follows Mary Louise Pratt, who defines it as a place where "peoples geographically and historically separated come into contact with each other and establish ongoing relations, usually involving conditions of coercion, radical inequality, and intractable conflict." See Pratt, *Imperial Eyes,* 6.
11 Arngrímsson, *Nýja Ísland;* Thor, *Icelanders in North America*.
12 In describing the Native inhabitants of the Icelandic reserve, Arngrímsson states, "The Salteaux [sic] were a peaceful people, who offered little resistance when the white man came and took their land. Like the animals they hunted, they were a semi-nomadic people, seldom settling for long in one place." Arngrímsson, *Nýja Ísland,* 194. Also see Thor, *Icelanders in North America,* 102–3.
13 Brydon, "Dreams and Claims," 164–90.
14 Perry, *On the Edge of Empire,* 19.
15 Pratt, *Imperial Eyes,* 10.
16 Alexander Morris to R.W. Scott, 21 April 1877, LAC, RG 6, A 1, vol. 28, file 536.
17 Michel Foucault, "The Politics of Health in the Eighteenth Century," in Michel Foucault, *Power/Knowledge: Selected Interviews and Other Writings, 1972-1977* (New York: Pantheon Books, 1980), 176.
18 Alison Bashford, "Medicine, Gender, and Empire," in *Gender and Empire,* ed. Philippa Levine (Oxford: Oxford University Press, 2004), 112–13.
19 Nayan Shah, *Contagious Divides: Epidemics and Race in San Francisco's Chinatown* (Berkeley: University of California Press, 2001), 3.
20 Esyllt W. Jones, "'Co-operation in All Human Endeavour': Quarantine and Immigrant Disease Vectors in the 1918–1919 Influenza Pandemic in Winnipeg," *Canadian Bulletin of Medical History* 22, 1 (2005): 58. See also Esyllt W. Jones, "Contact across a Diseased

Boundary: Urban Space and Social Interaction during Winnipeg's Influenza Epidemic, 1918-1919," *Journal of the Canadian Historical Association* 13, 1 (2002): 113–39; and Esyllt W. Jones, *Influenza 1918: Disease, Death and Struggle in Winnipeg* (Toronto: University of Toronto Press, 2007).

21 See Mary-Ellen Kelm, *Colonizing Bodies: Aboriginal Health and Healing in British Columbia, 1900-50* (Vancouver: UBC Press, 1998); Lux, *Medicine That Walks;* and Mary Jane McCallum, "The Last Frontier: Isolation and Aboriginal Health," *Canadian Bulletin of Medical History* 22, 1 (2005): 103–20.

22 Thomas, *Colonialism's Culture*, 116.

23 Alison Bashford, *Imperial Hygiene: A Critical History of Colonialism, Nationalism and Public Health* (New York: Palgrave Macmillan, 2004), 130.

24 AM, NR 0157, GR 1601, Survey notebooks nos. 651–54 and 674–78.

25 Harris, *Making Native Space*, 47.

26 Tough, 'As Their Natural Resources Fail,' 143–44.

27 See Rasporich, "Utopian Ideals," 352–77.

28 See, for example, the reports of Lord Dufferin's 1877 visit to the Icelandic reserve, in *Daily Free Press*, 17 September 1877.

29 Jackson, *Brot af Landnámssögu Nýja Íslands*, 33.

30 James Settee to CMS, 9 December 1872, CMSA, reel 55, CC1/O/57.

31 James Settee, Annual Report, 23 November 1875, CMSA, reel 55, CC1/O/57.

32 See Tough, 'As Their Natural Resources Fail,' 144–48.

33 Alexander Morris to R.W. Scott, 21 April 1877, LAC, RG 6, A 1, vol. 28, file 536.

34 "Elizabeth Fidler [sic], Claim for Loss of Houses and Improvements Occasioned by the Occupation of Icelandic Settlers," LAC, RG 15, D II 1, reel T-13113, vol. 409, file 105883.

35 John H. Ruttan to Alexander Morris, 6 April 1875, AM, Alexander Morris fonds, MG 12, B1, Correspondence series, reel M135, no. 981.

36 Ibid.

37 Egerton Ryerson Young, *By Canoe and Dog-Train among the Cree and Salteaux Indians* (London: Kelly, 1890), 168. The book places Young's visit in December 1877, but this is either a typographical or printing error as he moved to Port Perry, Ontario, in 1876. See Jennifer S.H. Brown, "Young, Egerton Ryerson," *Dictionary of Canadian Biography*, vol. 13, http://www.biographi.ca/en/bio/young_egerton_ryerson_13E.html.

38 Young, *By Canoe and Dog-Train*, 168-69.

39 Rossville Indians to Alexander Morris, 25 June 1874, AM, Alexander Morris fonds, MG 12, B1, Correspondence series, reel M135, no. 783.

40 "Norway House Agency. Correspondence regarding the Removal of Indians from Norway House to Grassy Narrows," LAC, RG 10, Black series, reel C-10107, vol. 3613, file 4060.

41 James Settee to CMS, 15 March 1875, CMSA, reel 55, CC1/O/57. Denominational rivalry may have played a role in Settee's opposition to the plan, as he may have feared Methodist encroachment in a community that was already associated with the Church of England.

42 Morris, *Treaties of Canada with the Indians*, 148. For a more detailed discussion of this case, see Winona Wheeler, "The Fur Trade, Treaty No. 5 and the Fisher River First Nation," in *Papers of the Rupert's Land Colloquium 2008*, ed. Margaret Anne Lindsay and Mallory Allyson Richard (Winnipeg: Centre for Rupert's Land Studies, 2010), 209–21.

43 John Taylor to the Minister of Agriculture, 31 August 1875, LAC, RG 17, A I 1, vol. 140, docket 14663. For more on Morris's assurance to Taylor that the Sandy Bar band would be removed, see John Taylor to John Lowe, 20 August 1876, LAC, RG 17, A I 1, vol. 166, docket 17253.

44 Þorsteinsson, *Saga Íslendinga í Vesturheimi*, 3:344–45. The quoted excerpt is my translation, edited by Ólafur Arnar Sveinsson.
45 Gerrard, *Icelandic River Saga*, 264–65.
46 I have been unable to determine whether the Big Island referred to in the name of the band was the Big Island (Mikley in Icelandic) that was part of the Icelandic reserve (now called Hecla Island) or Black Island (also called Big Black Island), which lies farther to the north and east. In the 1870s and 1880s, the names of the two islands were frequently switched on Canadian maps. See "Draft Letter of the Chief Inspector of Surveys. That the Names of Big Island and Big Black Island in Lake Winnipeg on Accompanying Map Should Be Reversed, [1884]," LAC, RG 15, D II 1, reel T-13044, vol. 324, file 77591.
47 Alexander Morris to David Laird, 8 July 1876, AM, Alexander Morris fonds, MG 12, B1, Letterbook series, reel M139, no. 352.
48 *Daily Free Press*, 23 September 1876.
49 One of these was evidently Ka-tuk-e-pin-ais himself. On 21 March 1877, health officer William Drever found the body of the "Old Chief Katuck-epinase" and three others at the Bad Throat River. See William Drever to Alexander Morris, 3 August 1877, AM, Alexander Morris fonds, MG 12, B1, Correspondence series, reel M137, no. 1517.
50 Several people who resided at Sandy Bar, including John Ramsay, did receive annuities at St. Peter's in 1875 and 1876. See Treaty Annuity Paylists, Treaties, 1, 2, 3, and 5, 1871–1876, LAC, RG 10, reel C-7135, vol. 9351, Treaty Annuity Paylists, Treaties 1, 2, 3, and 5, 1871–1876.
51 The correspondent for the *Free Press* gave the band's total number, including women and children, as forty. See *Daily Free Press*, 23 September 1876. My count, based on the 1875–79 treaty annuity records for the St. Peter's and Island (Treaty 5 Dog Head adhesion) bands, is sixty-one: eleven adult men, eleven adult women, twenty-five male children, twelve female children, and two older people of unspecified gender. It is entirely possible that not all of the sixty-one people I counted attended the Treaty 5 adhesion at Dog Head.
52 John Taylor to John Lowe, 20 August 1876, LAC, RG 17, A I 1, vol. 166, docket 17253.
53 Jackson, *Brot af Landnámssögu Nýja Íslands*, 31–37.
54 J.S. Lynch to J.A.N. Provencher, 11 April 1877, and J.A.N. Provencher to David Mills, 16 April 1877, LAC, RG 10, Black series, reel C-10112, vol. 3638, file 7213.
55 Ibid.
56 See *Daily Free Press*, 4 January 1877.
57 John Taylor to John Lowe, 22 September 1876, LAC, RG 17, A I 1, vol. 167, docket 17324.
58 Jackson, *Brot af Landnámssögu Nýja Íslands*, 32.
59 Fiddler was staying in the St. Peter's Indian Reserve at the time. She later claimed that John Taylor, Icelandic agent at Gimli, had ordered her to leave the area. See "Elizabeth Fidler [sic], Claim for Loss of Houses and Improvements Occasioned by the Occupation of Icelandic Settlers," LAC, RG 15, D II 1, reel T-13113, vol. 409, file 105883.
60 Sigtryggur Jónasson to John Lowe, 26 February 1877, LAC, RG 17, A I 1, vol. 183, docket 18913.
61 Gerrard, *Icelandic River Saga*, 219–20.
62 John Taylor to the Minister of Agriculture, 12 October 1876, LAC, RG 17, A I 1, vol. 170, docket 17669.
63 Sigtryggur Jónasson to John Lowe, 20 January 1877, LAC, RG 17, A I 1, vol. 179, docket 18595.

64 Jackson, *Brot af Landnámssögu Nýja Íslands,* 32; James Settee to CMS, 8 February 1877, CMSA, reel 55, CC1/O 57.
65 See Jón Steffensen, "Smallpox in Iceland," *Nordisk Medicinhistorisk Årsbok* 41 (1977): 41–56.
66 Hackett, *"A Very Remarkable Sickness,"* 105–6. On this epidemic, also see Jody F. Decker, "Tracing Historical Diffusion Patterns: The Case of the 1780-82 Smallpox Epidemic among the Indians of Western Canada," *Native Studies Review* 4, 1–2 (1988): 1–24.
67 Guðmundur Hálfdánarson, *Historical Dictionary of Iceland* (Lanham, MD: Scarecrow Press, 1997), 139–40; Paul Hackett, "Averting Disaster: The Hudson's Bay Company and Smallpox in Western Canada during the Late Eighteenth and Early Nineteenth Centuries," *Bulletin of the History of Medicine* 78, 3 (2004): 607–9.
68 Sigtryggur Jónasson to John Lowe, 20 January 1877, LAC, RG 17, A I 1, vol. 179, docket 18595.
69 *Daily Free Press,* 15 November 1876.
70 Drs. Young and J.S. Lynch to J.A.N. Provencher, 22 November 1876, AM, Alexander Morris fonds, MG 12, Ketcheson collection (hereafter B2), Telegram Book 3, no. 6.
71 "Report on Icelandic Colony in Keewatin (Mr. S. Jonassen [sic], Assistant Icelandic Agent)," Canada, *Sessional Papers of the Dominion of Canada,* vol. 8, 5th sess., 3rd Parliament, 1878, no. 9, 69.
72 Alexander Morris to R.W. Scott, 23 January 1877, AM, Alexander Morris fonds, MG 12, B2, Letterbook series, reel M141, no. 221.
73 See Treaty Annuity Paylists, 1875-1878, LAC, RG 10, reel C-7135, vols. 9351, 9352, 9353.
74 James Settee to CMS, 8 February 1877, CMSA, reel 55, CC1/O/57.
75 John Taylor to J.C. Taché, 15 January 1877, LAC, RG 17, A I 1, vol. 179, docket 1851; Jackson, *Framhald á Landnámssögu Nýja Íslands,* 100; Kristjanson, *The Icelandic People in Manitoba,* 67.
76 Alison Bashford, "Epidemic and Governmentality: Smallpox in Sydney, 1881," *Critical Public Health* 9, 4 (1999): 306.
77 The Council of Keewatin functioned only during the smallpox epidemic. It was never again reconstituted, leaving the Icelandic reserve under the direct authority of the lieutenant governor of Manitoba until 1881, when it was incorporated into the province. See Lewis H. Thomas, *The Struggle for Responsible Government in the North-West Territories, 1870-97,* 2nd ed. (Toronto: University of Toronto Press, 1978), 83–85.
78 See "Special Appendix A," Canada, *Sessional Papers of the Dominion of Canada,* vol. 8, 5th sess., 3rd Parliament, 1878, no. 10, xxix-xxx.
79 Alexander Morris to R.W. Scott, 28 June 1877, AM, Alexander Morris fonds, MG 12, B2, Letterbook series, reel M141, no. 264.
80 *Daily Free Press,* 23 July 1877.
81 "Special Appendix A," Canada, *Sessional Papers of the Dominion of Canada,* vol. 8, 5th sess., 3rd Parliament, 1878, no. 10, xxx.
82 Order-in-Council, PC 1877-0316, 1 May 1877, LAC, RG 2, A 1 a, reel C-3319, vol. 356.
83 David Armstrong, "Public Health Spaces and the Fabrication of Identity," *Sociology* 27, 3 (1993): 395.
84 Ibid.
85 Bashford, *Imperial Hygiene,* 11.
86 Alison Bashford and Claire Hooker, *Contagion: Historical and Cultural Studies* (London: Routledge, 2001), 39.

87 Alexander Mackenzie to Alexander Morris, 27 November 1876, and Alexander Morris to Alexander Mackenzie, 27 November 1876, AM, Alexander Morris fonds, MG 12, B2, Telegram Book 3, nos. 14 and 17.
88 *Daily Free Press,* 4 December 1876.
89 *Manitoba Herald,* 15 January 1877.
90 *Manitoba Herald,* 11 January 1877.
91 *Daily Free Press,* 22 June 1877.
92 Alexander Morris to R.W. Scott, 26 February 1877, AM, Alexander Morris fonds, MG 12, B2, Telegram Book 3, no. 59.
93 *Manitoban,* 16 September 1871.
94 Shortly after the epidemic, Provencher was embroiled in a scandal over his conduct, especially regarding his provision of supplies to the Indians. See Brian Titley, "Unsteady Debut: J.A.N. Provencher and the Beginnings of Indian Administration in Manitoba," *Prairie Forum* 22, 1 (1997): 21–46.
95 William Pennyfeather to Alexander Morris, 11 and 17 December 1876, AM, Alexander Morris fonds, MG 12, B1, Correspondence series, reel M136, nos. 1381 and 1384.
96 Dr. Willoughby Clark to J.A.N. Provencher, 1 February 1877, LAC, RG 10, Black series, reel C-10112, vol. 3638, file 7213.
97 "Friðjón Friðriksson," *Almanak Ólafur S. Thorgeirsson,* 1908, 33–35, my translation, with edits by Ólafur Arnar Sveinsson.
98 Henry Beddome to Alexander Morris, 13 April 1877, AM, Alexander Morris fonds, MG 12, B2, Correspondence series, reel M136, no. 1458.
99 C.A.P. Pelletier to Alexander Morris, 1 August 1877, included in John Taylor to the Minister of Agriculture, 5 July 1877, LAC, RG 17, A I 1, vol. 196, docket 2062.
100 John Taylor to John Lowe, 24 July 1877, LAC, RG 17, A I 1, vol. 198, docket 20421. Kristjanson, *The Icelandic People in Manitoba,* 52.
101 "Report of Icelandic Agent (Mr. John Taylor)," Canada, *Sessional Papers of the Dominion of Canada,* vol. 8, 5th sess., 3rd Parliament, 1878, no. 9, 64, 66.
102 Alexander Morris to R.W. Scott, 21 April 1877, LAC, RG 6, A 1, vol. 28, file 536.
103 Dr. W. Augustus Baldwin to Phoebe Lefoy, 13 March 1877, AM, New Iceland collection, MG 8, A 6-3.
104 John Taylor to J.C. Taché, 15 January 1877, LAC, RG 17, A I 1, vol. 179, docket 18531.
105 J.S. Lynch to Alexander Morris, 3 December 1876, AM, Alexander Morris fonds, MG 12, B1, Correspondence series, reel M136, no. 1377.
106 Sigtryggur Jónasson to John Lowe, 20 January 1877, LAC, RG 17, A I 1, vol. 179, docket 18595.
107 Sigtryggur Jónasson to John Taylor, 28 March 1877, LAC, RG 17, A I 1, vol. 187, docket 19318.
108 Henry Beddome to Alexander Morris, 13 April 1877, AM, Alexander Morris fonds, MG 12, B1, Correspondence series, reel M136, no. 1458.
109 William Drever to Alexander Morris, 3 August 1877, AM, Alexander Morris fonds, MG 12, B1, Correspondence series, reel M137, no. 1517.
110 Jackson, *Frá Austri til Vesturs,* 81.
111 J.S. Lynch to J.A.N. Provencher, 12 April 1877, and J.A.N. Provencher to Alexander Morris, 16 April 1877, AM, Alexander Morris fonds, MG 12, B1, Correspondence series, reel M136, nos. 1455 and 1461.

Notes to pages 117–23

112 Edmund A. Meredith to Alexander Morris, 13 July 1877, AM, Alexander Morris fonds, MG 12, B1, Correspondence series, reel M137, no. 1503.
113 *Heimskringla*, 23 November 1949.
114 *Framfari*, 13 March 1878, 145. Page numbers for *Framfari* are from the published English translation, Houser, *Framfari: 1877 to 1880*.
115 *Framfari*, 23 November 1878, 398.

CHAPTER 5: "PRINCIPAL PROJECTOR OF THE COLONY"

1 See Ray, *Indians in the Fur Trade*; and Sylvia Van Kirk, *"Many Tender Ties": Women in Fur-Trade Society in Western Canada, 1670-1870* (Winnipeg: Watson and Dwyer, 1980).
2 *British and Foreign Anti-Slavery Reporter*, 26 August 1840.
3 Sigtryggur Jónasson, "John Taylor og Elizabeth Taylor," *Syrpa: Mánaðarrit með myndum* 8, 4 (1920): 97–102.
4 Robert H. Schomburgk, *The History of Barbados; Comprising a Geographical and Statistical Description of the Island, a Sketch of the Historical Events since the Settlement, and an Account of Its Geology and Natural Productions* (London: Longman, Brown, Green and Longmans, 1848), 489.
5 See Chapter 4, "Filibustering, Piracy and the African Slave Trade," in W.T. Block, "A History of Jefferson County, Texas: From Wilderness to Reconstruction" (master's thesis, Lamar University, 1974), http://www.wtblock.com/wtblockjr/History%20of%20Jefferson%20County/Introduction.htm.
6 Morton, *Manitoba: A History*, 162.
7 Jónasson, "John Taylor og Elizabeth Taylor"; Wilhelm Kristjanson, "John Taylor and the Pioneer Icelandic Settlement in Manitoba and His Plea on Behalf of the Persecuted Jewish People," *Manitoba Historical Society Transactions*, 3rd ser., 32 (1975–76): 33–41.
8 See Kirsten McKenzie, *Scandal in the Colonies: Sydney and Cape Town, 1820-1850* (Melbourne: Melbourne University Press, 2004).
9 See David Lambert and Alan Lester, eds., *Colonial Lives across the British Empire: Imperial Careering in the Long Nineteenth Century* (Cambridge: Cambridge University Press, 2006), 2.
10 *Barbadian*, 1 July 1840.
11 See, for example, the reminiscences of Símon Símonarson, who was among New Iceland's first settlers. UMASC, Símon Símonarson fonds, Mss 34 (A. 80–04).
12 See Hall, *Civilising Subjects*.
13 John Taylor to the Minister of Agriculture, 31 December 1878, LAC, RG 17, A I 1, vol. 232, docket 23807.
14 On the inclusionary pretensions and exclusionary practices of British liberalism toward subject populations, see Mehta, *Liberalism and Empire*.
15 *Framfari*, 28 March 1879, 527. Page numbers for *Framfari* are from the published English translation, Houser, *Framfari: 1877 to 1880*.
16 The basic outline of Taylor's biography was given in a 1920 article written by his friend Sigtryggur Jónasson, assistant Icelandic agent. See Jónasson, "John Taylor og Elizabeth Taylor," 97–102. Additional details about the family's origins in Barbados are contained in an unpublished genealogy compiled by Mary Hearn, the wife of a descendant of one of Taylor's sisters. Ernest Wiltshire of Ottawa helped me to sketch out more of Elizabeth Mehetabel Jones's family background from his database of Barbadian planter families.

17 The National Archives, United Kingdom, (hereafter TNA), Office of Registry of Colonial Slaves and Slave Compensation Commission Records, T71, Barbados, St. Michael Parish, 1817, 1820, 1829, 1832, 1834.
18 "Accounts of Slave Compensation Claims; for the Colonies of Jamaica, Antigua, Honduras, St. Christopher's, Grenada, Dominica, Nevis, Virgin Islands, St. Lucia, British Guiana, Montserrat, Bermuda, Bahamas, Tobago, St. Vincent's, Trinidad, Barbadoes, Mauritius, Cape of Good Hope," *British Parliamentary Papers*, 1837–38, vol. 48 (215), 171.
19 *Barbadian*, 1 July 1840.
20 Pedro L.V. Welch, *Slave Society in the City: Bridgetown, Barbados, 1680-1834* (Kingston, Jamaica: Ian Randle, 2003), 69.
21 "The Humble Petition of Richard Taylor of the Parish of Saint Michael [Barbados]," TNA, CO 28/134/37, Barbados no. 61, folio 409.
22 Jónasson, "John Taylor og Elizabeth Taylor," 99. Thus far, I have been unable to determine which Nova Scotia institution Taylor attended.
23 See Chapters 4 and 5 in David Lambert, *White Creole Culture, Politics and Identity during the Age of Abolition* (Cambridge: Cambridge University Press, 2005).
24 "The Humble Petition of John Taylor, of the Island of Barbados, to the Secretary of State for These Colonies," as published in *Barbadian*, 8 July 1840.
25 *West Indian*, 6 July 1840.
26 Randolph B. Campbell, *An Empire for Slavery: The Peculiar Institution in Texas, 1821-1865* (Baton Rouge: Louisiana State University Press, 1989), 17.
27 Ibid., 23–24, 31–32.
28 Anonymous, *A Visit to Texas: Being the Journal of a Traveller through Those Parts Most Interesting to American Settlers, with a Description of Scenery, Habits, Etc.* (New York: Goodrich and Wiley, 1834), 10–11.
29 *West Indian*, 2 July 1840. Under the apprenticeship system, apprenticed labourers had the option of buying out their apprenticeship.
30 *Barbadian*, 4 July 1840.
31 "The Humble Petition of John Taylor, of the Island of Barbados, to the Secretary of State for These Colonies," as published in *Barbadian*, 8 July 1840. It is unclear which law Taylor was referring to. Under the 1806 Foreign Slave Trade Abolition Act (46 Geo. III, c. 52), it was permissible for British subjects to move slaves from one British West Indian island to another provided that they obtained permission from the Office of the Governor in the colony from which they embarked. However, the 1833 Slave Emancipation Act (3 & 4 Will. IV, c. 73) stipulated that former slaves could not be moved from one colony to another.
32 *Barbadian*, 1 July 1840.
33 Ibid.
34 Fred Lee McGhee, "The Black Crop: Slavery and Slave Trading in Nineteenth Century Texas" (PhD diss., University of Texas at Austin, 2000), 110.
35 "The Humble Petition of John Taylor, of the Island of Barbados, to the Secretary of State for These Colonies," as published in *West Indian*, 6 July 1840. On the Sabine Pass and slave trading, see Block, Chapter 4: "Filibustering, Piracy and the African Slave Trade," in "A History of Jefferson County."
36 Campbell, *An Empire for Slavery*, 42.
37 Ibid., 45.
38 *West Indian*, 9 July 1840.
39 TNA, CO 28/128/58, Barbados no. 110, folio 299.

40 Quoted in Campbell, *An Empire for Slavery*, 45.
41 *Barbadian*, 1 July 1840.
42 "The Humble Petition of John Taylor, of the Island of Barbados, to the Secretary of State for These Colonies," 15 April 1837, as published in *Barbadian*, 8 July 1840.
43 *West Indian*, 6 July 1840.
44 *Liberal*, 26 October 1839.
45 TNA, CO 28/127/12, Barbados no. 10, folios 103–4.
46 *West Indian*, 6 July 1840.
47 *Barbadian*, 1 July 1840.
48 TNA, CO 28/128/58, Barbados no. 110, folio 291.
49 TNA, CO 28/143/69, Barbados no. 33, folios 298–317.
50 *Barbadian*, 1 July 1840.
51 Ibid.
52 *Barbadian*, 8 July 1840.
53 *Liberal*, 15 July 1840.
54 TNA, CO 28/134/47, Barbados no. 72, folios 450–59.
55 TNA, CO 28/135/26, Barbados no. 99, folios 193–96.
56 Schomburgk, *The History of Barbados*, 138.
57 TNA, CO 28/156/13, Barbados no. 8, folios 126–37.
58 TNA, CO 28/160, folio 352.
59 John Taylor, n.d., John Taylor manuscript collection in the possession of the family of the late Donna Skardal, Baldur, Manitoba (hereafter Skardal Mss).
60 Ibid.
61 NA, CO 28/134/47 no. 72, folio 455.
62 See Philip Doddridge, *The Rise and Progress of Religion in the Soul: Illustrated in a Course of Serious and Practical Addresses, Suited to Persons of Every Character and Circumstance: With a Devout Meditation, or Prayer, Subjoined to Each Chapter* (1745; repr., Grand Rapids: Baker Book House, 1977).
63 John Taylor, untitled document dated London, 3 June 1844, Skardal Mss.
64 Her father, George H. Haines, was a founder of the Kingston Baptist Church. See *Register*, 2 February 1842.
65 Jónasson, "John Taylor og Elizabeth Taylor," 99, 102. For more on Taylor's nieces, see Ryan C. Eyford, "'Close Together, Though Miles and Miles Apart': Family, Distance, and Emotion in the Letters of the Taylor Sisters, 1881–1921," *Histoire sociale/Social History* 47, 96 (2015): 67–86.
66 Jónasson, "John Taylor og Elizabeth Taylor." Icelandic Canadian sources usually refer to the organization with which John Taylor was affiliated as the "British-Canadian Bible Society." I have been unable to find any organization of that name. However, the Upper Canada Bible Society, a branch of the British and Foreign Bible Society, was providing grants in support of "colportage among the shantymen in the lumbercamps" during this period. See Edward C. Woodley, *The Bible in Canada* (Toronto: J.M. Dent, 1953), 87.
67 Leopolda z Lobkowicz Dobrzensky, *Fragments of a Dream: Pioneering in Dysart Township and Haliburton Village* (Haliburton, ON: Municipality of Dysart, 1985), 229.
68 Extracts from the lost diary of Caroline (née Taylor) Christopherson in the possession of Bob Christopherson, Edmonton, Alberta. Bob's mother, Laura (née Anderson) Christopherson, made notes from the original diary, which was then owned by Caroline's daughter Sigurveig Dawe. See also *Daily Witness*, 8 April 1875.

69 *Daily Witness,* 8 April 1875.
70 John Taylor to the Minister of Agriculture, 5 June 1875, LAC, RG 17, A I 1, vol. 315, docket 14103.
71 John Taylor's principal contacts in Ottawa were probably John Bertram and James Hall, the Liberal MPs for Peterborough East and West. In September 1875, both men wrote the minister of agriculture, enthusiastically supporting Taylor's appointment as Icelandic agent. See LAC, RG 17, A I 1, vol. 140, dockets 14686 and 14688. Taylor may have had other contacts in cabinet or the upper echelons of the civil service; Wilhelm Kristjanson claims that Taylor had attended university with the "Minister of Immigration." Kristjanson, "John Taylor," 35. However, there was no minister of immigration during this period, as responsibility for immigration fell under the Agriculture portfolio. In 1875, the agriculture minister was Luc Letellier de St. Just, and the deputy minister was J.C. Taché, both francophones with whom Taylor would probably not have attended school. It is more likely that his upper-level contact was John Lowe, secretary of the department.
72 Mary Hearn, "The Hearn Family Story" (typescript, Clinton, ON, n.d.).
73 UMASC, Símon Símonarson fonds, Mss 34 (A. 80–04).
74 Ibid.
75 Macdonald, *Canada: Immigration and Colonization,* 40.
76 John Lowe to John Taylor, 15 September 1875, LAC, RG 17, A I 2, vol. 1513, 3.
77 For the smallpox epidemic, see Chapter 4; and Eyford, "Quarantined within a New Colonial Order," 57–78.
78 See Þór, "A Religious Controversy."
79 John Taylor to the Minister of Agriculture, 31 December 1878, LAC, RG 17, A I 1, vol. 232, docket 23807.
80 *Daily Free Press,* 3 August 1875.
81 Þorsteinsson, *Saga Íslendinga í Vesturheimi,* 2:336; Lindal, *The Icelanders in Canada,* 115. The Bible verse was Exodus 23:20.
82 Þorsteinsson, *Saga Íslendinga í Vesturheimi,* 2:336.
83 UMASC, Símon Símonarson fonds, Mss 34 (A. 80–04).
84 Ólafur Ólafsson from Espihóll to the Reverend Jón Bjarnason, 13 January 1876, Landsbókasafn Íslands (National and University Library of Iceland, hereafter Lbs.) Lbs. 4390, 4to., Bréfasafn séra Jóns Bjarnasonar í Winnipeg (Letter collection of the Reverend Jón Bjarnason in Winnipeg) (hereafter Lbs. 4390, 4to.).
85 John Taylor to Halldór Briem, 3 September 1883, Lbs. 34 NF, Bréfasafn Halldórs and Susie Briem (Halldór and Susie Briem letter collection) (hereafter Lbs. 34 NF).
86 Alexander Morris to Edward Blake, 5 November 1875, AM, Alexander Morris fonds, MG 12, B1, Letterbook series, reel M139, no. 306.
87 *Framfari,* 14 May 1879, 569.
88 Jónasson, "John Taylor og Elizabeth Taylor," 102.
89 See Hall, *Civilising Subjects,* 120–39.
90 John Taylor to the Minister of Agriculture, 1 January 1883, LAC, RG 17, A I 1, vol. 358, docket 38365.
91 John Taylor to Alexander Morris, 14 October 1875, AM, Alexander Morris fonds, MG 12, B1, Correspondence series, reel M139, no. 1133.
92 John Taylor to Alexander Morris, 30 October 1875, AM, Alexander Morris fonds, MG 12, B1, Correspondence series, reel M136, no. 1147.

93 Ólafur Ólafsson from Espihóll to the Reverend Jón Bjarnason, 13 January 1876, Lbs. 4390, 4to.
94 John Taylor to John Lowe, 28 November 1876, LAC, RG 17, A I 1, vol. 173, docket 17911.
95 On the role of Indian agents, see Carter, *Lost Harvests;* Robin Jarvis Brownlie, *A Fatherly Eye: Indian Agents, Government Power, and Aboriginal Resistance in Ontario, 1918-1939* (Don Mills: Oxford University Press, 2003).
96 John Taylor to John Lowe, 14 April 1879, LAC, RG 17, A I 4, vol. 1629.
97 John Taylor to the Minister of Agriculture, 31 December 1878, LAC, RG 17, A I 1, vol. 232, docket 23807.
98 Jackson, *Framhald á Landnámssögu Nýja Íslands,* 102.
99 John Taylor to Alexander Morris, 3 August 1875, AM, Alexander Morris fonds, MG 12, B1, Correspondence series, reel M136, no. 1066.
100 "Elizabeth Fidler, Claim for Loss of Houses and Improvements Occasioned by the Occupation of Icelandic Settlers," LAC, RG 15, D II 1, reel T-13113, vol. 409, file 105883.
101 John Taylor to James F. Graham, 15 March 1880, in "Clandeboye Agency - Claim to Land along the White Mud River by John Ramsay of St. Peter's Band," LAC, RG 10, Black series, reel C-10113, vol. 3649, file 8200.
102 "Memorial from Icelanders Tendering Thanks for the Government Loan and Making Suggestions as to Their Future Movements," March 1879, LAC, RG 17, A I 1, vol. 247, docket 25445.
103 Alexander Morris to R.W. Scott, 28 June 1877, AM, Alexander Morris fonds, MG 12, B2, Letterbook series, reel M141, no. 264.
104 John Lowe to John Taylor, 2 May 1877, LAC, RG 17, A I 6, reel T-132, vol. 1633, 217.
105 Ibid.
106 John Taylor to John Lowe, 14 April 1879, LAC, RG 17, A I 4, vol. 1629.
107 John Lowe to John Taylor, 5 June 1876, LAC, RG 17, "John Lowe's Secret and Confidential Letterbook" series (hereafter A I 5), reel T-131, vol. 1631, 92–93.
108 John Taylor to John Lowe, 13 July 1876, LAC, RG 17, A I 4, vol. 1629.
109 *Framfari,* 14 May 1879, 565–66.
110 Indenture contract between John Taylor and Everett Parsonage, 18 September 1875, New Iceland Heritage Museum, Gimli, MB.
111 Hilary Beckles, *A History of Barbados: From Amerindian Settlement to Nation-State* (Cambridge: Cambridge University Press, 1990), 109.
112 John Taylor to the Acting Lt. Governor of Keewatin, 17 May 1879, enclosed in J.S. Dennis to John Lowe, 11 July 1879, LAC, RG 17, A I 1, vol. 253, docket 26095.
113 John Taylor to John Lowe, 9 June 1879, LAC, John Lowe fonds, MG 29, E 18, vol. 19.
114 *Framfari,* 28 March 1879, 527.
115 *Framfari,* 17 July 1879, 626.
116 John Taylor to John Lowe, 28 February 1881, LAC, RG 17, A I 4, vol. 1629.
117 John Taylor to John Lowe, 5 September 1883, LAC, RG 17, A I 1, vol. 381, docket 41056; John Lowe to John Taylor, 29 May 1884, LAC, RG 17, A I 6, reel T-139, vol. 1642, 346.
118 Friðjón Friðriksson to Rev. Jón Bjarnason, 19 December 1880, UMIC, Friðjón Friðriksson papers. Typescripts in English translation are available at the Archives of Manitoba. See AM, New Iceland collection, MG 8, A 6–7.
119 John Taylor to John Lowe, 28 February 1881, LAC, RG 17, A I 4, vol. 1629.
120 John Taylor to Lord Lorne, 15 February 1882, LAC, Sir John A. Macdonald fonds, MG 26, A., reel C-4814, vol. 82, 31998–99.

121 John Taylor to Halldór Briem, 30 December 1883, Lbs. 34 NF.
122 John Taylor to Susie Briem, 17 February 1884, Lbs. 34 NF.
123 John Taylor to Halldór Briem, 21 April 1884, Lbs. 34 NF.
124 John Lowe to John Taylor, 18 July 1884, LAC, RG 17, A I 6, reel T-139, vol. 1642, 733.
125 Elizabeth Taylor to John Lowe, 20 August 1884, LAC, RG 17, A I 1, vol. 414, docket 45095.
126 Jónasson, "John Taylor og Elizabeth Taylor," 102.
127 *Framfari*, 14 May 1879, 569.
128 UMASC, Símon Símonarson fonds, Mss 34 (A. 80–04).
129 Friðjón Friðriksson to Rev. Jón Bjarnason, 19 December 1880, UMIC, Friðjón Friðriksson papers.
130 Jónasson, "John Taylor og Elizabeth Taylor," 102.
131 B.L. Baldwinson to A.M. Burgess, 12 December 1893, LAC, RG 76, I A 1, reel C-4680, vol. 22, file 389, part 2. These remarks were made in the context of Baldwinson's request to have his salary as Icelandic agent increased to $1,000 per year. He pointed out that Taylor had received $1,200 annually almost twenty years earlier.
132 Kristjanson, "John Taylor," 41.

Chapter 6: Becoming British Subjects

1 Arnason, "The Icelanders in Manitoba," 6–7. See also *Lögberg-Heimskringla*, 1 December 2000.
2 For the complete regulations that governed New Iceland's councils, see Walter J. Lindal, "The Laws and Regulations of New Iceland," *Icelandic Canadian* 50, 4 (1992): 210–22.
3 See, for example, Guðlaugur Magnússon, "Landnám Íslendinga í Nýja Íslandi," *Almanak Ólafur S. Thorgeirsson*, 1899, 35–38.
4 Sigtryggur Jónasson to John Taylor, 10 March 1877, enclosed in John Taylor to John Lowe, 31 March 1877, LAC, RG 17, A I 1, vol. 187, docket 19318.
5 See Þorsteinsson, *Saga Íslendinga í Vesturheimi*, 3:71–78; Kristjanson, *The Icelandic People in Manitoba*, 54–58; Lindal, *The Icelanders in Canada*, 138–50; Gerrard, *Icelandic River Saga*, 25; Arngrímsson, *Nýja Ísland*, 185–91; and Thor, *Icelanders in North America*, 107–9.
6 See S.J. Sommerville, "Icelanders in Canada," *Canadian Geographical Journal* 21, 4 (1940): 192–201; S.J. Sommerville, "The Twelve-Year Republic," *Icelandic Canadian* 3, 4 (1945): 5–7; and S.J. Sommerville, "Early Icelandic Settlements in Canada," *Papers Read before the Historical and Scientific Society of Manitoba, 1944-45* (1945): 25–43.
7 Morton, *Manitoba: A History*, 177.
8 Friesen, *The Canadian Prairies*, 261; Arnason, "The Icelanders in Manitoba"; Brydon, "Icelanders," 688.
9 In this respect, New Iceland's government was similar to the Council of Manitoba, a local administration created by the settlers of Portage la Prairie in the 1850s to address the shortcomings of Hudson's Bay Company rule. See *Globe*, 19 February 1869. In 1867–68, the Canadian settler Thomas Spence attempted to get recognition for the council but was informed by the Colonial Office that this was a non-legal body. See Morton, *Manitoba: A History*, 113–14.
10 Canada, *House of Commons Debates* (26 March 1878), 1398.
11 Michèle Dagenais, "The Municipal Territory: A Product of the Liberal Order?" in Constant and Ducharme, *Liberalism and Hegemony*, 202.
12 Thomas, *The Struggle for Responsible Government*, 85.

13 See Greer and Radforth, *Colonial Leviathan*, 10–11.
14 Curtis, *True Government by Choice Men?* 6.
15 Ian Radforth, "Sydenham and Utilitarian Reform," in Greer and Radforth, *Colonial Leviathan*, 84.
16 See ibid.
17 John Stuart Mill, *Considerations on Representative Government* (London: Parker, Son, and Bourn, 1861), 268.
18 Curtis, *True Government by Choice Men?* 10.
19 Dagenais, "The Municipal Territory," 207–8.
20 Bantjes, *Improved Earth*, 65–69.
21 Ibid., 89.
22 Ibid., 32.
23 John Taylor to John Lowe, 8 February 1877, LAC, RG 17, A I 1, vol. 180, docket 18671.
24 John Lowe to John Taylor, 2 May 1877, LAC, RG 17, A I 6, reel T-132, vol. 1633, 217.
25 See *An Act for the Temporary Government of Rupert's Land and the North-Western Territory when united with Canada*, S.C. 1869, 32–33 Vic., c. 3, and amendment in S.C. 1873, 36 Vic., c. 5; *An Act to make further provision for the Government of the North-West Territories*, S.C. 1871, 34 Vic., c. 16, and amendment in S.C. 1873, 36 Vic., c. 5; and Thomas, *The Struggle for Responsible Government*, 71.
26 See Thomas Michael Reynolds, "Justices of the Peace in the Northwest Territories, 1870-1905" (master's thesis, University of Regina, 1978).
27 John Taylor to Alexander Morris, 14 October 1875, AM, Alexander Morris fonds, MG 12, B1, Correspondence series, reel M136, no. 1133.
28 John Taylor to the Minister of Agriculture, 1 January 1877, LAC, RG 17, A I 1, vol. 179, docket 18518.
29 The other members of the bæjarnefnd were Jakob J. Jónsson and Jóhannes Magnússon. See Ólafur Ólafson from Espihóll to the Reverend Jón Bjarnason, 13 January 1876, Lbs. 4390, 4to.
30 John Taylor to John Lowe, 9 February 1876, LAC, RG 17, A I 1, vol. 151, docket 15109.
31 *Framfari*, 10 December 1877, 47. Page numbers for *Framfari* are from the published English translation, Houser, *Framfari: 1877 to 1880*.
32 John Taylor to John Lowe, 28 November 1876, LAC, RG 17, A I 1, vol. 173, docket 17911; John Taylor to John Lowe, 8 February 1877, LAC, RG 17, A I 1, vol. 180, docket 18671.
33 *An Act to amend and consolidate the laws respecting the North-West Territories*, S.C. 1875, 38 Vic., c. 49, s. 13.
34 The five were John Taylor, his brother William Taylor, his indentured servant Everett Parsonage, Edward Smith, a Canadian who had settled near Willow Point just prior to the creation of the reserve, and James Thomas Halcrow, an employee of Robert Fuller's sawmill on Big Island who homesteaded on the island after the mill closed.
35 *An Act respecting the North-West Territories, and to create a separate Territory out of part thereof*, S.C. 1876, 39 Vic., c. 21.
36 Canada, *House of Commons Debates* (17 February 1876), 86 and 195.
37 Sigtryggur Jónasson to John Lowe, 9 February 1877, LAC, RG 17, A I 1, vol. 178, docket 18408.
38 *Framfari*, 10 December 1877, 47.
39 *Framfari*, 22 December 1877, 57–58.
40 *Framfari*, 22 December 1877, 59.

41 *Framfari*, 14 January 1878, 77–81.
42 Sommerville, "Early Icelandic Settlements," 29–31.
43 This is consistent with the work of Walter Lindal and Professor Skuli Johnson. Lindal translated the word as "laws and regulations." Lindal, "The Laws and Regulations of New Iceland," 220. Johnson opted for "governmental regulations." See Sommerville, "Early Icelandic Settlements," 38–43.
44 *British North America Act*, 1867, c. 3, s. 92.
45 Murray S. Donnelly, *The Government of Manitoba* (Toronto: University of Toronto Press, 1963), 135. See also Gordon Goldsborough, *With One Voice: A History of Municipal Governance in Manitoba* (Portage la Prairie, MB: Association of Manitoba Municipalities, 2008), 6–7.
46 *An Act to amend and consolidate the laws respecting the North-West Territories*, S.C. 1875, 38 Vic., c. 49, s. 13.
47 "Lakething" was the translation that Sigtryggur Jónasson provided for Vatnsþing. Sigtryggur Jónasson to John Taylor, 10 March 1877, LAC, RG 17, A I 1, vol. 187, docket 19318. Walter Lindal translated Vatnsþing as "Lake District," which also accurately captures Jónasson's meaning. Lindal's assertion that "thing" in this context did not mean parliament or assembly, but rather a territorial division is confirmed by Jónasson's description of the colony government as "The Council *for* Lakething." See Lindal, "The Laws and Regulations of New Iceland," 220.
48 See Lindal, "The Laws and Regulations of New Iceland."
49 Karlsson, *The History of Iceland*, 261–65.
50 See Tables 2.1 and 2.2, on voting rights by province between 1867 and 1885, in Elections Canada, *A History of the Vote in Canada*, 2nd ed. (Ottawa: Office of the Chief Electoral Officer of Canada, 2007), 46–47.
51 Text from the Skuli Johnson translation, in Sommerville, "Early Icelandic Settlements," 38. Clergymen and resident schoolteachers were denied the right to vote.
52 On this issue in Iceland, see Guðmundur Hálfdánarson, "To Become a Man: The Ambiguities of Gender Relations in Late 19th and Early 20th Century Iceland," in *Political Systems and Definitions of Gender Roles*, ed. Ann-Katherine Isaacs (Pisa: Edizioni Plus, 2001), 44.
53 *Stjórnarlög Nýja Íslands*, IV kafli, 2 gr., *Framfari*, 14 January 1878, 78. In this instance and others referring to the published *Stjórnarlög Nýja Íslands*, I have consulted the original Icelandic version of *Framfari* in addition to Houser's translation.
54 I had hoped to solve this problem by examining the records from Árnesbyggð (River Point Settlement), the only New Iceland municipality for which a relatively complete set of records exists. The originals of these important documents are still in private hands, but Nelson Gerrard kindly permitted me access to his copies. Although the local census records indicate that there were two women-headed households in Árnesbyggð, I could not determine whether the women voted. Their participation would have been confirmed only if 100 percent of the Árnesbyggð electorate had voted. In fact, only a small portion did so.
55 Hálfdánarson, "To Become a Man," 46–47.
56 Catherine Lyle Cleverdon, *The Woman Suffrage Movement in Canada* ([Toronto]: University of Toronto Press, 1950), 22.
57 See Hálfdánarson, "Social Distinctions and National Unity," 763–79.
58 Karlsson, *The History of Iceland*, 261–65.
59 Gerrard, *Icelandic River Saga*, 210.

60 Sigtryggur Jónasson to John Lowe, 9 February 1877, LAC, RG 17, A I 1, vol. 178, docket 18408.
61 For an account of its development, see J.H. Aitchison, "The Municipal Corporations Act of 1849," *Canadian Historical Review* 30, 2 (1949): 107–22. Interestingly, as New Iceland's municipal regulations were being crafted, Baldwin's nephew Dr. William Augustus Baldwin was in the Icelandic reserve, serving as a medical officer for the Keewatin Board of Health (see pages 110, 115).
62 Sigtryggur Jónasson to John Taylor, 10 March 1877, LAC, RG 17, A I 1, vol. 187, docket 19318; also see *Framfari,* 14 January 1878, 77; and Lindal, "The Laws and Regulations of New Iceland," 211.
63 J.M. McEvoy, *The Ontario Township,* ed. W.J. Ashley (Toronto: Warwick and Sons, 1889), 11.
64 *An Act to divide the Province of Manitoba into Counties,* 1877, 40 Vic., c. 3.
65 McEvoy, *The Ontario Township,* 26–28, 40.
66 In general, the translations of terms from the *Stjórnarlög Nýja Íslands* used here are from Sigtryggur Jónasson's March 1877 description of the system. See Sigtryggur Jónasson to John Taylor, 10 March 1877, LAC, RG 17, A I 1, vol. 187, docket 19318. This document was not available to previous translators, including Walter Lindal. There are some differences between Jónasson and Lindal's translations of the terminology in the *Stjórnarlög Nýja Íslands;* Jónasson uses "foreman" rather than "reeve" to describe the head of the settlement committees. He also translates Vatnsþing as "Lakething," which is less precise than Lindal's "Lake District." See Lindal, "The Laws and Regulations of New Iceland," 220.
67 Lindal, "The Laws and Regulations of New Iceland," 214–17; Sigtryggur Jónasson to John Taylor, 10 March 1877, enclosed in John Taylor to John Lowe, 31 March 1877, LAC, RG 17, A I 1, vol. 187, docket 19318; *Framfari,* 14 January 1878, 77–80.
68 John Taylor to John Lowe, 20 May 1879, LAC, RG 17, A I 1, vol. 250, docket 25759.
69 See *Stjórnarlög Nýja Íslands,* VI kafli, *Framfari,* 14 January 1878, 78; and Lindal, "The Laws and Regulations of New Iceland," 213–14.
70 McEvoy, *The Ontario Township,* 39.
71 John Taylor to Alexander Morris, 10 January 1876, AM, Alexander Morris fonds, MG 12, B1, Correspondence series, reel M136, no. 1191; David Laird to Alexander Morris, 8 March 1876, AM, Alexander Morris fonds, MG 12, B1, Correspondence series, reel M136, no. 1230.
72 Sigtryggur Jónasson to John Taylor, 10 March 1877, enclosed in John Taylor to John Lowe, 31 March 1877, LAC, RG 17, A I 1, vol. 187, docket 19318.
73 *An Act respecting the North-West Territories, and to create a separate Territory out of part thereof,* S.C. 1876, 39 Vic., c. 21, ss. 7 and 12.
74 Sigtryggur Jónasson to John Taylor, 10 March 1877, enclosed in John Taylor to John Lowe, 31 March 1877, LAC, RG 17, A I 1, vol. 187, docket 19318.
75 *Stjórnarlög Nýja Íslands,* IX kafli, *Framfari,* 14 January 1878, 79–80.
76 *Stjórnarlög Nýja Íslands,* XIII kafli, 4 gr., *Framfari,* 14 January 1878, 80.
77 *Stjórnarlög Nýja Íslands,* XIII kafli, 1 gr., *Framfari,* 14 January 1878, 80; Lindal, "The Laws and Regulations of New Iceland," 217–18.
78 Sigtryggur Jónasson to John Taylor, 10 March 1877, enclosed in John Taylor to John Lowe, 31 March 1877, LAC, RG 17, A I 1, vol. 187, docket 19318. More documents from the council may have been transmitted to the Department of the Interior, but their whereabouts are unknown.

79 McEvoy, *The Ontario Township*, 32–35.
80 *Stjórnarlög Nýja Íslands*, X and XII kaflar, *Framfari*, 14 January 1878, 80.
81 *Stjórnarlög Nýja Íslands*, XVI kafli, *Framfari*, 14 January 1878, 81.
82 See, for example, "Abstract of Statistics for the Icelandic Colony for 1879, furnished by Fr. Fredrikssson [sic], County Warden," in John Taylor to John Lowe, 9 February 1880, LAC, RG 17, A I 1, vol. 272, docket 28126.
83 *Framfari*, 10 December 1877, 49.
84 *Stjórnarlög Nýja Íslands*, IV kafli, 7 gr., *Framfari*, 14 January 1878, 78.
85 Sigtryggur Jónasson to John Taylor, 10 March 1877, enclosed in John Taylor to John Lowe, 31 March 1877, LAC, RG 17, A I 1, vol. 187, docket 19318.
86 Ibid.
87 David Mills to John Taylor, 8 November 1877, University of Western Ontario, Archives and Research Collection Centre, David Mills papers, reel M-1241, vol. 2, 342.
88 Unfortunately, the documents forwarded to the Department of the Interior by the Department of Agriculture on this issue (John Taylor to John Lowe, 10 January 1877, LAC, RG 17, A I 1, vol. 202, docket 20830) have since been lost.
89 Donald John Arnold McMurchy, "David Mills: Nineteenth Century Canadian Liberal" (PhD diss., University of Rochester, 1968), 38; Thomas, *The Struggle for Responsible Government*, 8.
90 Canada, *House of Commons Debates* (22 March 1878), 1386.
91 Ibid.
92 *An Act to amend the Dominion Lands Act*, S.C. 1874, 37 Vic., c. 19, s. 8(3).
93 "Bill No. 23 An Act to establish Township Municipalities in the District of Keewatin," Canada, *Bills of the House of Commons, 1878, 5th Session, 3rd Parliament*, 1–33.
94 Canada, *House of Commons Debates* (22 March 1878), 1393.
95 John Lowe to John Taylor, 8 April 1878, LAC, RG 17, A I 6, reel T-134, vol. 1634, 36.
96 It was probably part of the missing Department of the Interior file on the Icelandic reserve.
97 Canada, *House of Commons Debates* (22 March 1878), 1389.
98 Canada, *House of Commons Debates* (26 March 1878), 1398.
99 *Framfari*, 24 January 1880, 729, contains an account of the 1880 elections. The minutes for the Árnes settlement committee end in 1880. Other settlement committees, such as the one for River settlement, may have lasted longer, but unfortunately their records do not survive.
100 *An Act to amend and consolidate the Acts relating to the Division of the Province of Manitoba into Counties and Municipalities, and Judicial Districts, and for the government of the same*, 1883, 46 and 47 Vic., c. 1; *Winnipeg Daily Sun*, 14 June 1883; Magnússon, "Landnám Íslendinga í Nýja Íslandi," 37.
101 See Donnelly, *The Government of Manitoba*, 135–37.
102 Canada, *House of Commons Debates* (26 March 1878), 1393.
103 Thomas, *The Struggle for Responsible Government*, 82–83, 87.
104 Sigtryggur Jónasson to John Taylor, 28 March 1877, enclosed in John Taylor to John Lowe, 31 March 1877, LAC, RG 17, A I 1, vol. 187, docket 19318.
105 *Framfari*, 16 July 1878, 299.
106 *Framfari*, 10 December 1877, 59.

Chapter 7: "Freemen Serving No Overlord"

1 *Daily Free Press*, 17 September 1877, 2.
2 Jackson, *Framhald á Landnámssögu Nýja Íslands*, 26.
3 See Arnason and Arnason, *The New Icelanders*, 3–8.
4 UMASC, Símon Símonarson fonds, Mss 34 (A. 80–04), translation by Wilhelm Kristjanson.
5 An Act to amend the Dominion Lands Act, S.C. 1874, 37 Vic., c. 19, s. 14 and s. 15. See Canada, *Dominion Lands Act, Consolidated, May 1876* (Ottawa: Queen's Printer, 1876), 46.
6 *Framfari*, 28 March 1879, 527. Page numbers for *Framfari* refer to the published translation, Houser, *Framfari: 1877 to 1880*.
7 Magnússon, "Landnám Íslendinga í Nýja Íslandi," 30–31.
8 Order-in-Council, PC 1875–0889, 13 September 1875, LAC, RG 2, A 1 a, reel C-3313, vol. 337.
9 Macdonald, *Canada: Immigration and Colonization*, 90–91.
10 See A.I. Silver, "French Canada and the Prairie Frontier, 1870-1890," *Canadian Historical Review* 50, 1 (1969): 11–36; Robert Painchaud, "The Catholic Church and the Movement of Francophones to the Canadian Prairies, 1870-1915" (PhD diss., University of Ottawa, 1976); and Sylvester, *The Limits of Rural Capitalism*, 13–14.
11 John Lowe to R.W. Scott, 8 August 1876, LAC, RG 17, "Reports and Memoranda" series (hereafter A I 13), reel T-1011, vol. 1976, 363.
12 Frank H. Epp, *Mennonites in Canada, 1786-1920: The History of a Separate People* (Toronto: Macmillan of Canada, 1974), 201.
13 John Lowe to R.W. Scott, 27 July 1876, LAC, RG 17, A I 13, reel T-1011, vol. 1976, 250.
14 Confidential Memorandum, John Lowe to R.W. Scott, 17 October 1876, LAC, RG 17, A I 4, vol. 1629.
15 Epp, *Mennonites in Canada*, 226.
16 Confidential Memorandum, John Lowe to R.W. Scott, 17 October 1876, LAC, RG 17, A I 4, vol. 1629.
17 John Taylor to J.A. Grahame, 3 September 1875, LAC, RG 17, A I 4, vol. 1629.
18 J.H. McTavish to the Minister of Agriculture, 14 September 1875, LAC, RG 17, A I 4, vol. 1629.
19 Confidential Memorandum, John Lowe to R.W. Scott, 17 October 1876, LAC, RG 17, A I 4, vol. 1629.
20 John Lowe to John Taylor, 15 September 1875, LAC, RG 17, A I 2, vol. 1513, 3.
21 Order-in-Council, PC 1875–0976, 8 October 1875, LAC, RG 2, A 1 a, reel C-3313, vol. 338.
22 D.A. Smith to John Lowe, 18 January 1876, enclosed in Confidential Memorandum, John Lowe to R.W. Scott, 17 October 1876, LAC, RG 17, A I 4, vol. 1629.
23 Order-in-Council, PC 1877–813, 27 August 1877, LAC, RG 2, A 1 a, reel C-3320, vol. 359.
24 "Report of the Select Standing Committee on Immigration and Colonization," Canada, *Journals of the House of Commons of the Dominion of Canada*, 4th sess., 3rd Parliament, 1877, Appendix 6:5.
25 Order-in-Council, PC 1877–296, 13 April 1877, LAC, RG 2, A 1 a, reel C-3319, vol. 355.
26 John Lowe to R.W. Scott, 18 September 1876, LAC, RG 17, A I 13, reel T-1011, vol. 197, 290.
27 John Lowe to R.W. Scott, 23 September 1876, LAC, RG 17, A I 1, vol. 169, docket 17528.
28 John Lowe to R.W. Scott, 27 July 1876, LAC, RG 17, A I 13, reel T-1011, vol. 197, 250; John Lowe to R.W. Scott, 18 September 1876, LAC, RG 17, A I 13, reel T-1011, vol. 197, 290.
29 John Taylor to John Lowe, 6 November 1875, LAC, RG 17, A I 1, vol. 145, docket 15147.

30 John Lowe to John Taylor, 16 December 1875, LAC, John Lowe fonds, MG 29, E 18, vol. 4.
31 John Taylor to Alexander Morris, 10 January 1876, AM, Alexander Morris fonds, MG 12, B1, Correspondence series, reel M136, no. 1191A; John Taylor to Chief Commissioner J.A. Grahame, 10 January 1876, AM, Hudson's Bay Company Archives, D. 20/6–7, Commissioner's Inward Correspondence (General), no. 50.
32 John Taylor to John Lowe, 9 February 1876, LAC, RG 17, A I 1, vol. 151, docket 15109.
33 John Lowe to John Taylor, 23 February 1876, LAC, John Lowe fonds, MG 29, E 18, vol. 4.
34 Þorsteinsson, *Saga Íslendinga í Vesturheimi*, 3:25.
35 John Lowe to John Taylor, 2 October 1876, LAC, John Lowe fonds, MG 29, E 18, vol. 4.
36 John Lowe to John Taylor, 2 May 1877, LAC, RG 17, A I 6, reel T-132, vol. 1633, 217.
37 John Lowe to Isaac Burpee, 7 February 1877, LAC, RG 17, A I 13, reel T-1011, vol. 1976, 376.
38 "Memorandum: Icelandic Expenditure," n.d., LAC, RG 17, A I 13, reel T-1013, vol. 1982, 192.
39 John Lowe to John Taylor, 2 May 1877, LAC, RG 17, A I 6, reel T-132, vol. 1633, 217 (emphasis in original).
40 Macdonald, *Canada: Immigration and Colonization*, 121–22.
41 Ibid., 212.
42 Ibid., 213.
43 John Lowe to John Taylor, 2 May 1877, LAC, RG 17, A I 6, reel T-132, vol. 1633, 217.
44 *An Act to amend the Dominion Lands Act*, 1874, 37 Vic., c. 19, s. 14 and s. 15.
45 This figure is based on the Department of Agriculture's estimate of $135 to provision and supply a family of five for one year. See John Lowe to R.W. Scott, 8 August 1876, LAC, RG 17, A I 13, reel T-1011, vol. 1976, 363.
46 *An Act to amend the Dominion Lands Act*, S.C. 1874, 37 Vic., c. 19, s. 14 and s. 15.
47 "Report of the Select Standing Committee on Immigration and Colonization," Canada, *Journals of the House of Commons of the Dominion of Canada*, 5th sess., 3rd Parliament, 1878, A2-20, A2–21.
48 John Lowe to R.W. Scott, 10 August 1876, LAC, RG 17, A I 13, reel T-1011, vol. 1976, 273.
49 "Report of the Select Standing Committee on Immigration and Colonization," in Canada, *Journals of the House of Commons of the Dominion of Canada*, 5th sess., 3rd Parliament, 1878, A2-20, A2–21.
50 Gerrard, *Icelandic River Saga*, 221.
51 John Taylor to John Lowe, 9 September 1878, LAC, RG 17, A I 1, vol. 231, docket 23765.
52 *Framfari*, 4 February 1879, 443.
53 Gerrard, *Icelandic River Saga*, 211.
54 John Taylor to Alexander Morris, 1 March 1876, AM, Alexander Morris fonds, MG 12, B1, Correspondence series, reel M136, no. 1227.
55 *Framfari*, 6 March 1879, 498–99.
56 *Framfari*, 13 March 1879, 510.
57 *Framfari*, 17 July 1879, 620–28.
58 John Taylor to John Lowe, 20 May 1879, LAC, RG 17, A I 1, vol. 250, docket 25759.
59 "Memorial from Icelanders Tendering Thanks for the Government Loan and Making Suggestions as to Their Future Movements," March 1879, LAC, RG 17, A I 1, vol. 247, docket 25445.
60 John Taylor to John Lowe, 20 May 1879, LAC, RG 17, A I 1, vol. 250, docket 25759.
61 *Framfari*, 14 May 1879, 569.

62 "Memorial from Icelanders Tendering Thanks for the Government Loan and Making Suggestions as to Their Future Movements," March 1879, LAC, RG 17, A I 1, vol. 247, docket 25445.
63 See Weaver, *The Great Land Rush*, 81–87.
64 Ibid., 245.
65 "Report of the Select Standing Committee on Immigration and Colonization," Canada, *Journals of the House of Commons of the Dominion of Canada*, 5th sess., 3rd Parliament, 1878, A2-20, A2-21.
66 John Lowe to John Taylor, 28 February 1878, LAC, RG 17, A I 6, reel T-134, vol. 1633, 491.
67 Sigtryggur Jónasson to the Minister of Agriculture, 24 September 1877, LAC, RG 17, A I 1, vol. 202, docket 20828. *Framfari*, 7 January 1879, 433.
68 John Lowe to John Taylor, 2 October 1876, LAC, RG 17, A I 2, reel T-116, vol. 1517, 136; *Framfari*, 7 January 1879, 434–35.
69 *Framfari*, 23 December 1878, 430; Journal 'A,' 1875, and Journal 'B,' 1876, Lbs. 511-512, fol.; Journal 'C,' 1876–77, Lbs. 514, fol.
70 "Memorial from Icelanders Tendering Thanks for the Government Loan and Making Suggestions as to Their Future Movements," March 1879, LAC, RG 17, A I 1, vol. 247, docket 25445 (emphasis in original).
71 *Framfari*, 17 July 1879, 626.
72 John Lowe to John Taylor, 28 February 1878, LAC, RG 17, A I 6, reel T-134, vol. 1633, 491; John Lowe to John Taylor, 15 June 1878, LAC, RG 17, A I 2, reel T-117, vol. 1522, 63.
73 See *Framfari*, 7 January 1879, 434–35, and 17 July 1879, 620–28.
74 John Taylor to John Lowe, 1 June 1878, LAC, RG 17, A I 1, vol. 225, docket 23142.
75 *Framfari*, 14 May 1879, 565–66.
76 John Lowe to John Taylor, 26 May 1879, LAC, RG 17, A I 6, reel T-134, vol. 1635, 80.
77 John Taylor to John Lowe, 9 June 1879, LAC, John Lowe fonds, MG 29, E 18, vol. 19.
78 *Framfari*, 23 April 1879, 542.
79 Ibid.
80 *Framfari*, 2 September 1879, 661–62.
81 *Framfari*, 14 June 1878, 266–67.
82 *Framfari*, 28 March 1879, 527.
83 Ibid.
84 J.S. Lynch to J.A.N. Provencher, 12 April 1877, AM, Alexander Morris fonds, MG 12, B1, Correspondence series, reel M136, no. 1456; Alexander Morris to David Mills, 29 June 1877, AM, Alexander Morris fonds, MG 12, B1, Letterbook series, reel M138, no. 148.
85 See the memoirs of Árni Sigurðsson Mýrdal in *Heimskringla*, 23 December 1953. This assertion appears to be borne out by the fact that Ramsay did not include his land at Sandy Bar in his later claims for compensation.
86 John Taylor to James F. Graham, 15 March 1880, included in "Clandeboye Agency – Claim to Land along the White Mud River by John Ramsay of St. Peter's Band," LAC, RG 10, Black series, reel C-10113, vol. 3649, file 8200.
87 John Taylor to Lieutenant Governor Cauchon, 29 June 1878, included in "Elizabeth Fidler [sic], Claim for Loss of Houses and Improvements Occasioned by the Occupation of Icelandic Settlers," LAC, RG 15, D II 1, reel T-13113, vol. 409, file 105883.
88 *An Act to Amend and Consolidate the Acts Respecting Indians* [Indian Act], 1876, 39 Vic., c. 18, s. 70.

89 "List of Patents Issued in the Icelandic Reserve," 1888, LAC, RG 15, D II 1, reel T-13824, vol. 572, file 174672.
90 Friðjón Friðriksson, Jóhann Briem, and Þorgrímur Jónsson to John Taylor, 15 March 1883, LAC, RG 17, A I 1, vol. 366, docket 39363; John Taylor to John Lowe, 25 January 1884, LAC, RG 17, A I 1, vol. 395, docket 42612.
91 John Lowe to George Newcomb, 30 August 1883, LAC, RG 17, A I 2, reel T-119, vol. 1542, 54.
92 George Newcomb to John Lowe, 15 September 1883, LAC, RG 17, A I 1, vol. 382, docket 41183; "The Icelandic Reserve - Report of George Newcomb, Dominion Lands Agent," Canada, *Sessional Papers of the Dominion of Canada*, vol. 7, 2nd sess., 5th Parliament, 1884, no. 12, 14-17.
93 John Lowe to John Taylor, 20 November 1883, LAC, RG 17, A I 6, reel T-138, vol. 1640, 983.
94 John Lowe to John Mortimer Courtney, 10 January 1883, LAC, Department of Finance fonds, RG 19, E 2 e, vol. 299, file 22.
95 Magnússon, "Landnám Íslendinga í Nýja Íslandi," 33.

Conclusion

1 See Bouchard, "Family Reproduction," 475–510.
2 G.M. Sproat to J.H. Pope, Letters 'A,' 'B,' and 'C,' 27 March and 1 April 1872, LAC, RG 17, A III 2, vol. 2397.
3 *Lögberg,* 28 November 1946.

Bibliography

ARCHIVAL SOURCES

Archives of Manitoba (AM)

Government Records

Department of Mines and Natural Resources
- Federal Department of the Interior Homestead Files, NR 0215
- Land Surveyors' Field Books, NR 0157, GR 1601
- Township Plans, NR 0212

Legislative Assembly
- Sessional Papers, LA 009, GR 174

Premier's Office Files, EC 0016
- Thomas Greenway fonds, GR 1662
- John Norquay fonds, GR 553

Private Records

Lieutenant Governors Papers
- James Cox Aikens fonds, MG 12, D1
- Joseph Edouard Cauchon fonds, MG 12, C1
- Alexander Morris fonds, MG 12, B1 and B2
- Sir John Christian Schultz fonds, MG 12, E1

New Iceland Collection, MG 8

Hudson's Bay Company Archives

Section 'D' - Governor's Papers and Commissioner's Office

Archives of Ontario (AO)
- Department of Immigration fonds, RG 11

Birmingham University Library, Birmingham, UK
Church Missionary Society Archive (CMSA)
- Original Letters and Papers of Rev. James Settee Senior, 1845-1846, 1852-1878, reel 55, CC1/O/57

Landsbókasafn Íslands (National and University Library of Iceland, Lbs.)
- Bréfasafn séra Jóns Bjarnasonar í Winnipeg (Letter collection of the Reverend Jón Bjarnason in Winnipeg), Lbs. 4390, 4to.
- Bréfasafn Halldórs and Susie Briem (Letter collection of Halldór and Susie Briem), Lbs. 34 NF.
- Bréfasafn Benedikt Jónssonar á Auðnum (Letter collection of Benedikt Jónsson of Auðnir), Lbs. 4415, 4to.
- Journal 'A' and 'B,' Lbs. 511-512, fol.
- Journal 'C,' Lbs. 514, fol.

Library and Archives Canada (LAC)
Government Records
- Department of Agriculture fonds, RG 17
- Department of Employment and Immigration fonds, RG 76
- Department of Finance fonds, RG 19
- Department of Indian Affairs and Northern Development fonds, RG 10
- Department of the Interior fonds, RG 15
- Department of Justice fonds, RG 13
- Department of Militia and Defence fonds, RG 9
- Department of Secretary of State fonds, RG 6
- Office of the Governor General of Canada fonds, RG 7
- Post Office Department fonds, RG 3
- Privy Council Office fonds, RG 2

Private Records
- Edward Blake fonds, MG 27, I D 2
- Alexander Burgess fonds, MG 29, E 114
- Edgar Dewdney fonds, MG 27, I C 4
- Frederick Temple Hamilton-Temple-Blackwood, 1st Marquess of Dufferin and Ava fonds, MG 27, I B 3
- David Laird fonds, MG 27, I D 10
- John Lowe fonds, MG 29, E 18
- Sir John A. Macdonald fonds, MG 26, A
- Alexander Mackenzie fonds, MG 26, B
- David L. Macpherson fonds, MG 27, I D 12
- William McDougall fonds, MG 27, I C 6
- Edmund Allen Meredith fonds, MG 29, E 15
- John Henry Pope fonds, MG 27, I D 14

- Richard William Scott fonds, MG 27, II D 14
- Clifford Sifton fonds, MG 27, II D 15
- Sir Donald A. Smith fonds, MG 29, A 5
- Edward Watkin fonds, MG 24, E 17
- Thomas White fonds, MG 27, I D 19

The National Archives, United Kingdom (TNA)
- Colonial Office and predecessors: Barbados, Original Correspondence, CO/28
- Office of Registry of Colonial Slaves and Slave Compensation Commission Records, T71

New Iceland Heritage Museum, Gimli, MB
- Everett Parsonage document collection

Private Archival Collections
- Bob Christopherson, Edmonton, AB
- Nelson Gerrard, Arborg, MB
- Donna Skardal, Baldur, MB (Skardal Mss)

University of Manitoba Archives and Special Collections (UMASC)
- Skapti Arason fonds, Mss Sc 154 (A. 96–43)
- Símon Símonarson fonds, Mss 34 (A. 80–04)

University of Manitoba Icelandic Collection (UMIC)
- Friðjón Friðriksson papers

University of Western Ontario, Archives and Research Collections Centre
- David Mills papers

Newspapers and Periodicals
Almanak Ólafur S. Thorgeirsson, Winnipeg, 1895–1954
Barbadian, Bridgetown, Barbados, 1835–48
British and Foreign Anti-Slavery Reporter, London, 1840
Daily Free Press, Winnipeg, 1872–85
Daily Sun, Winnipeg, 1883
Daily Times, Winnipeg, 1879–85
Daily Witness, Montreal, 1875
Framfari, Lundi (Riverton), 1877–80
Globe, Toronto, 1869–85
Heimskringla, Winnipeg, 1886–1959
Liberal, Bridgetown, Barbados, 1837–43
Lögberg, Winnipeg, 1888–1959
Lögberg-Heimskringla, Winnipeg, 1959-
Manitoba Herald, Winnipeg, 1877
Manitoban, Winnipeg, 1871
Norðanfari, Akureyri, Iceland, 1873–80
Register, Montreal, 1842

Standard, Winnipeg, 1874–79
Times, London, 1875–76
Weekly Free Press, Winnipeg, 1872–85
West Indian, Bridgetown, Barbados, 1839–40

OTHER SOURCES

Aitchison, J.H. "The Municipal Corporations Act of 1849." *Canadian Historical Review* 30, 2 (1949): 107–22. http://dx.doi.org/10.3138/CHR-030-02-01.

Akenson, Donald Harman. "The Historiography of English-Speaking Canada and the Concept of Diaspora: A Sceptical Appreciation." *Canadian Historical Review* 76, 3 (1995): 377–409. http://dx.doi.org/10.3138/CHR-076-03-04.

–. *The Irish in Ontario: A Study in Rural History.* Montreal and Kingston: McGill-Queen's University Press, 1984.

Anderson, Alan Betts. "Assimilation in the Bloc Settlements of North-Central Saskatchewan: A Comparative Study of Identity Change among Seven Ethno-Religious Groups in a Canadian Prairie Region." PhD diss., University of Saskatchewan, 1972.

Anderson, Benedict. *Imagined Communities: Reflections on the Origin and Spread of Nationalism.* Rev. ed. London: Verso, 2006.

Anderson, Kay. *Vancouver's Chinatown: Racial Discourse in Canada, 1875–1980.* Montreal and Kingston: McGill-Queen's University Press, 1991.

Anonymous. *A Visit to Texas: Being the Journal of a Traveller through Those Parts Most Interesting to American Settlers, with a Description of Scenery, Habits, Etc.* New York: Goodrich and Wiley, 1834.

Armstrong, David. "Public Health Spaces and the Fabrication of Identity." *Sociology* 27, 3 (1993): 393–410. http://dx.doi.org/10.1177/0038038593027003004.

Arnason, David, and Vincent Arnason, eds. *The New Icelanders: A North American Community.* Winnipeg: Turnstone Press, 1994.

Arnold, David. *Imperial Medicine and Indigenous Societies.* Manchester, UK: Manchester University Press, 1988.

Avery, Donald. *"Dangerous Foreigners": European Immigrant Workers and Labour Radicalism in Canada, 1896–1932.* Toronto: McClelland and Stewart, 1979.

–. *Reluctant Host: Canada's Response to Immigrant Workers, 1896–1994.* Toronto: McClelland and Stewart, 1995.

Backhouse, Constance. *Colour-Coded: A Legal History of Racism in Canada, 1900–1950.* Toronto: University of Toronto Press, 1999.

Ballantyne, Tony. *Orientalism and Race: Aryanism in the British Empire.* New York: Palgrave, 2002.

Bantjes, Rod. *Improved Earth: Prairie Space as Modern Artefact, 1869–1944.* Toronto: University of Toronto Press, 2005.

Barber, Marilyn. *Immigrant Domestic Servants in Canada.* Ottawa: Canadian Historical Association, 1991.

Bashford, Alison. "Epidemic and Governmentality: Smallpox in Sydney, 1881." *Critical Public Health* 9, 4 (1999): 301–16. http://dx.doi.org/10.1080/09581599908402942.

–. *Imperial Hygiene: A Critical History of Colonialism, Nationalism and Public Health.* New York: Palgrave Macmillan, 2004.

Bibliography

Bashford, Alison, and Claire Hooker. *Contagion: Historical and Cultural Studies*. London: Routledge, 2001.

Bayly, C.A. *Imperial Meridian: The British Empire and the World, 1780–1830*. London: Longman, 1989.

Beckles, Hilary. *A History of Barbados: From Amerindian Settlement to Nation-State*. Cambridge: Cambridge University Press, 1990.

Belich, James. *Replenishing the Earth: The Settler Revolution and the Rise of the Anglo-World, 1783–1939*. Oxford: Oxford University Press, 2009. http://dx.doi.org/10.1093/acprof:oso/9780199297276.001.0001.

Bell, Winthrop Pickard. *The Foreign Protestants and the Settlement of Nova Scotia: The History of a Piece of Arrested British Colonial Policy in the Eighteenth Century*. Fredericton: Acadiensis Press, 1990.

Berger, Carl. *The Sense of Power: Studies in the Ideas of Canadian Imperialism, 1867–1914*. Toronto: University of Toronto Press, 1970.

–. *The Writing of Canadian History: Aspects of English-Canadian Historical Writing since 1900*. 2nd ed. Toronto: University of Toronto Press, 1993.

Bertram, Laurie K. "'Fight Like Auður': Gender, Ethnicity, and Dissent in the Career of Salome Halldorson, Social Credit MLA, 1936–41." Master's cognate research paper, McMaster University, 2004.

–. "New Icelandic Ethnoscapes: Material, Visual, and Oral Terrains of Cultural Expression in Icelandic-Canadian History, 1875–Present." PhD diss., University of Toronto, 2010.

–. "Public Spectacles, Private Narratives: Canadian Heritage Campaigns, Maternal Trauma and the Rise of the Koffort (Trunk) in Icelandic-Canadian Popular Memory." *Material Culture Review* 71 (2010): 39–53.

Bessason, Haraldur. "A Few Specimens of North American-Icelandic." *Scandinavian Studies* 39, 2 (1967): 115–46.

Biggs, C. Lesley, and Stella Stephanson. "In Search of Gudrun Goodman: Reflections on Gender, 'Doing History' and Memory." *Canadian Historical Review* 87, 2 (2006): 293–316. http://dx.doi.org/10.1353/can.2006.0042.

Block, W.T. "A History of Jefferson County, Texas: From Wilderness to Reconstruction." Master's thesis, Lamar University, 1974. http://www.wtblock.com/wtblockjr/History%20of%20Jefferson%20County/Introduction.htm.

Bolt, Christine. *Victorian Attitudes to Race*. London: Routledge and Kegan Paul, 1971.

Bouchard, Gérard. "Family Reproduction in New Rural Areas: Outline of a North American Model." *Canadian Historical Review* 75, 4 (1994): 475–510. http://dx.doi.org/10.3138/CHR-075-04-01.

Boucher, Alan. *The Iceland Traveller: A Hundred Years of Adventure*. Reykjavík: Iceland Review, 1989.

Bradbury, Bettina. "Pigs, Cows, and Boarders: Non-wage Forms of Survival among Montreal Families, 1861-1891." *Labour/Le Travail* 14 (Fall 1984): 9–46.

–. *Working Families: Age, Gender, and Daily Survival in Industrializing Montreal*. Canadian Social History Series. Toronto: McClelland and Stewart, 1993.

Brown, Jennifer S.H., and Elizabeth Vibert. *Reading beyond Words: Contexts for Native History*. Peterborough: Broadview Press, 1996.

Brownlie, Robin Jarvis. "'A Better Citizen Than Lots of White Men': First Nations Enfranchisement – an Ontario Case Study, 1918–1940." *Canadian Historical Review* 87, 1 (2006): 29–52.

–. *A Fatherly Eye: Indian Agents, Government Power, and Aboriginal Resistance in Ontario, 1918–1939*. Don Mills: Oxford University Press, 2003.

Brownlie, Robin Jarvis, and Mary-Ellen Kelm. "Desperately Seeking Absolution: Native Agency as Colonialist Alibi?" *Canadian Historical Review* 75, 4 (1994): 543–56.

Brydon, Anne. "Dreams and Claims: Icelandic-Aboriginal Interactions in the Manitoba Interlake." *Journal of Canadian Studies/Revue d'Etudes Canadiennes* 36, 2 (2001): 164–90.

–. "Icelanders." In *Encyclopedia of Canada's Peoples*, ed. Paul Robert Magocsi, 685–700. Toronto: Multicultural History Society of Ontario and University of Toronto Press, 1999.

–. "Inscriptions of Self: The Construction of Icelandic Landscape in Nineteenth Century British Travel Writings." *Ethnos* 60, 3 (1995): 243–63. http://dx.doi.org/10.1080/001418 44.1995.9981520.

Buckner, Phillip A., ed. *Canada and the British Empire*. New York: Oxford University Press, 2008.

Burchell, Graham, Colin Gordon, and Peter Miller, eds. *The Foucault Effect: Studies in Governmentality*. Chicago: University of Chicago Press, 1991. http://dx.doi.org/10.7208/chicago/9780226028811.001.0001.

Burton, Antoinette M., ed. *After the Imperial Turn: Thinking with and through the Nation*. Durham, NC: Duke University Press, 2003. http://dx.doi.org/10.1215/9780822384397.

–. *At the Heart of the Empire: Indians and the Colonial Encounter in Late-Victorian Britain*. Berkeley: University of California Press, 1998.

Burton, Richard Francis. *Ultima Thule; or a Summer in Iceland*. 2 vols. London: Nimmo, 1875.

Campbell, Randolph B. *An Empire for Slavery: The Peculiar Institution in Texas, 1821–1865*. Baton Rouge: Louisiana State University Press, 1989.

Canada, Department of Agriculture. *Nýa* [sic] *Ísland í Kanada*. London: Gilbert and Rivington, 1875.

Carter, Sarah. *Aboriginal People and Colonizers of Western Canada to 1900*. Toronto: University of Toronto Press, 1999.

–. "'Daughters of British Blood' or 'Hordes of Men of Alien Race': The Homesteads-for-Women Campaign in Western Canada." *Great Plains Quarterly* 29, 4 (2009): 267–86.

–. *Lost Harvests: Prairie Indian Reserve Farmers and Government Policy*. Montreal and Kingston: McGill-Queen's University Press, 1990.

–. "'They Would Not Give Up One Inch of It': The Rise and Demise of St. Peter's Reserve, Manitoba." In *Indigenous Communities and Settler Colonialism*, ed. Zoë Laidlaw and Alan Lester, 173–93. Basingstoke, UK: Palgrave Macmillan, 2015.

Chilton, Lisa. *Agents of Empire: British Female Migration to Canada and Australia, 1860s–1930*. Toronto: University of Toronto Press, 2007.

Cleverdon, Catherine Lyle. *The Woman Suffrage Movement in Canada*. [Toronto]: University of Toronto Press, 1950.

Constant, Jean-François, and Michel Ducharme, eds. *Liberalism and Hegemony: Debating the Canadian Liberal Revolution*. Toronto: University of Toronto Press, 2009.

Cooper, Frederick, and Ann Laura Stoler. *Tensions of Empire: Colonial Cultures in a Bourgeois World*. Berkeley: University of California Press, 1997. http://dx.doi.org/10.1525/california/9780520205406.001.0001.

Crampton, Jeremy W., and Stuart Elden. *Space, Knowledge and Power: Foucault and Geography*. Aldershot, UK: Ashgate, 2007.

Crawford, Kenneth Grant. *Canadian Municipal Government*. Canadian Government Series No. 6. Toronto: University of Toronto Press, 1954.

Curthoys, Ann, and Marilyn Lake. *Connected Worlds: History in Transnational Perspective*. Canberra, Australia: ANU E Press, 2005.

Curtis, Bruce. *The Politics of Population: State Formation, Statistics, and the Census of Canada, 1840–1875*. Toronto: University of Toronto Press, 2001.

–. *True Government by Choice Men? Inspection, Education, and State Formation in Canada West*. Toronto: University of Toronto Press, 1992.

Daschuk, James. *Clearing the Plains: Disease, Politics of Starvation, and the Loss of Aboriginal Life*. Regina: University of Regina Press, 2013.

Dawson, Carl A. *Group Settlement: Ethnic Communities in Western Canada*. Toronto: Macmillan, 1936.

Decker, Jody F. "Depopulation of the Northern Plains Natives." *Social Science and Medicine* 33, 4 (1991): 381–93. http://dx.doi.org/10.1016/0277-9536(91)90319-8.

–. "Tracing Historical Diffusion Patterns: The Case of the 1780-82 Smallpox Epidemic among the Indians of Western Canada." *Native Studies Review* 4, 1–2 (1988): 1–24.

Dick, Lyle. *Farmers "Making Good": The Development of Abernethy District, Saskatchewan, 1880–1920*. Ottawa: National Historic Parks and Sites, Canadian Parks Service, 1989.

Dobrzensky, Leopolda z Lobkowicz. *Fragments of a Dream: Pioneering in Dysart Township and Haliburton Village*. Haliburton, ON: Municipality of Dysart, 1985.

Doddridge, Philip. *The Rise and Progress of Religion in the Soul: Illustrated in a Course of Serious and Practical Addresses, Suited to Persons of Every Character and Circumstance: With a Devout Meditation, or Prayer, Subjoined to Each Chapter*. Grand Rapids: Baker Book House, 1977 (originally published 1745).

Dollar, Clyde D. "The High Plains Smallpox Epidemic of 1837-38." *Western Historical Quarterly* 8, 1 (1977): 15–38. http://dx.doi.org/10.2307/967216.

Donnelly, Murray S. *The Government of Manitoba*. Toronto: University of Toronto Press, 1963.

Dufferin and Ava, Frederick Temple Blackwood. *Letters from High Latitudes: Being Some Account of a Voyage, in 1856, in the Schooner Yacht "Foam," to Iceland, Jan Mayen, and Spitzbergen*. 3rd ed. London: John Murray, 1857.

Elbourne, Elizabeth. *Blood Ground: Colonialism, Missions, and the Contest for Christianity in the Cape Colony and Britain, 1799–1853*. Montreal and Kingston: McGill-Queen's University Press, 2002.

–. "The Sin of the Settler: The 1835-36 Select Committee on Aborigines and Debates over Virtue and Conquest in the Early Nineteenth-Century British White Settler Empire." *Journal of Colonialism and Colonial History* 4, 3 (2003). http://dx.doi.org/10.1353/cch.2004.0003.

–. "Word Made Flesh: Christianity, Modernity, and Cultural Colonialism in the Work of Jean and John Comaroff." *American Historical Review* 108, 2 (2003): 435–59. http://dx.doi.org/10.1086/533242.

Elections Canada. *A History of the Vote in Canada*. 2nd ed. Ottawa: Office of the Chief Electoral Officer of Canada, 2007.

Elliott, Bruce S. *Irish Migrants in the Canadas: A New Approach*. Montreal and Kingston: McGill-Queen's University Press, 1988.

Emmer, P.C., and Magnus Mörner, eds. *European Expansion and Migration: Essays on the Intercontinental Migration from Africa, Asia, and Europe*. New York: Berg, 1992.

Epp, Frank H. *Mennonites in Canada, 1786–1920: The History of a Separate People*. Toronto: Macmillan of Canada, 1974.

Errington, Elizabeth Jane. *Emigrant Worlds and Transatlantic Communities: Migration to Upper Canada in the First Half of the Nineteenth Century*. Montreal and Kingston: McGill-Queen's University Press, 2007.

Etherington, Norman. *Missions and Empire*. Oxford: Oxford University Press, 2005.

Ewanchuk, Michael. *Spruce, Swamp and Stone: A History of the Pioneer Ukrainian Settlements in the Gimli Area*. Winnipeg: privately printed, 1977.

Eyford, Ryan C. "'Close Together, Though Miles and Miles Apart': Family, Distance, and Emotion in the Letters of the Taylor Sisters, 1881–1921." *Histoire sociale/Social History* 47, 96 (2015): 67–86. http://dx.doi.org/10.1353/his.2015.0012.

–. "From Prairie Goolies to Canadian Cyclones: The Transformation of the 1920 Winnipeg Falcons." *Sport History Review* 37, 1 (2006): 5–18.

–. "Icelandic Migration to Canada, 1872-1875: New Perspectives on the 'Myth of Beginnings.'" Master's thesis, Carleton University, 2003.

–. "Quarantined within a New Colonial Order: The 1876-1877 Lake Winnipeg Smallpox Epidemic." *Journal of the Canadian Historical Association* 17, 1 (2006): 55–78. http://dx.doi.org/10.7202/016102ar.

FitzGibbon, Mary Agnes. *A Trip to Manitoba or, Roughing It on the Line*. Toronto: Rose-Belford, 1880.

Foucault, Michel. *Power/Knowledge: Selected Interviews and Other Writings, 1972–1977*. New York: Pantheon Books, 1980.

Francis, R.D., and Howard Palmer, eds. *The Prairie West: Historical Readings*. 2nd rev. and expanded ed. Edmonton: Pica Pica Press, 1992.

Freeman, George, ed. *Pembina County Pioneer Daughter Biographies*. Vol. 1, *Icelandic Settlements of Akra/Cavalier, Gardar, and Mountain North Dakota*. Grand Forks, ND: Laxa Press, 2007.

Friedmann, Harriet. "World Market, State, and Family Farm: Social Bases of Household Production in the Era of Wage Labor." *Comparative Studies in Society and History* 20, 4 (1978): 545–86. http://dx.doi.org/10.1017/S001041750001255X.

Friesen, Gerald. *The Canadian Prairies: A History*. Toronto: University of Toronto Press, 1987.

–. "Space and Region in Canadian History/Les concepts d'espace et de région en histoire de Canada." *Journal of the Canadian Historical Association* 16, 1 (2005): 1–48. http://dx.doi.org/10.7202/015725ar.

Friesen, Richard J. "Saskatchewan Mennonite Settlements: The Modification of an Old World Settlement Pattern." *Canadian Ethnic Studies* 9, 2 (1977): 72–90.

Gabaccia, Donna R. *Militants and Migrants: Rural Sicilians Become American Workers*. New Brunswick, NJ: Rutgers University Press, 1988.

Gandhi, Leela. *Postcolonial Theory: A Critical Introduction*. New York: Columbia University Press, 1998.

Garner, John. *The Franchise and Politics in British North America, 1755–1867*. Ottawa: University of Toronto Press, 1969.

Gates, Paul W. "Official Encouragement to Immigration by the Province of Canada." *Canadian Historical Review* 15, 1 (1934): 24–38. http://dx.doi.org/10.3138/CHR-15-01-02.
Gerrard, Nelson. *Icelandic River Saga*. Arborg, MB: Saga Publications, 1985.
Gjerde, Jon. *From Peasants to Farmers: The Migration from Balestrand, Norway to the Upper Middle West*. Cambridge: Cambridge University Press, 1985.
–. *The Minds of the West: Ethnocultural Evolution in the Rural Middle West, 1830–1917*. Chapel Hill: University of North Carolina Press, 1997.
Gjerset, Knut. *History of Iceland*. New York: Macmillan, 1924.
Goldsborough, Gordon. *With One Voice: A History of Municipal Governance in Manitoba*. Portage la Prairie, MB: Association of Manitoba Municipalities, 2008.
Greer, Allan, and Ian Radforth, eds. *Colonial Leviathan: State Formation in Mid-Nineteenth-Century Canada*. Toronto: University of Toronto Press, 1992.
Guðmundsson, Böðvar. *Bréf Vestur-Íslendinga*. Vol. 1. Reykjavík: Mál og menning, 2001.
Gunnlaugsson, Gísli Ágúst. *Family and Household in Iceland, 1801–1930: Studies in the Relationship between Demographic and Socio-economic Development, Social Legislation and Family and Household Structures*. Acta Universitatis Upsaliensis. Studia Historica Upsaliensia. Uppsala: S. Academiae Ubsaliensis, 1988.
Gwyn, Sandra. *The Private Capital: Ambition and Love in the Age of Macdonald and Laurier*. Toronto: McClelland and Stewart, 1984.
Hackett, Paul. "Averting Disaster: The Hudson's Bay Company and Smallpox in Western Canada during the Late Eighteenth and Early Nineteenth Centuries." *Bulletin of the History of Medicine* 78, 3 (2004): 575–609. http://dx.doi.org/10.1353/bhm.2004.0119.
–. *"A Very Remarkable Sickness": Epidemics in the Petit Nord, 1670–1846*. Winnipeg: University of Manitoba Press, 2002.
Hálfdánarson, Guðmundur. "Defining the Modern Citizen: Debates on Civil and Political Elements of Citizenship in Nineteenth-Century Iceland." *Scandinavian Journal of History* 24, 1 (1999): 103–16. http://dx.doi.org/10.1080/03468759950115872.
–. *Historical Dictionary of Iceland*. Lanham, MD: Scarecrow Press, 1997.
–. "Old Provinces, Modern Nations: Political Responses to State Integration in Late Nineteenth and Early Twentieth Century Iceland and Brittany." PhD diss., Cornell University, 1991.
–. "Severing the Ties: Iceland's Journey from a Union with Denmark to a Nation-State." *Scandinavian Journal of History* 31, 3 (2006): 237–54. http://dx.doi.org/10.1080/03468750600930878.
–. "Social Distinctions and National Unity: On Politics of Nationalism in Nineteenth-Century Iceland." *History of European Ideas* 21, 6 (1995): 763–79. http://dx.doi.org/10.1016/0191-6599(95)00068-2.
–. "To Become a Man: The Ambiguities of Gender Relations in Late 19th and Early 20th Century Iceland." In *Political Systems and Definitions of Gender Roles*, ed. Ann-Katherine Isaacs, 43–51. Pisa: Edizioni Plus, 2001.
Haliburton, R.G. *The Men of the North and Their Place in History; A Lecture Delivered before the Montreal Literary Club, March 31st, 1869*. Montreal: Lovell, 1869.
Hall, Catherine. *Civilising Subjects: Colony and Metropole in the English Imagination, 1830–1867*. Chicago: University of Chicago Press, 2002.
Hall, D.J. *Clifford Sifton*. Vol. 1, *The Young Napoleon, 1861–1900*. Vancouver: UBC Press, 1981.

–. *Clifford Sifton*. Vol. 2, *A Lonely Eminence, 1901–1929*. Vancouver: UBC Press, 1985.
Harris, R. Cole. *Making Native Space: Colonialism, Resistance, and Reserves in British Columbia*. Vancouver: UBC Press, 2002.
–. *The Reluctant Land: Society, Space, and Environment in Canada before Confederation*. Vancouver: UBC Press, 2008.
–. *The Resettlement of British Columbia: Essays on Colonialism and Geographical Change*. Vancouver: UBC Press, 1997.
Harrison, Mark. *Climates and Constitutions: Health, Race, Environment and British Imperialism in India, 1600–1850*. Oxford: Oxford University Press, 1999.
Hearn, Mary. "The Hearn Family Story." Clinton, ON, privately printed, n.d.
Higham, John. *Strangers in the Land: Patterns of American Nativism, 1860–1925*. New Brunswick, NJ: Rutgers University Press, 1955.
Hind, Henry Youle. *Narrative of the Canadian Red River Exploring Expedition of 1857 and of the Assiniboine and Saskatchewan Exploring Expedition of 1858*. London: Longman, Green, Longman, and Roberts, 1860. http://dx.doi.org/10.5962/bhl.title.82399.
Hoerder, Dirk. *Creating Societies: Immigrant Lives in Canada*. Montreal and Kingston: McGill-Queen's University Press, 1999.
–. *Cultures in Contact: World Migrations in the Second Millennium*. Durham, NC: Duke University Press, 2002. http://dx.doi.org/10.1215/9780822384076.
–, ed. *Labor Migration in the Atlantic Economies*. Westport, CT: Greenwood Press, 1985.
Hoerder, Dirk, and Leslie Page Moch, eds. *European Migrants: Global and Local Perspectives*. Boston: Northeastern University Press, 1996.
Houser, George, ed. *Framfari: 1877 to 1880*. Gimli, MB: Gimli Chapter Icelandic National League of North America, 1986.
Iacovetta, Franca. *Such Hardworking People: Italian Immigrants in Postwar Toronto*. Montreal and Kingston: McGill-Queen's University Press, 1992.
Jackson, Thorleifur Jóakimsson. *Brot af Landnámssögu Nýja Íslands*. Winnipeg: Columbia Press, 1919.
–. *Frá Austri til Vesturs: Framhald af Landnámssögu Nýja-Íslands*. Winnipeg: Columbia Press, 1921.
–. *Framhald á Landnámssögu Nýja Íslands*. Winnipeg: Columbia Press, 1923.
Jacobson, Matthew Frye. *Whiteness of a Different Color: European Immigrants and the Alchemy of Race*. Cambridge, MA: Harvard University Press, 1998.
Jónasson, Sigtryggur. *The Early Icelandic Settlements in Canada*. Transaction 59 of the Historical and Scientific Society of Manitoba. Winnipeg: Manitoba Free Press, 1901.
–. "John Taylor og Elizabeth Taylor." *Syrpa: Mánaðarrit með myndum* 8, 4 (1920): 97–102.
Jones, Esyllt W. "Contact across a Diseased Boundary: Urban Space and Social Interaction during Winnipeg's Influenza Epidemic, 1918-1919." *Journal of the Canadian Historical Association* 13, 1 (2002): 119-39. http://dx.doi.org/10.7202/031156ar.
–. "'Co-operation in All Human Endeavour': Quarantine and Immigrant Disease Vectors in the 1918–1919 Influenza Pandemic in Winnipeg." *Canadian Bulletin of Medical History* 22, 1 (2005): 57–82.
–. *Influenza 1918: Disease, Death and Struggle in Winnipeg*. Toronto: University of Toronto Press, 2007.
Jónsson, Guðmundur. "Institutional Change in Icelandic Agriculture, 1780-1940." *Scandinavian Economic History Review* 41, 2 (1993): 101–28. http://dx.doi.org/10.1080/03585522.1993.10415863.

Jónsson, Guðmundur, and Magnús S. Magnússon. *Hagskinna: Sögulegar hagtölur um Ísland/Icelandic Historical Statistics*. Reykjavík: Hagstofa Íslands, 1997.
Jónsson, Jakob. "Þegar Nýja Ísland var sjálfstætt ríki [When New Iceland was an independent state]." *Eimreiðin* 49 (1943): 116–26.
Karatani, Rieko. *Defining British Citizenship: Empire, Commonwealth, and Modern Britain*. London: Frank Cass, 2003.
Karlsson, Gunnar. "The Emergence of Nationalism in Iceland." In *Ethnicity and Nation Building in the Nordic World*, ed. Sven Tägil, 33–61. Carbondale: Southern Illinois University Press, 1995.
–. *The History of Iceland*. Minneapolis: University of Minnesota Press, 2000.
Kelm, Mary-Ellen. *Colonizing Bodies: Aboriginal Health and Healing in British Columbia, 1900–50*. Vancouver: UBC Press, 1998.
Kjartansson, Helgi Skúli. "Emigrant Fares and Emigration from Iceland to North America, 1874-1893." *Scandinavian Economic History Review* 28, 1 (1980): 53–71. http://dx.doi.org/10.1080/03585522.1980.10407907.
–. "Icelandic Emigration." In *European Expansion and Migration: Essays on the Intercontinental Migration from Africa, Asia, and Europe*, ed. P.C. Emmer and Magnus Mörner, 105–19. New York: Berg, 1992.
–. "The Onset of Emigration from Iceland." *American Studies in Scandinavia* 9, 1 (1977): 87–93.
Kjartansson, Helgi Skúli, and Steinþór Heiðarsson. *Framtíð handan hafs: Vesturfarir frá Íslandi, 1870–1914*. Reykjavík: Háskólaútgáfan, 2003.
Kristinsson, Júníus. *Vesturfaraskrá, 1870–1914: A Record of Emigrants from Iceland to America, 1870–1914*. Reykjavík: Sagnfræðistofnun Háskóla Íslands; distributed by Sögufélag, 1983.
Kristjanson, Wilhelm. "John Taylor and the Pioneer Icelandic Settlement in Manitoba and His Plea on Behalf of the Persecuted Jewish People." *Manitoba Historical Society Transactions*, 3rd ser., 32 (1975–76): 33–41.
Lalonde, André. "Settlement in the North-West Territories by Colonization Companies, 1881-1891." PhD diss., Laval University, 1969.
Lambert, David. *White Creole Culture, Politics and Identity during the Age of Abolition*. Cambridge: Cambridge University Press, 2005.
Lambert, David, and Alan Lester, eds. *Colonial Lives across the British Empire: Imperial Careering in the Long Nineteenth Century*. Cambridge: Cambridge University Press, 2006.
Landon, Fred. "The Evolution of Local Government in Ontario." *Ontario History* 42, 1 (1950): 1–5.
Lefebvre, Henri. *The Production of Space*. Oxford: Blackwell, 1991.
Lehr, John C. "The Government and the Immigrant: Perspectives on Ukrainian Block Settlement in the Canadian West." *Canadian Ethnic Studies* 9, 2 (1977): 42–52.
Lester, Alan. "British Settler Discourse and the Circuits of Empire." *History Workshop Journal* 54, 1 (2002): 24–48. http://dx.doi.org/10.1093/hwj/54.1.24.
–. *Imperial Networks: Creating Identities in Nineteenth-Century South Africa and Britain*. London: Routledge, 2001.
Levine, Philippa, ed. *Gender and Empire*. Oxford: Oxford University Press, 2004.
Lindal, Walter J. *Canada Ethnica II: The Icelanders in Canada*. Winnipeg: Viking Press, 1967.

–. "The Laws and Regulations of New Iceland." *Icelandic Canadian* 50, 4 (1992): 210–22.
Little, Jack I. "Colonization and Municipal Reform in Canada East." *Histoire sociale/Social History* 14, 27 (1981): 93–121.
–. *Crofters and Habitants: Settler Society, Economy, and Culture in a Quebec Township, 1848–1881*. Montreal and Kingston: McGill-Queen's University Press, 1991.
Loewen, Royden. *Family, Church and Market: A Mennonite Community in the Old and the New Worlds, 1850–1930*. Toronto: University of Toronto Press, 1993.
Loo, Tina. *Making Law, Order, and Authority in British Columbia, 1821–1871*. Toronto: University of Toronto Press, 1994.
Loveridge, D.M. "The Garden of Manitoba: The Settlement and Agricultural Development of the Rock Lake District and the Municipality of Louise, 1878-1902." PhD diss., University of Toronto, 1987.
Lux, Maureen K. *Medicine That Walks: Disease, Medicine and Canadian Plains Native People, 1880–1940*. Toronto: University of Toronto Press, 2001.
Lytwyn, Victor P. *Muskekowuck Athinuwick: Original People of the Great Swampy Land*. Winnipeg: University of Manitoba Press, 2002.
Macdonald, Norman P. *Canada: Immigration and Colonization, 1841–1903*. Aberdeen, UK: Aberdeen University Press, 1966.
Mackie, Richard. "The Colonization of Vancouver Island, 1849-1858." *BC Studies* 96 (1992): 3–40.
Mackintosh, William A. *Prairie Settlement: The Geographical Setting*. Toronto: Macmillan, 1934.
Magnússon, Magnús S. *Iceland in Transition: Labour and Socio-economic Change before 1940*. Lund: Ekonomisk-historiska föreningen i Lund, 1985.
Martin, Chester. *"Dominion Lands" Policy*. Carleton Library Series No. 69. Toronto: McClelland and Stewart, 1973.
Matthiasson, John S. "Icelandic Canadians in Central Canada: One Experiment in Multiculturalism." *Western Canadian Journal of Anthropology* 4, 2 (1974): 49–61.
–. "The Icelandic Canadians: The Paradox of an Assimilated Ethnic Group." In *Two Nations, Many Cultures: Ethnic Groups in Canada*, ed. Jean Elliott, 331–41. Toronto: Prentice Hall, 1979.
McCallum, Mary Jane. "The Last Frontier: Isolation and Aboriginal Health." *Canadian Bulletin of Medical History* 22, 1 (2005): 103–20.
McCracken, Jane. "Stephan G. Stephansson: Icelandic-Canadian Poet and Freethinker." *Canadian Ethnic Studies* 15, 1 (1983): 33–53.
McEvoy, J.M. *The Ontario Township*. Ed. W.J. Ashley. Toronto University Studies in Political Science No. 1. Toronto: Warwick and Sons, 1889.
McGhee, Fred Lee. "The Black Crop: Slavery and Slave Trading in Nineteenth Century Texas." PhD diss., University of Texas at Austin, 2000.
McIntosh, Andrea L. "In Plain Sight: The Development of Western Icelandic Ethnicity and Class Division, 1910-20." PhD diss., University of Manitoba, 2005.
McKay, Ian. "The Liberal Order Framework: A Prospectus for a Reconnaissance of Canadian History." *Canadian Historical Review* 81, 4 (2000): 617–45. http://dx.doi.org/10.3138/CHR.81.4.617.
–. *The Quest of the Folk: Antimodernism and Cultural Selection in Twentieth-Century Nova Scotia*. Montreal and Kingston: McGill-Queen's University Press, 1994.

McKenzie, Kirsten. *Scandal in the Colonies: Sydney and Cape Town, 1820–1850*. Melbourne: Melbourne University Press, 2004.
McLaren, John, A.R. Buck, and Nancy E. Wright, eds. *Despotic Dominion: Property Rights in British Settler Societies*. Vancouver: UBC Press, 2005.
McMurchy, Donald John Arnold. "David Mills: Nineteenth Century Canadian Liberal." PhD diss., University of Rochester, 1968.
Mehta, Uday Singh. *Liberalism and Empire: A Study in Nineteenth-Century British Liberal Thought*. Chicago: University of Chicago Press, 1999.
Mill, John Stuart. *Considerations on Representative Government*. London: Parker, Son, and Bourn, 1861.
Miller, J.R. *Compact, Contract, Covenant: Aboriginal Treaty-Making in Canada*. Toronto: University of Toronto Press, 2009.
–. *Skyscrapers Hide the Heavens: A History of Indian-White Relations in Canada*. Toronto: University of Toronto Press, 1989.
Milligan, Frank Archibald. "The Lieutenant-Governorship in Manitoba, 1870-1882." Master's thesis, University of Manitoba, 1948.
Milloy, John S. "The Early Indian Acts: Developmental Strategy and Constitutional Change." In *As Long as the Sun Shines and the Water Flows: A Reader in Canadian Native Studies*, ed. I.A.L. Getty and A.S. Lussier, 56–64. Vancouver: UBC Press, 1983.
Mitchell, Timothy. *Colonising Egypt*. Berkeley: University of California Press, 1991.
Morris, Alexander. *Nova Britannia, or, Our New Canadian Dominion Foreshadowed; Being a Series of Lectures, Speeches and Addresses*. Toronto: Hunter, Rose, 1884.
–. *The Treaties of Canada with the Indians of Manitoba and the North-West Territories, Including the Negotiations on Which They Were Based, and Other Information Relating Thereto*. Toronto: Belfords, Clarke, 1880.
Morton, Arthur S., and Chester Martin. *History of Prairie Settlement/"Dominion Lands" Policy*. Toronto: Macmillan, 1938.
Morton, W.L. "The Extension of the Franchise in Canada: A Study in Democratic Nationalism." *Canadian Historical Association: Report of the Annual Meeting* 22, 1 (1943): 72–81.
–. *Manitoba: A History*. Toronto: University of Toronto Press, 1957.
Mouat, Jeremy. "Situating Vancouver Island in the British World, 1846-49." *BC Studies* 145 (2005): 5–30.
Newton, Melanie J. *The Children of Africa in the Colonies: Free People of Color in Barbados in the Age of Emancipation*. Baton Rouge: Louisiana State University Press, 2008.
Ólafsson, Jón. *Alaska: Lýsing á landi og lands-kostum, ásamt skýrslu innar íslenzku sendinefndar: um stofnun íslenzkrar nýlendu*. Washington, DC, 1875.
Oswald, Elizabeth Jane. *By Fell and Fjord; or, Scenes and Studies in Iceland*. London: Blackwood and Sons, 1882.
Owram, Doug. *Promise of Eden: The Canadian Expansionist Movement and the Idea of the West, 1856–1900*. Toronto: University of Toronto Press, 1980.
Painchaud, Robert. "The Catholic Church and the Movement of Francophones to the Canadian Prairies, 1870-1915." PhD diss., University of Ottawa, 1976.
Palmer, Howard. "Escape from the Great Plains: The Icelanders in North Dakota and Alberta." *Great Plains Quarterly* 3, 4 (1983): 219–23.
–. *Patterns of Prejudice: A History of Nativism in Alberta*. Toronto: McClelland and Stewart, 1982.

–, ed. *The Settlement of the West*. Calgary: University of Calgary and Comprint, 1977.

Pálsson, Hjörtur. *Alaskaför Jóns Ólafssonar 1874*. Reykjavík: Menningarsjóður, 1975.

Peers, Laura Lynn. *The Ojibwa of Western Canada, 1780 to 1870*. Winnipeg: University of Manitoba Press, 1994.

Perry, Adele. *On the Edge of Empire: Gender, Race, and the Making of British Columbia, 1849–1871*. Toronto: University of Toronto Press, 2001.

Perry, Adele, Esyllt Jones, and Leah Morton, eds. *Place and Replace: Essays on Western Canada*. Winnipeg: University of Manitoba Press, 2013.

Pratt, Mary Louise. *Imperial Eyes: Travel Writing and Transculturation*. New York: Routledge, 1992. http://dx.doi.org/10.4324/9780203163672.

Ramirez, Bruno. *On the Move: French-Canadian and Italian Migrants in the North Atlantic Economy, 1860–1914*. Toronto: McClelland and Stewart, 1991.

Rasporich, A.W. "Utopian Ideals and Community Settlements in Western Canada, 1880-1914." In *The Prairie West: Historical Readings*, ed. R. Douglas Francis and Howard Palmer, 352–77. Edmonton: Pica Pica Press, 1992.

Ray, Arthur J. "Diffusion of Diseases in the Western Interior of Canada, 1830-50." *Geographical Review* 66, 2 (1976): 139–57. http://dx.doi.org/10.2307/213577.

–. *Indians in the Fur Trade: Their Role as Trappers, Hunters, and Middlemen in the Lands Southwest of Hudson Bay, 1660–1870*. Toronto: University of Toronto Press, 1974.

–. "Smallpox: The Epidemic of 1837-38." *The Beaver* 306, 2 (1975): 8–13.

Reynolds, Thomas Michael. "Justices of the Peace in the Northwest Territories, 1870-1905." Master's thesis, University of Regina, 1978.

Richtik, James Morton. "The Agriculture Frontier in Manitoba: Changing Perceptions of the Resource Value of Prairie and Woodland." *Upper Midwest History* 3 (1983): 55–61.

–. "Chain Migration among Icelandic Settlers in Canada to 1891." *Scandinavian Canadian Studies* 2 (1986): 73–88.

–. "A Historical Geography of the Interlake Area of Manitoba." Master's thesis, University of Manitoba, 1964.

–. "Manitoba Settlement, 1870 to 1886." PhD diss., University of Minnesota, 1971.

–. "Mapping the Quality of Land for Agriculture in Western Canada." *Great Plains Quarterly* 5, 4 (1985): 236–48.

–. "The Policy Framework for Settling the Canadian West, 1870-1880." *Agricultural History* 49, 4 (1975): 613–28.

Roediger, David R. *The Wages of Whiteness: Race and the Making of the American Working Class*. Rev. ed. London: Verso, 1999.

Rutherdale, Myra, and Katie Pickles. *Contact Zones: Aboriginal and Settler Women in Canada's Colonial Past*. Vancouver: UBC Press, 2005.

Sandwell, R.W. "The Limits of Liberalism: The Liberal Reconnaissance and the History of the Family in Canada." *Canadian Historical Review* 84, 3 (2003): 423–50. http://dx.doi.org/10.3138/CHR.84.3.423.

–. *Contesting Rural Space: Land Policy and Practices of Resettlement on Saltspring Island, 1859–1891*. Montreal and Kingston: McGill-Queen's University Press, 2005.

Schomburgk, Robert H. *The History of Barbados; Comprising a Geographical and Statistical Description of the Island, a Sketch of the Historical Events since the Settlement, and an Account of Its Geology and Natural Productions*. London: Longman, Brown, Green and Longmans, 1848.

Scott, James C. *Seeing Like a State: How Certain Schemes to Improve the Human Condition Have Failed.* New Haven: Yale University Press, 1998.
Shah, Nayan. *Contagious Divides: Epidemics and Race in San Francisco's Chinatown.* Berkeley: University of California Press, 2001.
Silver, A.I. "French Canada and the Prairie Frontier, 1870-1890." *Canadian Historical Review* 50, 1 (1969): 11–36. http://dx.doi.org/10.3138/CHR-050-01-02.
Skilling, H. Gordon. *Canadian Representation Abroad: From Agency to Embassy.* Toronto: Ryerson Press, 1945.
Soja, Edward W. *Postmodern Geographies: The Reassertion of Space in Critical Social Theory.* London: Verso, 1989.
Sommerville, S.J. "Early Icelandic Settlements in Canada." *Papers Read before the Historical and Scientific Society of Manitoba, 1944–45* (1945): 25–43.
–. "Icelanders in Canada." *Canadian Geographical Journal* 21, 4 (1940): 192–201.
Spence, Thomas. *The Prairie Lands of Canada.* Montreal: Gazette Printing House, 1879.
Steffensen, Jón. "Smallpox in Iceland." *Nordisk medicinhistorisk årsbok* 41 (1977): 41–56.
Stoler, Ann Laura. *Race and the Education of Desire: Foucault's History of Sexuality and the Colonial Order of Things.* Durham, NC: Duke University Press, 1995.
St-Onge, Nicole J.M. *Saint-Laurent, Manitoba: Evolving Métis Identities, 1850–1914.* Regina: University of Regina, Canadian Plains Research Center, 2004.
St-Onge, Nicole, Carolyn Podruchny, and Brenda Macdougall, eds. *Contours of a People: Metis Family, Mobility and History.* Norman: University of Oklahoma Press, 2012.
Swyripa, Frances. *Wedded to the Cause: Ukrainian-Canadian Women and Ethnic Identity, 1891–1991.* Toronto: University of Toronto Press, 1993.
Sylvester, Kenneth Michael. "Immigrant Parents, Ethnic Children, and Family Formation in the Early Prairie West." *Canadian Historical Review* 84, 4 (2003): 585–612. http://dx.doi.org/10.3138/CHR.84.4.585.
–. *The Limits of Rural Capitalism: Family, Culture, and Markets in Montcalm, Manitoba, 1870–1940.* Toronto: University of Toronto Press, 2001.
Taylor, Bayard. *Egypt and Iceland in the Year 1874.* New York: G.P. Putnam's Sons, 1875.
Taylor, Greg. *The Law of the Land: The Advent of the Torrens System in Canada.* Toronto: Osgoode Society for Canadian Legal History/University of Toronto Press, 2008.
Thomas, Brinley. *Migration and Economic Growth: A Study of Great Britain and the Atlantic Economy.* 2nd ed. Cambridge: Cambridge University Press, 1973.
Thomas, Lewis H. *The Struggle for Responsible Government in the North-West Territories, 1870–97.* 2nd ed. Toronto: University of Toronto Press, 1978.
Thomas, Nicholas. *Colonialism's Culture: Anthropology, Travel, and Government.* Princeton: Princeton University Press, 1994.
Thomson, Don W. *Men and Meridians: The History of Surveying and Mapping in Canada.* 3 vols. Ottawa: Queen's Printer, 1966.
Thor, Jónas. *Icelanders in North America: The First Settlers.* Winnipeg: University of Manitoba Press, 2002.
Titley, Brian. "Unsteady Debut: J.A.N. Provencher and the Beginnings of Indian Administration in Manitoba." *Prairie Forum* 22, 1 (1997): 21–46.
Tobias, John L. "Protection, Civilization, and Assimilation: An Outline History of Canada's Indian Policy." *Western Canadian Journal of Anthropology* 6, 2 (1976): 13–30.
Tough, Frank. *'As Their Natural Resources Fail': Native Peoples and the Economic History of Northern Manitoba, 1870–1930.* Vancouver: UBC Press, 1996.

Tracie, Carl J. *"Toil and Peaceful Life": Doukhobor Village Settlement in Saskatchewan, 1899–1918*. Regina: Canadian Plains Research Center, 1996.
Trow, James. *Manitoba and North West Territories: Letters ... Together with Information Relative to Acquiring Dominion Lands, Cost of Outfit, Etc.* Ottawa: Department of Agriculture, 1878.
–. *A Trip to Manitoba*. Quebec City: Marcotte, 1875.
Tyman, John Langton. *By Section, Township and Range: Studies in Prairie Settlement*. Brandon, MB: Assiniboine Historical Society, 1972.
–. "The Disposition of Farm Lands in Western Manitoba, 1870-1930: Studies in Prairie Settlement." D. Phil. diss., Oxford University, 1970.
Valverde, Mariana. *The Age of Light, Soap, and Water: Moral Reform in English Canada, 1885–1925*. Toronto: McClelland and Stewart, 1991.
Van Kirk, Sylvia. *"Many Tender Ties": Women in Fur-Trade Society in Western Canada, 1670–1870*. Winnipeg: Watson and Dwyer, 1980.
Vanderhill, Burke G., and David E. Christensen. "The Settlement of New Iceland." *Annals of the Association of American Geographers* 53, 3 (1963): 350–63. http://dx.doi.org/10.1111/j.1467-8306.1963.tb00454.x.
Voisey, Paul Leonard. *Vulcan: The Making of a Prairie Community*. Toronto: University of Toronto Press, 1988.
Wakefield, Edward Gibbon. *A View of the Art of Colonization in Present Reference to the British Empire; in Letters between a Statesman and a Colonist*. Reprints of Economic Classics. New York: A.M. Kelley, 1969 (originally published 1849).
Walters, Thorstina. *Modern Sagas: The Story of the Icelanders in North America*. Fargo: North Dakota Institute for Regional Studies, 1953.
–. *Saga Íslendinga Norður-Dakota*. Winnipeg: City Printing and Publishing, 1926.
Warkentin, John H. "Western Canada in 1886." *Transactions of the Historical and Scientific Society of Manitoba* 3, 20 (1965): 85–116.
Weaver, John C. *The Great Land Rush and the Making of the Modern World, 1650–1900*. Montreal and Kingston: McGill-Queen's University Press, 2003.
Welch, Pedro L.V. *Slave Society in the City: Bridgetown, Barbados, 1680–1834*. Kingston, Jamaica: Ian Randle, 2003.
Wheeler, Winona. "The Fur Trade, Treaty No. 5 and the Fisher River First Nation." In *Papers of the Rupert's Land Colloquium 2008*, ed. Margaret Anne Lindsay and Mallory Allyson Richard, 209–21. Winnipeg: Centre for Rupert's Land Studies, 2010.
Williams, Raymond. "Base and Superstructure in Marxist Cultural Theory." *New Left Review* 82 (1973): 3–16.
Wilson, Catharine Anne. *A New Lease on Life: Landlords, Tenants and Immigrants in Ireland and Canada*. Montreal and Kingston: McGill-Queen's University Press, 1994.
–. *Tenants in Time: Family Strategies, Land, and Liberalism in Upper Canada, 1799–1871*. Montreal and Kingston: McGill-Queen's University Press, 2009.
Wolf, Kirsten. "Emigration and Mythmaking: The Case of the Icelanders in Canada." *Canadian Ethnic Studies* 33, 2 (2001): 1–15.
Woodley, Edward C. *The Bible in Canada*. Toronto: J.M. Dent, 1953.
Woodsworth, J.S. *Strangers within Our Gates, or Coming Canadians*. Toronto: Frederick Clarke Stephenson, 1909.
Woollacott, Angela, Desley Deacon, and Penny Russell, eds. *Transnational Lives: Biographies of Global Modernity, 1700-Present*. London: Palgrave Macmillan, 2010.

Young, Robert J.C. *Postcolonialism: An Historical Introduction.* Oxford: Blackwell, 2001.

Þór, Jónas. "A Religious Controversy among Icelandic Immigrants in North America, 1874-1880." Master's thesis, University of Manitoba, 1980.

Þorsteinsson, Þorsteinn Þ., and Tryggvi J. Oleson. *Saga Íslendinga í Vesturheimi.* 5 vols. Winnipeg and Reykjavík: Þjóðræknisfélag Íslendinga í Vesturheimi, 1940–53.

Index

Note: Page numbers in *italics* indicate illustrated material.

abolition, 121, 124, 126, 134
Aboriginal population. *See* Indigenous population
adoptions, 133, 135. *See also* kinship groups
Afro-Barbadian resistance movement, 124
agriculture: agricultural settlers, 51, 53, 75, 82, 85; Indigenous agriculture, 89; pastoral agriculture, 82; plantation agriculture, 48–49, 120; prairie farming, 88–89. *See also* farms/farming; homesteads
Akureyri, 82, 86
Alaska, 37, 88
Allan Steamship Line, 7, 23, 36, 42, 77–78, 79, 86, 187
Alþingi, 27, 28
Ames, Thomas, 124–25
Amherst Island, 49
Anderson, Benedict, 25
Anglo-Canadians, 45, 62–63, 64, 135–36, 161, 186
Annand, William, 193n4
anti-slavery movement, 123, 124, 127
Arason, Benedikt, 69–70, 92
Arason, Skapti, 88, 91
Árnesbyggð (River Point Settlement), 94, 151, 224n54, 226n99

Arngrímsson, Guðjón, 99, 142, 212n12
assimilation, 17, 54, 63, 64, 101, 132, 134–35, 189, 190
Austrian (steamship), 79, 80, 209n20

Bad Throat River, 105, 116
Baldwin, William Augustus, 110, 115–16, 225n61
Baldwinson, Baldwin L., 42, 71–72, 140, 222n131
Ballantyne, Tony, 16
Bantjes, Rod, 18, 145, 146
Baptist Church, 121, 128, 130, 133
Barbadian (Bridgetown), 123, 127
Barbados, 126–28, 138, 218n29
Bashford, Alison, 101, 111
Bayly, Christopher, 15–16
Beatty, Walter, 67
Beaumont Committee of Safety, 125
Beddome, Henry, 110, 114–15
Benjamínsson, Kristmundur, 178
Beren's River, 110
Bertram, John, 220n71
Big Island band, 105, 107, 117–18, 214n46
Bjarnason, Jón, 72, 133, 161, *177*
Björnsson, Sigurður Jósúa, 77, 94

Björnsson, Sveinn, 182
Black River, 116
Blood Vein band, 105
Bolt, Christine, 25
Brazil, 86
Bridgetown, Barbados, 123, 127
Briem, Halldór, 133, 135, 139, *177*, 182
Briem, Jóhann, 154, 155
British and Foreign Bible Society, 130, 219n66
British colonialism. *See* colonialism
British Columbia, 27, 55–57, 149
British North America Act, 149, 156, 160
British North American Colonial Empire, 31–32
Broken Head, 113
Bryce, George, 63
Brydon, Anne, 99
Bunster, Arthur, 27
Burgess, A.M., 71
Burton, Antoinette, 16
Burton, Richard Francis, 30–31, 74, 187
By Fell and Fjord (Oswald), 29

cadastral survey, 67, 145. *See also* Dominion Lands Survey system
Canada: Bureau of Statistics, 26; expansion idealism, 31, 33, 50, 62; immigration and colonization goals, 86, 167. *See also* Department of Agriculture; Department of the Interior; Dominion Lands Act; North-West Territories
Canada First movement, 32, 33
Canada West, 121, 129, 151
Canadian (steamship), 79
Canadian Land and Emigration Company, 130
Canadian Pacific Railway (CPR), 5, 47, 51–52, 57, 60–61, 69–70, 89–90, 95, 188
Canadian Shield, 77–78
Carberry, 139
Central Canadian Land Co., 57
Chinese immigrants, 27, 149
Christopherson, Sigurður, 88, 139
Church of England, 128
citizenship: municipal government, 156–58; rights and responsibilities, 87, 145, 185; settlers' pathway to, 10, 148. *See also* municipal systems
civilization, hierarchies of, 30
Clark, Willoughby, 114
class, 7, 24–27, 145–46, 149, 161, 189–90
climate, 32–33, 35, 37, 44, 85
Codd, Donald, 45, 47, 89
colonialism: British contexts, 49–51, 54–55, 191; colonial nationalism, 24; cultural stereotypes, 99; defined, 13–15, 102; disease, 97–98, 101, 111, 116; idealism, 31, 33, 50
colonization/colonization reserves: attitudes toward, 62–64; authority over Canadian Northwest, 188–91; colonization companies, 59–61; ethno-religious groups, 61–62, 187–88; farming colonies, 55–57; government support, 165; history and development, 8–9, 48–51, 55, 58, 102; nominal reserves, 61–62; private schemes, 52–53, 59–61; *sanitizing-colonizing*, 101, 116; segregation policies, 189; systematic forms, 49–51, 188; Wakefield theory, 49–51
colporteur (travelling Bible salesman), 129–30
Committee on Immigration and Colonization, 74
communes/commune system, 65, 77, 83, 150
community histories, 18–19
contact zone, 99, 212n10. *See also* settler/Indigenous relations
Continental liberalism, 87
cordon sanitaire, 110–15
cottars, 82, 84
Council of Keewatin, 110, 215n77
Council of Manitoba, 222n9
Cree, 8, 47, 98–99, 103, 107–8
Crooks, Adam, 36
Curtis, Bruce, 145

Dagenais, Michèle, 144–45
Daily Free Press (Winnipeg), 41, 108, 109, 113, 132, 214n51
Dakota Territory, 73, 91, 160, 176, 181, 184, 190

Daley, J.J., 27
Danish settlements, 45, 59
Daschuk, James, 98
Davis, R.A., 111, 113
Dawson, Carl, 17, 187
debt, 175, 179, 182–83, 190
debt-slavery, 138
Decker, Jody, 98
demographics: first colonists, 75–78; household size and composition, 92–94; Icelandic reserve, 109; Indigenous population, 103, 108–9; Large Group (Stóri Hópurinn), 78–87; pre-treaty communities, 103; smallpox epidemic, 108
Denmark, 27–28, 201n26
Dennis, J.S., 59, 65, 67
Department of Agriculture: emigrant recruitment, 33–38, 40, 43, 187; Immigration Branch, 3, 5, 26, 33–38; immigration policy, 167–68, 173; Keewatin Townships and Municipalities Bill, 143–44, 156–60, 190, 226n88; New Iceland colonization, 131, 146, 166–67, 170–71, 228n45; *Nýja Ísland í Kanada* (New Iceland in Canada), 38, 89
Department of the Interior: debt records and land patents, 184; Dominion Lands Branch, 5; Indian Affairs Branch, 5; land survey and registration, 67; municipal government, 146
"desirability" concept, 23–24, 26–27, 34–38, 43, 44, 187
Dewdney, Edgar, 27
district councils, 154–55, 160, 176
Dixon, William, 22–23
Doddridge, Philip, 128
Dog Head band, 105, 110, 136, 214n51
Dominion Lands Act: citizenship path, 10; enforcement, 175, 181; group settlements, 164, 165, 173–74; "Hamlet Clause," 66; history and definition, 5, 47–55, 58, 59–60, 64, 205nn20–21; Icelandic reserve support, 65–67, 69, 72, 190; land distribution, 52–53, 188–89, 205n25; New Iceland, 65–67, 72; private colonization schemes, 59–60, 61; private property regime, 48; railway company settlements, 61; repayment of loan and land ownership, 165, 184; revisions to (1876), 65–67, 173–74; Treaty Indians land claims, 183. *See also* homesteads
Dominion Lands Survey system: completion, 190; components, 51–53, 205n25; land survey and registration, 67; odd-numbered sections, 69–72; reserves and surveyed land, *46*; smallpox epidemic, 146; townships, *53*, 151; uniform survey grid, 47–48, *70*, 92
Dominion of Canada, 27, 33
Doukhobors, 43, 64
Doupe, Joseph, 67
Drever, William, 116
Dufferin, Lord (Frederick Hamilton-Temple-Blackwood): as authority on Iceland, 22–23, 29–30, 35, 74, 187; Gimli visit, 41, 163–64; J. Taylor correspondence, 130; *Letters from High Latitudes*, 22–23, 30–31; support for New Iceland, 182, 184, 190
Durham, Lord (John George Lambton Durham), 145
Dysart Township, 130

education: citizenship training, 156; Icelandic immigrants, 83–84, 130, 134, 190; land sales endowment, 52; national character, 31–32, 41, 156; responsibility for, 18, 134, 148, 153. *See also* schools/school lands
Elbourne, Elizabeth, 16
elections/elected officials, 147–48, 155, 158. *See also* franchise policy/enfranchisement
emancipation era, 120
emigrant recruitment, 33–38, 40, 43, 187
Ennis, James, 42
epidemics: government response to, 109–15; land administration, 98. *See also* smallpox
European Romantic movement, 24–25, 29, 43
European settler colonialism, 101
Exodus, Book of, 132
Eyfjörð, Jakob Sigurðsson, 91
Eyjólfsson, Stefán, 92

Index

family. *See* households; kinship groups
farms/farming: farm colonies, 47, 55–57, 189; farm names, 68–69, 92; in Iceland, 82–83; industrial farm plan, 130, 139; prairie farming, 88–89. *See also* agriculture; homesteads
Fiddler, Elizabeth, 103, 107, 135–36, 183
Fish, Hamilton, 37
Fisher River, 104, 117
fish/fisheries, 82, 85, 89–90, 114, 118–19
Fleming, Sanford, 34
Florida, 140
Foreign Slave Trade Abolition Act, 218n31
Fort Alexander, 102, 113, 114
foster children, 76
Foucault, Michel, 12, 15, 100–1, 111, 145
Framfari (Icelandic reserve newspaper): background, 176; debt/debt repayment, 138, 182–83; Dominion Lands Act, 69–71; election records (1880), 226n99; emigrant recruitment, 42; letter on Monkman, 119; municipal government structure, 148, 155–56; out-migration, 95, 164, 181; property rights, 182; reserve system, 190; Secret Deal letter, 137
Franchise Bill (1885), 149
franchise policy/enfranchisement, 10, 52–53, 147–50, 157. *See also* elections/elected officials
freedom of movement, 85, 138, 164, 180–82
"free grant" lands, 77–78, 174–75. *See also* homesteads
French Canadians, 45, 59, 167
Friðriksson, Friðjón, 60, 71–72, 88, 114, 131–32, 139, 140, 192
Fuller, Robert, 223n34
fur trade, 98, 103, 110

Galveston Bay, Texas, 125
Gaspé, 34
gender, 145–46, 149, 161, 189–90
German settlements, 45, 49, 58
German Society of Montreal, 58
Gerrard, Nelson, 18–19, 142
Gimli, County of, 160
Gimli: Dufferin visit, 41, 163–64; founding and history, 7, 33, 65–68, 95, 101, 160; and J. Taylor, 130–41; Monkman visit, 118; municipal government, 148; smallpox epidemic, 100, 110, 116
Gíslason, Albert, 91
Glenelg, Lord (Charles Grant), 126
Globe (Toronto), 41–42
government loan, 163–85; calculation of amount, 170–71, 228n45; formal acknowledgment, 179–81, *180*; granting, 166–70; HBC as loan guarantor, 168–69; homesteads as security, 168, 173, 179; loan records, 79, 80; purpose of, 90, 171–72; repayment, 173–83; Secret Deal letter, 176–79. *See also* property/property improvements
Gradual Civilization Act (1857), 10
Grahame, James A., 168
Gramsci, Antonio, 15
Grant, Ulysses S., 37
grasshoppers, 89, 168, 170
Grassy Narrow, 103, 104
Gravenhurst, 90
Greer, Allan, 144–45
Grey, Charles, 127
group settlements, 47–64; benefits, 56–57, 64; Dominion Lands Act, 164, 165, 173–74; ethno-religious groups, 61–62, 187–88; farming colonies, 55–57; group colonization, 35–39, 57, 58, 59, 61; history and definition, 47–51, 55, 74; liberalism theories, 187–88; shared migration experience, 77–78, 82
Gunsell, William, 125
Guðmundsdóttir, Rebekka, 109
Guðmundsdóttir, Valdís, 92, *93*
Guðrún, Jóhanna, *93*

Hackett, Paul, 98
Haines, Mary Elizabeth, 129
Halcrow, James Thomas, 223n34
Half-breed reserves, 45, *46*, 62–63, 103, 186. *See also* Métis
Hálfdánarson, Guðmundur, 28, 87
Haliburton, Richard Chandler, 187
Haliburton, Robert Grant, 32–33
Halifax, 78
Hall, Catherine, 16

Hall, James, 220n71
Hamilton, Captain, 126–27
Hannesdóttir, Oddný, 80
Harris, Cole, 50
HBC. *See* Hudson's Bay Company (HBC)
Heiðarsson, Steinþór, 19, 86
Hind, Henry Youle, 7, 31
homesteads: accounts, 155–56; acquisition of properties, 163–64; Dominion Lands Act, 64, 80, 158, 173, 188; forced seizure, 138, 159, 165, 181–82; free grant homesteads, 51–52, 53, 64, 163–64; goals, 186; "pre-emption" status, 52; similarities with Iceland, 92–94; treaty Indians, 183; US Homestead Act, 51. *See also* farms/farming; land claims; patents (titles); property/property improvements
households/household formation, 81, 83, 92–95. *See also* kinship groups
House of Commons, Keewatin Bill debates, 159–60
Howard, Thomas, 105
Hudson's Bay Company (HBC): Dufferin Gimli visit, 164; Icelandic Deputation, 47; land grants and reserves, 5, 31, 33, 50, 52, 53, 186; and New Iceland, 59, 71, 168–69; smallpox epidemic, 108

Iceland: Canadian relations with, 27–28; emigration/emigration recruitment, 28, 35, 38, 40, 42–43, 86, 91–92, 187; European romantic notions of, 24–25, 29, 41, 43, 187, 190; geographic district map, 78; government structure, 77, 150–51; history, 27–28; internal migration, 84–86; isolation, 24, 29, 40–41, 100, 190; literary heritage, 28–29, 33, 41; Mount Askja eruption, 37–38, 79; nationalism movement, 24–25, 27–29, 54, 82, 86, 99, 201n26; Norse language, 24, 29; socio-economic patterns, 81–87; travel writing, 29–31; *Vesturfaraskrá* (emigrant register), 83
Icelander's River, 102, 103, 148
Icelanders' Society in America, 211n69
Icelandic colonization reserve. *See* New Iceland
Icelandic colony. *See* New Iceland
Icelandic Deputation: government support, 92, 95, 104; membership, 45, 118; selection of colony site, 7, 10, 47, 82, 88–91, 135, 168, 188; site report, 38, 211n69
Icelandic immigrants, 73–95; character assessment, 36–37, 39–40, 117–18, 173; common migration experience, 73, 91, 94–95; demographic profiles, 11–12, 42, 75–87, 209n8, 209n13, 209n19, 209n23, 210n33; as "desirable" immigrants, 27, 35, 40, 43, 44, 74; financial aid, 90, 171–72; first group, 73–78; geographic origins in Iceland, 77, 82, 209n20, 210n68; goals and aspirations, 54, 75, 95, 186, 188, 190–91; Large Group (Stóri Hópurinn), 79–87; settler/Indigenous relations, 96, 99–100, 104–6, 135–36, 161, 190–92, 212n10, 212n12. *See also* immigration policy; New Iceland (Nýja Ísland)
Icelandic nationalism, 24–25, 27–29, 41, 54, 72, 82, 86–88, 99, 201n26
Icelandic reserve. *See* New Iceland
Icelandic River Saga (Gerrard), 18–19
immigration policy: Canadian expansion idealism, 33, 50, 62; climate, 32–33, 35, 37, 44, 85; colonization projects, 35–39, 40, 42–43, 46, 178–79; goals, 23–24, 25, 186; immigrant reserves, 16–17, 146; inclusion/exclusion components, 25–26; pathway to citizenship, 10, 148; per capita value of, 26; resettlement of immigrants, 18, 58, 75, 78, 86, 91–92, 95, 98, 187; social views of, 15. *See also* "desirability"; emigrant recruitment
imperialism, 13–14, 30
indenture contracts, 124–25, 126, 137, 138, 164, 180, 181. *See also* labour
Indian Act, 5, 52, 161, 183, 193n6
Indian agents, 134
Indian reserves, 20, 45, 46, 56, 186. *See also* Indigenous population; reserves/reserve systems
Indians. *See* Indigenous population
Indigenous population: agriculture, 89; appropriation of land, 117–18; Canadian

Index

mythic narratives, 99; definitions, 193n6; Indigenous settlements, 101–3, 104, 186, 189; racial notions of, 25–26; resettlement, 104, 167; residential schools, 15; responses to colonialism, 98, 191–92; sanitation practices, 116–17; settler/Indigenous relations, 96, 99–100, 104–6, 135–36, 161, 190–92, 212n10, 212n12; smallpox epidemic, 107–9. *See also* land claims; race/racial articulation

individualism, 23, 36

industrial farm plan, 130, 139

isolation: Iceland, 24, 29, 40–41, 100, 190; mitigation of, 56, 137; New Iceland, 75, 95, 99, 111, 188

Jack Fish band, 105
Jacobsen, Matthew Frye, 200n12
Jamaica, 133, 140
Jefferson, Thomas, 24
Jenkins, Edward, 36, 38, 201n43
Jewish refugees, 139
Jóhannesson, Páll, 65, 134, 147, 164
Jónasson, Einar, 88
Jónasson, Sigtryggur, *177*; assistant Icelandic agent, 131, 172, 175–76; background, 35, 209n23; Dominion Lands Act enforcement, 182; formal acknowledgment of loan, 179–81; Icelandic Deputation, 7, 38, 45, 47; immigrant debts, 60, 138; and John Taylor, 124, 140, 217n16; land claims, 69, 211n84; municipal government, 142, 143, 146–48, 160, 162, 226n78; New Iceland, 42, 88, 90, 91, 164, 172; smallpox epidemic, 108, 109, 116
Jónsson, Björn, 77, 156
Jónsson, Þorgrímur, 107, 108
Jónsson, Jakob J., 182, 223n29s
Jónsson, Jón, 107
Jónsson, Kristján, 88
Jónsson, Páll, 175
justice, administration of, 153–54
justice of the peace, 133, 147, 176

Karlsson, Gunnar, 85–86
Ka-tuk-e-pin-ais, 105, 116–17
Keewatin, 40, *112*

Keewatin Act, 110, 147–48, 154
Keewatin Board of Health, 109–11, 115, 117, 225n61
Keewatin District elections, 147–48
Keewatin Townships and Municipalities Bill, 143–44, 156–60, 190, 226n88
Kelm, Mary-Ellen, 100–1
Kingston, Canada West, 129
Kinmount, 36, 78, 87–88, 90, 92
kinship groups: adoptions, 133, 135; blended families, 76–77, 81–82; foster children, 76; kinship-based migration, 77, 91, 94–95, 99, 103, 188. *See also* households/household formation
Kjartansson, Helgi Skúli, 19, 86
Krieger, William C., 33, 38, 40, 42
Kristinsson, Júníus H., 19, 211n68
Kristjanson, Wilhelm, 140–41, 142, 220n71
Kristófersson Sigurður, 88, 139

labour: apprenticed labourers, 218n29; bonded labour, 84–85, 137–38; family labour, 76; indenture contracts, 124–25, 126, 137, 138, 164, 180, 181; statute labour system, 154, 155
"Lakething" (*Vatnsþing*) administrative unit, 224n47
Lake Winnipeg, 47, 73, 75, 89–90, 98, 103, 188
Lake Winnipeg Indian treaty negotiations, 90
Lambertsen, Guðmundur, 86
land claims: Elizabeth Fiddler, 103, 107, 135–36, 183; homesteaders, 67, 69, 94, 106, 211n84; Indigenous population, 8, 47, 52, 90, 183; John Ramsay, 106, 136, 183, 189, 229n85; Sandy Bar band, 99, 105–6, 117–18, 136, 183. *See also* property/property improvements
land/land grants: British colonial practice, 48–49, 102; communal pattern of land use, 65, 77, 83, 150; land appropriations during smallpox epidemic, 117–18; land surveys, 51, 67, 116–17, 145; proprietary grants, 188; social engineering, 55, 58–59. *See also* Dominion Lands Survey system; patents (titles); reserves/reserve system

Large Group (Stóri Hópurinn), 79–87; characteristics, 74–75, 81; choice of settlement location, 91; geographic origins, 79; impact on New Iceland, 79, 171; smallpox, 96–97
Lashley, April, 125–26
Laurier, Wilfrid, 55
law enforcement, 147, 154
Leeward Islands, 125
Lefebvre, Henri, 54
Lester, Alan, 16
Letters from High Latitudes (Dufferin), 22–23, 30–31
liberalism/liberal theory, 8, 13–15, 31–32, 87, 165–66, 185
liberty: acquisition of property, 163; freedom of movement, 85, 138, 164, 180–82; personal liberty and debt, 138, 164, 165, 182; slavery/racial equality, 123, 126, 127; theories on, 14, 20, 32. *See also* property/property improvements
Lindal, Walter, 142, 225n66
livestock, 82–83, 86, 138
local government. *See* municipal system
Loewen, Royden, 17, 75
Lorne, Lord (John Campbell), 139
Lowe, John, 4; colonization policy, 12, 58, 136; Icelandic immigration, 22, 35, 38, 40, 173; and J. Taylor, 40, 220n71; land grant policies, 69, 169, 172, 174, 179; municipal governments, 146–47, 148, 159; New Iceland, 4–5, 41–42, 68, 73, 135, 170, 181–82, 193n4; Secret Deal letter, 176–79
"Loyalists," 184
lumber camps, 130
Lundi, 67, 101
Lutheranism, 23, 133
Lux, Maureen, 100–1
Lynch, James Spencer, 39–41, *39*, 183; Indigenous land compensation, 183; New Iceland report, 100; smallpox epidemic, 106–9, 115, 116, 117

Macdonald, John A., 55, 66, 160
Macdonald, Norman, 23, 44
MacGregor, Evan, 126
Mackenzie, Alexander, 3, 58–59, 113, 160–61, 166–67, 172
Mackintosh, W.A., 9, 187
Macpherson, C.B., 14
magistrates, 138, 154
Magnússon, Eiríkur, 38
Magnússon, Guðlaugur, 166
Magnússon, Jóhannes, 223n29
Mair, Charles, 42–43
Manitoba: ethno-religious settlements, 9–10, 27, 45, 58–59, 63; Historical and Scientific Society of Manitoba, 143; history, 33, 143; quarantine map, *112*; reserves/reserve system, 6, 45–47, *46*, 62–63
Manitoba Act (1870), 5, 45
Manitoba and North West Railway, 61
Manitoba Herald (Winnipeg), 113
Manitoba Municipal Act (1873), 149
Manitoban (steamship), 77–78, 92
marriage, 83–84, 85, 87
Master and Servants Act, 138
Mattson, Hans, 35
McDougall, William, 34, 35
McKay, Ian, 8–9, 14–15
McPhillips, George, 65, 67–68
McTavish, J.H., 168–69
Mehta, Uday Singh, 15
Mennonites, 9–10, 27, 45, 58–59, 63–64, 75, 167–70, 188
Meredith, Edmund Allen, 22
Metis, 5, 8, 33, 34, 45, 63, 98–99, 161, 193n6
migration, 16–17, 77
military garrison, 113, 115
militia unit, 134
Mill, John Stuart, 145
Mills, David, 59, 143, 144, 156–62, *157*, 190
Milwaukee, 37
Minnesota, 78, 91
Mitchell, Peter, 159
Monkman, Joseph, 47, 118–19, *118*
Montreal Daily Witness, 130
Moore, William, 126
Mormonism, 91
Morris, Alexander: Canadian expansion schemes, 31–32; Indigenous land claims,

Index 255

8, 47, 90, 183; New Iceland, 39, 47, 90, 100, 171; nineteenth-century racial theories, 187; Norway House Cree relocation, 103–4; reserves justice systems, 134, 147; smallpox epidemic, 109–10, 111, 113, 117
Morris, William, 29
mortgages, 164–65, 174–75, 178–80, 185. *See also* property/property improvements
Morton, Arthur, 61
Morton, W.L., 143
Moses, 132
Mount Askja eruption, 37–38, 79
Mount Cashell, Lord (Stephen Moore), 49
municipal government, 143, 146–48, 153, 159, 223n34
municipal systems, 142–62, 225n61; background, 145, 155–56, 160, 190; basic structures of governance, 133–34; citizenship, 156–58; compared to Iceland system, 150–51; conflict resolution, 154; Council of Manitoba, 222n9; districts/district councils, 151, 154–55; elections/election policy, 147–50, 223n34, 224n54, 226n99; governmentality concept, 12–13; hierarchical structure, 141, 145–46, 161; institution building, 146–48; "Lakething" (*Vatnsþing*) administrative unit, 224n47; protest and resistance, 146; reeves, 153; settlements (*byggð*), 67, 151; taxation, 153, 155–56; townships, 151–53. *See also* citizenship; settlements
Muskoka, 36, 77–78

national community, 24–25, 29
Native populations. *See* Indigenous population
Netley Creek, 103
Newcomb, George, 184
New Iceland (Nýja Ísland): assessment, 40–41, 63, 74, 100; boundary disputes, 69–72; demographics, 42, 83, 109; dissolution, 137, 191; Dufferin visit, 41, 163–64; founding, 36, 59, 65, 67, 68, 69, 73, 172; government property debate,
164, 165; growth and development, 79–87; hardships, 92, 138–39, 160; history, 7–8, 36, 43, 45–48, 59, 60, 73–75, 87–91; and Indigenous population, 95–96, 98–99, 104–6, 135–36, 161, 190–92, 212n10, 212n12; isolation, 75, 95, 99, 111, 188; living conditions, 115–17, 132; Lowe visit, 41–42; Mackenzie colonization policy, 3, 160–61, 166–67, 172; as mission community, 133–34; myths/mythology, 142–43; outcome, 184–85; out-migration, 95, 117, 137–38, 160, 164–65, 176, 181–82, 190–91; preserving Icelandic culture, 87–88; quarantine, 101, 110–15, *112*, 114, 132; settler aspirations, 82; smallpox epidemic, 39, 108, 115–17; socio-economic patterns, 84; spatial management and public health, 101, 116–18; as speculation, 182–83; village settlement plan, 65, *66*. *See also* homesteads; municipal systems; reserves/reserve systems
New Iceland Colonial Reserve, 8, 104–6
New Iceland in Canada (*Nýja Ísland í Kanada*) immigration pamphlet, 38, 89
New Iceland Printing Company, 176
New York Tribune, 29, 30
Norse language, 24, 29, 30
Northern Pacific Railroad, 57, 174
northern races: emigration recruitment policy, 33–34; European Romantic notion, 24–25, 41, 43; racial superiority, 24, 32–33, 74, 187. *See also* race/racial articulation
North-West Emigration Aid Society, 33
North-West Mounted Police, 147, 154
North-West Territories: Canadian expansion, 47, 50, 62, 161, 186; Dominion Lands survey, *46*; farming colonies, 47, 55–57; government systems, 144, 147–48; justice system, 147, 154
North-West Territories Act, 149
North-West Territories Council, 161
Norway House, 8, 47, 102, 103–4, 110, 135–36
Norway/Norwegian immigrants, 34–35
Norðanfari (newspaper; Iceland), 86
Nova Scotia, 39, 49, 78, 79, 91

Nýja Ísland í Kanada (New Iceland in Canada) immigration pamphlet, 38, 89

Oddleifsson, Gestur, 118–19
Ojibwe, 8, 98–99, 103, 107–8, 113
Ólafsson, Ólafur: background, 176; land/property disputes, 106, 175–76, 180, 183; Lutheranism, 133; New Iceland offices, 134, 136, 147, 150–51, 153; out-migration, 137
Ólafsson, Eggert, 28
Ólafsson, Erlendur, 95
Ólafsson, Jón, 37, 88
old Norse race, 41
Ontario, 36, 77, 78, 79, 91, 154
Osenbrugge, Ferdinand, 60
Oswald, Elizabeth Jane, 29

Palliser, John, 31
Palmerston, Lord (Henry John Temple), 126
Parsonage, Everett, 137, 139, 223n34
pastoral agriculture, 82
patents (titles): applying for, 52, 71, 158, 184; government loan repayment, 61, 164, 174–75, 184; granting of, 80, 179, 183–85; Indigenous population, 183; registering, 190
paternalism, 12, 20, 123, 133–34, 161, 162
paupers, 84, 85
Pelletier, C.A.P., 115
Perry, Adele, 16, 197n53
Pétursson, Björn, 119, 138, 165–66, 182, 183
Phoenician (steamship), 79
Portage la Prairie, 222n9
Pratt, Mary Louise, 30, 212n10
Prescod, Samuel Jackman, 126, 127
Prince Edward Island (PEI), 49
property/property improvements: immigrant homesteads, 163–65, 168–69, 175, 184–85, 190; Indigenous property, 5, 103, 106, 135–36, 183, 189, 229n85; loan repayment and property ownership, 165–66, 179, 182; mortgage on property improvements, 164–65, 174–75, 178–80, 185; political and civil rights, 10, 12, 74, 143, 145–46, 149–50, 157–58; private property rights, 14, 20, 48, 51, 54, 146, 179, 182–83, 190; public health measures, 100, 110, 113, 116; seizure of, 138, 159, 165, 181–82; taxation, 153, 155–56; value of, 49, 57–59, 175, 178–79. *See also* homesteads; land claims; patents
proprietary grants, 188
Provencher, J.A.N., 106, 108, 114, 136, 216n94
public health and governance, 98, 100–1, 109–13, 111, 146
Punk Island, 116

quarantine, 3, 100, 110–15, *112*, 117, 146. *See also* smallpox epidemic
Quebec, 22
Quebec City, 34, 36, 42

race/racial articulation: biological determinism, 134; and climate, 32–33, 35, 44; cultural stereotypes, 99–100; defined, 200n12; franchise restrictions, 149; hierarchical systems, 122–23, 134, 141, 145–46, 161, 189–90; Icelandic population, 24–25, 39–40, 117–18; liberty and racial equality, 123, 126, 127; racial baptism, 31; racially defined reserves, 117; smallpox epidemic, 100, 115–17; theories on, 25–26, 32–33, 35, 44, 64, 187; white racial privilege, 191. *See also* "northern races"
Radforth, Ian, 144–45
railway reserves, 45–47, *46*, 52, *53*, 57, 60–63, 174, 186
Ramsay, John: property claim, 106, 136, 183, 189, 229n85; relations with Icelanders, 99, 118, 191–92; smallpox epidemic, 110, 116
Rask, Rasmus Christian, 29
Rasporich, A.W., 17, 54
Red River/Red River Colony, 8, 31, 33, 45, 49, 68, 90, 98–99, 104
Red River Valley, 89
Reid, J. Lestock, 105
religion, 22–23
remittances, 80
Republic of New Iceland, 142–43

Republic of Texas, 125
reserves/reserve systems: defined, 102; development and administration, 5–7, 47–51; land reserve/colonization policy, 58–59; net effect, 54–55; nominal reserves, 61–62; racially segregated, 101, 117; as social laboratories, 189; and sovereignty, 50–51; spatial practices, 9–10, 12, *46*, 47–48; Wakefield theory, 49–51, 55. *See also* colonization/colonization reserves; Indian reserves; New Iceland
resettlement of immigrants, 18, 58, 75, 78, 86, 91–92, 95, 98, 187. *See also* immigration policy
Richtik, James Morton, 205n20
Riel, Louis, 34, 39–40
roads/road construction, 67–68, 89–90, 101, 131, 142, 150, 153–55, 166, 172
Roediger, David, 200n12
Rogers, Samuel, 125–26
Rosseau, 36, 77–78
Rossville Methodist mission, 103
Rowan, Robert F., 59
Roy, Fernande, 14
Rupert's Land, 50, 156
Rural Municipality of Gimli, 160
Ruttan, John H., 103

Sabine Pass, 125
Salteaux, 212n12
Sandy Bar (Icelandic town), 67, 96–97, 101
Sandy Bar (Indigenous village), 102–3, 116
Sandy Bar band: land disputes and claims, 99, 105–6, 117–18, 136, 183; smallpox epidemic, 108, 109, 116; treaty negotiations, 105–6
sanitation, 101, 111, 115, 189
sanitzing-colonizing, 101
Saskatchewan, 61, 145
Scandinavian immigration, 34–35
schools/school lands: Dominion Land Act set-asides, 52, *53*, 71; Icelandic immigrant settlements, 63, 66, 102, 133–34, 153–54; Indian residential schools, 15; national school, 134; responsibility for, 153–54, 159, 161
Schultz, John Christian, 33, 39

Scott, Richard William, 43
Scott, William Duncan, 43–44
Scottish Canadian Allan Steamship Line. *See* Allan Steamship Line
Scottish settlements, 49, 58
secret ballot, 158–59
Secret Deal letter, 137–38, 176–79, 180
Select Standing Committee on Immigration and Colonization, 26, 26–27, 196n42
self-sufficiency, 165, 173
Selkirk, 47
Selkirk, Lord (Thomas Douglas), 49
Settee, James, 96, *97*, 102, 104, 108, 109, 213n41
Settee, Sarah, 109
settlements (*byggðir*): background, 101–2, 151–53; settlement committees, 160, 226n99; settlement officials, 153–56. *See also* municipal systems
settler/Indigenous relations, 96, 99–100, 104–6, 135–36, 161, 190–92, 212n10, 212n12
settler societies, 25–26, 111–12
Shah, Nayan, 100
Shantz, J.Y., 167–68
Shaw, David, 58
Shrewsbury, William, 124
Sifton, Clifford, 61–62, 64
Sigurðsson, Árni, 229n85
Símonarson, Símon, 67, 68, 92–94, *93*, 95, 131, 140
Simonsen, J.H., 35
Slave Emancipation Act (1833), 218n31
slavery/slave trade, 120, 121–25, 127, 181, 218n31
smallpox epidemic: aftermath, 114–15; colonization and surveillance practices, 146; cordon sanitaire, 110–15; Council of Keewatin, 110, 215n77; hygiene regimes, 111; mortality rate, 189; outbreak, 39, 96–97, 106–7, 170, 171; quarantine, 3, 100, 110–15, *112*, 117, 146; racial articulation, 100; spatial practices and public health, 19–20, 146, 189; spread of and response to, 107–15; vaccine/vaccinations, 114
Smith, Donald A., 169

Smith, Edward, 223n34
social engineering, 55, 56–59, 189
social welfare arrangements, 93–94
Société de Colonisation de Manitoba, 59, 167
socio-economic patterns: agricultural economy, 85; climate, 85; household size and composition, 92–94; Icelandic immigrants, 11–12, 210n33; per capita value of productive immigrants, 26; pre-treaty communities, 102–3; Red River Colony, 98–99; rigid economy schemes, 170–73
Sommerville, Steina Jónasina, 142–43
spatial practices, 96–119; colonization and surveillance, 145–46; land administration and public health, 98, 100–11, 116–17, 189; segregation on racial grounds, 111–12; surveys, 51, 67, 116–17, 145. *See also* colonization/colonization reserves; Dominion Lands Survey system; smallpox; treaties
Spence Thomas, 63
Sproat, Gilbert Malcolm, 55–58, 189
St. Andrews, 139
Stefánsson, Magnús, 116
Stjórnarlög Nýja Íslands (government regulations of New Iceland), 148–49, 151, 153–54, 156, 224n53, 225n66
St. Michael's parish, Bridgetown, 123
Stoler, Ann Laura, 16, 25–26
St. Patrick (steamship), 77–78, 79, 92
St. Peters/St. Peter's band, 8, 45, 103, 104, 105, 113, 214n51
Sveinsson, Friðrik, 106
Swiss immigration, 58
Sydenham, Lord (Charles Poulett Thomson), 145
Sylvester, Kenneth, 17
systematic colonization theory, 49–51

Taché, Alexandré Antonin, 167
taxation/taxation policy, 153, 155–56
Taylor, Bayard, 29, 30
Taylor, Carrie, 134
Taylor, Elizabeth, 140
Taylor, John, 120–41, *121*; Baptist missionary, 121, 129–30; Barbados, 122–24; and Department of Agriculture, 40, 87–88, 131, 146; founding of New Iceland, 36, 59, 65, 67, 68, 69, 73, 172; Gimli life and household, 130–41, 155; Icelandic agent, 12, 20, 122, 130–41, 131, 146, 172, 220n71, 222n131; Icelandic Deputation, 7, 45, 47, 90, 92, 122, 130, 135; industrial farm plan, 130, 139; justice of the peace, 133; religious transformation, 121, 128–29; relocation and death, 139–40; Secret Deal letter, 137–38, 176–79; slavery/slave trade, 120, 121–25, 127, 181, 218n31; smallpox epidemic, 106–9, 115, 131; Texas/Texas affair, 122, 124–26, 128; trial and prison term, 121, 122, 126–28. *See also* municipal systems; New Iceland
Taylor, Richard, 123
Taylor, Rose, 133, 140
Taylor, Susie, 135
Taylor, William Stewart, 129, 130, 135, 139, 209n19, 223n34
Texas/Texas affair, 122, 124–26, 128
Thingvalla, 61
Thomas, Lewis H., 144
Thomas, Nicholas, 13, 101
Thor, Jónas, 75, 99, 142
Thorlaksson, Páll, 136, 137, 176–78, *177*
Tiger Hills, 184
Times (London), 38
Toronto Globe, 3–4
townships, 53, 151–53, 173
trade regimes, 85, 86
traditional rural society, 86–87
transatlantic migrant transportation, 86
travel writing, 30
treaties: Treaty 1, 8, 105, 214n51; Treaty 2 (1871), 105; Treaty 4, 9–10; Treaty 5 (1875), 104, 105, 214n51
Treaty Indians, 183
treaty negotiations, 105–6
Trinidad, 140
Trow, James, 63
Turner, Frederick Jackson, 9, 144

Ukrainians, 64
United Iceland Colony, 54, 89
United States: Homestead Act (1862), 51; Icelandic immigration, 37; railway land grants, 174
utopias, group settlement projects as, 17–18, 54

vaccine/vaccinations, 114
Vancouver Island, 50
Vaughn, A.H., 47
Vesturfaraskrá (emigrant register), 83
Victoria Railway Line, 36
village committee (*bæjarnefnd*), 134, 147, 223n29
Völuspá (The seeress's prophecy), 33

wage labour, 190
Wakefield, Edward Gibbon, 49–51, 54–55, 58–59
Weekly Free Press (Winnipeg), 62, 63

West Indian (Bridgetown), 218n29
West Indies, 120, 133, 138, 140
White Mud River, 8, 102, 103–4, 105, 107, 135–36, 183
white settlers/white settler society, 11, 16, 51, 55, 74, 120–21, 183, 191
Whittaker, Edward, 125, 126
Willow Point Settlement, 7, 156, 164
Windward Islands, 126
Winnipeg Dominion Lands Office, 71
Wisconsin, 7, 78, 86, 90, 91, 211n69
women, 145, 150, 224n54
Wood, Edmund Burke, 182
Woodsworth, J.S., 43

Young, David, 108
Young, Egerton Ryerson, 103, 213n37
Young, Robert J.C., 13

Þorláksson, Árni, 65
Þorsteinsson, Þorsteinn, 142